Victorian Infidels

Edward Royle

Lecturer in History, University of York

Victorian Infidels

The Origins of the British Secularist Movement
1791–1866

Manchester University Press
Rowman & Littlefield Publishers

Published by the University of Manchester
at the University Press
316–24 Oxford Road, Manchester M13 9NR

ISBN 0 7190 0557 4

USA

Rowman & Littlefield Publishers
81 Adams Drive, Totowa, N.J. 07512

US ISBN 0 87471 509 1

The publication of this book has been
assisted by an award from the
Twenty-seven Foundation

Printed in Great Britain
by Butler & Tanner Ltd,
Frome and London

Contents

Abbreviations

A.A.C.A.N.	Association of All Classes of All Nations
A.H.R.	*American Historical Review*
A.P.U.	Anti-Persecution Union
B.L.	Bradlaugh papers, National Secular Society, London
B.M. Add. Mss.	British Museum, Additional Manuscripts
C.N.	Cowen papers, Newcastle upon Tyne Public Library
H.B.	Holyoake papers, Bishopsgate Institute, London
H.C.	Holyoake papers, Co-operative Union, Manchester
I.I.S.H.	International Institute of Social History, Amsterdam
L.S.S.	London Secular Society
L.S.U.	Lancashire Secular Union
N.C.F.S.	National Community Friendly Society
N.M.W.	*New Moral World*
N.R.U.	Northern Reform Union
N.S.S.	National Secular Society
O.C.	Owen papers, Co-operative Union, Manchester
P.L.	Public library
P.M.G.	*Poor Man's Guardian*
R.S.	Rational Society
Tr.H.S.L.C.	*Transactions of the Historical Society of Lancashire and Cheshire*
W.R.S.A.	West Riding Secular Alliance
W.R.S.U.	West Riding Secular Union

Notes

Note references have usually been gathered together at the end of each paragraph, in which case the order of the notes is that of the items to which they refer.

Introduction

Victorian Britain was a Christian country. That is, its laws and institutions, supported by the courts and public opinion, aided by a variety of Churches and sects, upheld and declared the Christian religion. The whole tone of Victorian middle-class life was religious, and the Churches enjoyed a great period of prosperity and success. But contemporaries were well aware that the foundations of religion in society were precarious: intellectual doubt threatened the very basis of biblical Christianity on the one hand, and mass infidelity among the lower orders disturbed and challenged pious consciences on the other.

The growth of industrial society in the nineteenth century, with its increasingly urban, class-conscious and secular outlook, was the background to the development of an all-out radical attack on the political and religious establishment of the country. The origins of this establishment can be traced to the Restoration, when the political and religious clock had been put back in an effort on the part of the governing class to suppress the memory and achievements of the Commonwealth period. Church and State had then been wedded in a marriage of mutual convenience in which orthodox Christianity was regarded as the very basis of the law and the constitution. Gradually during the course of the nineteenth century this constitution came under attack and was eroded: dissenters and Roman Catholics were admitted into the political fold, the franchise was extended to the first of the new classes to find its identity—the middle class—and by the 1850s even Quakers and Jews were allowed civil rights.

The turn of those lower down the social scale was to come next. In pre-industrial society attacks on orthodox Christianity were not uncommon, but they were usually made in the name of orthodox Christianity. Irreligion in its true sense of an attack on the established religion became common only with the development of industrial society, and was usually associated amongst the lower orders with the general radical attack on the Church–State constitution.[1] To this extent, irreligion was motivated by the same concerns which stirred the Nonconformist attack on the establishment, and the mid-century leaders of ultra-radical free-thought were to find they had much in common with the middle-class

radicalism of Richard Cobden. Even Mr Gladstone became their radical
hero in time. But radical infidelity was much more than this. It was
also a creed which rejected the values of established society, and these
values were sometimes expressed more cogently by middle-class Nonconformists than by the Anglicans of the social establishment. Irreligion
was very much a part of that ultra-radical movement which was
mounted in Britain in the last decade of the eighteenth century as part
of the European response to the French revolution, and which was sustained in the nineteenth century until the constitution had been sufficiently modified to admit men of all classes and of all, or no, creeds.

The two men most responsible for giving form and content to this
attack were Thomas Paine and Robert Owen. Paine, though, lived only
on the fringes of modern society: his ultra-radicalism in politics still
belonged largely to pre-industrial England and was more concerned
with interest groups than with classes, and his irreligion halted at
deism and the new religion of theophilanthropy. Thomas Paine as the
nineteenth-century radicals knew him was mediated to them by Richard
Carlile, who made him a more crude but more appealing figure. Robert
Owen was a complete contrast. He also thought in older social terms,
but his message was appropriate to the new conditions; whilst he remained a conservative deist, most of his followers were radicals, and a
good number of them seized upon his attacks on religion and his enlightenment rationalism as an integral part of his wider social
schemes.

Class concepts for the first time became important in ultra-radical
politics in the generation following the peace of Vienna in 1815, and
feelings of class solidarity were whipped up by the popular press of
the 1820s, '30s and '40s. The aim of this 'blasphemous and seditious
press' was two fold: to maintain the attack on the constitution at home,
and to mount a parallel attack abroad on the *ancien régime* as re-
established at Vienna. The Holy Alliance, of which aristocratic, Tory
Britain was seen to be a part, was the object of much political and
religious abuse. But although ultra-radicalism can be said to have had
certain general aims, there was no unified radical movement, and
though most men were influenced by Paine and Owen, the ambiguous
nature of their writings led different people to interpret them with
differing degrees of extremism. It is probably true to say that only a
minority of ultra-radicals were root-and-branch opponents of all religion,
just as only a very few were total anarchists in political matters.

In the 1830s Owen's political conservatism served to emphasise this
disunity. Followers of Paine, particularly those most influenced by
Carlile, responded mainly to the appeal of Owen's moral crusade, which

involved an attack on religion, while political reformers turned to Chartism. Owen's followers split further when some chose to emphasise the social schemes whilst others continued to concentrate on the irreligious aspects of Owenism. This study of mid-Victorian freethought is concerned largely with this latter group of Owenites, as it was they who most faithfully embodied the aspirations of the Paine–Carlile irreligious tradition, and their methods were the same. Carlile himself could not agree with Owen, and stood in the background, but other leaders of the blasphemous and seditious press—notably Henry Hetherington and James Watson—were very much involved and provided a backbone of continuity. The leadership, though, passed to a number of Owen's social missionaries, who found in the local structure of Owenism a far better propagandist organisation than either Carlile or Hetherington had managed to establish in the 1820s and '30s. The first of these new Owenite leaders was Charles Southwell, but the most influential was George Jacob Holyoake.

This book is concerned primarily with Holyoake's efforts to adjust the ultra-radical infidel tradition to the new conditions which emerged in mid-nineteenth-century Britain, and as such it can suggest in miniature a number of social changes which were of far wider importance. In the 1840s Owenism had failed to realise its social aims, Chartism had failed to achieve its political aims, and the infidels had failed to storm the gates of the establishment. In the 1850s, therefore, radicals of all three persuasions had to rethink their strategies. With the failure of the Owenite community at Queenwood in 1846, most of the former Owenite local organisation, or such as remained, passed to Holyoake and his followers, whilst a great deal of local energy was absorbed in the attempt to set up trading stores. Co-operation in the community became the slogan, instead of co-operation in communities. Withdrawal was replaced by participation, hostility by compromise, revolutionary change by gradual transformation. The same happened to the Chartist movement, and possession of the vote came for many to symbolise acceptance within the existing system rather than the first step towards a radical alteration of the system. Holyoake and his followers were involved in both these changes, and Holyoake himself was one of the first working-class leaders to advocate 'individual' Owenism as well as Chartist co-operation with the middle classes. In the same way his own freethought movement responded to the times, and in 1851 was renamed Secularism as a symbolic break with the older labels of atheism and infidelity.

Secularism therefore contained within its aims and membership many of the social tensions and changes of the 1850s. At a time when

respectable 'honest doubt' was first making its claims on public attention, the Secularists were expressing similar views for similar reasons,
though they have not attracted similar attention from intellectual
historians. Perhaps this is because they produced little that was intellectually original, but their arguments, which were largely based on
eighteenth-century ideas, may serve to correct the impression that what
men like Darwin had to say came as a totally unexpected blow to the
religious world. Where the Secularists did differ from the 'honest
doubters' was in their preoccupation with politics. Partly because of
their tradition, and partly because they were excluded from civil rights
on account of their beliefs, the Secularists were political as well as
intellectual radicals, and their agitation was organised as a political
movement. Their concern was to open up the establishment, and their
campaign was for the creation of a secular, pluralistic, open society in
place of one based on a closed, aristocratic constitution and the Christian ideology. Sympathy with these aims came from some middle-class
radicals and intellectuals, most notably John Stuart Mill, whose essay
On Liberty (1859) may stand as the most cogent plea for the sort of
society which the Secularists wanted.

The period between the failure of Chartism in 1848 and the enfran-
chisement of urban householders in 1867 is one of the most important
in the whole of the nineteenth century, but until recently it has been
one of the most neglected. In the 1850s attitudes which had been
assumed two or more generations earlier were beginning to be abandoned: the aristocracy of labour, which had been the backbone of
working-class movements in the earlier decades of rising class-consciousness, began to find in Liberalism a political creed which could be shared
with men of other classes, and which could embody its own radical
aspirations. Political liberalism included religious liberalism, and with
the formation of the Liberal party the foundations of the modern
secular State were laid. This is not to claim that the Secularists themselves were overwhelmingly important in this process, but they were a
part of it and were used by their leaders as a powerful pressure group.

This aspect of Secularism is best known in connection with Charles
Bradlaugh's efforts to enter Parliament in the 1880s, but Bradlaugh's
aims and achievements can be understood only against the background
of the 1840s and '50s. Because Secularism is now so closely identified
with Bradlaugh's name, the history of the movement, and in particular
the role of G. J. Holyoake, has been distorted. Holyoake had already
provided for Bradlaugh the ideological foundations and the organisation for the National Secular Society, which Bradlaugh established in
1866. Holyoake forged the link between the Chartism and Owenism of

the 1840s and the Reform League and the Secularism of the late 1860s. Though other veterans such as Lloyd Jones continued to be active, Holyoake more than anyone else was responsible for perpetuating in these years the remnants of ultra-radical local organisation, which might otherwise have been lost. Bradlaugh's movement would not have been the same without this earlier work.

Holyoake is therefore the central figure in this book, and inescapably so. Though I am not here attempting a biography of his early life, so much of the man is involved in the movement that it is impossible as well as undesirable to separate the two. The personal approach is also dictated by the nature of the sources. Most of the periodicals of the freethought movement from 1841 to 1866 were edited by Holyoake, and his *Reasoner* (1846–61) forms the basis of this study. He also laid the intellectual foundations of the movement, writing over a hundred pamphlets during this period, and his private papers constitute the largest source of unpublished material. There were other, lesser, leaders —most importantly Charles Southwell and Robert Cooper—but the material on them is not so abundant. Both left scraps of autobiography and a few pamphlets and edited periodicals from time to time, and their letters to Holyoake and Owen are in those respective collections, but there is little else. Most of what is available is incorporated in this study. Charles Bradlaugh is a different matter, but his papers are disappointingly thin for this period of his life. He entered freethought in 1849 but did not become important until the late 1850s, and only with the formation of the National Secular Society in 1866 did he become dominant. I have therefore treated him as he seems to have been regarded by his contemporaries: he was a promising newcomer, welcomed by the movement, but perhaps resented by some of the older leaders, including Holyoake; he was certainly not a central figure before 1861 and he did not assume full editorial control of the *National Reformer*, except for a few months, until after John Watts's death in 1866. By restricting this study to the years before he reached supremacy in the movement I hope to avoid casting the shadow of hindsight too far across the earlier history of Secularism. Each period is worth studying in its own right.

There are other reasons, though, for concluding this study in the early 1860s, which in many ways marked the end of an era. First, the Queenwood bankruptcy came before Chancery in 1861 and was settled in 1863, thus bringing to an end the Owenite story which had been started in 1839 and which had been tied up with the development of freethought ever since. Only after the final Queenwood settlement could Owenism rest in peace. Secondly, the last of the major restrictions on the press, against which Hetherington had struggled in the 1830s, was removed by Mr Gladstone in 1861 with the abolition of the Paper Duties and another radical cause was settled—or almost settled. Thirdly, the first nail was driven in the coffin of the *ancien régime* when Italy was liberated in 1861 (France under Napoleon III was regarded as no better than France under the Bourbons). Admittedly much remained to be done, and a vast amount of liberal legislation had to wait until Mr Gladstone's first and greatest reforming Ministry, but by the 1860s the mood of politics had been set and the country was preparing for change. The new developments of the 1850s were completed when the cause of Italy brought Palmerston and Gladstone together to form the Liberal Party, cementing at the top what the forces of popular liberalism were achieving beneath the surface.[2] When Palmerston died in 1865, men instinctively felt that a new age was about to begin. Russell and Derby also retired, and that age of transition, which forms the background to this study, had come to an end. The early 1860s saw one of those strange breaks in history which theoretically should not happen but which in practice do. As in Parliament, so in radicalism in general and in ultra-radical freethought in particular, there was a change of generations. Southwell emigrated in 1856 and died in 1860; Cooper retired in 1858 and died in 1868; Owen died in 1858; John Watts died in 1866; Joseph Barker was reconverted to Christianity in 1863. The men who had been so important in the 1840s and 1850s had largely gone by the late 1860s, except for Holyoake. Holyoake had been twenty in 1837, when the Owenite movement was getting under way at the Manchester congress; when the Political Union was being revived in his native Birmingham; when the *Northern Star* was being started in Leeds; and when a committee of London radicals was starting to draft the People's Charter. Bradlaugh at that time was four, and therein lay a significant difference between the two generations. The older men had many links with Chartism and socialism and had known the hopes and frustrations of those early years. The later generation was merely the inheritor of a tradition, and those older men who survived—Holyoake, W. J. Linton, G. J. Harney, Thomas Cooper—stood outside the mainstream of events. Men like George Howell and Charles Bradlaugh were to rise to take their places, just as in the 1880s they in their turn were to be supplanted by a new generation of socialists in the Social Democratic Federation and the Independent Labour Party.[3]

The sources for a study of radical freethought in this earlier period are somewhat limited. Apart from the writings of the various leaders and their periodicals, references are few and far between. Local newspapers do not add much, for, except in unusual circumstances which were normally quoted verbatim in the Secularist press, the local freethinkers attracted little attention. Numerically they were often insignificant, so that even detailed local studies, such as have reshaped the history of Chartism, can often contribute little, especially for the early years of Secularism between 1840 and 1866. What local studies do reveal, however, is the close connection between the various movements which made up British working-class radicalism during these years—the continuity between the Zetetic Society, Owenism and Secularism in Glasgow, for example, or the links between West Riding Chartism and Secularism, and the involvement of some of Richard Oastler's men in Huddersfield Secularism.

What is true of local studies is also true of individual personalities. Much of the evidence is tantalisingly fragmentary and it is difficult to add features to the bare bones of the names which flit in and out of the periodicals. The historian of any one movement is in danger of not recognising his obscure characters as the equally obscure participants in other radical movements. In a biographical appendix I have tried to piece together a few details which may, in the absence of other information, help towards a general understanding of the interconnectedness of the various radical movements and their personalities in early and mid-Victorian Britain.

In the footnotes I have tried to note the major sources, which are also listed in the bibliography. As much of the text is based on a close study of the weekly periodicals of freethought I have spared the reader the tedium and expense of detailed references, except where these seemed to be of particular importance.

Finally I should like to thank Dr G. Kitson Clark, who supervised the original research out of which this book grew, and Professor J. F. C. Harrison and Professor H. J. Perkin, who gave a later version of the manuscript the benefit of their much-needed criticisms. I am also immensely grateful to the Co-operative Union, Manchester, for allowing me to make the first systematic study of the Holyoake papers, and particularly to the late Desmond Flanagan, who helped me as he helped so many other students of Co-operative history. Mr D. Tribe and Mr J. S. L. Gilmour have allowed me to borrow books from their private collections, and I am also indebted to Mr D. R. Webb of the Bishopsgate Institute, Mr W. McIlroy of the National Secular Society, and to the librarians and staffs of the British Museum reading room, the University library, Cambridge, the Bodleian Library, Oxford, the International Institute of Social History, Amsterdam, and the city libraries of Birmingham, Leeds, Leicester, Manchester, Newcastle upon Tyne and

Sheffield. Others whom I wish to thank include Dr D. E. D. Beales, Professor A. Briggs, Dr S. Budd, Dr J. W. Burrow, Dr C. B. Campbell, Dr R. G. Garnett, Mr J. Salt, Dr F. B. Smith, and the Rev. J. Sturdy. My gratitude is due, finally, to the Master and Fellows of Selwyn College, Cambridge, where most of this book was written, and to my wife, who patiently endured while most of this book was being written.

Notes
1 C. B. Campbell, *Towards a Sociology of Irreligion* (London, 1971), pp. 2–5.
2 J. Vincent, *The Formation of the Liberal Party* (London, 1966), *passim.*
3 E. Royle, *Radical Politics, 1790–1900* (London, 1971), pp. 76–9.

I

Heritage

a
The age of reason

'Our soundest knowledge is, to know that we know him not; *and our safest eloquence concerning Him is our silence*; therefore it behoveth our words to be wary and few.'[1] So wrote Richard Hooker, the father of English divines, but he was not questioning the existence of God, only a detailed knowledge of His attributes; and this was the primary concern of thinkers both Christian and non-Christian throughout the eighteenth century. Men differed not over the existence of God but over the reasons they could give for belief in such an existence.

The eighteenth century did not have any one philosophy of 'Enlightenment' and there were many cross-currents in the European thought of the century, but so far as the nineteeth-century freethinkers were concerned it was primarily the age of reason. Nothing was to be taken on trust, save that there were general laws of nature awaiting discovery by the rational observer. The dilemma of religious belief in an age of reason had already been put by John Dryden in his *Religio Laici* (1682):

> How can the *less* the *Greater* comprehend?
> Or *finite Reason* reach *Infinity*?
> For what could *Fathom* GOD were *more* than *He*.[2]

Revelation was therefore necessary to supplement reason. This was the basis of the great theological synthesis worked out by St Thomas Aquinas.

In the age of reason a serious attempt was made to attain a knowledge of God not by revelation but purely by reason, by scientific induction from known data, and some of the basic philosophical problems of eighteenth-century thought arise out of this attempt. Did the emphasis on reason mean that revelation was irrelevant? What if the rational evidence for the existence and nature of God contradicted the revealed evidence of the Bible? If everything could be seen to operate according to natural laws, what room was there for miracles? Even more disturbing, if the course of life were determined by such natural laws, what room was there for human free will?

These were some of the problems with which the great minds of the eighteenth century tried to grapple, and the starting point for many was the work of the seventeenth-century French philosopher René Descartes (1596–1650). Beginning with the individual human mind, Descartes assumed from his awareness of his own existence that there are certain self-authenticating first principles; that there is a distinct antithesis between subject and object, between soul and matter; and that knowledge is absolute and therefore independent of matter.[3] This theme of dualism—the antithesis of spirit and matter—runs right through the thought of the eighteenth and nineteenth centuries, and one of the aims of the rationalists was to reconcile the two.

John Locke attacked the first of Descartes' three principles by challenging the possibility of innate ideas. Even the idea of God, he argued, was not inborn but was attributable to sense impressions, stored in the memory and arranged by the mind. Ideas were, for Locke, not self-authenticating but dependent upon external evidence, and the most powerful evidence in favour of Christianity was that of miracles.[4] Locke offered this as a reasonable and sincere defence of his faith, but the weaknesses in his argument were there for others to probe more deeply. To base a belief in God on external evidence created the possibility of an idea of God contradictory to that revealed in Scripture, and to appeal to miracles in an age of reason was to presume that the laws of nature were not universally applicable. In one way and another, Locke's theory of ideas underlay much of eighteenth- and nineteenth-century freethought.

A second great influence on thought in the age of reason was the 'new philosophy' associated with the names of Bacon and Newton. The scientific method of observation and induction, which appeared to reveal the physical laws of the universe, had great appeal to the educated and popular mind alike as a suitable approach to all knowledge. Attempts were made to discover laws of nature, not only in astronomy and physics but also in ethics and morality, and the quest for a science of human nature occupied the minds of, among others, Thomas Hobbes (1588–1679), David Hume (1711–76) and Jeremy Bentham (1748–1832). When George Berkeley (1685–1753), Bishop of Cloyne, tried to refute Locke's theory of ideas, he could do so only at the expense of Descartes' second principle, that mind and matter are utterly distinct and reconciled only in the mind of God. Instead, Berkeley argued, nothing can exist without either perceiving or being perceived, and ideas can therefore have no existence except in the mind. Thus mind acts upon matter rather as a force acts on an atom, and the great mind behind the whole universe, sustaining it and giving it cohesion, is God.[5]

This was a fundamental idea of the age of reason. The universe was pictured as comprising units of inert matter governed by forces acting upon them. Every effect had its cause, and the prime mover of the universe was God. The existence and nature of God were therefore to be demonstrated by a scientific study of the Creation, which would naturally lead the observer to the Creator. Alexander Pope neatly summed up this argument in his *Essay on Man* (1733–34):

> Say first, of God above, or man below,
> What can we reason, but from what we know?
> Of man, what see we but his station here,
> From which to reason, or to which refer?[6]

This religion, centred on man and reason, was far different from the Christianity which had divided Europe in more than a century of civil and religious wars. The immediacy of a revealed, personal God, who was also Saviour, was replaced by a more impersonal concept. Although some Christian apologists, like Samuel Clarke, continued to emphasise the importance of revelation, they generally conceded much ground to the deists in that both Christian and non-Christian writers assumed the virtues of a natural and rational religion.

There was little room in this rational and designed universe for the arguments of atheists. John Ray, one of the earliest in a long line of clergymen who combined natural philosophy with natural theology, wrote in 1691 *The Wisdom of God Manifested in the Works of Creation*, in which he considered and rejected the possibility of atheism:

> it seems to me impossible [he wrote] that Matter divided into as minute and subtle Parts as you will or can imagine, and those moved according to what Catholick laws soever can be devised, should without the Presidency and Direction of some intelligent Agent, by the mere agitation of a gentle Heat, run itself into such a curious Machine, as the Body of Man is.[7]

A deist, the third Earl of Shaftesbury (1671–1713), was no less adamant in dismissing the atheistical notion of chance: he defined 'a perfect atheist' as 'one who believes nothing of a designing principle or mind, nor any cause, rule, or measure of things, but *chance*—so that in nature neither the interest of the whole nor of any particulars can be said to be in the least designed, pursued, or aimed at'.[8] The nineteenth-century atheist could accept this definition with pride, but such a position was almost untenable in the age of reason. The notion of chance was absurd when the beauties and functionalism of the human eye were considered.

The argument from design was first used by the Dutch mathematician

Nieuentytt in the seventeenth century, and continued to be popular until
the 1830s, when eight weighty volumes of *Bridgewater Treatises* were
composed. The writer most associated with natural theology, however,
was not one of the Bridgewater authors but William Paley (1743–1805).
In his *Natural Theology; or Evidence of the Existence and Attributes
of the Deity, collected from the Appearance of Nature* (1802) the argument from design is given its most lucid expression, and the atheist is
ridiculed for not seeing the Creator of the world in the works of his hand,
just as the watchmaker can be seen in the skilful design and workmanship
of a watch. But Paley was not unaware of the weakness of this reasoning
as an argument in favour of the Christian God. Rather, he announced
in his preface, his justification of Christianity—as opposed to mere
deism—was to be found in his other works, most notably *A View of the
Evidences of Christianity* (1794), in which he appealed to the historical
evidences of miracles and auxiliary evidences of the Bible, such as
prophecy.

These historical evidences formed the major areas of dispute between
deists and Christians in the eighteenth century. John Toland, in his
Christianity not Mysterious (1696), argued that there was nothing intel-
ligible in the New Testament which could not also be rationally understood. Revelation was therefore superfluous. The Christian reply was
that, although the truths of revelation were to be attested by reason,
human reason was not able, of itself, to understand all the mysteries of
the universe. This argument assumed that nothing in the Christian
revelation was, in fact, contrary to reason and the religion of nature.
Deists were quick to point out that this was not so. Matthew Tindal
contrasted the God of Nature with the Jewish God of the Bible. Another
'moral philosopher' argued that if the so-called revelations of the Koran
could be subjected to the cold criticism of natural reason, then so also
could the revealed truths of the Bible.[9] Either Christianity was the same
thing as deism, or, according to arguments used by rational Christians
themselves, it was less than perfect. The opponents of Christianity therefore concentrated on those aspects of Christian thought which seemed
contrary to reason—miracles, prophecy and the resurrection of Christ.

The resurrection—the most important miracle recorded in the Bible
—was the crucial issue, and a controversy about it was started by Thomas
Woolston. His *Six Discourses on the Miracles of our Saviour* (1727–9)
treated all miracles, including the resurrection, as allegorical. Bishop
Sherlock replied in 1729 with the *Trial of the Witnesses*, which set out
the orthodox reasons for believing the New Testament account of the
resurrection. This prompted Thomas Chubb to subject the resurrection
to some elementary historical criticism: the Gospels, he said, were written

long after the event by persons who were not themselves witnesses, and so would not be treated as reliable forms of evidence in a court of law.[10] Three years later Peter Annet wrote a more extreme reply, in which he treated Sherlock's witnesses as vulgar cheats. Meanwhile one of the most prominent of the early freethinkers, Anthony Collins, had used historical criticism to call prophecy into question. If the New Testament were a fulfilment of the Old, then the prophecies of the Old Testament should relate to the New. In fact, he claimed, they did not; and in many cases the books of prophecy—such as Daniel—had been written long after their supposed date of composition.[11]

At the same time as men were probing with their reasons the problems of theology, religion continued to be for a great many people an emotional and irrational affair of the heart. The great period of English deism came in the late seventeenth and early eighteenth centuries, and in the succeeding half-century a change in mood, associated with the romantic and gothic revivals, prepared the way for the Evangelical awakening of religion in England.

The Evangelicals appealed to the heart and not to the head. They restored the emphasis on Christ as Saviour of the world. Their doctrine of the Holy Spirit brought back God from the outer reaches of the mechanistic universe and restored Him to an immediate role in the life of sinful man. A man was to be justified by his faith in Christ and in the atoning power of Christ's death. By contrast, a deistic pamphleteer in 1746 was finding contrary to reason the whole notion of a Son of God who was God himself, and unnatural the idea of an atoning death for the sins of others.[12] Deism and Christianity stood opposed to each other. The Evangelicals taught Christians not to base their faith on the intellectual presuppositions of the deists, but to stand firm by the word of God —revelation, not reason.

All Christians based themselves on the Bible, but there was a difference in approach between the Evangelicals and the rational theologians. William Paley was content to argue for the validity of the Christian evidences, and he was not unduly disturbed by minor criticisms of the sacred texts. He was aware of discrepancies, but did not find them important. Christians who were more committed to a literal and fundamentalist interpretation of the Bible, however, were to find that their faith was increasingly under attack from scholars. Rational Christians were alarmed that the Evangelicals might actually be contributing to the spread of infidelity, and one conservative commentator at the end of the eighteenth century blamed 'Mystics, Muggletonians, Millennaries, and a variety of eccentric characters of different denominations' for 'their ridiculous mode of defending, or enforcing, their different Christian tenets', which 'only increased the objections to the Christian Belief, in the minds of those persons before unhinged by the subtleties of Infidels'.[13]

The attack on the Bible was, however, real enough, and even the most reasonable of men had, in time, to modify their approach to its sacred word. Elementary biblical criticism had been current for a century and more before the Evangelical revival began. In the *Leviathan* (1651) Thomas Hobbes had pointed out that Moses could not have written that part of the book of Deuteronomy which admits that the whereabouts of Moses's grave are not known 'to this day'; and he made a number of other such observations about the dating of various books in the Old Testament.[14] More important, in 1670 Baruch Spinoza (1632–77) had published in Holland his *Tractatus Theologico-politicus*, which offered 'the first serious analytical criticism of the Old Testament'.[15] English thought in general lagged behind that of the Continent. In 1739 Samuel Parvish, a Guildford bookseller, cautiously suggested a late date for the writing of the Mosaic law, but the really significant development in studies of the Pentateuch came in 1753, when Jean Astruc, a French physician, distinguished the separate Elohim and Yahwist accounts of the Creation in the first chapters of Genesis. So, gradually, the knowledge was acquired with which the literal truth of the Bible could be seriously called into question. The climax came at the end of the eighteenth century when Alexander Geddes (1737–1802), a Scottish Roman Catholic priest, produced a new translation of the Bible (1793) in which he dated the Pentateuch from the time of King Solomon; and in a later work, *Critical Remarks on the Holy Scriptures* (1800), he treated the Mosaic account of the Creation as a myth. Geddes was censured by his bishops; he was an isolated figure in Britain, and his works were never reprinted, but he had some influence on the Continent. In Germany Vater popularised his ideas and developed the hypothesis that the Pentateuch was really based on the journals of Moses but was not written up until long after his death.[16]

German scholars also turned their attention to the New Testament, and examined the Gospels as individual historical documents. F. D. E. Schleiermacher (1768–1834) denied the authenticity of the Pauline authorship of the Epistle to Timothy; K. G. Bretschneider (1776–1848) argued that the Gospel according to St John was not written by St John the apostle; G. L. Bauer (1755–1806) offered mythical interpretations of biblical events; J. A. L. Wegscheider (1771–1849) cited pagan parallels to the virgin birth. 'It is a curious thing,' wrote J. J. Ampère from Bonn in 1827, 'the scientific audacity with which these good theologians, despite their sincere faith, discuss the documents of that faith. One publicly declares that the Pentateuch is not of Moses; another rejects the Gospel

of St John; another that of St Matthew.'[17] But the German theologians
were able to pursue their scholarship because they had found a new
basis for their faith. Schleiermacher treated religion as a matter of con-
templating the eternal—an experience of piety; knowledge was a different department of life from religion. The mystical quality of the Gospel
of St John transcended mere historical criticism.

In England E. B. Pusey (1800–82) appreciated this fact, and his book,
*An Historical Enquiry into the Probable Causes of the Rationalist
Character of the Theology of Germany* (1826–30), was one of the few
English works which the Germans found it worthwhile translating into
their own language, but such a pietistic defence of theological enquiry—
Pusey feared he would be called a Methodist—depended upon the reality
of the religious experience. For many men the horizon of their ideas
remained that of rational thought, and German ideas were only slowly
received in England. When H. H. Milman's *History of the Jews* was
published (anonymously) in 1829 it caused such a public outcry that the
publisher had to stop the series of which it formed a part. Dean Stanley,
the Broad Church leader, later called Milman's work 'the first decisive
introduction of German theology into England, the first palpable indication that the Bible could be studied like any other book, that the characters and events of the sacred history could be treated at once both
critically and reverently'.[18] Four years earlier Connop Thirlwall had
translated Schleiermacher's *Critical Essay on the Gospel of St Luke*
(1821), which offered an interpretation incompatible with verbal literal-
ism. Schleiermacher's name became synonymous with infidelity, and
Thirlwall's chances of ecclesiastical preferment were sadly stunted.
Another German name which came to epitomise in England the secular
and critical spirit of Continental theology was that of D. F. Strauss
(1808–74), whose *Life of Jesus* (1835), translated into English by George
Eliot in 1845, became one of the works to precipitate the mid-Victorian
'crisis of faith'.

Most people in England, however, were unaware of all this. The Bible
continued for them to be the literally true word of God, and their faith
depended upon it. The spread of historical criticism seemed a cruel blow
to honest churchmen working to save souls, but it seemed a timely justification to the rationalists, who, for over a century, had been challenging
revelation in the name of reason.

More dramatic than the quiet work of obscure German theologians,
and more sinister because more widely discussed, were the discoveries
of the geologists. A scholar might be wrong about the dating of the
Pentateuch—and he could always be ignored—but the evidence of
geology was the evidence of one of the most popular sciences, and the

evidence presented by geologists against the literal truth of Genesis was compelling.

In the eighteenth century religion had not been in conflict with science. In the grand synthesis of the natural theologians, the works of God declared and confirmed the revealed word of God. But as Thomas Burnett had cautioned in 1690, ' 'Tis a dangerous thing to ingage the authority of Scripture in disputes about the Natural World, in opposition to Reason, lest Time, which brings all things to light, should discover that to be evidently false which we had made Scripture to assert'.[19] The book of Genesis clearly described the Creation as a series of miraculous, God-inspired events which had occurred, according to Archbishop Ussher's chronology, as recently as 4004 B.C. The formation of the world must therefore have been as dynamic as its continuance, for the instruction of man and to the glory of God, had been static. This view became increasingly less tenable in the late eighteenth and early nineteenth centuries.

Two schools of thought developed among geologists as to the nature of the Creation. The most numerous body agreed with the natural theologians that the present condition of the earth was static and that the whole work of creation had been the product of a series of catastrophic periods of activity. Available evidence seemed to support this. The existence of fossils, for example, confirmed the fact of a universal flood. A. G. Werner, Professor of Mineralogy at Freiburg in Saxony, argued that the different types of rock recorded different periods of activity in the creation of the world. By contrast, James Hutton of Edinburgh led the minority view in concerning himself not with the origins of the world but with its contemporary processes, and he put forward the theory that the forces of change are continually operative.

Hutton's views had serious implications for the Biblical account of the Creation. The Wernerian school had assumed, if not Archbishop Ussher's chronology, then at least some comparatively recent date for the formation of the world; but Hutton saw 'no vestige of a beginning— no prospect of an end'. Richard Kirwan, president of the Royal Irish Academy, led the opposition to Hutton's theory, which he regarded as being more dangerous than the opinions of Thomas Paine. John Playfair of Edinburgh defended Hutton and dismissed the horror of those who 'would have us consider their Geological speculations as a commentary upon the text of Moses'. He found a confirmation, rather than a denial, of the God of the natural theologians in the uniformity of creation according to the processes set out by God in the beginning—whenever that was.[20]

New techniques confirmed the inadequacy of the traditional Mosaic chronology. The crust of the earth was shown to have been formed over a long period, and there was evidence that animal life had existed at the same time as some of the rocks were being laid. William Smith, a civil engineer and amateur geologist, worked out the correct succession of the strata of England and Wales. He found that given sets of beds tended to contain the same species of shells over vast and widely separated areas. At the same time, in France, J.-B. Lamarck (1744–1829) was systematising the zoology of invertebrates, while Georges Cuvier (1769–1832) was developing the techniques of vertebrate palaeontology and fitting the animal creation into the geological time scale. The old-established belief in the 'chain of being', from God down to the meanest of his creatures, was shown to be wanting. Animals had existed which were now extinct, and different fossils were to be found in strata from different eras. This was shocking only to biblical fundamentalists. The short time scale had to be abandoned, but otherwise the new techniques enhanced the catastrophic interpretation of the creation of the world.

The most sophisticated attempt to reconcile the latest scientific knowledge with the Bible was made by William Buckland of Oxford. In his inaugural lecture to the Readership in Geology in 1819, he aimed 'to shew that the study of Geology has a tendency to Confirm the evidences of Natural Religion; and that the facts developed by it are consistent with the accounts of the Creation and Deluge recorded in the Mosaic writings'. He acknowledged that there were many who still doubted the continued superintendence of God, 'maintaining that the system of the Universe is carried on by the force of the laws originally impressed on matter, without the necessity of fresh interference or continued supervision on the part of the Creator', but he felt capable of meeting such objections. Natural theology clearly showed 'that the secondary causes producing these convulsions have operated at successive periods, not blindly and at random, but with a direction to beneficial ends . . .' The clearest evidence in favour of divine intervention was the creation of animals, for 'it is demonstrable from Geology that there was a period when no organic beings had existence: these organic beings must therefore have had a beginning subsequently to this period; and where is that beginning to be found, but in the will and *fiat* of an intelligent and all-wise Creator?' So the catastrophists appeared to have the better of the argument, and it remained for the uniformitarians to show how animals could possibly have appeared without divine intervention. Some men, such as Lamarck, attempted this, but their arguments did not carry much conviction.[21]

Buckland realised that Natural Theology used in this way did not appear to be entirely consistent with the first chapters of Genesis but he

was confident that there was no basic contradiction. Genesis did not deny
the existence of previous worlds or deal with any natural history other
than that connected with the present world as prepared for the habitation of man. As for the six days of Creation, they could simply be interpreted as six eras during which God had prepared the scene for Adam
and all the other animals of the present creation. Thus Buckland was
prepared to allow a much longer period of time than had been traditionally accepted, but his whole thesis rested on one assumption: that
'the evidence of all facts that have yet been established in Geology
coincides with the records of Sacred History and Profane Tradition to
confirm the conclusion, that *the existence of mankind* can on no account
be supposed to have taken its beginnings before that time which is
assigned to it in the Mosaic writings'.[22]

This was written between 1818 and 1820. Some five years later
McEnery, a Roman Catholic priest, found human remains alongside
those of extinct mammals in Kent's Cavern, near Torquay. Out of
deference to Buckland he did not publish his findings, but in 1828
Tournal de Narbonne did publish an account of human remains found
in a cave at Bise among the bones of mammals which Cuvier had dated
as belonging to the Quaternary epoch.[23] Could it be that man, created
by God in His own image and set a little lower than the angels, was just
another of the animals? What was man's place in nature?

The same question was also being posed by some biologists and
medical practitioners, and a materialistic interpretation of life was
becoming possible—although still highly improbable. Materialists in
the eighteenth century did not deny the existence of God *a priori*, and a
few, like Joseph Priestley, even remained Christians, but the general
effect of the materialistic argument was either to relegate God to the
beginning, when he had first imposed his immutable natural laws upon
matter, or by *a posteriori* reasoning to abolish him altogether.

What the materialists challenged was the dualistic concept of mind
and matter, as modified by Bishop Berkeley. They rejected the Newtonian concept of the atom as a permanently designed structure which
participated in a world of change and yet remained itself unchanged.
Matter, they argued, was active not passive, and they sought the origin
of motion not in some external guiding Power and Intelligence but in
the properties of matter itself. The greatest of the French materialists,
Baron d'Holbach, made this distinction clear:

> If, by 'Nature', we understand a mass of dead material, devoid of all
> properties and entirely passive, we shall doubtless be compelled to search
> outside this Nature for the principle of its movements. But if by Nature
> we understand that which it really is, a whole of which the various parts

have various properties, behave in accordance with these properties, and
are in a state of perpetual interaction upon each other—then we shall
have no need to have recourse to supernatural forces in order to account
for the objects and the phenomena that we see.[24]

The causes of change were not to be sought in the will of an external
being, even one which operated through the properties of matter, but in
the interaction of matter with its material environment, a theory derived
from Locke's sensationalist theory of knowledge, which Berkeley had
been at great pains to contradict. Taken to its logical conclusions,
this materialism had serious consequences for the theological view of
man.

First, it implied that mind, hitherto the repository of the divine light
in man and the feature which distinguished man from the animals, was
no more than a function of the brain. Joseph Priestley (1733–1804), the
Unitarian divine, philosopher and chemist, tentatively reached this conclusion. Simple observation suggested to him that

> the power of sensation or perception, and thought, as belonging to man,
> have never been found but in conjunction with a certain *organised
> system of matter*, and, therefore, that those powers necessarily exist in,
> and depend upon, such a system. . . . Had we formed a judgment concern-
> ing the necessary seat of thought, by the *circumstances that universally
> accompany it*, which is our rule in all other cases, we could not but have
> concluded, that in man it is a property of the *nervous system*, or rather of
> the *brain*.

If this were indeed true, then man could be fitted into the general animal
creation, and yet another argument for divine intervention and special
creation would have been discredited. Medical opinion, though, did not
in general support this extreme conclusion, and Christian apologists like
Buckland felt secure. Small doubts, however, did begin to creep in, and,
as with natural theology, the apologists adopted positions which subsequent scientific discoveries made untenable. Cabanis (1757–1808), a
French physician, advanced a materialistic theory of the brain which,
when propagated in England by Dr T. C. Morgan in 1819, resulted in
Morgan losing his practice; and when Sir William Lawrence (1783–
1867), in his introductory lecture to the College of Physicians, went so
far as to doubt the inspiration of Genesis on medical grounds, his lectures
were refused a copyright (1822)—though, contrary to what was intended,
this facilitated their circulation amongst freethinkers. Not until 1870
was the unitary nature of the central nervous system and the brain finally
accepted by all informed opinion.[25]

Secondly, if mind were as much a fiction as the universal flood, then
what of the divine Mind in the universe? The seventeenth-century Dutch

philosopher Spinoza had abandoned Cartesian dualism and put forward
instead a system of mystical pantheism in which everything was reduced
to attributes of the single substance, God. Some freethinkers adopted this
philosophy, and, lacking the mystical element, transformed its pantheism
into virtual atheism. Others adopted the 'nebular hypothesis' to explain
the origin of the universe. This theory had originated with the Greek
atomists, and dismissed the problem of the Creator by dispensing with
the Creation. The Renaissance scholar Bruno had revived this theory,
and it was developed in the eighteenth century by Immanuel Kant (1755)
and by the Marquis de Laplace (1749–1827), whose *Exposition du
système du monde* was translated into English in 1809 and was used by
Sir John Herschel in his influential *Treatise on Astronomy* (1833). The
Creator, if not rendered a dispensable hypothesis by Laplace, had been
banished to the very beginnings of time.[26]

How, then, had the animals been created? The most important
answer to this question came from Lamarck, the French zoologist,
whose major contribution to nineteenth-century thought was the concept of evolution. He claimed that life had originated in matter as the
result of a series of physical and chemical reactions. Living matter
had then evolved, producing higher and more complex organisations,
finally resulting in man. Intelligence had appeared in the lowest
mammals, and had increased with the development of the nervous
system. 'Every fact or phenomenon observed in a living body is, at one
and the same time, a physical fact or phenomenon and a product of
organisation.'[27] The problem was to explain why the organisation of
matter should change, why organisms should grow and develop.
Lamarck tried to account for this in what is the most unsatisfactory part
of his whole system, his theory of the will, according to which living
bodies exert themselves to exist in their environment, and so adapt
themselves to it. The result of such adaptation was that some organisms
fell into disuse and decay, whilst others were developed. These acquired
characteristics were then transmitted to the next generation, and so
on. This 'development hypothesis' was plainly inadequate, but it had
great appeal in the first half of the nineteenth century, influencing,
among others, Herbert Spencer and Charles Darwin. It was expounded
in the popular *Chambers's Information for the People*, and written
on at length in the freethought journals.[28] In 1844 it was given its
most popular Victorian form in Robert Chambers's *Vestiges of the
Natural History of Creation*, a totally unsatisfactory work which shows
both the strength and the weakness of Lamarck's theory. It was un-
scientific, and yet it pointed in the right direction, and those Christians
who felt their arguments fortified in the face of the ignorance of the

scientists were to be rudely shocked when in 1859 Charles Darwin offered a more plausible version of the development hypothesis, which accounted for change in terms of random variation and the survival of the fittest.[29]

Genesis against geology; mind against materialism. These were the issues which, in the early nineteeth century, contributed to the growing sense that science was in opposition to the Christian faith. As new scientific knowledge became available, so the latest positions of the Christian apologists had to be abandoned. The crisis of faith reached a climax in the mid-century decades, but the roots reach back to the Enlightenment.

The freethinkers, however, did not escape all intellectual difficulties themselves, for a natural consequence of materialism was determinism. The French Encyclopaedist Baron d'Holbach had written in his great work on natural law, *Système de la Nature* (1770):

> Man always deceives himself when he abandons experience to follow imaginary systems. He is the work of nature. He is submitted to her laws. He cannot deliver himself from them. He cannot step beyond them, even in thought.[30]

The implications of this belief in the all-pervasiveness of natural law were worked out by the necessitarian philosophers, and one of the earliest of them, Thomas Hobbes, set out the basic definitions on which the theory depended:

> *Liberty*, and *necessity* are consistent: as in the water, that hath not only *liberty*, but a *necessity* of descending by the channel; so likewise in the actions which men voluntarily do; which, because they proceed from their will, proceed from *liberty*; and yet, because every act of man's will, and every desire, and inclination proceed from some cause, and that from another cause, in a continual chain, whose first link is in the hand of God the first of all causes, proceed from *necessity*. So to him that could see the connection of those causes, the *necessity* of all men's voluntary actions, would appear manifest.[31]

This theme was developed by Anthony Collins, *Philosophical Inquiry Concerning Human Liberty* (1715); David Hume, *An Inquiry Concerning Human Understanding* (1748); David Hartley, *Observations on Man* (1749); and was transmitted to the nineteenth century in the writings of Joseph Priestley, *The Doctrine of Philosophical Necessity Illustrated* (1777).

The necessitarians and natural law philosophers argued that everything has a cause, whether we are aware of it or not. In the psychology of man we call this cause 'motive'—that is, circumstances so influence man through his passions that the object of his will is determined by them. But this was not mere mechanical determinism, because man has the power of reason, which influences the way his will is motivated. By experience, man learns that certain causes have certain effects, and this very knowledge represents a change in circumstances. So, by studying nature, man is able to escape: his actions are all necessary, but they are not beyond his control. In this form the doctrine of necessity reached the nineteenth century, and found its clearest expression in Charles Bray's widely read book *The Philosophy of Necessity*, published in 1841. Bray defined the doctrine as follows:

> The doctrine of necessity, in plain language, means that a man could in no case have acted differently from the manner in which he did act, supposing the state of his mind, and the circumstances in which he was placed, to be the same; which is merely saying, that the same causes would always produce the same effects. Men are prone to suppose that they could have done otherwise, because, in reviewing their conduct, its consequences—the experience resulting from it—are mixed up with the motives that decided them before, so that if they had to decide over again, different circumstances must be taken into calculation.[32]

Here Bray's teaching is very little different from that put forward by Robert Owen as 'the doctrine of circumstances' and although Owen never admitted having read the works of the necessitarians of the eighteenth century, it is hard to escape the conclusion that he had absorbed some of their ideas. Bray himself was an Owenite for a time, and his book was advertised in the *New Moral World*.

The doctrine of necessity made a profound impression on nineteenth-century thought. In Priestley's hands it became a philosophical justification for mutual improvement and social reform. Far from encouraging fatalism, it stimulated men to activity:

> . . . the apprehension that their endeavours to promote their own happiness will have a certain and necessary effect, and that no well-judged effort of theirs will be lost: instead of disposing them to remit their labour, will encourage them to exert themselves with redoubled vigour; and the *desire of happiness* cannot but be allowed to have the same influence upon all systems.[33]

In terms of morality this led to the doctrine of Utilitarianism. The source and standard of morals was transferred from the will of God to the will of man and those forces influencing the will of man. Conduct was made the consequence of rational appetite—the product of the passions considered by reason in the light of experience—and man was presumed to be basically selfish, pursuing his own happiness and avoiding pain. On these axioms Jeremy Bentham sought to construct for the ethical world a *Principia* such as Newton had provided for the physical.

But Bentham was only one of several Utilitarian thinkers: John Gay, David Hartley, David Hume, Joseph Priestley, William Godwin and William Paley all used the same sorts of arguments.

Philosophical necessity, with all its implications, was therefore one of the most important legacies of the Enlightenment. It enabled the idea of regularity in nature to be combined with an exaltation of the powers of reason, and it provided a secular system of ethics to match the secularised concept of natural law. It also provided a secular theology for deism and the religion of nature. Science was the new providence, education was to be the redeemer of mankind; for by understanding and controlling circumstances, man could shape the human clay. In this grand scheme for the perfectibility of man the old notions of original sin and salvation found little place. When Priestley visited Paris in 1774 the philosophers he met marvelled that he could continue to be a Christian. Reason had grappled with the problems of life and had reached conclusions in opposition to those of the Christian revelation. Nineteenth-century freethought found its basic doctrines ready-made in the philosophy of the Enlightenment.

b

Thomas Paine

The roots of the Painite tradition can be traced back to the civil war in the middle of the seventeenth century, when 'Oliver's preachers' had challenged the religious and political structure of England,[34] and freethought matured in the coffee-house society of the Restoration, where politics and religion were inextricably linked. John Toland was not only one of the first writers to push Locke's freethinking Christianity into deism, he was also an ardent republican and author of lives of Milton and Harrington.[35] The law of land recognised this close connection: in 1671 Sir Matthew Hale made it explicit in his notorious ruling that 'Christianity is parcel of the laws of England', and when Thomas Woolston was later tried for publishing his *Six Discourses on the Miracles of Our Saviour* Chief Justice Raymond acted on the principle that 'whatever strikes at the very root of Christianity tends manifestly to a dissolution of the Civil Government'.[36] Nevertheless, English deism was able to remain respectable so long as it was confined to the respectable such as the great aristocrats, Shaftesbury, Bolingbroke and Herbert of Cherbury. Those violent opinions on religious and political matters which the seventeenth-century tumults had uncovered were again suppressed, and affairs of Church and State in eighteenth-century England enjoyed a superficial calm which was only occasionally troubled by suggestions of turbulence below.

When such turbulence emerged it was instantly branded 'infidelity'— a word used to describe unorthodox beliefs of any kind which were held by or shared with members of the lower orders. When Thomas Cooper lectured on 'The early English Freethinkers' in 1848 he included such names as Herbert of Cherbury, Hobbes, Shaftesbury, Bolingbroke, Gibbon and Hume, but he drew special attention to Thomas Chubb as 'our first *working-man freethinker* registered in the history of English Literature'. Chubb (1679–1747) was a chandler who belonged to a little debating society in Salisbury, and it is with such men and such obscure societies that the origins of the British freethought movement are to be found: Jacob Ilive (1705–68), for example, was a printer from Bristol who lectured in the London halls on the 'Religion of Nature'. In 1753 he was pilloried three times and sentenced to three years' hard labour for writing a pamphlet against divine revelation. The most notorious of all these early infidels was Peter Annet (1693–1769), a former dissenting minister who eked out a living as a schoolmaster and who, like Ilive, lectured in the London halls. Also like Ilive, he was punished for his efforts. In 1761 he published the first freethought journal, the *Free Inquirer*, in which he ridiculed the Holy Scriptures, and for this blasphemy was sentenced at King's Bench in 1762 to a pillorying, a fine and a year's hard labour.[37]

Annet was a member of one of the most famous of all the London debating clubs, the Robin Hood Society, which met at the 'Robin Hood and Little John Inn' off the Strand. This society was open to all who paid a sixpenny admission charge, and about five thousand people attended each year to discuss all manner of topics, literary, religious and political. The Robin Hood Society closed down in 1773, but W. H. Reid, who gives a contemporary description of these early London societies, reported a similar sort of place off Oxford Road where a 'Priest of Nature' delivered lectures in 1775–76, and 'a pretty numerous circle' who met in the Hoxton district between 1776 and 1793.[38]

Writing in 1800, Reid noticed similarities between such societies in England, France and Germany, and he also compared the English situation in the mid-seventeenth and late eighteenth centuries. It is certainly true that the radicals of Western Europe and North America shared a common intellectual heritage, and although deism in England had made little progress after 1750 the ideas of the previous hundred years were borrowed and matured in France. Toland's *Letters to Serena* (1704) were translated into French by d'Holbach in 1768 under the title of *Lettres Philosophiques*, and two years later d'Holbach used Toland's argument for materialism in his own *Système de la Nature*. The leading intellectuals of the French Enlightenment were deists: d'Alembert, d'Holbach, Diderot, Condorcet, Turgot and Buffon all advocated the religion and philosophy of Nature. In the late eighteenth and early nineteenth centuries their works were translated into English and were read in Britain and North America. Reid complained that a translation of Voltaire was to be had in sixpenny parts and that second-hand copies could be bought for a penny.[39]

This was of little significance before the revolution broke out in France. Only afterwards did contemporaries see the dangers inherent in the literature and societies of the Enlightenment. In 1798 a pamphlet on *French Philosophy* credited Voltaire, d'Alembert, Diderot, Turgot, d'Holbach and Rousseau with causing the French revolution: 'If the influence of religion be removed from the minds of men,' the author noted, 'civil laws will be found utterly ineffectual for the preservation of order in society, and universal anarchy must ensue.'[40] This was, perhaps, an exaggeration, but the general effect of the literature of the Enlightenment was to promote a rational and radical criticism of existing institutions and ideas. To this extent, reason was the parent of revolution.

Events in France after 1789 inspired ultra-radicals throughout Europe, and the obscure debating societies and clubs of Britain found new life. The Society of United Irishmen, founded in Dublin late in 1791, increased its influence, particularly in Lancashire and western Scotland; the London Corresponding Society, started early the following spring, articulated the demands of the artisans and others among the lower orders in the capital who had not really shared in earlier movements for parliamentary reform, and branches of the London Corresponding Society, calling themselves Corresponding or Constitutional Societies, were soon established also in Sheffield, Manchester, Norwich, Derby, Southwark and other centres of population. The government acted quickly to suppress them. When the Scottish radicals called a series of General Conventions in 1792 and 1793, two of the leaders, Thomas Muir and the Reverend T. F. Palmer, were transported for inciting discord between king and people. In November 1793 the Scots organised a 'British Convention of Delegates of the People associated to obtain universal suffrage and annual parliaments', to which representatives came from Ireland and London. The L.C.S. delegates, Margarot and Gerald, were arrested and transported. The following year, when the L.C.S. organised its own general meetings in London, twelve of its leading members were arrested, and three—Thomas Hardy, John Horne Tooke and John Thelwall—were indicted but then acquitted by a jury. This

c

led the government to take extra powers. Habeas Corpus was suspended in May 1794, despite the protests of Sheridan and a minority of Whigs in the Commons, and the following year, after incidents at the opening of Parliament, two Acts were introduced, one to make more rigorous the law on treason, the other to restrict the right of public meeting. The radical societies were driven underground, and when John Binns and John Gale Jones visited Birmingham on behalf of the L.C.S. they too were arrested.

The government was genuinely afraid. The radicals seemed to be in alliance with the French, the navy was mutinous, and Ireland was seething with rebellion. The United Irishmen were active in Britain: Binns and Father O'Coigly were founding groups of United Englishmen around Liverpool and Manchester, and similar groups of United Scotsmen were being started in Glasgow and Ayrshire. Radicals were said to be learning French in readiness for an invasion. But as the government took even greater powers the radical organisations were suppressed. Ireland was put down (1798) and annexed (1801), the laws against the press were strengthened (1798 and 1799), corresponding societies were made illegal (1799), the laws against combinations of workpeople were revised (1799 and 1800), and the suspension of Habeas Corpus was continually renewed.[41]

Into this world of radical hopes and failures the writings of Thomas Paine were published, circulated and avidly read. Paine stands at a fountainhead of political and religious freethought, but he was not an original thinker. His writings present the conclusions of the Enlightenment, bound up with the nascent infidelity of Chubb, Ilive and Annet, and sealed with the revolutionary fervour of France. Until the English artisan became reconciled to the political and ecclesiastical establishment, itself growing more liberal, after 1848, the tradition of Paine remained a dominant theme among the leaders of the British working-class movement. His teachings were repeated with little or no change for two generations and more.[42]

Paine was born in Thetford, Norfolk, in 1739, the son of an artisan, and he went into the Excise service, but it was as a radical journalist in America during the War of Independence that he made his reputation. In 1787 he returned to Europe, hoping for a revolution in the Old World such as he had witnessed in the New. In 1790 Edmund Burke, who had supported the American revolution, led the forces of reaction in Britain when he published his celebrated *Reflections on the Revolution in France*, in which he attacked a lecture by Richard Price, a leading Unitarian, in defence of the French. Paine rushed into print in 1791 with a reply, justifying the French against Burke. This was the *Rights of Man*,

Part 1, which sold at three shillings a copy and earned the praise of even moderate reformers. In 1792 Paine published Part 2, which was a different sort of work: it was cheap and it was seditious. Paine vigorously attacked the follies of the so-called British constitution, the hallowed settlement of 1689, and the hereditary Hanoverian monarchy. He expressed himself clearly as a root-and-branch republican.

In 1791, according to the Dean of Norwich, writing half a century later, 'Thomas Paine, in reply to "Burke's Reflections", published his pestilent work, the "Age of Reason" '.[43] Paine did nothing of the kind, but this sort of mistake illustrates the confusion which persisted in the minds of respectable commentators between Paine's political and religious radicalism. Paine did not write the *Age of Reason* until 1794, when, as an exile in Paris, he was alarmed to see the French people rushing headlong into atheism, and he was, in fact, a very religious man with some extremely conservative theological views. In the *Rights of Man* he had written, 'Every religion is good that teaches man to be good; and I know of none that instructs him to be bad.' Paine was a humanist and a deist, and in Paris he tried to give his beliefs an institutional form by starting a Society of Theophilanthropists, the object of which, in the words of Samuel Adams, was ' . . . *to renovate the age* by inculcating in the minds of youth *the fear and love of the Deity and universal philanthropy*'. Paine once described himself as 'a man who considers the world as his home, and the good of it in all places as his object'.[44]

In his theological writings Paine was more conservative than Priestley and the French philosophers. He accepted the conclusions of Newtonian science without question or modification; he rejected materialism: 'Motion is *not a property* of matter,' he wrote, ' . . . Motion, or change of place, is the effect of an external cause acting upon matter.' He believed in immortality as 'consciousness of existence . . . not dependent on the same form or the same matter'. That is, by maintaining the dualism of matter and spirit he rejected the resurrection of the body; whereas Priestley, by rejecting the dualism, managed to keep the resurrection of the body. Paine also recognised the possibility of miracles, not because the Deity acts contrary to the laws of nature but because 'unless we know the whole extent of those laws, and of what are commonly called the powers of nature, we are not able to judge whether anything that may appear to us wonderful or miraculous be within, or be beyond, or be contrary to, her natural power of acting'. Paine's psychological theory was merely an extension of the watch metaphor: 'The main spring which puts all in motion corresponds to the imagination; the pendulum which corrects and regulates that motion corresponds to the judgment; and the hand and dial, like the memory, record the operation.' Behind the mechanism sat the great Maker: 'God is the power of first cause, nature is the law, and matter is the subject acted upon.' There was little in this to arouse controversy. Paine was in the mainstream of the natural theologians. Like Paley a few years later, he used the argument from design to prove the existence of God. ' ... *the creation is of itself demonstration of the existence of a Creator,*' he wrote. 'When we see a watch, we have a positive evidence of the existence of a watchmaker, as if we saw him.'[45]

Part 1 of the *Age of Reason* was handed to the American diplomat and freethinker Joel Barlow as Paine was being arrested as an enemy alien during the Terror. While in the Luxembourg prison, awaiting the guillotine which never came, Paine composed Part 2, which, like Part 2 of the *Rights of Man*, contained the negative side of his thought. In it he launched a savage attack on Christianity, which justified his reputation as an infidel and which provided his readers with a standard criticism of Christian orthodoxy. His starting point was the absurdity of the doctrines of Christianity, and he began in moral revulsion against the atonement which presented God Almighty as 'a passionate man who killed His son when He could not revenge Himself in any other way'. Such a religion corrupted human values by placing itself above the needs of humanity. 'It is a want of feeling,' he wrote in an essay *On Church Bells*, 'to talk of priests and bells while so many infants are perishing in the hospitals, and aged and infirm poor in the streets, from the want of necessaries.' His own religion, in contrast, proclaimed, in a phrase which rang down the decades, 'One good schoolmaster is of more use than a hundred priests.'[46]

The cornerstone of the Christian system was the Bible, so Paine's main object in the *Age of Reason*, Part 2, was 'to show that the Bible is spurious, and thus, by taking away the foundation, to overthrow at once the whole structure of superstition raised thereon'. The criticisms which he offered are not very profound—a mixture of crudity and common sense with a little genuine insight. As W. H. Reid noted, 'Mr Paine's observations, under this character, might be corrected by many school-boys. With him, neither metaphor nor allegory is allowable in religion!' But, as Reid himself realised, this was where the biblical fundamentalists played into the freethinkers' hands.[47]

Paine first of all rejected the Bible on the well-trodden grounds of incompatibility with nature. 'For my own part,' he protested, 'my belief in the perfection of the Deity will not permit me to believe that a book so manifestly obscure, disorderly, and contradictory can be His work. I can write a better book myself.' Secondly, he rejected the Bible because 'It is a history of wickedness that has served to corrupt and brutalize mankind; and, for my part, I sincerely detest it as I detest everything that is cruel'. A third reason was that the Bible made impossible claims for itself, on which were founded incredible doctrines. Genesis was 'an anonymous book of stories, fables and traditionary or invented absurdities, or of downright lies', and yet on this book depended the doctrine of the atonement for Adam's sin, for 'To have made Christ to die on account of an allegorical tree would have been too bare faced a fable'. Fourthly, the Bible, both as a book and as a source of teaching, was neither outstanding nor original when compared with the writings of the other great religions. Lastly, Paine pointed out the internal contradictions of the Bible, distinguishing between the Elohim and Yahwist stories in Genesis 1 and 2, and suggesting that Job, a gentile book, was the oldest part of the Bible, while the Mosaic law had not been known until the time of Josiah.[48]

This was Paine's theological contribution to the radical tradition. Building on the early eighteenth-century deists, he added little. His significance was that in plain English he spoke out beyond the educated few to the semi-literate, and even illiterate, many, and he spoke with the twin tongues of infidelity in religion and politics at a time of political and social upheaval. 'Infidelity has already overthrown one of the greatest kingdoms in Europe,' lamented a contemporary work on French philosophy.[49] To call the Bill of Rights 'a bill of wrongs, and of insult', and to assert that 'In every land throughout the universe the tendency of the interest of the greatest number is in the direction of good rather than of evil', confirmed reformers and conservatives alike among the respectable classes in their belief that infidelity was political dynamite.[50] One leader of the reform movement of the 1780s, the Reverend Christopher Wyvill, feared that 'If Mr Paine should be able to rouze up the lower classes, their interference will probably be marked by wild work, and all we now possess, whether in private property or public liberty, will be at the mercy of a lawless and furious rabble'.[51] For a decade Paine looked as though he might do just that, and for a further fifty years his name inspired hopes or fears of its accomplishment.

There was a close connection between the growth of the radical clubs and the spread of radical literature. The reports of the House of Commons Committees of Secrecy, 1794, and 1799, and the observations of W. H. Reid, all suggest that the popularity of the literature was due to the work of the clubs. The London Corresponding Society reprinted and circulated the *Rights of Man* in a cheap edition which had sold over 200,000 copies by 1795. In Sheffield the Constitutional Society was reported to have reprinted the work at sixpence and then to have had it read aloud at public meetings. The *Age of Reason* was circulated in a similar way, and

the Bishop of London complained that it was being read even among the
miners of Cornwall. The L.C.S. also reprinted Volney's *Ruins of Empires*
(translated by Joel Barlow), d'Holbach's *System of Nature* and North-
cote's *Life of David*, and began a series of weekly halfpenny reprints of
Annet's works. Prosecution then halted their proceedings, and plans for
cheap editions of other works, both French and English, had to be
abandoned.[52]

The impact of this activity on a local situation is described in Reid's
account of the infidel societies of London. Discussion groups had long
existed in coffee houses and inns, but they became more extreme in the
1790s, as they discussed and debated the ideas put forward by Paine,
Voltaire, Rousseau and other favourite authors. One such society met at
the Green Dragon in Fore Street, near Cripplegate, where meetings were
held on Wednesday and Sunday evenings in the spring of 1795. The
magistrates tried to control such places by threatening their landlords'
licences, and the Green Dragon society was hounded from tavern to
tavern throughout the East End until, in 1797, it spent its last two
months in the safety of Hoxton, beyond the jurisdiction of the City.
Other east London clubs met in Bunhill Row, Whitechapel, Spitalfields
and Shoreditch, while two societies met in the West End, one of which
survived until 1798. The literature also gave rise to its own organisations
and, according to Reid, one group met in a Bethnal Green garden on
Sundays to read and discuss the *Age of Reason*, whilst others studied
Voltaire and Godwin.[53]

This expansion of organisations and extremist literature promised
much for the coming of the revolution to England as it already had to
the United States and France. Contemporaries were acutely aware of the
similarities between events on both sides of the English Channel, and
perhaps even more aware of the dreadful precedents of the seventeenth
century in England. Radical ideas had permeated society, and the
dangerous and turbulent classes were talking about religion and politics
in a critical and rebellious manner. Reid described the 1790s as 'the first
period in which the doctrines of Infidelity have been extensively circulated among the lower orders', and the London Corresponding Society,
which expanded rapidly in 1794 and 1795, he described as 'the sole
medium which, for the first time, made infidelity as familiar as possible
with the lower orders'. London apprentices, the original 'roundheads',
were admitted to the discussion clubs 'according to the modern notions
of equality'. Necker had noticed the same trend in France, and Reid
compared the club localities of London with the Parisian *fauxbourg* of
St Antoine. Parliament was told by its Committee of Secrecy that the
royalist and republican parties, dormant since 1688, had 'now returned

to the charge with a rage and animosity equal to that which characterized our ancestors during the civil wars in the reign of Charles the First'.[54]

Yet in 1800 W. H. Reid thought that the worst was over. The government's policy of repression seemed to have worked. Public opinion had hardened behind the forces of law and order, which were too strong for the radicals. In 1792 Thomas Erskine had defended the *Rights of Man*; five years later he led the prosecution against the *Age of Reason*. Moreover radical opinion was itself divided. The *Age of Reason* was never as popular as the *Rights of Man*, and the decision of the London Corresponding Society to publish the *Age of Reason* split its own ranks when a number of religiously orthodox radicals broke away from the parent body. A further division resulted from the infiltration of the society by the extremist United Irishmen. There was also a change in attitude to the war. In 1793 the radicals had seen the war against France as an aristocratic campaign against the republican ideal, but by 1800 this ideal was sadly tarnished. The forces of reaction had set in, not only in Britain and Ireland but also in France itself. The 1802 Concordat with the Papacy, by which Napoleon restored the Catholic faith in France, marks the end of the decade of revolution.

During these years, despite the setbacks, a revolutionary tradition had been born. Ideals had been conceived, hopes expressed and ideas shared in the 1790s. No amount of political repression could conceal this. As Reid concluded, 'though their meetings are no longer holden; still as scattered individuals, they are sufficiently numerous to do considerable mischief; the Atheistical class in particular seem most incorrigible'. The radicalism of the next two generations was to look back to the 1790s for its origins and inspiration. When Ben Brierley wrote in 1895 about Failsworth, near Manchester, he recalled with pride the Jacobin Club which had met a century earlier to read 'Voltaire, Mirabeau, and other great thinkers which the French Revolution sent to the fore'. As G. J. Holyoake somewhat whimsically noted in his *History of Co-operation*, 'Historical knowledge was a weak point of the people. Those of them who were politicians believed that the history of the world began with the French Revolution.'[55]

c
Richard Carlile

Ultra-radicalism was repressed rather than stamped out during the Napoleonic wars, and when the economic situation took a turn for the worse in 1812 discontent began to emerge once more. With the peace came even greater economic dislocation, and the popular movement flared up again. Twenty years of economic development gave this post-war radicalism a much broader social and geographical basis and, as the provinces and employees in the new industries were caught up in the campaign, the balance of forces began to shift from London to the north, where ultra-radicalism was gaining a new bitterness from incipient working-class consciousness.

The radical press led the way, and through it the ideas of the 1790s were once more made current among the lower orders. Chief among the propagators of Painite ideology was Richard Carlile, a Devon tinsmith who knew nothing of radical politics until he came to London in 1813.[56] In 1816 he read Paine's *Rights of Man* for the first time and was caught up in the world of the radical publishers and newsagents. The following year he began to hawk the *Black Dwarf* and fell in with another young admirer of Paine, W. T. Sherwin, who had just started a radical paper of his own boldly called the *Republican*. Then Sherwin married and gained greater discretion: the paper was renamed *Sherwin's Political Register* and Carlile was asked to take over its publication, together with Sherwin's shop at 183 Fleet Street. Carlile was almost immediately arrested for selling William Hone's *Parodies on the Book of Common Prayer* and was thrown into gaol for eighteen weeks, where he completed his radical education by reading the *Age of Reason*. His course now seemed clear: his mission was to expose and denounce kingcraft and priestcraft, and he achieved this in two ways. First, he reissued the works of Paine and other freethought classics; secondly, when the government tried to stop him, he became a martyr and throughout the country built up groups of followers who were dedicated to his cause.

His publishing output was considerable. The backbone of his efforts was his weekly periodical, *Sherwin's Political Register*, which he restarted under its original title of *Republican* in August 1819, and which he continued to publish, with intermissions, until the end of 1826. At first the paper offered sixteen pages of large octavo for twopence, but after the Blasphemous and Seditious Libels Act came into force in 1820, making small, cheap papers illegal, he doubled the number of pages and put up the price to sixpence. In the early days the circulation was over ten thousand—fifteen thousand during the crisis of 1819—but by the end it was scarcely in four figures. As Carlile commented in 1826, ' "The Republican" has not had the most extensive circulation; but its effect has been powerful where it has been read.'[57] The contents were nearly always the same: comments on some outrageous action by the govern-ment; an extract—perhaps a long one if other copy was short—from a freethought classic; local reports and correspondence; and controversies about obscure religious or political points. Even from gaol, Carlile dominated the paper, and most of the original articles were from his pen.

Carlile's first reaction after reading the *Age of Reason* was to reprint it, and this he did in two half-guinea volumes in December 1818. The initial sale at this price was not great—a hundred copies were sold in the first month—but at the same time he also began a number of other reprints in cheaper forms: Paine's *Common Sense* and *Rights of Man* were issued in weekly parts along with *Sherwin's Political Register*, the *Rights of Man* appeared both in a half-crown volume and in a two-volume edition which cost £1, and other reprints were later made available in a weekly series entitled the *Deist or Moral Philosopher*. At first the government took no action, for 1818 was a comparatively quiet year on the political front and Carlile seemed to pose no threat, but early in 1819 a private body calling itself the 'Society for the Suppression of Vice' began a prosecution.[58] The only immediate consequence of this action was an increase in the sale of the *Age of Reason*. After Peterloo in August 1819, however, the government grew too alarmed to let the matter rest. Carlile had been present at Peterloo, published an account of what had happened, and was thereupon arrested on a charge of seditious libel. But when his trial came on at the Guildhall in October 1819 the earlier blasphemy charges were preferred. He was convicted and sentenced to two years in prison and a fine of £1,000 for publishing the *Age of Reason*, and to one year in prison and a fine of £500 for publishing Elihu Palmer's *Principles of Nature*. He was sent to Dorchester gaol, and, as he refused to pay the fines or to enter into £1,000 securities for life, he was not in fact released until November 1825.

The effect of this trial and punishment was the opposite of what had been intended. Two thousand copies of the *Age of Reason* were sold in six months. The work was also read out by Carlile in court as part of his defence and was therefore allowed a legal circulation in the verbatim reports of the trial, which sold ten thousand twopenny numbers. Trade at Carlile's shop—now called 'The Temple of Reason'—was brisk, and, although the sheriff's officers cleared the stock and closed the premises when Carlile was convicted, first Carlile's wife, Jane, and then his sister, Mary Ann, soon reopened the shop and carried on the business until they too were arrested and sent to Dorchester gaol. Even this did not stop the production of blasphemous works. Volunteers kept the shop open and not only continued to sell the *Republican*, the works of Paine and Palmer and the report of the trial, but also undertook new ventures, including an issue of the Koran in threepenny numbers. Then in 1826, when Carlile was able to resume his work in person, he started a Joint Stock

Book Company which reissued, among other works, nine numbers of
Annet's *Free Inquirer*, the French classic *Bon Sens* and Shelley's *Queen
Mab*, which was based on Mirabaud's (d'Holbach's) *System of Nature*.[59]
Great as had been the efforts of the London Corresponding Society to distribute the works of freethought in the 1790s, the nineteenth-century
radicals owed their familiarity with the writings of the Enlightenment
mainly to Carlile. The Painite tradition might not have existed if Carlile
had not revived it after the French wars. He was not a modest man, but
his own summary of his achievement up to the end of 1822 is in this
respect not far wrong:

> Thomas Paine's 'Age of Reason' was the first serious and honest attack ever
> made upon the Christian idolatry in this country. Many sneers and jeers
> were passed upon it, from the time of what is called the glorious Revolu-
> tion in this country, down to the close of the last century; but nothing like
> a serious attack until the first part of the 'Age of Reason' appeared . . .
>   Just calculate how many persons may read one copy of 'Age of Reason,'
> if it be taken care of. I know several persons, who have kept copies, which
> they purchased of me in 1819, in constant use, in the way of lending them
> up to this time, and instances where a single copy has gone through fifty
> families, all approving as they read. This is the way to calculate the power
> of the Printing Press. Had the 'Age of Reason' kept circulating from its
> first appearance, as it has within these last four years, it would ere this,
> have undermined the Christian idolatry of this country; but it is notorious
> that it was spell bound for twenty years, with the exception of a few copies
> put forth by Daniel Isaac Eaton. From December 1818, to December 1822
> nearly twenty thousand copies will have gone into circulation. 'Let Cor-
> ruption rub out that if she can,' as Mr Cobbett said of his forty thousand
> Registers.[60]

Carlile's second achievement was to bind together the beginnings of
ultra-radical organisations throughout the country. During the initial
period of persecution, when the whole radical press was under attack,
formal organisation had hardly been necessary, but after 1821 the building up of radical groups in the provinces was undertaken as a matter of
deliberate policy.

Before 1819 Carlile had been but one radical leader among many.
Cobbett, with his *Register*, and Wooler, with his *Black Dwarf*, were the
real leaders of the 'blasphemous and seditious press', while Cobbett and
Hunt dominated the political scene. But the prosecutions which were
begun in 1819 against the metropolitan and provincial publishers and
vendors of radical literature had marked Carlile out as an important
national leader. In all twenty-five informations were laid against ten
London booksellers for distributing Carlile's publications, while Swann
of Macclesfield, Russell of Birmingham, Mann of Leeds and Marshall of
Glasgow, among others, all had Carlile's works mentioned in their indict-

ments. The stand taken subsequently by Carlile and his family, together
with his long martyrdom in Dorchester gaol, merely added to his stature
at a time when, in the normal course of events, interest and support
might have been expected to have fallen away.[61]

The Fleet Street shop had to be kept open, not only as a matter of
principle but also out of sheer necessity, for Carlile could only be kept
in gaol so long as there was an adequate income to meet his wants. In
October 1820 he launched his first appeal: 'If half a dozen persons were
resolved successively to oppose the Vice Society, their prosecutions would
become of the greatest advantage to the propagation of good principles,'
he wrote in the *Republican*, and, although the paper ceased publication
in 1821, when it was re-started in January 1822 its pages show that his
appeal had not gone unheeded.[62] Little groups of sympathisers had
begun to meet in towns and villages throughout the country to send their
pennies and sixpences to Carlile and other 'victims', and when Jane and
Mary Ann Carlile were imprisoned in the autumn of 1821 they began
also to send volunteers to fill the breach. In this way a generation of
local radical leaders was given its political education.

Organisations seem to have been first started in December 1821, when
the 'Edinburgh Freethinkers' Zetetick Society', led by James and Robert
Affleck, was formed to support Carlile. They had a library and held
lecture meetings on Sunday evenings, and in February 1822 they were
able to send twenty-nine subscriptions to the victim fund.[63] A similar sort
of thing happened in Leeds, where a meeting of 'The Friends of Rational
Liberty', chaired by James Watson, celebrated Carlile's birthday on 8
December: fifty-three people were present, two of whom—Watson and
Humphrey Boyle—were shortly to go to London as volunteers in Fleet
Street.[64] In London itself a society was started for propagating 'Deistical
Principles through the medium of Lectures, Discussion, Publication of
Tracts, &c. &c.', and in May 1822 a Zetetic Society was announced which
entered into correspondence with the Edinburgh Zetetics.[65] The idea of
local radical or Zetetic clubs to support Carlile spread rapidly. Subscriptions had already begun pouring in from Huddersfield, where the
friends of Carlile were organised by Abel Hellawell, a tinplate worker,
and from the neighbouring villages of Marsden and Almondbury. The
first major occasion for a large number of gatherings was the anniversary
of Paine's birthday, 29 January 1822, and early in February the reports
began to appear in the *Republican*: sixty men and women reformers had
met at Ashton; a guinea had been collected at Bath; a Paine Club had
been founded at Birmingham; three pounds came from Sheffield; and
eighteen subscriptions were made in the village of Stokesley, near Stock-
ton, where the health of Paine had been drunk in pure water.[66]

Other towns and villages followed this lead in the next few months. Excepting Edinburgh and London, most of the activity came from the West Riding, Lancashire and Cheshire. As early as 1819 there had been a group of Carlile sympathisers in Stockport, led by William Perry, and, encouraged by letters from him and James Watson of Leeds, the Friends of Free Discussion in Manchester met in May 1822 to consider ways of helping Carlile.[67] They launched an appeal for funds, and Manchester and Bolton, Leeds and Huddersfield emerged in the *Republican* as centres of support for Carlile.

The loyalty of these local radicals to Carlile's cause was cemented by the sufferings of their own members who had gone to help in Fleet Street. By the time Leeds celebrated Paine's birthday in 1822, Humphrey Boyle was already in Newgate, together with W. V. Holmes, Joseph Rhodes and John Barkley. James Watson, who made the main speech at the Leeds dinner in 1822, also went to London later the same year and soon joined the others in Newgate, for selling Palmer's *Principles of Nature*: Stockport gave special support to Joseph Swann, the Stockport hatter who spent four and a half years in Chester gaol for selling the *Republican* in Macclesfield; and Nottingham felt a special sympathy for Susannah Wright, the local lace-mender who had been the first to take on the Fleet Street shop when Mary Ann Carlile went to prison in 1821. The Scottish blasphemy laws were far harsher than the English, and the Edinburgh Zetetics had their own problems when James Affleck was prosecuted for using blasphemous expressions and the society was forcibly closed. Among the books seized by the police from the Society's library were Mirabaud's *System of Nature*, Shelley's *Queen Mab*, Voltaire's *Philosophical Dictionary*, and Owen's *Essays on the Formation of Character*. Affleck, however, was irrepressible, and in 1824 he set himself up in business as a bookseller, only to be imprisoned for three months for selling the *Republican* and the *Theological Works* of Paine.[68]

The year 1824 also saw a renewed series of prosecutions in London. Between 1819 and 1822 most of the prosecutions had been instigated either by the Society for the Suppression of Vice or the Constitutional Association, but neither had been outstandingly successful.[69] The 1824 prosecutions were largely the result of a final drive against the Fleet Street house by the Home Office under Robert Peel. William Haley, Richard Hassall, William Cochrane, Thomas Riley Perry and Michael John O'Connor were all tried at the Old Bailey in June 1824 and sentenced to between six months and three years in prison for publishing the *Republican*, the *Age of Reason* and Palmer's *Principles of Nature*. In Newgate Campion, Hassall and Perry produced their own *Newgate Monthly Magazine or calendar of men, things and opinions*, while in

Fleet Street the radical work continued. The failure of these prosecutions prompted Peel to modify his policy. There were no further arrests after 1824, and in November 1825 Carlile's fines and securities were remitted. After six years he was again free.[70]

During these years Carlile's publications and imprisonment had made a lasting impression on English radicalism. The support given to him had been enormous: over £1,400 had been collected for him between 1819 and 1825, largely in poor men's pennies and sixpences. In 1822 alone almost £900 had been sent in by fifty-seven localities throughout Great Britain. Nearly £400 of this came from London, but other towns which sent totals of over £20 were Edinburgh, Huddersfield, Leeds, Manchester, Nottingham and Stockport. Zetetic and similar societies flourished: between forty and fifty localities seem to have had pro-Carlile groups of radicals, and about half of these reported organised societies.[71]

All sorts of people rallied to Carlile, but they were mostly artisans and shopkeepers; as the Lord Advocate said of the Edinburgh Zetetic Society in 1823, it 'was attended by the lowest description of persons; not a person above a grocer belonged to it'. The Sheffield society was started by seven basketmakers; at Bolton the membership included a number of weavers; the ropemakers of Shadwell sent several contributions in the London lists.[72] There were old men and young men. There were veterans like John Gale Jones, a prominent member of the London Corresponding Society who was brought back into radicalism by the shock of the Peterloo massacre; and, more obscurely, men like John Andrew of Hattersley, a sexagenarian who in 1829, said Carlile, 'boasts of having been of our opinions before we were born', and Daniel Nield of Ripponden who had been brought up in a clothier's family but who had educated himself to be a surgeon and was a long-standing deist.[73] Then there were young men who, like Carlile, knew of the 1790s only through the literature and the stories told by the older men. Amariah Batty, a dyer and threadmaker of Castleton in the North Riding, was twenty-eight in 1822: he had renounced Christianity after discussing the Carlile case in 1819, and had been led on from the *Age of Reason* to the works of Mirabaud, Volney and Voltaire. Another young man was Richard Hassall, a Dorset carter who, after visiting Carlile in Dorchester gaol, volunteered for the Fleet Street shop; his radical education was completed in Newgate.[74]

Carlile's release from gaol in November 1825 was widely celebrated the following January on Paine's birthday, but as soon as he ceased to be a martyr his support began to fall away. In gaol he had begun to acquire pretensions. Manchester lamented that full shares in the Joint Stock Book Company were £100 each; tickets for the Paine celebration at the City of London Tavern in 1826 cost half a guinea each, and only seventy-

five people came, out of an expected three hundred. Carlile closed the
Republican at the end of 1826 and he wanted to start a more respectable
stamped newspaper instead but his efforts failed when he fell ill with
asthma and rheumatic pains brought on by his long imprisonment, and
when Richard Hassall, who was to have edited the new paper, died sud-
denly at the age of twenty-five. The Book Company languished too, for
lack of funds.[75] Meanwhile Carlile's views about religion were changing
and he was falling under the influence of one of the most curious infidels
of all—a renegade clergyman, the Reverend Robert Taylor.[76]

After rejecting Christianity and then attempting to recant, Taylor had
been forced to leave the Church of England and to become a lecturer on
deism. He went to Ireland, and in Dublin he issued a series of deistical
tracts entitled the *Clerical Review* and started a Society of Universal
Benevolence, but at only his second Sunday meeting the students of
Trinity College caused a riot, so he decided to return to London. He
arrived in the summer of 1824, was quickly accepted by John Gale Jones
and the other radicals, and started a Christian Evidence Society, to which
he lectured at the Crown and Anchor tavern on reasons for not believing
the Christian evidences. In prison Carlile heard of and welcomed this
new ally, although when he was released and met Taylor in person he
was not at first so impressed. Taylor was a deist and not an atheist, and
his attempts to introduce an infidel 'liturgy' into his 'services' were
greeted by Carlile with derision and characterised as hypocrisy. Gradually, however, Carlile was won over to Taylor's point of view, and their
friendship grew. Carlile came to appreciate the intellectual strength
which the former clergyman was able to bring to the cause. Mostly the
freethought movement had borrowed from the works of the Enlightenment, but Taylor wrote his own. His arguments were esoteric and novel,
based partly on a historical criticism of the biblical texts and partly on
comparative religion, mythology and philology. The *Diegesis*, his major
work, which he wrote in Oakham gaol in 1828, became a new freethought
classic.

Taylor was imprisoned for blasphemy in 1828, and this cemented his
friendship with Carlile. The latter, who had started a new periodical, the
Lion, at the beginning of 1828, kept it on at a loss to give Taylor an outlet for his views. The renewal of persecution brought new strength both
to Carlile and to his supporters in the country as help again poured in
from the provinces and subscriptions from Birmingham and Bristol,
Ashton and Aberdeen, Leeds and Leicester, Hyde and Halifax mounted
for the new martyr. The same men who had been the backbone of
Carlile's support in 1822 –5 were again to the fore: Joshua Matley of
Ashton, Joseph Russell of Birmingham, John Heys of Bolton, James and

Robert Affleck of Edinburgh, John Smith of Leeds, Elijah Riddings of Manchester and many more. There were also scores of new names, some of which, like that of Lawrence Pitkethly of Huddersfield, were to become familiar in the radical periodicals of the coming generation.[77]

When Taylor was released in February 1829, he and Carlile decided to go on an 'Infidel Mission' to these faithful followers, and an 'Infidel Rent' was proposed to pay for their efforts. They first went to Cambridge, where Taylor issued debating challenges to all the heads of colleges and pinned copies, written in Latin and Greek, on the door of the university library. But when no action was taken by the university (other than that of depriving their lodging-house keeper of his licence) they left for Wisbech and the north. At first the results were disappointing. There was no open support at Wisbech, although funds had been received from the town; they were unable to hire a hall in Nottingham; and even in Leeds only eighty or ninety people paid a shilling to hear them speak in the Music Hall. Bradford and Manchester were equally thin in their support, but Stockport was very encouraging, there was a full house at Ashton, and the meeting at Huddersfield was thought very satisfactory.[78]

The ground in Lancashire had, to some extent, been prepared by one of the most interesting of all the converts to Zeteticism, Rowland Detrosier. This young radical had worked in the mills of Manchester as a boy, but he had risen to respectability in the Swedenborgian 'Bible Christian' Church. Patronised by Joseph Brotherton, he had been given charge of the pulpit of Mount Brinksway chapel, near Stockport, but a debate with members of the local Zetetic Society had converted him to deism, and early in 1828 he had submitted a defence of deism to Carlile's *Lion*. At first he was allowed to keep his pulpit, but after allowing Carlile to speak from it in September 1827 he lost his position and returned to Manchester, where he became a leading advocate of working-class education. Detrosier had an enormous personal following in Lancashire and Cheshire, and his independent adherence to the sort of ideas which Taylor and Carlile were advocating in London suggests a widespread acceptance of unorthodoxy in the textile towns of the north-west on which the London leaders could easily build.[79]

On the whole the 1829 tour confirmed the pattern of support suggested in the periodicals. Lancashire, Cheshire and the West Riding were the strongholds, but even here Carlile's appeal was limited to a relatively small group of activists, who only in times of crisis could have a widespread influence out of all proportion to their actual numbers. In Leeds, for example, despite the lack of mass support at Carlile's meetings, five stalwarts—four of whom had been among the first contributors to Carlile's cause in 1822—planned to raise £150 in £2 shares to build a lecture room; and in 1829 the energies of such men throughout the country raised £243 5s 6d for the Infidel Rent, more than enough to meet the propagandist expenses of the year's work. Taylor and Carlile were therefore reasonably satisfied when they returned to London, and they hoped to make another provincial tour in 1830, but, because of the renewed reform crisis which began in that year, they decided to concentrate all their efforts in London. Carlile hired the Rotunda as a lecture theatre for the radicals, and started another weekly paper, the *Prompter*, in which to advocate the cause of reform.[80]

Robert Taylor was one of the main attractions at the Rotunda. On Sundays he delivered what he called 'sermons' from his 'Devil's Pulpit' in the Rotunda, and he himself was dubbed by Henry Hunt as the 'Devil's Chaplain'. Both he and Carlile were soon in trouble again, and the Home Office kept notes on what was said in the Rotunda lectures. Carlile was sentenced in January 1831 to two years in the Giltspur Street Compter for publishing an address 'To the Insurgent Agricultural Labourers' in the *Prompter*, and Taylor was indicted for delivering two blasphemous lectures on Good Friday and Easter Sunday 1831, and was sentenced to two years in the Horsemonger Lane gaol.[81] Subscriptions again poured in, although not quite so many as formerly, and old names mixed with new in lists of supporters from the usual places. In London friends kept in progress the work of the absent leaders: James Watson opened the Finsbury chapel for discussions on four evenings a week, and the tradition of help from the provinces was kept up by Eliza Sharples, who came from Bolton to help Gale Jones in keeping the Rotunda open.[82]

This was the last time, though, that this sequence of events was to be repeated. Taylor married a wealthy supporter after his second imprisonment and retired to Tours. Carlile took Eliza Sharples as his new partner —both in marriage and in work—and she completed the ascendency of Taylor's views in his mind. He underwent a kind of spiritual conversion and for the last ten years of his life the earlier atheist was scarcely recognisable as he fumbled through mysticism and mythology towards an allegorical interpretation of Christianity. In May 1832 he announced in another brief publication, the *Isis*:

> I declare myself a convert to the truth as it is in the Gospel of Jesus Christ. I declare myself a believer in the truth of the Christian religion . . . I declare for the spirit, the allegory, and the principle, and challenge the idolatrous pretenders to Christianity to the field of discussion.

He made one more excursion into politics, in 1833, when he started an unstamped paper, the *Gauntlet*, and toured the country enrolling three thousand Volunteers to force the government to cut taxes. Then the following year he suffered his last imprisonment, for causing a public nuisance when he protested against the Church rates by displaying in his Fleet Street shop window the effigies of a distraining officer and a bishop, the latter arm in arm with the devil. But he no longer had anything important to say to his followers. Even in 1830 the *Prompter* had sold no more than a thousand copies, most of them in London and Lancashire.[83]

Richard Carlile's greatest achievement had been to establish the tradition of Thomas Paine. 'I would fain rouse the inhabitants of Sheffield,' he wrote in 1822, 'by calling upon them to come forward, not to support this or that man, but to support those principles which are laid down in the writings of Thomas Paine.'[84] There were, of course, some radicals who had been converted to such principles in the 1790s—men like John Gale Jones of the London Corresponding Society, Clio Rickman, the friend of Paine who chaired an American Independence celebration among the London radicals in 1822, as well as ordinary subscribers to Carlile's cause, like B. Randal of Portsea, who called himself 'an old man forty years firm and steady in the principles of Mirabaud', and Joseph Law of Bradford, who signed himself 'a disciple of Paine of 30 years' standing'. To these Carlile added a large number of converts who first met Paine through the publication of the 1820s.[85]

Carlile transmitted the ideas of Paine, but he was not entirely lacking in self-interest when he stressed the rigid orthodoxy of the Painite tradition, and he was not himself entirely faithful to that tradition in all respects. When he had urged the Sheffield radicals to be true to Paine he had really been levelling a sharp blow at Henry Hunt. He disapproved strongly of Hunt's Great Northern Radical Union in 1822, by which Hunt was hoping to secure his own election to Parliament. For Carlile, Paine had become more than the name of a great radical: he had been transformed into a symbol for root-and-branch republicanism as defined by Carlile himself, and so the name was to be used by Carlile as an instrument with which to attack other radical leaders.[86] And in the same way, in time, his own name was to be joined to that of Paine in a new standard of orthodoxy to be hoisted by competing groups of ultra-radicals in the next generation. Rather like Marxist Leninism, the Paine–Carlile tradition was established as the ideology of the ultra-radicals.

At times Carlile's writings accurately reflect the spirit of Paine. In 1822, in an open letter to Canning, he defined republicanism and deism in terms consistent with those used by Paine in the *Rights of Man* and the *Age of Reason*, but the previous year he had in fact renounced Paine's deism and put in its place that very kind of materialistic atheism against which the *Age of Reason* had been written.[87] In the last number of the *Republican* Carlile admitted to this revisionism and stated his own

D

principles in words which accurately set out the revised character of the tradition:

> No profession is made of having added any thing to the soundness and utility of Mr Paine's political principles, other than in the extended publicity given to them, but a profession is made of having added much to the soundness and utility of his theological principles. He made or defended a system and kept a god, we have ventured to ask—WHAT IS GOD? We find no one to answer the question with an intelligible sentence, and finding no one to answer the question, having no answer of our own, we have found that an honest inquirer after truth can and should proceed without the use of the word god.[88]

Carlile's followers do not seem to have been unduly disturbed by the reversal in the religious teaching of the tradition. Thomas Turton of Sheffield wrote that he was 'an admirer of three, but not three in one, Mirabaud, Thomas Paine and Richard Carlile', although Paine here was the odd man out in that he was not a materialist; and Elijah Riddings of Manchester wrote of 'the sublime truths contained in the inestimable productions of Diderot, Voltaire, Condorcet, Volney, Paine, Palmer, &c.' when in fact Paine's *Age of Reason* may well have been written to counter the influence of Condorcet.[89] Such fundamental differences were easily glossed over because deists and atheists alike were anti-Christian. 'Atheism', indeed, was sometimes no more than a variety of anti-clericalism. Both Paine and Carlile were at one in their detestation of the Church and the Christian theology, and their followers of all views were quite happy with this. Carlile's supporters found no difficulty in following him from deism to atheism and then back again to some form of deism, so long as the slogans 'kingcraft' and 'priestcraft' were interjected at frequent intervals.

In the 1830s Carlile ceased to be personally important and the radical leadership passed to other men, some of whom, like Lovett, did not share Carlile's religious views, and others of whom, like Hetherington, shared the views but did not like Carlile. The struggle against the restrictions placed on the press by the laws of blasphemous and seditious libel was supplanted by the campaign against the financial burdens, especially that of the newspaper stamp, and the analysis of the country's ills in terms of kingcraft and priestcraft gave way in part to the more subtle analysis of the socialists. Carlile's personal eclipse, though, did not destroy his influence in the radical world. Only superficially did one radical organisation replace another, for though there were several competing heads there was only one body. The number of radicals in any but the largest towns was strictly limited and had to provide followers for all kinds of radical causes. Just as the churches were dismayed that their

congregations did not share their sectarian intolerance, but were prepared to give both church and chapel a try, so the radical organisations
were like little sects, and their leaders were distressed to find that their
adherents were equally ready to listen to their rivals. The acrimony to be
found between the leaders in their periodicals was rarely reflected in the
provincial and local societies, and this lack of discrimination was very
often a cause of the violent quarrels at the centre.

This natural eclecticism among radical followers explains why, in the
1830s, Carlile's supporters quite readily turned to work for Henry
Hetherington and the *Poor Man's Guardian*, although Carlile himself
remained implacably hostile to Hetherington and his friends. The leader
on the wane might feel deprived and jealous, but for the followers a new
movement meant a new hero and a new set of ideas to be added to the
old ones, even when the heroes were rivals and the ideas were incompatible. A man like James Watson, who matured into a national figure during
these years, was able to support Carlile, Hetherington and Owen all at
the same time. In this way the radical tradition was built up. Carlile's
atheism was added to Paine's deism; O'Brien's socialist analysis of society
was added to Carlile's kingcraft –priestcraft diagnosis of the country's
ills. Reform was the goal, and all efforts in that general direction were in
the right direction, despite the personality conflicts which often obscured
the fundamental unity of much of British radicalism.

d
Robert Owen

Owenism, according to the Reverend J. R. Beard, was 'the form in which
the broken and scattered forces of Infidelity, not long since marshalled
under the leadership of Taylor and Carlile, have rallied and found a
temporary refuge and support', but it was more than just that: it contained many contradictory and even conflicting elements.[90] It was in
some ways a 'class' movement, and yet it was officially of 'All Classes of All
Nations'; it was democratic, and yet it was also extremely paternalistic;
it represented a new departure in radicalism, and yet it was still a continuation of the old. The source of these differences in attitude, which eventually led to differences within the movement, lies largely in the character
of the founder of the system, Robert Owen.

Owen was a successful capitalist, a self-made man who had picked up at
second hand some of the rationalist social and educational theories of
the Enlightenment, and he had achieved international fame by developing his schemes at the New Lanark cotton community. Whilst at New

Lanark, at the very beginning of the nineteenth century, his mind had set
in its eighteenth-century framework. Under the influence of Godwin,
though not necessarily from a reading of *Political Justice*, he came to
believe

> That Man is a *compound being*, whose character is formed of his constitu-
> tion, or organisation at birth, and of the effects of external circumstances
> upon it, from birth to death; such original organisation and external
> influences continually acting and re-acting each upon the other.[91]

Education in its fullest sense was therefore the key which would unlock
the gate back into Paradise, and New Lanark, an isolated community,
was the ideal place for an experiment. Owen's success there convinced
him of the infallibility of his own ideas, and other people of the
possibility of their truth.

His first venture in the publication of his views was a short speech at a
dinner given in Glasgow in 1812 in honour of Joseph Lancaster, in which
he explained

> Any general character, from the best to the worst, from the most ignorant
> to the most enlightened, may be given to any community, even to the
> world at large, by the application of proper means; which means are to a
> great extent at the command and under the control of those who have
> influence in the affairs of men.[92]

The last phrase betrayed the nature of Owen's thought. He was essentially
a conservative, a lover of order and harmony in society, and singularly ill-
fitted to become a popular leader. He did not at first even seek the support of working men. At New Lanark he was a benevolent despot, and
throughout his life he looked to governments and to the wealthy for their
patronage, and appealed to the titled and the influential to transform the
face of social England. His first opportunity came immediately after the
French wars when the government was concerned with the problem of
the poor. Owen generalised his New Lanark experience and put forward
a plan for communities—villages of co-operation where the forces of
capitalist production could be harnessed for the well-being of all. Not
surprisingly, this idea proved too radical for the committee set up in 1816
by the Association for the Relief of the Manufacturing and Labouring
Poor, under the chairmanship of the Archbishop of Canterbury; and a
select committee of the House of Commons, the following year, did not
even call Owen to give his evidence. He was left to publicise his views in
the newspapers and at a series of public meetings which he called at the
London Tavern in the summer of 1817.

Between 1817 and 1824 Owen unfolded the full extent of the plans which he had first conceived at New Lanark. His basic principles were set out in his four *Essays on the Formation of Human Character* (1813 – 1814), which expanded upon the Glasgow speech of 1812, but he began to think of communities not only as a solution to the problem of the poor but also as a scheme for promoting the practical happiness and regeneration of all mankind. Mr Owen the philanthropist was becoming Mr Owen the prophet of a new way of life.

Not till 1819 did Owen issue his first address to the working classes— and this was a plea for rational toleration of the classes by each other, stating that 'the rich and the poor, the governors and the governed, have really but one interest'. The radical leaders were not convinced: the *Black Dwarf* urged him to 'let the Poor alone', Cobbett thought the proposed buildings looked like monasteries and dubbed the communities 'parallelograms of paupers'; and a vote of thanks to Owen after his London Tavern meeting on 14 August 1817 was defeated. Yet his views fell on fertile ground, his criticisms of orthodox political economy were favourably received, and his ideas were gradually taken up by the leaders of the working classes, who, like himself, were not content to accept the new and rigid system of the capitalist economy as immutable. The radicals began to find in Owen's ideas a new philosophy of life, which was nicknamed 'Owenism'.[93]

One of the first groups of working men to espouse the cause formed, in 1821, a Co-operative and Economical Society in London. Its members were mostly printers, including Henry Hetherington, and they produced a journal entitled the *Economist*, edited by George Mudie, in which the word Owenite was first used. The object of the Society was to form an association 'for improving the condition of the working classes during their continuance in their present employments', and a start was made in Spa Fields, where twenty-one families lived individually but arranged their housekeeping, eating and education on a communal basis. The project had collapsed by 1823. Several other community schemes were also reported in the *Economist*, but none of them lasted. The most important was that at Orbiston, near Motherwell, founded by Abram Combe and A. J. Hamilton of Dalzell, which lasted until 1827. Owen supplied the basic ideas for such schemes, but other men took the initiative and Owen himself always regarded their efforts as mere half-hearted tinkerings with the old immoral world. In 1824, he therefore left Europe for North America, where he sought to put his plans into effect at New Harmony, in Indiana.[94]

When he returned in 1829 he found that 'Owenism' had developed out of all recognition. The attempt to form communities had given way, temporarily if not permanently, to less ambitious co-operative schemes centred on the trading store. The original idea of the store was to raise funds for a community, and it appears to have developed independently in several different places, notably in London and Brighton. In London a number of radicals had, in 1824, formed a society to propagate Owen's system. Their aim was to set up a community within fifty miles of London, but by 1827 they had raised less than a tenth of the capital required and so they opened a general store at their meeting place in Red Lion Square. In Brighton, the co-operators, led by Dr William King, did the same thing in the same year. The first storekeeper at Red Lion Square was James Watson, and when he retired at the end of 1829 William Lovett succeeded him. In this way the leading radicals of the next genera-tion were attracted to Owenism, and what had been no more than a quasi-sect, following the strange views of a factory-master-turned-philanthropist, was on the way to becoming a mass movement. The ideas of the new co-operators were spread by Dr King's *Brighton Co-operator*, and James Watson acted as a 'co-operative missionary' when he went north to visit his Yorkshire relations. In 1830 he was lecturing in Leeds, Halifax, Dewsbury, Huddersfield and Wakefield, and William Pare of Birmingham and Alexander Campbell of Glasgow were similarly occupied in their own areas. Co-operative societies multiplied like rabbits throughout the north, and when the first Co-operative Congress was held in Manchester in 1831, over three hundred societies were in existence, of which fifty-six sent representatives of their 300,000 members and £6,000 trading capital.[95]

The vision of the community began to wane as the stores provided a more realistic and immediate objective, and some societies started dis-tributing their profits as dividends on purchases, but their astonishing and rapid progress naturally led on to other schemes. The co-operative movement was still primarily concerned to provide an alternative to the competitive capitalist economy, and its members sought to implement the labour theory of value by setting up a number of 'labour exchanges' at which goods of equal labour value could be exchanged without recourse to money. The London co-operators started an Exchange Bazaar in 1830, the North West of England United Co-operative Society started one in Lancashire in 1832, and Owen set up his own—the National Equitable Labour Exchange—in Gray's Inn Road, London, also in 1832.[96] At first he characteristically appealed to wealthy patrons for support, but the Exchange's main users were London artisans, who in 1833 set up the United Trades Association to run it. For the first, and perhaps the last, time in his career, Owen sensed the tremendous economic power of the working classes to re-shape society by their own efforts, and as the ranks of trade unions were swelled with working men disillusioned with the political reform of 1832, Owen prepared another huge scheme to channel their energies. He put aside the little organisations of the past, and called in London a congress to establish a Grand National Moral Union of the Productive Classes, which, early in 1834, was turned into the ill-fated Grand National Consolidated Trades Union.

The failure of the G.N.C.T.U. was important for the development of the working-class movement, but not for Owen himself. The radicals reacted by returning to politics as the only sure way of achieving reform, and the London co-operators, who in 1831 had formed the National Union of the Working Classes, in 1836 started the London Working Men's Association. Owen, on the other hand, was more than ever convinced that he alone knew the secret by which the regeneration of society could be accomplished, and the time was now ripe for him to declare his knowledge to the world. He had quarrelled with the other leaders of Owenism, including J. E. Smith, the editor of the *Crisis*, and he had abandoned the G.N.C.T.U. before its final collapse, so the way was now clear for him to take over the Charlotte Street premises of the Labour Exchange for his latest organisation, the Friendly Association of the Unionists of All Classes of All Nations. He also started another journal, the *New Moral World*, which on 1 May 1835 announced the Association of All Classes of All Nations.[97]

Owen now put the past firmly behind him. The 'system of shop and store-keeping' was abandoned, and the A.A.C.A.N., 'discarding all temporising or half measures, boldly adopted the entire principles of the Rational System of Society'. Its declared object was

> . . . to effect peaceably, and by reason alone, an entire change in the character and condition of mankind, by establishing over the world, in principle and practice, the religion of charity for the opinions, feeling, and conduct of all individuals, without distinction of sex, class, sect, party, country, or colour, combined with a well-devised, equitable, and natural system of united property; which public property is to be created by the members of the Association, without infringing upon the rights of any private property now in existence. . . .

This was to be attained by the establishment of branch associations, the creation of a new public opinion by means of public meetings, lectures, discussions, missionaries and cheap publications, and, most importantly, by the establishment of 'Communities of United Interest' where all the members of the Association could be educated and employed.[98]

Progress was at first slow, and Owen still looked primarily to M.P.s and wealthy friends for support. Popular interest was expressed in Birmingham, Worcester and Northampton, but when the first annual congress was held in London only one provincial delegate attended—from Manchester and Salford. The heart of the new movement was not to be in London but in the provinces, which had most enthusiastically supported the co-operative and trade union movements a few years earlier. This was recognised when the second annual congress met at the Salford Social Institution in 1837.

The Manchester area had a continuous record of co-operative history. When the Salford store in Great George Street had closed in 1831 the Manchester friends, led by Lloyd Jones, had converted it into an Evening and Sunday School for youths and adults. This school exerted considerable influence in the Manchester area and became a seed-bed for Owenite leaders and lecturers. Even before Owen had set up the A.A.C.A.N. the socialists of Salford were organising themselves into five classes of ten people to discuss the social system, and, fired with missionary zeal, they were planning to persuade their friends in Bolton to adopt a similar sort of organisation.[99] Other groups of loyal co-operators survived elsewhere and looked to Robert Owen for a new lead. In Birmingham, Glasgow, Liverpool, Northampton and Paisley, as well as in Bolton and Salford, committees were reported to be busy during 1836, and they were soon acquiring premises in which to hold their meetings. The Salford co-operators again led the way, collecting subscriptions for a hall which was opened for Sunday lectures at the very beginning of 1836; Bolton followed when James Rigby of Manchester opened the former Rose Hill Chapel for meetings in Bolton on Easter Sunday 1836; and in Birmingham, the Allison Street schoolrooms were hired for lectures.[100] Membership expanded rapidly. By Easter, Salford was claiming over a hundred members; Bolton had sixty, not counting another eighty children in the Sunday school; and when Robert Owen came north on a lecture tour his reception was overwhelming. The new Bolton and Salford halls were filled to overflowing, and Joseph Smith of Salford and John Finch of Liverpool had to give subsidiary lectures to those who could not get in. By the end of the year Salford could boast three hundred members, and an additional hall had had to be hired in Peter Street, Manchester. Owen filled this with an audience of two thousand in February 1837.[101]

Congress met at the Salford Social Institution in May, and was attended by thirty-two different localities from all over the country: the affairs of the A.A.C.A.N. were put on a regular basis, the name of 'Socialist' was officially adopted, and the last and most important stage in the development of Owenism had begun. Between 1837 and 1845, radicals in over a hundred towns throughout Great Britain came under the influence of Owenite views, and a sophisticated system of organisation and propagation, not unlike that of the Methodists, was created, with lecturers, public halls, missionary districts, circuits, class meetings, and the weekly penny subscription. The 1837 congress appointed the first two missionaries, James Rigby of Manchester and Alexander Campbell of Glasgow, to assist Owen in propagating his system; and a Social Missionary and Tract Society was established. The *New Moral World*, with G. A. Fleming of Manchester as its editor, was transferred from London to Manchester, and the A.A.C.A.N., enrolled under the Friendly Societies Acts, was given a hierarchy of organisation, with a Central Board consisting of a Home Department in Manchester and a Foreign Department in London. Owen, of course, was the President and Social Father.[102]

The movement then grew rapidly. By the end of 1837 there were branches or prospects of branches in twenty-four towns and villages. G. A. Fleming toured Lancashire rallying supporters and encouraging the formation of societies, and the Manchester lecturers were also ready to help their Yorkshire friends. Lloyd Jones opened an institution in Dewsbury, Fleming and Rigby opened premises in Halifax and Bradford, and Joshua Hobson gathered together the socialists in Leeds, and reported, 'In a short time we shall want the missionaries from Manchester.'[103] A series of monthly meetings was begun at Brighouse, and in Huddersfield, which had the first Yorkshire branch, the hired premises proved too small after only three months and a prospectus had to be issued for building a new Social Institution. During the course of 1837 seven more halls were opened in Lancashire, including one at Liverpool, and other parts of the country were rapidly caught up in the new stream of energy which Manchester had generated. Birmingham and Bristol followed Salford, Bolton and Stockport among the earliest branches of the A.A.C.A.N., missions were sent in the Midlands to Walsall and Coventry, Norwich reported activity, and in July a metropolitan branch of the A.A.C.A.N. was announced. Local men joined the official missionaries in the task of propagating the system.

The speed with which these socialist groups appeared and grew suggests that they already had strong roots. Although the A.A.C.A.N. was new, Owen was building on the co-operative movement, and, as in Salford, continuity of leadership can be traced in many towns. The degree of perseverance which the co-operators showed after the failures of the early 1830s, and their willingness to trust Owen and his organisations yet again, illustrates the magnetic appeal which his personality and views must have had, and this was enhanced in the textile districts of the north, where Owen was also advocating a reduction of the working week in factories and was joining in the opposition to the New Poor Law. Despite the set-backs to his views and the growth of the political reform movement (with which Owen had little sympathy) many of the inhabitants of the growing industrial towns still found inspiration in his vision of a new society, free from the ills of the competitive capitalist system.

But Owen was able to build on more than just his past following. He was also able to draw on other radical groups for support, and there is at least some indication that many of the former followers of Carlile were attracted to Owenism in the mid-1830s. James Hewitt, secretary of the branch at Macclesfield, C. J. Haslam, a member of the Manchester Central Board, and Lawrence Pitkethly, secretary of the West Riding District Meeting, had all been subscribers to Carlile's cause. There was also some continuity of meeting-places, the Blackfriars Rotunda being an obvious example, but the clearest indication of a connection between the Zetetic Societies of the 1820s and the A.A.C.A.N. comes in a *New Moral World* report from Glasgow. Alexander Campbell, the socialist missionary, had been one of Carlile's supporters as early as 1824 and had been imprisoned in 1833 for his part in the struggle of the un-stamped press; he was also a dedicated Owenite, manager of the Orbiston community, one of the first men to suggest the 'divi.' principle for co-operative stores, and the leader of co-operation in Glasgow. At a meeting of Glasgow and Paisley socialists in 1837, chaired by James Paterson (who had subscribed to Taylor's cause in 1828), James Nockles, the Glasgow secretary, gave an account of the Zetetic Society for the past year, and Alexander Campbell outlined the progress of socialism in England. The meeting was then to have gone to Glasgow Green for a Sunday evening gathering in the open air, but, as Campbell had been forbidden only the previous week to hold such meetings, the police compelled him to retire to the Zetetic Society's hall in Nelson Street, which the socialists shared with the Zetetic Society. Here, at least, the Zetetic and Socialist societies overlapped, if they did not completely lose their separate identities, and the Glasgow Socialists were always to main-tain a preference for 'eclectic' views.[104]

By the time of the next congress, held in Salford in May 1838, the A.A.C.A.N. had assumed national proportions. Four additional mission-aries were appointed, who were soon able to report activity from all over the country, and Owen himself found followers even in East Anglia. Manchester was losing its monopoly, and after the congress the *New Moral World* and Central Board were transferred to Birmingham, where the 1839 congress—despite complaints from Manchester—was held. The years 1838–39 saw a further period of rapid expansion: there were by May 1839 over fifty branches, and lectures had been delivered in a great many other places as well. Six of the branches had over a hundred and fifty members, ten others had between fifty and a hundred and fifty, and a further thirty-eight existed with fewer than fifty members.[105] As with the churches, though, adherents and people who heard the lectures far outnumbered those who were committed and paid-up members. The *New Moral World* could proudly announce that 'The cloud, originally no bigger than a man's hand, has been gradually waxing in magnitude'.[106]

The millennium was not to dawn so easily, and in the years following 1839 the Owenites had to face two difficult challenges. An external threat was posed by public opinion in general, and by certain clergymen in particular, who saw in socialism a threat to moral standards and Christian doctrine. This in itself would probably not have greatly harmed the Owenites—as the *New Moral World* declared under its masthead each week, 'Silence will not retard its progress: and opposition will only give increased celerity to its movements'—but the Owenites faced a second threat to their survival when internal differences of opinion began to appear, and the combination of the two was to prove fatal.

The internal problem which faced the Owenites was one of strategy. The final aim of the A.A.C.A.N. was to establish a community, and from the beginning this was what had attracted working men. The Salford congress in 1837 had set up a National Community Friendly Society alongside the A.A.C.A.N. to realise this aim, and in 1839 the two societies were united to form the Universal Community Society of Rational Religionists. At the same time an estate was acquired on which to commence a community at Queenwood in the parish of East Tytherley in Hampshire. The basic problem of the new community was finance. Working men could not, on their own, provide all the money necessary to set up a community, especially on the grand scale which Owen envisaged, when short time and unemployment were threatening the Industrial north. The dislocation of the textile industry during the black years of 1839–42 increased the impatience for a community and at the same time removed from working men the slim chance of their being able to create their own. Other difficulties, such as the poor quality of the estate chosen and the unsuitability of the northern Owenites to work it, merely added to the problem.

The story of Queenwood is largely one of false optimism, extravagance and misfortune, ending in bankruptcy.[107] Its effect on the U.C.S.R.R. was catastrophic. Owen, with his grand schemes for community, demonstrated how far he was out of touch with the needs and abilities of his followers: he continually emphasised 'all classes of all nations', while they were primarily interested in the working classes of the British nation. As working-class funds failed, Owen appealed to capitalists to finance the community, but the effect of this was to transfer control of the

U.C.S.R.R.'s work to an outside body, the Home Colonisation Society, which Owen and a number of his friends, including Frederick Bate, William Galpin and Henry Travis, had set up in 1840. The members of the Home Colonisation Society laid down four conditions on which they would help the U.C.S.R.R., and after considerable heart-searching and hesitation early in 1841, the Central Board finally gave way on all four points.[108] As a consequence the Society was able to proceed with Owen's elaborate and expensive plans for building a residential community, to be entitled Harmony Hall, on the Queenwood estate, but the next annual congress was to discover the price. The Central Board recommended to the delegates when they met at Manchester in May 1841 that the experiment should be taken out of the hands of the ordinary members and that the democratic constitution of the Society at branch and national level should be drastically curtailed. Owen proposed to introduce what was called the 'elective paternal' system of government, which when fully implemented, would mean that at both national and local levels the members could continue to elect their president, but that he should then have power to nominate all the other officers, except the treasurer and auditors.[109] Democracy was being pushed out, and the ordinary members of the Society were torn between their eagerness to build a community on the one hand and their distrust of capitalists and their love of freedom on the other.

During the course of the next year the implications of the 'elective paternal' system for the Central Board, and hence for the whole of the Society's policy, became apparent. Owen was, of course, elected president, and the movement fell increasingly under his sway and under the control of the Home Colonisation Society. In June 1841 the central office of the U.C.S.R.R. was moved from Holborn to the premises of the Home Colonisation Society in Pall Mall; Galpin became general secretary in August; and Owen gradually took over the *New Moral World*, so that, by the end of the year, Fleming could be dismissed as editor and control of the paper could be vested in the Central Board alone.[110]

This increasing autocracy also resulted in a decline in the position and importance of lecturers. Initially the Owenite movement had been built up by the lecturers, but once the community had been established their role was called into question. Enough time had been spent attacking the follies of the old immoral world, and the moment had now arrived to commence building the new. If men could not be won over by argument, they might at least be convinced by example and practical demonstration. Further, as the community began to swallow up more and more of the Owenites' resources, the missionary organisation was proving too costly. Halls of Science had to be heated, lit and paid for, and the lecturers themselves had expenses and needed a salary. These things could no longer be afforded, and so the Central Board decided in 1842 to discontinue the formal propagandist structure on which the original success of the Society had been based.[111]

Many men accepted this, for the reasons given: they too wanted to hasten the day when they would be able to leave the old world and enter the community, and they were prepared to follow Owen, whatever he suggested, provided he seemed to be leading them nearer their goal. But there was another reason why the Central Board wished to abandon the missionaries, and it was not a reason which all the lecturers were likely to accept. The ordinary members and many of the lecturers had been brought up in the Paine–Carlile tradition, and had learned their radicalism through the blasphemous and seditious press. In Owenism they had found a philosophy congenial to their own ideas, and they relished the way in which the Christian Church could be attacked and its theology ridiculed with the weapons of Owenite thought. But to attack the old immoral world was hardly constructive, and capitalists were not likely to invest money in an organisation which had a reputation for undermining religion. Owenism was scarcely respectable, and so the Central Board had to take the blaspheming lecturers in hand. If Owenism was to succeed, its image at the grass roots would have to be changed. And it was out of the tension generated within the socialist movement between the democratic radicalism of the Paine–Carlile tradition and the capitalistic paternalism of Robert Owen that an independent British freethought movement was born.

Notes

1 R. Hooker, *Ecclesiastical Polity*, I, s. 2, quoted by G. J. Holyoake, *The Origin and Nature of Secularism* (London, 1896), pp. 99–100.
2 J. Dryden, *Religio Laici*, vv. 39–41.
3 R. Descartes, *Discourse on Method* (1637); *Meditations* (1642)—see L. Stephen, *English Thought in the Eighteenth Century*, (London, 1876), I, pp. 19–33.
4 J. Locke, *An Essay Concerning Human Understanding* (1706); *The Reasonableness of Christianity* (1695)—see Stephen, *op. cit.*, I, pp. 36–8, 100–1.
5 G. Berkeley, *Essay towards a New Theory of Vision* (1709); *Treatise Concerning the Principles of Human Knowledge* (1710)—see Stephen, *op. cit.*, I, pp. 40–3.
6 A. Pope, *Essay on Man*, I, vv. 17–20.
7 J. Ray, *Wisdom of God*, p. 304, quoted by B. Willey, *The Eighteenth Century Background* (London, 1962), p. 42.
8 Quoted in *Oracle*, 6 November 1841.

9   'A moral philosopher', *Deism Fairly Stated and Fully Vindicated* . . .
    (second edition, London, 1746), pp. 85–6.
10 T. Chubb, *Discourse on Miracles* (London, 1741).
11 See L. Stephen, *op. cit.*, i, pp. 186–277.
12 *Deism Fairly Stated*, p. 41.
13 W. H. Reid, *The Rise and Dissolution of the Infidel Societies in this
    Metropolis* . . . (second edition, London, 1800), p. 19. The same point had
    been made against John Wesley in a book reviewed in the *Annual Register*
    (1762), appendix, pp. 239–47.
14 T. Hobbes, *Leviathan*, ch. XXXIII.
15 E. M. Gray, *Old Testament Criticism* . . . (New York, 1923), p.86.
16 J. M. Robertson, *A History of Freethought in the Nineteenth Century*,
    (London, 1929), i, pp. 129, 133–6.
17 *Ibid.*, p. 131.
18 J. Hunt, *Religious Thought in England in the Nineteenth Century*
    (London, 1896), p. 114.
19 T. Burnett, *Theory of the Earth*, preface, quoted by B. Willey, *op.cit.*,
    p. 38.
20 C. C. Gillispie, *Genesis and Geology* (Cambridge, Mass., 1951), pp. 49–56,
    73–9.
21 W. Buckland, *Vindiciae Geologicae* (Oxford 1820), dedication, pp. 18–19,
    21.
22 *Ibid.*, p. 23.
23 J. M. Robertson, *op.cit.*, i, p. 117; G. Daniel, *The Idea of Prehistory*
    (London, 1964), pp. 42–3.
24 Paul Thyry, Baron d'Holbach (1675–1760), *Système de la Nature*, i, p. 24,
    quoted and translated by B. Willey, *op. cit.*, p. 152.
25 J. Priestley, *Disquisitions relating to Matter and Spirit* . . . (London, 1777),
    s. III, pp. 26–7; J. M. Robertson, *op.cit.*, i, pp. 118–23; R. M. Young, *Mind,
    Brain and Adaptation in the Nineteenth Century* (Oxford, 1970), p. 225.
26 Robertson, *op. cit.*, i, pp. 113–14.
27 J.-B. Lamarck, *History of Invertebrate Animals* (1812–22), I, pp. 53 ff.,
    quoted by J. C. Greene, *The Death of Adam* (Iowa, 1959), p. 155.
28 E.g. *Co-operative Magazine* (1826); *Oracle* (1841–3).
29 R. M. Young, 'The impact of Darwin on conventional thought', in A.
    Symondson (ed.), *The Victorian Crisis of Faith* (London, 1970), pp. 13–35.
30 Quoted in *Half Hours with the Freethinkers*, 15 February 1857
31 T. Hobbes, *Leviathan*, ch. XXI.
32 C. Bray, *The Philosophy of Necessity* (London, 1841), quoted in *N.M.W.*,
    23 April 1842. See also R. K. Webb, *Harriet Martineau* (London, 1960),
    pp. 80–4.
33 J. Priestley, *The Doctrine of Philosophical Necessity Illustrated* (London,
    1777), s. VIII, p. 97.
34 W. H. Reid, *op. cit.*, p. 41.
35 E. Twynam, *John Toland, Freethinker, 1670–1722* (privately printed,
    1968); F. Venturi, *Utopia and Reform in the Enlightenment* (Cambridge,
    1971), pp. 57–62.
36 W. H. Wickwar, *The Struggle for the Freedom of the Press, 1819–32* (London, 1928), pp. 25–6.
37 *Reasoner*, 15 November 1848; E. Twynam, *Peter Annet, 1693–1769*

(London [1938]), p. 11 and *passim*; L. Stephen, *op. cit.*, i, pp. 163–6; J. M. Robertson, *A Short History of Freethought* (London, 1899), p. 320.

38 E. Twynam, *op. cit.*, pp. 1–2; W. H. Reid, *op. cit.*, pp. 87, 90–2.

39 B. Willey, *op. cit.*, p. 152; E. Twynam, *John Toland*, p. 8; W. H. Reid, *op. cit.*, p. 88. For early North American freethought see G. A. Koch, *Republican Religion* (New York, 1933).

40 *French Philosophy* (Sheffield, 1798), *passim*, especially p. 24.

41 See the *Report from the Committee of Secrecy of the House of Commons relative to the Proceedings of different Persons and Societies in Great Britain and Ireland engaged in a Treasonable Conspiracy, 15 March 1799*, Hansard xxxiv, cols. 579–657; also G. A. Williams, *Artisans and Sansculottes* (London, 1968), and G. S. Veitch, *The Genesis of Parliamentary Reform* (London, 1965).

42 M. D. Conway, *The Life of Thomas Paine* (New York and London, 1892); A. O. Aldridge, *Man of Reason* (London, 1960); P. Foner (ed.), *The Complete Writings of Thomas Paine* (New York, 1945). For the Painite tradition see H. Collins (ed.), *The Rights of Man* (London, 1969), introduction; and E. Royle, *Radical Politics*.

43 Quoted in *Reasoner*, 10 March 1847.

44 *Rights of Man*, Part 2 (1792)—Foner, i, p. 442; *Letter to Samuel Adams* (1803)—Foner, ii, p. 1437; *Letter to the Right Honorable the Marquis of Lansdowne* (1787)—Foner, ii, p. 1265.

45 *The Existence of God* (1797)—Foner, ii, p. 751; *Age of Reason*, Part 2 (1795)—Foner, i, p. 592; *Age of Reason*, Part 1 (1794)—Foner, i, p. 507; *Essay on Dream* (1802)—Foner, ii, p. 843; *The Existence of God* (1797)—Foner, ii, p. 752; *On the Religion of Deism* (1804)—Foner, ii, p. 798.

46 *Age of Reason*, Part 1—Foner, i, p. 497; *On Worship and Church Bells* 1797)—Foner, ii, pp. 758–9.

47 *Age of Reason*, Part 2—Foner, i, p. 554; W. H. Reid, *op. cit.*, p. 70.

48 *The Prosecution of the Age of Reason* (1797)—Foner, ii, p. 737; *Age of Reason*, Part 1—Foner, i, p. 474; Part 2—Foner i, p. 528; *On the Religion of Deism*—Foner, ii, p. 800; *Prosecution of the Age of Reason*—Foner, ii, p. 737; *Extracts from a Reply to the Bishop of Llandaff* (1810)—Foner, ii, pp. 764–88.

49 *French Philosophy*, p. 24.

50 *Rights of Man*, Part 2—Foner, i, p. 383; *An Answer to Four Questions on the Legislative and Executive Powers* (1792)—Foner, ii, p. 531.

51 Quoted by E. P. Thompson, *The Making of the English Working Class* (London, 1965), p. 24.

52 H. Collins, *op. cit.*, p. 36; B. Simon, *Studies in the History of Education, 1780–1870* (London, 1960), pp. 182–3; W. H. Reid, *op. cit.*, pp. 29, 6–7.

53 *Ibid.*, pp. 10–13, 18, 8.

54 *Ibid.*, pp. 3, 16, 17, iv; *Annual Register* (1794), p. 267.

55 W. H. Reid, *op. cit.*, p. 116; B. Brierley, *Failsworth, my native village . . .* (Oldham, 1895), pp. 15–16; G. J. Holyoake, *History of Co-operation* (London, 1906), i, p. 10.

56 The best source for Carlile's life, apart from the *Republican*, is the biography by his daughter, Theophila Carlile Campbell, *The Battle for the Freedom of the Press as Told in the Story of the Life of Richard Carlile* (London, 1899). Neither of the more recent biographies is definitive–G. A.

Aldred, *Richard Carlile, agitator* (third edition, Glasgow, 1941) and G. D. H. Cole, *Richard Carlile* (London, 1943). G. J. Holyoake, *The Life and Character of Richard Carlile* (London, 1849) is useful but not always reliable. Much of what follows is based on W. H. Wickwar, *op. cit.*

57 *Republican*, 30 June 1826.

58 Popularly known as the Vice Society, it was founded in 1802 and later merged with the Proclamation Society (founded 1787), which had been responsible for the original prosecution of the *Age of Reason*—W. H. Wickwar, *op. cit.*, pp. 35–7.

59 *Ibid.*, pp. 90–6; *Republican*, 31 March, 17 November, 29 December 1826. For an eye-witness account of the Fleet Street struggle see B. B. Jones, *Reasoner*, 5 June 1859, parts of which are reprinted in E. Royle, *op. cit.*, pp. 104–5. The Fleet Street shop was originally at No. 183. Carlile moved to No. 55 in January 1819, to 5 Water Lane in January 1823, to 84 Fleet Street in September 1823, to No. 135 in July 1825, and to No. 62 in June 1826.

60 *Republican*, 1 November 1822.

61 W. H. Wickwar, *op. cit.*, pp. 96–114. Carlile later said that 'the cessation of prosecution was my political death'—quoted by P. Hollis, *The Pauper Press* (Oxford, 1970), p. 117.

62 *Republican*, 2 October 1820.

63 *Ibid.*, 18 January, 22 February 1822.

64 *Ibid.*, 11 January 1822.

65 *Ibid.*, 4 January, 3 May, 25 October, 13 December 1822.

66 *Ibid.*, 18 January–15 March 1822.

67 *Ibid.*, 28 June 1822.

68 W. H. Wickwar, *op. cit.*, pp. 217–19; *Republican*, 24 May, 6 December 1822, 25 April 1823, 23 January, 24 September, 10 October 1824.

69 'The Constitutional Association for opposing the Progress of Disloyal and Seditious Principles', founded 1820, was a secular counterpart to the Vice Society. It was popularly known as 'The Bridge Street Gang' after its offices near Blackfriars Bridge—Wickwar, *op. cit.*, pp. 180–4. For the failure of the two societies see *ibid.*, pp. 180–204.

70 *Ibid.*, pp. 229–38; *Republican*, 21 May, 4, 11 June, 30 July 1824, 25 November 1825.

71 *Ibid.*, 30 December 1825, 27 December 1822.

72 *Ibid.*, 25 April 1823, 23 August, 10, 17 May 1822.

73 *Ibid.*, 28 June 1822; *Lion*, 31 July 1829; *Republican*, 30 April 1824.

74 *Ibid.*, 18 January 1822, 17 November 1826.

75 *Ibid.*, 28 July, 6 January, 3 February, 8 December 1826; *Lion*, 4 January 1828.

76 For Taylor's career see G. A. Aldred, *The Devil's Chaplain* (Glasgow, 1942) and H. Cutner, *Robert Taylor* (London, n.d.).

77 *Republican*, 9 April 1824, 15, 29 April, 16 December 1825, 11 August 1826; also H. Cutner, *op. cit.*, pp. 42–53. For Pitkethly, see appendix v.

78 The mission is reported in *Lion*, 29 May–25 September 1829, and there is also a brief account in the prefaces to the bound editions of the *Devil's Pulpit* (London, 1831–32).

79 G. A. Williams, *Rowland Detrosier: a working class infidel, 1800–34* (York, 1965); *Lion*, 18 January, 9, 16 May 1828.

80 *Ibid.*, 17 July, 25 December 1829.
81 *Prompter*, 27 November 1830, 29 January, 23 April, 9 July 1831; *Devil's Pulpit*, 3, 10 June 1831.
82 G. D. H. Cole, *op. cit.*, pp. 25–6. There is a reference to 'a lady' at Bolton in the *Lion*, 14 August 1829.
83 *Isis*, May 1832, quoted by Cole, *op. cit.*, p. 26; P. Hollis, *op. cit.*, p. 211; W. H. Wickwar, *op. cit.*, p. 296; *P.M.G.*, 21 September 1833.
84 *Republican*, 23 August 1822.
85 *Ibid.*, 2 August (Rickman), 7 June (Randal), 27 September 1822 (Law).
86 E.g. *Lion*, 23 October 1829.
87 *Republican*, 27 September 1822; Carlile, *Address to Men of Science . . .* (London, 1821).
88 *Republican*, 29 December 1826.
89 *Ibid.*, 23 August, 20 September 1822; A. O. Aldridge, *op. cit.*, p. 230.
90 J. R. Beard, *The Religion of Jesus Christ defended from the assaults of Owenism* (London, 1839), preface, quoted in *Reasoner*, 18 August 1847.
91 R. Owen, *Outline of the Rational System of Society . . .* (London, n.d.), p. 2.
92 R. Owen, *The Life of Robert Owen, written by himself*, (London, 1857–1858), I, p. 266.
93 *Ibid.*, IA, p. 230; F. Podmore, *Robert Owen* (London, 1923), pp. 240–1; G. D. H. Cole, *The Life of Robert Owen* (third edition, London, 1965), p. 204.
94 W. H. G. Armytage, *Heavens Below* (London, 1961), pp. 92–5; R. G. Garnett, *The Ideology of the Early Co-operative Movement* (Canterbury, 1966), p. 7.
95 G. J. Holyoake, *History of Co-operation*, I, pp. 71, 76–7, 82, 100; Podmore, *op. cit.*, pp. 374–91, 423; James Watson to Holyoake, 24 December 1872, H. C. 2142.
96 A branch was opened at the Rotunda; the Exchange moved to 14 Charlotte Street, Fitzroy Square, in 1833–Podmore, *op. cit.*, pp. 402–22.
97 *N.M.W.*, 1 November 1834, 23 May 1835.
98 *Ibid.*, 4 July 1840, 9, 16, 23 May 1835.
99 L. Jones, *The Life, Times and Labours of Robert Owen* (fifth edition, London, [1912]), pp. 286–93; B. Simon, *op. cit.*, pp. 214–15; *N.M.W.*, 14 March, 14 November 1835.
100 *Ibid.*, 2 January, 2 April, 19 March 1836.
101 *Ibid.*, 7 May, 11, 25 June, 12 November 1836, 4 March 1837.
102 *Ibid.*, 3 June 1837.
103 *Ibid*, 21 October 1837 (Leeds), 16 December 1837 (Dewsbury), 23 September 1837 (Halifax), 11 November 1837 (Bradford), 6 May 1837 (Brighouse), 9 December 1837 (Huddersfield).
104 *Ibid.*, 9 September 1837, 19 October 1839; *Reasoner*, 14 August 1850, 21 November 1858; *National Reformer*, 12 July 1862. For Alexander Campbell see appendix v.
105 *N.M.W.*, 26 May 1838, 8 June 1839; A.A.C.A.N. minute book, 8 April 1839.
106 *N.M.W.*, 27 October 1838.
107 See F. Podmore, *op. cit.*, pp. 530–65; R. G. Garnett, 'Robert Owen and community experiments', in S. Pollard and J. Salt (eds.), *Robert Owen, Prophet of the Poor* (London, 1971), pp. 53–61.

108 *N.M.W.*, 13 February 1841; A.A.C.A.N. minute book, 14–20 February 1841.
109 *N.M.W.*, 29 May, 26 June 1841.
110 A.A.C.A.N. minute book, 4 June, 29 August, 12 December 1841.
111 *Ibid.*, 29 May 1842.

2

Infidelity, 1841–50

a
Infidel socialism

Owen's attitude towards religion was as ambiguous as his attitude towards politics: in both he appeared to be more radical than he actually was, and although men's impressions of what he meant changed, he himself remained remarkably consistent throughout his long life. The grounds of his opposition to religion had been set out in the third *Essay on the Formation of Character* (1814). There he argued that Christianity was to be opposed, not on anti-clerical or any other of the popular grounds, but for sober, rational and moral reasons. Owen was, and remained, an eighteenth-century deist, a follower of the rational religion of Nature. He believed in harmony, and found Christianity to be inconsistent and opposed to harmony because it failed to recognise the fundamental principle of human nature, that

> the will of man has no power whatever over his opinions; he must, and ever did, and ever will believe what has been, is, or may be impressed on his mind by his predecessors and the circumstances which surround him.[1]

But because Christianity was to be opposed, that did not mean it was to be challenged violently in the manner of Carlile. Rather, if men were truly the products of their environment and education, then they were also its victims. Christians could not be held responsible for their irrational beliefs, so they should be helped to see the truth, not ridiculed and slandered. Hence the tone of Owen's infamous *Address*, delivered at the City of London Tavern on 21 August 1817. In this speech he tried to explain

> If the new arrangements proposed really possess all the advantages that have been stated, why have they not been adopted in universal practice, during all the ages which have passed?

His answer built up to a climax of rhetoric, in which we can clearly hear the millenarian tone of his approach:

> My Friends, a more important question has never yet been put to the sons of men: Who *can* answer it? Who *dare* answer it,—but with his life in his

59

hand; a ready and willing victim to truth, and to the emancipation of the
world from its long bondage of disunion, error, crime, and misery?

Behold that victim! On this day—in this hour—even now—shall those
bonds be burst asunder, never more to reunite while the world shall last,
What the consequences of this daring deed shall be to myself, I am as
indifferent about as whether it shall rain or be fair tomorrow. Whatever
may be the consequences, I will now perform my duty to you, and to the
world; and should it be the last act of my life, I shall be well content, and
know that I have lived for an important purpose.

Then, my friends, I tell you, that hitherto you have been prevented from
even knowing what happiness really is, solely in consequence of the errors
—gross errors—that have been combined with the fundamental notions of
every religion that has hitherto been taught to men. And, in consequence,
they have made man the most inconsistent, and the most miserable being
in existence. By the errors of these systems he has been made a weak,
imbecile animal; a furious bigot and fanatic; or a miserable hypocrite;
and should these qualities be carried, not only into the projected villages,
but *into Paradise itself, a Paradise would no longer be found!*[2]

And so the speech went on, attacking religion as the source of disharmony
in the world. He was making the rationalist's assumption that if the
truth were only declared, men would see it, recognise it as the truth, and
accept it in their lives. If they did not at first hear the message, then
Owen saw his task to be to repeat it until they did hear him; and so, with
boring monotony, he was to repeat himself for the rest of his life.

This particular revelation at the London Tavern received more attention than Owen's similar statements in the third *Essay*, chiefly because he
spent a great deal of money publicising the speech in the press, but his
disclosures about religion did not mark such a crisis in his life as he himself expected or as his biographers have suggested. New Lanark continued
to attract visitors: between 1815 and 1825 twenty thousand names occur
in the visitors' book, and in 1819 a deputation from Leeds, comprising
Edward Baines, Robert Oastler and John Cawood, found 'it is quite
manifest that the New Lanark system has a tendency to improve the
religious character'. Owen did not overnight become a social outcast for
his heresy, although certain members of Parliament, such as Lord
Lascelles and William Wilberforce, were quite prepared to use Owen's
views to discredit the causes with which he was associated, such as poor
law and factory reform. Even in 1822 Owen had no difficulty in finding
support for his British and Foreign Philanthropic Society, to which
£45,000 was subscribed by Owen's respectable friends.[3]

Complaints about the pernicious effects of Owen's theological opinions
become common only after 1828. 'The question of *religion* was not
productive of much dissension until Mr Owen's return from America,
when his "Sunday Morning Lectures" excited the alarm of the religious

portion of their members, and caused great numbers to secede from them,' William Lovett later wrote of the impact of Owen's views on the co-operative movement.[4] These Sunday morning lectures, delivered at the London Tavern in 1829 and at several other London halls during 1830 and 1831, were attended by a miscellany of London radicals, including some of the followers of Carlile and Taylor, and on at least one occasion Taylor himself was present and addressed the meeting from the floor. Only at this time, against a background of economic depression and mounting popular political unrest, did Owenism come to be identified with the infidelity of Carlile and Taylor. In other words, Owen's infidelity lay not so much in the nature of his opinions as in the company with whom he shared them.

During the 1830s, as Owen's views on religion were popularised, they were also vulgarised, and the negative aspects of his beliefs came to be emphasised at the expense of the positive. Owen did nothing to discourage this, and his vigorous and wholesale attacks on the established institutions of society, in which he ran together the rationalist and socialist critiques, encouraged the more radical among his supporters; he told an audience at the Charlotte Street Institution in 1834

> The chief of these Satanic institutions over the world, varied in different countries somewhat in form and name, yet always essentially the same, are the priesthood, the lawyers and magistrates, the military, the unnatural and artificial union of the sexes, individual and national competition and contests, and the consequent single-family or universally disuniting arrangements of society, and the metal circulating medium of wealth.[5]

Owen did not really mean any of this in an aggressive or vindictive sense, but, despite his good intentions, his views did damage to the co-operative movement, which had taken his inspiration but not his direct leadership. In 1827 the *Co-operative Magazine* thought Owen's 'religio-phobia' unnecessary, Lovett's comments on secessions from the movement have already been noted, and John Gray, another patron of the co-operators, asked the secretary of the London Co-operative Society in 1831, 'What has the eternal doctrine of *'necessity'* to do with roast beef?' and wished the Society a happy deliverance from 'the religious mania with which you are at present afflicted'.[6] The 1832 Co-operative congress passed a resolution dissociating the movement from Owen's peculiar views, but the decision was a dead letter. Owen himself was oblivious of the harm he was doing, and his followers were too well prepared by the teachings of Paine and Carlile to abandon what they felt to be the most relevant part of his message.

Two aspects of Owen's work and thought isolated him from the respectable and influential world in the 1830s and threw him almost entirely upon the resources of the infidel-radicals: his practice of debating his views with clergymen and other champions of Christianity, and his lectures on marriage.

These lectures, delivered in 1835 and inaccurately reported in the *New Moral World* at the time, were set before the world at large in 1838 when Joshua Hobson published the reporter's version as a book, later entitled *Lectures on the Marriages of the Priesthood of the Old Immoral World*. The style was sensationalist; marriage was declared to be 'a Satanic device of the Priesthood to place and keep mankind within their slavish superstitions, and to render them subservient to all their purposes'; and in 1844 'A Lecturer of Seven Years' Standing' gave his opinion that the publication of the *Lectures on Marriage* had '*done all the harm that is usually attributed to the anti-religious lectures that have been given, and the theological discussions that have taken place*'.[7] Certainly they provided opponents of Owenism with the amunition they needed, but the lecturer in question was probably deliberately under-estimating the effect which men like himself had had on the platform. Owen had first debated his case in public in 1829 when he had discussed with the Reverend Alexander Campbell in Cincinnati such familiar propositions as 'That all the religions of the world have been founded on the ignorance of mankind', and in 1837 he had resumed the practice in England when he had discussed his views in Manchester with the Reverend John H. Roebuck, a Warrenite minister. This was the signal for an increasingly frequent number of similar debates, lectures and discussions held during the next few years by Owen and his missionaries with the self-appointed champions of the Christian faith. Owen himself was always gentle, and repeated his boring platitudes with infinite patience and with thorough disregard for his opponents' arguments—a debate was still a lecture for him; but some of his missionaries were more provocative, and, with audiences taking sides, discussions often became occasions for acrimonious interchanges which Owen felt to be appropriate only in the old immoral world.

Between 1839 and 1841 religious objections to socialism reached a climax and grew in intensity of feeling as Owenite activities spread throughout the country. During these years $2\frac{1}{2}$ million tracts were circulated, 40,000 of them being given away during the course of one year and a further half-million being handed out during the Birmingham congress (1839) alone. In twelve months fifty formal discussions were held with the clergy, nearly 1,500 lectures were given (including over six hundred on theological and ethical subjects), and three hundred and fifty towns were regularly visited by fourteen missionaries. Total audiences were estimated at between ten and twelve thousand a week, and the circulation of the *New Moral World* doubled between October 1838 and June 1840.[8]

All this coincided with a period of economic dislocation and mounting Chartist unrest—as Lloyd Jones recalled, 'the whole of the manufacturing districts were in a state of activity, and lecturers were sent up and down in all directions to address the people'. So far as the government was concerned, Owenism was only a minor part of this general activity, but the reactionary *Quarterly Review* thought the Owenites a 'great and spreading sect' and some clergymen believed that the socialists were a more insidious threat to the State than the Chartists, since their leaders criticised marriage and told their audiences that man was not responsible for his actions. The Owenites themselves concluded, rather melodramatically, that the real reason why they were opposed by the clergy was because they advocated 'education in positive knowledge, and not in mystical faith—education in the works of nature, and therefore it is *Atheistical* and *Blasphemous* in the eyes of Bishops and Priests, who trade and fatten on the credulity of the people'.[9]

The increased activity of the Owenites was made apparent in two very obvious forms: new communities and monumental Halls of Science. The physical presence of these symbols of infidelity stirred local men to action. Events at Liverpool were typical. The local leader there was John Finch, founder of the first Liverpool co-operative store in 1829, and secretary to the local branch of socialists, who in 1838 held their meetings in the Tarlton Street Institute. Audiences of a thousand were attracted to the Institute, so the members decided to issue shares and start building their own hall. Finch laid the foundation stone in June 1839 in Lord Nelson Street, and by December the work was completed. The erection of this hall stirred up religious opposition. Fielding Ould, a popular open-air preacher, began a campaign against the infidels, and at a meeting called by the No Popery Association to petition the Queen against Finch, the hall and socialism Finch, who had the courage to attend, was assaulted.[10] Similar prejudice was to be found elsewhere. In Huddersfield, first the persons who had agreed to provide the land for the new hall, and then the men who had been hired to build it, broke their contracts, and Josiah Rhodes, the local socialist lecturer, was given notice by his Wesleyan employer. In Bradford the hall was built without mishap, but then the local gas company refused to supply the building.[11] Such local irritations filled socialists with anger against Christians and their religion, and made it difficult for the Central Board to apply Owen's doctrine of calm and rational toleration.

Apart from Queenwood, the most important Owenite community was that at Manea Fen in Cambridgeshire, where William Hodson had

started an unofficial experiment on a small scale. His community had
the same effect on rural Cambridge as the Nelson Street Hall had on
urban Liverpool, and the Christian Advocate to the University urged
'clergy and religious persons' to 'be on their guard against the extension
of these emissaries of infidelity among the country parishes' and to 'take
measures to avert these flagitious and wicked attempts'.[12] One man, John
Brindley, sometime schoolmaster at March, near Manea, needed no such
prompting. In December 1838 he had issued a challenge to the Birmingham socialists to debate with him, and for the next few years he was
usually to be found at the heart of any organised opposition to the
Owenites and their views. During the course of 1839 he made a number
of appearances in several towns in the West Midlands, Lancashire and
the West Riding: in September the No Popery Association invited him to
Liverpool to help in their campaign against the Nelson Street Hall, and
in June 1840 he was lecturing in the Potteries with great effect. One of the
local employers, Enock Wood of Burslem, turned off any of his men who
were Owenites; Owen himself was locked out of the theatre at Newcastle
under Lyme, which he had hired for a lecture; and Alexander Campbell
was ragged when he attempted to hold a meeting, but the police would
make no arrests. The following year, when Owen was due to open the
new Broadmead Hall of Science in Bristol, Brindley went there first to
prepare a welcome: Owen's books were burned in public, Owen himself
had to retire to London, and the fittings inside the new hall were damaged in a riot. When Lloyd Jones lectured there on the next two nights
he had to have police protection.[13]

If the Owenites were as popular as they themselves sometimes thought,
why were they so easily made the objects of popular fury? The reception
which the crowd gave the Owenites in the Potteries is in marked contrast to that experienced by Thomas Cooper there in 1842. The fact is
that, unlike Chartism at its height, Owenism was almost exclusively confined to the 'respectable' among the working classes. Police reports arising
out of the agitation of 1840 agreed that 'these persons consisted of the
most skilled, well-conducted, and intelligent of the working class', and
even in the textile districts of the north, where Owenism came closest to
being a broadly based popular movement, its teachings on co-operation
and self-help were beyond the pockets, and its doctrine of necessity was
beyond the comprehension, of many working men.[14] On the other hand,
no great financial or intellectual qualifications were needed to understand and practise the teachings of John Brindley, or, for that matter, of
Thomas Cooper. The popular orator could appeal to the basic instincts
of the mob. Lloyd Jones, who knew this sort of people well, later said,
'Had Owen and his followers not been grossly misrepresented, and the

doctrines they taught designedly misinterpreted by men whose object it was to excite the worst prejudices in a class below that of our ordinary working people, it is fair to surmise that no disturbance would have taken place.'[15] This was to some extent true, but the perversion was not always deliberate, and Owen's views lent themselves to the kind of treatment they received. Joseph Barker, for example, who at this period of his life was a New Connexion minister in Gateshead, wrote to the *Gateshead Observer* in 1840:

> ... The whole of their writings are aimed at the overthrow of society, and all their proceedings are in opposition to every principle on which society is founded. They openly profess that their intentions are to do away with all religions, to abolish all existing arrangements and institutions of society, to do away with marriage, to destroy all single family arrangements, to have property, women and children thrown into one common stock, and to live and herd together like beasts of the field.[16]

Barker no doubt believed every word of this, and the Owenites, like many other minorities in history, were to be persecuted not so much for what they believed but for the threat they were thought to pose to society.

Clergymen and other public men petitioned Parliament to take action, and the Owenites themselves petitioned for an investigation of their true beliefs, but Lord Melbourne's Whig government preferred to do nothing. This complacency infuriated Henry Phillpotts, the Bishop of Exeter, who was one of the most vocal of the old-fashioned High Anglicans left in the House, but his religious attack on the socialists looked to some contemporaries suspiciously like a political attack on the Whig government and its Home Secretary, Lord Normanby.

The Whigs were anathema to the Bishop, to the man who had elevated him to his see (Wellington), and to the rest of the diehard Tories. Since 1830 they had witnessed an attack on the time-honoured constitution, a threat to the Church in both England and Ireland, and finally an insult to the Queen—for Melbourne had allowed Owen to attend court on 26 June 1839 to present in person a petition in favour of socialism to his old patron's daughter. Lord John Russell, Home Secretary in 1838, had summed up the nature of Whiggism when he had publicly stated that 'He thought the people had a right to free discussion. It was free discussion which elicited truth . . . It was not from free discussion . . . that governments had anything to fear; there was fear when men were driven by force to secret combinations; there was the fear, there was the danger, and not in free discussion.'[17] Phillpotts decided to put an end to such liberal nonsense. At the opening of the new session in January 1840 the Bishop announced his campaign, and Normanby reaffirmed the government's resolution to do nothing.[18]

Phillpotts was not content to let matters rest, and in the next few weeks he hounded the government until Melbourne finally agreed to set up an inquiry, and a circular letter was issued to all Lords Lieutenant, to be read out at the quarter sessions, commanding magistrates to make a diligent search for books of a blasphemous and seditious nature.[19] This letter was directed at least as much against Chartism as Socialism, and resulted in only one major enforcement of the blasphemy laws—the prosecution of the radical publishers, Hetherington, Cleave and Heywood, for publishing C. J. Haslam's *Letters to the Clergy of All Denominations*—and it was an almost total failure. When Hetherington and Watson began proceedings against four respectable London publishers of Shelley's *Queen Mab*, which had been indicted many years before, the case against Heywood was dropped, Cleave was fined £20 but his gaol sentence was remitted, and no action was taken against Hetherington until the Reverend Hugh Stowell of Salford and the Bishop of Exeter stirred up the dust, and then Hetherington was given the shortest possible sentence of four months.[20]

Although the central government was reluctant to act against the socialists, certain local clergymen and magistrates were all too keen to use their considerable powers to suppress infidelity. Manchester lay at the heart of Owenite activity, and the Salford socialists had made rapid progress in the 1830s. Late in 1838 they had extended their activities still further when they had opened the Carpenters' Hall in Manchester for lectures, and such was their success that they then began to make plans for a new hall in Campfield, off Deansgate. Owen laid the foundation stone for this in August 1839, the old Salford Social Institution was closed at the end of the year and the socialists looked forward to the opening of their new premises, the largest of their kind in Manchester.[21] The Reverend J. W. Kidd, incumbent of nearby St Matthias's Church, Campfield, was not pleased: eager socialists who gathered at the building site on Sunday mornings disturbed his services, and feeling ran high on both sides. With the help of Hugh Stowell, Kidd formed a committee 'for the counter-action and suppression of that hideous form of infidelity which assumes the name of Socialism', and the attempt this committee made to suppress socialism in Manchester illustrates the difficult legal position which people of unorthodox beliefs had to face in early Victorian England.[22]

The lower hall of the Campfield building was opened early in 1840, and the main hall on 7 June. Within a week Kidd was prosecuting the three door stewards for taking money on a Sunday, contrary to 39 George III, cap. 79, s. 15. The Owenites claimed exemption from this Act on the grounds that the Hall of Science was registered as 'intended to be used as a place of religious worship by an assembly of protestants, called rational religionists', but in accordance with the Act of 57 Geo. III, cap. 19, s. 26, the court ruled that the socialists could not show that the money was collected for charitable purposes unless the accused took an oath and gave evidence. Being infidels, they were unable to take an oath, and so each of the stewards was fined £20. Next, in view of the defence offered by the socialists, Mr Kidd caused Robert Owen, James Rigby and Robert Buchanan to be summoned to take the oath of a dissenting preacher. Owen and Rigby lived beyond the jurisdiction of the court, but Buchanan was asked to take the oath. He refused, unless he were also allowed to explain what he means by it. Within a week he was back in court, this time to face a charge from the curate of St Matthias's. Again he refused to swear and he was fined 50s, but after a further two months he at last agreed to take the oath, which he had opposed on principle rather than because of its content.[23]

This incident in itself might not have been important. On balance the socialists had done well out of the Bishop of Exeter's campaign. Socialist-baiting was and continued to be the concern of only a minority of the clergy, assisted by self-appointed crusaders like John Brindley. Phillpotts focused this opposition for a few months at the beginning of 1840, but, as Lord Normanby himself remarked, 'When the right rev. Prelate gave himself credit for having given a check to the Socialists, it must be admitted that he had also given them very much importance.'[24] The significance of the Manchester prosecutions was that they precipitated a crisis of conscience within the Owenite movement and at last forced the Central Board to make a clear ruling on the attitude of socialists to the Christian religion.

Owen's conduct was never entirely consistent, so far as his followers could tell, but in an address 'To the Social Missionaries' prepared for the 1839 congress he had said,

> You will no longer find it advantageous or necessary to contend with the religious prejudices of the old world . . . you will best overcome the errors that have been forced into the human mind, by mildly and calmly placing self-evident truths before them . . . By attacking error in any other manner, or in any other spirit, you violate your own principles, and act in opposition to your religion of charity. The period for these religious contests has already ceased with all minds approaching rationality.[25]

Most of the lecturers ignored him, but as the financial needs of the Queen-wood community became more and more pressing after 1840 Owen's theoretical objections to controversy were supplemented by the weighty practical arguments of his capitalist friends, and the Central Board began to adopt a more actively conciliatory attitude towards Christianity. Some socialist lecturers felt that, although Owen was right in principle, the hostility of the clergy had to be met in kind, and the split which this divergence produced in the Owenite ranks deepened as the Central Board and the *New Moral World* seemed more and more to be neglecting all principle and to be conciliating religious opinion for monetary gain. The movement was, in the eyes of such lecturers, selling its soul for the sake of Queenwood and the capitalist creditors. When Robert Buchanan was prosecuted in Manchester, the *New Moral World* saw no moral reason why he should not take the oath of a dissenting preacher; and when a second social missionary, Lloyd Jones, was required by magistrates at Bristol to take the oath and prepared to do so 'without a moment's hesitation', his readiness to accept some sort of Christianity divided the socialists still further.[26] William Chilton, a member of the Bristol branch, wrote to G. J. Holyoake in December 1841:

> Prepare yourself for a separation, you are now *virtually* divorced from your adopted—she is playing the *whore* with the priests or priestcraft, and rank disease befouls her veins. Did you mark that L. Jones, *on behalf of the Social Body*, undertook to prove, that *they* believed in a *personal and intelligent God*. I congratulate you upon your conversion; when did *you* have your call?[27]

Chilton had grounds for concern. The Central Board was shifting rapidly from opposition to controversy to a positive adoption of a pseudo-Christian religion. When the Edinburgh socialists had applied for a U.C.S.R.R. branch charter in February 1840 they stated that 'We regard the objects for which we seek to be associated with you as strictly of a moral and economical, and not at all of a theological character, as involving no collision with the different religions of mankind, except in so far as these religions are opposed to the fundamental facts of our system.' The difficulty lay in the interpretation put upon this last phrase. The Central Board went so far as to express its 'complete concurrence in your opinion, that Socialism is in harmony with the Christian religion, interpreted by enlightened reason', but as local socialists found their way forward blocked by religious prejudice they took a different line. When Henry Jeffery went to Edinburgh as lecturer in 1841 he found the branch 'a hybrid, unitarian kind of concern. The members were fond of hearing the nonsense sometimes spoken about "Socialism being genuine, primitive, practical or some other sort of Christianity". A word against religion nearly frightened them from their seats.' But he had not been deterred, and a year later they were taking their 'strong meat like men'. When J. C. Farn tried the same policy in Liverpool, the Central Board warned him that if he repeated his offence he would be dismissed.[28] Farn, like Jeffery, simply ignored this, but another social missionary reacted more strongly against Owen and the official policy. This was Charles Southwell, who has been called one of the 'imperfectly white sheep' of the freethinking family.

Southwell was a rough and impetuous man, and, on his own account, had always been this way inclined. In the early 1830s he had opened an ultra-radical bookshop near Stretton Ground, Westminster, to supply the needs of the ultra-radical movement, and then he had joined with others in starting a Rational School, at which he delivered his maiden speech in support of the vendors of the blasphemous and seditious press. As the re-form agitation died down he began to look round for something else to do, and when the Foreign Enlistment Act was suspended in 1835 he volun-teered for the British Legion formed to fight in Spain for Queen Isabella and the 'liberals' against the Carlists. He did this, characteristically, not out of great feeling for principle but 'with the hope of bettering my condition, through some lucky accident, or some bold *coup de main*'. He failed in this, and in 1837 returned home, penniless and ill with fever.[29]

Southwell was, by nature, an adventurer—a fighter with a love of the dramatic; and it was not long before his love of controversy revived, prompting him to set himself up as an open-air lecturer on anti-theological subjects on Kennington Common. This brought him to the notice of the Lambeth Owenites, and when the London missionary, Frederick Hollick, was unable to fulfil an engagement at the Lambeth Social Institution, Southwell was invited in his place, and he soon be-came a regular lecturer at the branch. By the end of 1839 he was rapidly becoming one of the most popular freethought lecturers in London. As a convert to socialism, he debated the 'Five Fundamental Facts' of Owen's system with Richard Carlile at Lambeth, and early in 1840 he went on a lecture tour of Yorkshire. His reputation grew, probably because he combined a bluntness of speech with a histrionic platform manner which must have been very entertaining, and, at the same time as the Bishop of Exeter was condemning socialism in the Lords, Southwell was becoming the foremost campaigner for infidel socialism in the country.[30] His message was clear, as he told his audiences.

> It is religion which leaveneth the whole lump of human society; and he is a shallow politician who would reconstruct society without knowing what kind of leaven the religious leaven is.[31]

The socialists were impressed by their new star, and at the 1840 congress his name was mentioned as that of a possible social missionary or lecturer if he passed the required examination. This he must have done, for in June 1840 the Central Board approved an application by the London socialists to have him as a missionary in their district, but at the end of the year he was transferred to Birmingham in place of T. S. Mackintosh, who had been moved on to Leeds.[32]

Southwell was no respecter of persons—God, man, or Robert Owen— and he later claimed that he had asked the 1840 congress to appoint a committee to consider the philosophical and verbal inaccuracies of '*all* the authorized works' of the Society. A man of action like Southwell felt Owen's doctrine that 'The character of man is formed for and not by him' could not be true. Man was, rather, both the creature and the creator of circumstance. Southwell may here have mistaken the date of his first challenge to Owen's authority, but he certainly did clash with Owen the following year when he asked for a missionaries' textbook other than the *Book of the New Moral World*, and he spoke out strongly against both the plans for the East Tytherley community and the proposed 'elective paternal' system of government.[33] The 1841 congress report says nothing of Southwell's intervention, beyond the phrase 'After some observations from Messrs. Southwell and Goddard . . .', and so the text of Southwell's speech is to be found only in his *Confessions*, written eight years later, but the speech seems to catch the same phrases as the debate of which it was a part and the tone is so typical of both Southwell and Owen that it is useful to set out Southwell's recollections in full:

> Almost the first 'great truth' he told this memorable Congress was, that old things could not last another month; and, after delivering himself of that 'great truth,' he proceeded to assure the delighted Missionaries that they and they only, knew the causes of existing evils; and that they, and they only, knew how to remedy them. Though myself a Missionary I was hard of belief; to me it appeared too good to be true; and I ventured to suggest that, instead of wasting time on chimerical subjects, we should employ it in considering how to deal with tangible and really useful questions. I went on to say that, in my opinion, the public mind was not prepared for a total change of society; and expecting, as Mr Owen did, to be called in, by government, to prescribe for all our political diseases, was expecting foolishly. I added, that what we really needed was an efficient corp of Missionaries, whose sole mission should be the honourable one of preparing the popular mind for a reception of those truths, without which Socialism must ever be ranked among the dreams of dreamy minded men . . . This speech called up Mr Owen, who, petulantly waving his hand, declared I was not a practical man,—that the only practical man was himself,—that, before the lapse of three months, old things would pass away and all become new, and government must call him in to save the sinking state, or rather to create another state upon the parrollellogram-matic [*sic*] principle, . . . that the time for agitating the public mind was passed, and the golden age about to commence.[34]

Though Southwell's realism found little favour in a vote taken immedi-ately afterwards, he was voicing a growing fear among the socialists. They were interested in socialism as a democratic movement for the material improvement, self-help and education of the working classes, and, so long as religion appeared opposed to these things, socialists were bound to be anti-religious. This view was both highly principled and severely practical. Owen, on the other hand, was concerned to divert all the energies of the movement into creating a working model of the new moral world on the Tytherley estate in Hampshire. He had no concept of a popular movement, but his scheme remained popular because he seemed to offer the most immediate and tangible way out of the socially destructive capitalist system and into the haven of the new moral world. The paradox is that Southwell, the man of violence, was the equivalent in the socialist movement of William Lovett in the Chartist movement—both men advocated lectures and education as the means to improvement; whereas Owen, the man of peace, was the equivalent of Feargus O'Connor or even of J. R. Stephens—advocates of direct action and the immediate realisation of their aims. They promised the millennium.

The major concern of the 1841 congress was to encourage the capitalists of the Home Colonisation Society. Lloyd Jones recalled how they 'superseded the old society, by causing such alterations to be made in its contitution as reduced it to a subordinate position, in which it became a follower and helper with little or no power of initiation in anything that required the spending of money, or that involved the safety of what was, or what might be, invested'. Southwell voiced the reaction of the rank and file when he wrote of the Central Board shortly afterwards, 'you are fast dwindling into a community of pedlars, with souls so slavish as to think of nothing but driving a hard bargain in the national sale of human industry . . . Your party is now held together rather by its interests than its principles.'[35] In the person of Southwell the opposition to Owen, the Queenwood capitalists and the Central Board's attempt to placate Christian public opinion was finding its focus, but so long as Owen could offer hope at Queenwood the infidel radicals were likely to find only a minority of socialists who were prepared openly to support them.

The 1841 congress sent Southwell to Bristol for three months, but there the local socialists were dismayed at the heterodoxy of his opinions, while he grew more and more angry at what he regarded as the time-serving hypocrisy of the capitalist-minded Central Board. Finally, in disgust, he resigned his lectureship and started his own paper in opposition to the *New Moral World*. His chief collaborator in this venture was William Chilton, one of the few members of the Bristol branch who agreed with Southwell's irreligious views. Together, Chilton later wrote, they had many conversations upon their peculiar opinions, and 'often regretted that there was no publication in existence, nor never had been, advocating and defending unqualified atheism'. Southwell proposed that, with the help of an engraver named Field, they should start such a paper. Chilton was to be the printer and Southwell was to provide the copy, and so the *Oracle of Reason* was born.[36]

Positive doubts had not come to Southwell until a fellow workman at Broadwood's piano works, where he had been employed as a youth, had given him a copy of Timothy Dwight's *Sermons*. 'I read this,' he later recalled, 'and a feeling, like an electric shock, struck through my frame; all my thoughts and feelings underwent a change, and I became, involuntarily and without any choice of my own, what I now am—an Atheist.'[37] Despite the suddenness of his intellectual conversion, he accepted, a 'sentimental theism' until 1838, when he recommenced his lecturing in London. Chilton too claimed that he was an intellectual convert to atheism, but the book which had persuaded him was the Bible. Indeed, like many of the atheist leaders, he went out of his way to deny that the man who rejected Christianity solely out of moral disgust could really be considered an atheist at all.[38] The religious history of the young man who was soon to join them and become 'the second priest of the *Oracle*' was entirely different. This was G. J. Holyoake, whom Southwell had first met when he was the social missionary in Birmingham.

George Jacob Holyoake was born on 13 April 1817 in Birmingham, the eldest son and second child of George Holyoake, a skilled whitesmith who held 'a position of responsibility' at the Eagle Foundry, and of Catherine Groves, a religious woman who brought her children up in the strict puritan manner. The young Holyoake was totally dissimilar from the young Southwell. He was contemplative, whereas Southwell was rebellious; his outlook was sympathetic to religion and he retained a religious frame of mind throughout his life, discarding Christianity slowly, painfully and, in his later years, reluctantly. It was in 1836 that his infant faith began to broaden, mainly through the company he kept at the Birmingham Mechanics' Institute, where Daniel Wright, a Unitarian, was teacher of the evening classes, and William Hawkes Smith, another Unitarian but also a socialist, was a leading member. Smith was a religious socialist, and one can perhaps trace his influence on Holyoake's overall development, but a more immediate impact was made on the young man by two of his contemporaries in the classes, John Griffin Hornblower, who first took him to hear Robert Owen, and Frederick Hollick, who introduced him to a study of phrenology and guided him along the path to socialism. In February 1838 Holyoake joined the Association of All Classes of All Nations, and in May he met George Combe, the renowned phrenologist. His career now gathered pace, and by September, when he went on a walking holiday in the north, he was known to and knew most of the socialist leaders. The following year he was married to Ellen Williams at the new civil Registry Office, and began looking for a better job than that of whitesmith, which he had practised under his father. He had experience as a teacher in the Mechanics' Institute classes, and held several private appointments, but Hollick, who had gone to Sheffield as stationed lecturer in 1839, urged him to apply to the Owenites, and in 1840 was able to inform him that the Leeds congress had 'marked down' his name. Holyoake had already acquired valuable experience as a substitute for T. S. Mackintosh, the Birmingham social missionary, and during 1840 he had risen rapidly in the local socialist hierarchy. In April he had opened the Birmingham District Rational Schools at the Allison Street School rooms, in June he had been instrumental in acquiring the lease of the Lawrence Street Chapel for the Owenites, in July he joined the Birmingham District Central Board, and in August he was elected president of the Birmingham local branch. He was invited to lecture in Worcester the same month, and was shortly afterwards appointed stationed lecturer there by the Central Board.[39]

The sort of man Holyoake was in 1840 can be seen from testimonials which accompanied his first application for a socialist lectureship. In his capacity as secretary to the Birmingham District Board L. G. Hornblower wrote:

> His morals we know to be unimpeachable; while of his mental acquirements, much, very much might be said without doing adequate justice to him in that respect . . . As a Lecturer we have found him exceedingly pleasing and highly instructing—evincing much research, and an intimate acquaintance with the various Philosophies of the Ancient & Moderns, not excluding the one taught by ourselves; as a Disputant, the few opportunities he has had of displaying his talents would lead me to conclude that Truth will never suffer in his hands, while his active business habits will render him of infinite value to any Branch who may be so fortunate as to secure his services.[40]

Hollick privately expanded this eulogy:

> The *solid attainments* & habits of *business like precision* and punctuality—joined to an indomitable perseverance, I do not know his equal [*sic*].
> It is my opinion that in any Branch where the members need putting into Business habits; instructing in useful Knowledge, and in short, for *surely* progressing he would be an invaluable acquisition. His qualifications as a Calligraphist—Arithmetician—Mathematician—Book Keeper &c. &c. would be what is chiefly wanted in many places, & would qualify him for general conductor of any Branch. While his powers of reasoning, & his general Knowledge of our principles, would make him perfectly capable of advocating our views in public.[41]

Holyoake was, in fact, the ideal of the self-improved artisan: intelligent, industrious, economical; an educator and an organiser. These qualities

F

were to make him a national figure in future years, but there were some serious deficiencies. He lacked personal magnetism and was not a good public speaker. One contemporary remembered him as 'a young man, tall and slim, with dark hair and a thin, falsetto voice', and even Hollick admitted in his testimonial, 'His oratorical powers, & physical capabilities I know are enough for ordinary Lecturing, if not adapted to large & noisy assemblies.'[42] Holyoake was not physically strong: he was some-times racked with pain, his eyes were weak, and on occasions after 1847 he suffered from temporary blindness. But as he grew older and further from the physical deprivations of youth he grew stronger, and actually outlived most of his contemporaries. Age had the opposite effect on his other weakness, which was a psychological one. His intellectual capacity was great, and he suffered the emotional insecurity of one who has out-grown his own background but has not been accepted by another. As a result, Holyoake was pedantic and pretentious, a snob who readily criticised his equals and eagerly sought to please his betters. Particularly when under pressure, he was all too ready to seek the company of men of a higher social rank than himself, whom he thought of as being of his own intellectual level and who would therefore appreciate him.

In May 1841 the socialists in Sheffield decided to open a day school at the Hall of Science and Holyoake was appointed as both lecturer in the hall and teacher in the schools. His experience in Birmingham with the Mechanics' Institute classes and with the District Board Rational schools fitted him admirably for the task, and he put a great deal of effort into his work, writing to the Central Board about his plans and employing a 'curate', Thomas Paterson of Brighton, out of his own meagre salary.[43] There was little sign of rebellion in the young man: the Central Board urged him to implement the 'elective paternal' system of government in his branch, and this had been done by the following congress; on the same day as the *Oracle of Reason* was first issued, Holyoake was approving of the 'fresh and improved' tone of the *New Moral World*, of which Owen had become the virtual editor. Moreover, he was personally obliged to the Central Board for a loan of £10, but events at the close of 1841 transformed this tranquil situation and the subsequent course of Holyoake's life.[44]

b
The Anti-Persecution Union

The *Oracle of Reason* was at first highly successful, selling on average about four thousand copies a week. In theology it was thoroughly radical:

'in a word, we war not with the church, but the altar; not with forms of worship, but worship itself; not with the attributes, *but the existence, of deity*'.[45] Its tone was erratic, its reception mixed and the greatest compliment paid was that of imitation. A month after the *Oracle*, in December, Frederick Hollick brought out his *Atheist and Republican*, and from the north came a paper entitled the *Blasphemer*, while, on a more educated level, Hetherington was already publishing his *Freethinker's Information for the People* modelled on *Chambers's Information* and providing a mass of detail on geology, zoology, and comparative religion from which freethought lecturers and writers were able to draw their examples and ideas. Cheap periodical copies of Voltaire's *Philosophical Dictionary*, Godwin's *Political Justice* and Strauss's *Life of Jesus* were also advertised in the radical press at this time.

There was nothing unusual in the fact that individual Owenites should publish their views in independent publications. Robert Buchanan had started his *Rational Religionist* at the beginning of 1841, and G. A. Fleming published a paper called the *Union, a Monthly Record of Moral, Social and Educational Progress* after his dismissal from the *New Moral World* early in 1842. Radical leaders had to have their own papers to communicate their special ideas, and ephemeral periodicals could soon be produced at little capital cost. Despite a later claim that the *Oracle* was 'the only exclusively ATHEISTICAL print that has appeared in any age or country', the *Oracle* should be more accurately viewed as only one of a number of similar papers which were produced both in the years of social tension following the Napoleonic wars and again in the 'hungry forties'.[46]

What set the *Oracle* apart from its contemporaries was not its message but its language. Goodwyn Barmby, president of the London Communist Propaganda Society, echoed the feelings of many ultra radicals when he wrote of the *Oracle* in his *Promethean*:

> it is the action of speaking from old memory, and a worthless production, a lilliputean printed disgrace, a pigmean illiterate dishonour to the cause of dissent from christianity. . . . When we say the *Oracle* attacks christianity with the same bigotry and intolerance, and with the same Billingsgate abuse as that with which the Christian attacks the Infidel, we speak the truth, and say enough to dishonour it.[47]

Even Richard Carlile shared this view and thought that the return to the former style of propaganda, which he had pioneered, was a mistake. He inquired of the *Oracle*, 'What is all this splutter and clatter about god?...', and wrote to Holyoake after the latter had become editor, 'You, Southwell, and others, are now where I once was, resting upon the mere flippant vulgarisms of what you and the world consent to call atheistic

Infidelity, regulating your amount of wisdom by a critical contrast with other people's folly. Nothing that you say leads to any settlement of the dispute between you and them.'[48] Carlile was quite right. The *Oracle* reads like the *Republican* of 1822, and, like Carlile, the editors of the *Oracle* were eventually to calm down. But also like him, they were first to suffer imprisonment.

Southwell was deliberately provocative: Christianity was deprived of its capital 'C', and in the fourth issue he wrote an article entitled 'The Jew Book' which opened with these choice words:

> That revoltingly odious Jew production, called BIBLE, has been for ages the idol of all sorts of blockheads, the glory of knaves, and the disgust of wise men. It is a history of lust, sodomies, wholesale slaughtering, and horrible depravity; that the vilest parts of all other histories, collected into one monstrous book, could scarcely parallel! Priests tell us that this concentration of abominations was written by a God; all the world believe priests, or they would rather have thought it the outpourings of some devil![49]

Southwell was immediately arrested for blasphemous libel, by order of Sir James Wood, a Bristol magistrate and a Methodist, and at the Quarter Sessions in the New Year Sir Charles Wetherall sentenced him to a year in gaol and a fine of £100.

Southwell and Chilton were now more than ever determined to keep the *Oracle* open: no. 5 was brought out on time by Chilton, but no. 6 was delayed until the New Year while Chilton looked round for a new editor. He was reluctant to put himself in a position of danger, as he thought he could be of most use behind the scenes, and so Southwell suggested Holyoake for the post. The later was at first reluctant, but when he grasped the point of principle involved, he readily agreed.[50]

As with so many other radicals, the prosecution of free speech led Holyoake from moderation to extremism and Southwell's arrest precipitated action among many socialists who were beginning to doubt the wisdom and honesty of the course being followed by the Owenite Central Board under the influence of the Home Colonisation Society. Maltus Questell Ryall, a member of the Lambeth branch where Southwell had first joined the Owenites, quickly formed a committee of London freethinkers for the defence and support of Southwell, while in Sheffield Holyoake was busy in December issuing an address to the socialist branches on Southwell's behalf.[51] One of these addresses reached Ryall and his London Committee, and Ryall immediately volunteered to help with the *Oracle*. In accepting the editorship of the paper, Holyoake had also been automatically accepted as the new leader of the infidel socialists.

In January 1842 he delivered a lecture in Sheffield on 'The Spirit of

Bonner in the Disciples of Jesus', in which he proclaimed that 'the persecution of my friend . . . has been, within these few weeks, the cradle of
my doubts and the grave of my religion. My cherished confidence is gone,
and my FAITH IS NO MORE.' This was the last stage on Holyoake's road to
atheism. Intellectual conviction was to come during the next twelve
months. Until this time, he had been anticlerical rather than antitheistic.
The preaching of the Reverend John Angell James had given him a
'silent terror of Christianity', he later recalled when tracing the development of his views; his baby sister Eliza had died in 1829 while his mother
was out paying the Church rates and Easter dues; and he clearly remembered the shattering blow dealt to his faith when he had first realised that
prayer was not answered literally and positively.[52] The nature of his
early opposition to Christianity is brought out in an address which he
issued on arrival at his first lecturing station in 1840:

> . . . And is it not time that Sectarian bitterness should give way to the
> noble feeling of desire to better the condition of the swarms of poor our
> land unfortunately contains? Distress, like the Angel of Death, is again
> sweeping over them. They have toiled, but others have consumed;
> abundance of their creating surrounds them, and they are left to starve,
> with the choice only of the gloomy degrading Poor House or the pre-
> mature grave. *Is this right?* Those whose duty it is to cry to heaven against
> the sufferings of the poor, sing Te Deums in honours of bloody victories,
> or thank God our Taxes are increased and tell us to be content! They
> live in luxury, while their professed Master had not, nor the children of
> their common Father have not, where to lay their heads. *Is this
> Christianity?* If the poor man asks for his Political rights, he is told he is
> too ignorant to have them. He is not too ignorant *to toil and starve*, but
> only to *obtain redress*. But, whatever may be the obstacle, true, useful,
> practical knowledge is the only infallible means of removing it. The pray-
> ing of Eighteen Centuries has only left us without even the sign of a better
> state. Faith without *works* has been very '*dead*'; and we must work out our
> own salvation.[53]

This was the authentic voice of socialism as understood by the artisans
and factory workers of the manufacturing districts, which was ignored
by the capitalists on the Central Board, and which was barely understood
by Robert Owen. This was the cry of socialists moved by the forces which
stirred the Chartists, and which, eager to sweep away privilege in Church
and State, drew strength from the radical tradition of Paine and Carlile. It
was agreement on this issue—about the purpose of socialism and the need
to speak out—which made Holyoake a sympathiser with Southwell in
December 1841. Their views on religion coincided only in the heat of the
moment, and even then Holyoake's plans were decidedly more moderate.
   Holyoake's attitude to theological discussion appeared over-scrupulous
to his more vocal colleagues. Early in 1842 he was writing to other

socialist lecturers, advocating a plan for divorcing theology from socialism by the establishment of separate theological discussion classes
within the socialist branches. Ryall was enthusiastic about the plan,
Chilton had no choice, as the Bristol president forced him to resign from
the branch and forbear lecturing in the Hall of Science, but Henry
Jeffery, the Edinburgh lecturer, rejected the scheme as impracticable.[54]
This division of opinion was to persist and it reappeared in the Secularist
movement. Each party thought his plan was the practical one: in theory,
Holyoake was right and his attempt to divorce socialism from theology
was consistent with Owen's teachings, but in fact Jeffery's was the more
realistic attitude. So far as the Central Board was concerned, anything
which might upset confidence in the Queenwood community was to be
condemned.

The difficulty with Holyoake's plan became apparent when he was
invited to lecture at Cheltenham on 24 May on the subject of 'Home
Colonisation as a means of superseding Poor Laws and Emigration'.
About a hundred Chartists and socialists gathered in the Mechanics'
Institute to hear him. The socialists had been well prepared by the efforts
of J. B. Lear, leader of the Cheltenham socialist class, and a series of
letters on home colonisation had appeared in the local press during
March. The Christians were also ready, inspired by their militant pastor,
the Reverend Francis Close, who was the sworn enemy of all Catholics,
Tractarians and socialists. At the end of the lecture a local preacher
named Maitland asked what place was assigned to God in the socialist
community. Holyoake's reply, according to an eye-witness, was as follows:

> He made some remarks about Education and said 'for his part he thought
> the people of this Country ought not to have any religion, they were too
> poor,' he said 'for my part I am of no religion at all' he said 'those that
> professed religion were worshippers of Mammon' 'for my part I don't
> believe there is such a thing as a God' he said when he was speaking of the
> people of this Country being too poor— 'If I could have my way I would
> place the Deity on half-pay as the Government of this Country did the
> subaltern officers' [sic].[55]

'This reply was indecorous,' Holyoake later admitted, but he had no real
alternative except to answer to this effect. A freethinking poet in the town
had already been forced to recant, and W. J. Linton, writing in the Odd-
Fellow, had charged the socialists with hypocrisy, so Holyoake felt that
he must take his stand alongside Southwell. He fully realised the consequences of his action as he made his way to Bristol to visit Southwell,
and Lear with George and Harriet Adams, the local radical booksellers,
prepared for the expected trial.[56] On 2 June he returned to Cheltenham
to attend a meeting on the right of free speech, after which he was
arrested on a common law charge of blasphemy and hastened away to

Gloucester gaol before bail could be arranged. Reaction to these events was mixed. The Adams, though not themselves atheists, offered copies of the *Oracle* for sale, whereupon they too were arrested. Sympathetic meetings were held in Manchester, Stockport and Macclesfield, though the latter was not well attended, and even William Galpin sent a personal note of sympathy, but the Newcastle and Sunderland socialists refused to contribute to the defence fund and the branches at Bristol and Sheffield showed little sympathy for their former social missionaries.[57]

Holyoake's arrest and trial were among the greatest events of his life. The halo of martyrdom confirmed him as the undisputed leader of radical freethought, and he was to appeal to it as evidence of his loyalty to the cause whenever he was later challenged with accusations of expediency. The events of 1842 therefore figure largely in his own accounts of his life and they need to be put rather more securely in their context. Holyoake was by no means the only man to be arrested for his beliefs in these years: in 1840 William Lovett and John Collins had been arrested and kept in Warwick gaol for nine days without trial; Sir James Graham, the Conservative Home Secretary in 1842, had more to worry about than Holyoake or even the whole socialist movement. The largest single issue in his correspondence during May and June is the division in the Scottish Kirk, and in July and August he was preoccupied with the 'Plug Plot' riots in Manchester and district. It was egotistical nonsense for Holyoake to claim, as he later did, that the Home Secretary had acted specially to transfer his trial from the Quarter Sessions to the Assizes—a Bill had been introduced months before to relieve magistrates of certain duties, including that of hearing cases in which they were not likely to be impartial.[58]

The Holyoake case was lifted out of the ordinary by the reaction of the London radicals to it. While Southwell could be held to have deserved his fate, Holyoake was a much better victim for propaganda purposes in the long struggle for freedom of belief and expression. He was kept in Gloucester gaol until 18 June and then released on bail to enable him to prepare his own defence. After a brief visit to Birmingham he went to London for the first time, an experience which broadened his outlook and deepened his knowledge of political radicalism. He went to the House of Commons to hear John Arthur Roebuck, the M.P. for Bath, who had taken up with the Home Secretary the irregular detention of Holyoake without bail; he joined in discussions at several metropolitan coffee houses; and he lectured at the John Street Institution and the Rotunda. J. Humphreys Parry, then a law student, helped draw up the defence for reasons which many radicals of all views shared—that 'the great principle which you and I commonly advocate and of which you are now the martyr, is not atheism or any other ism, but the right of every man to promulgate his opinions upon every subject without incurring civil penalty'. Even Richard Carlile reappeared on the scene, although he was heartily opposed to Southwell's ideas and methods. He had been recommended by his Sheffield friend, Thomas Turton, to look sympathetically on the young man, and he came to treat Holyoake like a son and the heir to his tradition. He was delighted that another martyr had joined the freethought ranks, and cheerfully wrote to him about his own days in Dorchester gaol. He busied himself trying to convince Sir Robert Peel that Holyoake really was a Christian after all, but by this time Holyoake most certainly was not; he wrote with irony to his wife from Gloucester on Sunday, 14 August, the day before his trial, 'I have been to the Cathedral to hear a sermon but was not converted.' He also told her that Carlile had brought him 'some beautiful raspberry vinegar to drink tomorrow' at the trial.[59]

Holyoake needed the refreshment. He began his defence speech at 11.45 a.m. and did not finish until 9.10 p.m. During this time he treated the Assizes, presided over by Mr Justice Erskine, to a detailed history of the case; he explained the reasons for his disbelief in God and for his belief in the independent nature of morality; he discoursed on the nature of persecution; and he examined the legality of the indictment. At about 4.00 p.m. Erskine tried to cut him short by telling him that 'If you can convince the jury that your only meaning was that the incomes of the clergy ought to be reduced, and that you did not intend to insult God, I should tell the jury you ought not to be convicted.' This was exactly what Holyoake had meant, but he could hardly admit it now. His hatred against Christianity had been roused; London had proclaimed him a hero; Carlile was at his side. Such a tame admission followed by the anticlimax of an acquittal was out of the question. W. J. Fox was not the only person to think 'you forced your own conviction on yourself'.[60] Holyoake was, nevertheless, treated comparatively lightly: whereas Southwell had been imprisoned for a year, Holyoake was sentenced to only six months in Gloucester gaol, and George Adams, who had been tried on the same day for selling the *Oracle*, was sentenced to one month.

For Holyoake the period of his imprisonment was one of intense activity. He wrote over two thousand letters, and in response to attempts made to convert him back to Christianity with the apologetic works of Leslie and Paley, he formed the intellectual basis of his atheism by writing *Paley Refuted in his Own Words*, which became a standard freethought work, and *A Short and Easy Method with the Saints*, which examined Christianity in the light of its fruits. Then, in October 1842, came the deepest confirmation of his hatred of Christianity, when he was told that his elder daughter, Madeline, had died, partly owing to malnutrition—an event which he recalled with bitterness for the rest of his life.

The events of 1842 made a deep impression not only on Holyoake himself but on public opinion in general. 'Asmodeus', writing in the *Cheltenham Mercury* in 1891, recalled 'with what an intense feeling of indignation, I as a blossoming young sage, regarded his cruel persecution by a clique of degraded local superstitionists'.[61] The prosecutions of 1842 had stirred up a nest of hornets such as had not troubled the courts since the most provocative years of the 1820s, and it is fitting that Carlile himself should have blessed the new movement which was based on the activities of the radical press.

The first aim of the infidel radicals was to keep the *Oracle* going and thus to demonstrate to the authorities that imprisonment and persecution could not suppress Southwell and his friends. The editorial office, which had temporarily been moved from Bristol to Sheffield by Holyoake, was transferred to 8 Holywell Street, London, in June or July 1842 and Holyoake's name ceased to appear on the front page at the end of August. The new editor was Holyoake's former 'curate', Thomas Paterson, assisted by Maltus Ryall, who appears to have been the business manager. Paterson had the bluster of Southwell but not his ability, and the quality and circulation of the *Oracle* declined rapidly. Ryall did not have Holyoake's business abilities, and Chilton continued only behind the scenes. The circulation of the paper was hampered by problems of distribution: unstamped papers could not be transmitted free through the post and so had to be sent by parcel to provincial agents who would then pass the copies to local newspaper sellers, but no respectable agents would handle the *Oracle*. This meant that very often the paper was unobtainable. J. C. Farn wrote, 'It is absolutely necessary that some new arrangements should be made to promote the sale of the *Oracle;* I KNOW that great difficulties stand in the way of its circulation even in Newcastle, Leeds, and Manchester districts; if it cannot be obtained readily in these quarters, you may easily guess the difficulties elsewhere.'[62] Such arrangements as could be made were on an *ad hoc* basis. For example, Mr Roche of the Macclesfield Hall of Science handled the paper there, while in Sheffield Holyoake's good friend and experienced vendor of blasphemous and seditious literature, G. J. Harney, was the agent. Sales of the paper did not meet costs and the second volume, begun in November 1842, was made possible only by a donation of £40 from W. J. Birch, one of that group of middle-class patrons who helped the working-class freethought movement to exist.

The second aim of the radicals was to assist their imprisoned leaders. The London Committee, which Ryall had organised on Southwell's

behalf, had not done much; Ryall was inclined to let matters slip and
had looked to Holyoake for leadership. 'Try to concoct a good plan for
carrying on an extensive plan of agitation or support for the persecuted.
We must draw something up together. I have hitherto been prevented
from directing my attention to the subject,' he wrote to Holyoake in his
dilatory way, but before Holyoake could do much he had himself been
arrested and the impetus to form an Anti-Persecution Union actually
came from large public meetings held in the Birmingham Hall of Science
and the London John Street Institution whilst Holyoake was on bail.
Ryall was appointed general secretary of the Union, and Holyoake's
brother-in-law, Edward Nichols, was made provincial secretary in
Birmingham, assisted by Chilton and Paterson.[63]

The object of the Anti-Persecution Union (A.P.U.) was defensive and
not offensive: 'They appeal not to free thinkers only, but to those of
whatever sect or party who would uphold the Right of Private Judgement and Free Discussion for all, whether Christian, Jew, Turk, Theist,
or Atheist.'[64] The first victims to receive aid were, quite naturally, Southwell, Holyoake and George Adams. Holyoake was in the least fortunate
position as he had a growing family to support. Mrs Holyoake received
ten shillings a week from the A.P.U., but her husband was left dependent
upon the goodwill of his Sheffield friends, John Fowler and Paul
Rodgers. His prison diet was bad, and even after a petition to Sir James
Graham had resulted in an extension of his study hours, he was allowed
neither light nor fire. Southwell fared much better. He was well treated
and liberally supplied by Thomas Whiting of Bristol, though there was
later some dispute as to how much the A.P.U. should pay towards such
'necessaries' as the bottled stout which Southwell had received. The
Union also refused to contribute towards the £100 fine which had to be
paid before Southwell could be released. Eventually the fine was reduced
to £50 and paid off with a loan raised by Southwell's brother, and the
prisoner was released on 6 February, 1843.[65]

The third object of the infidels was to maintain a vigorous defence of
the liberty of expression. This was achieved defensively in two major
and several minor legal contests undertaken by the A.P.U. and offensively
by the provocative actions of individual ultra-radicals. Thomas Paterson,
who as editor of the *Oracle* was accepted as the leader of the atheists
during the time of Southwell's and Holyoake's imprisonment, began in
the manner of Carlile, placarding the windows of his bookshop at 8
Holywell Street with posters about 'The Existence of CHRIST, alias the
Baby God disproved' and other messages appropriate to the season of
Christmas 1842. Large crowds gathered outside the shop and when the
law intervened Paterson treated it with contempt. He ignored a sum-

mons to appear at Bow Street on 24 December because he did not want to spoil his Christmas, but finally he appeared late in January, when he was tried on four counts under 2 & 3 Victoria cap. 47, s. 56, charged with displaying obscene literature in a public thoroughfare, and convicted on all three cases actually presented to a total of one month's imprisonment in Tothills prison. He emerged, ill, martyred, and quite unrepentant, ready to repeat his offences when a new field of activity was opened up in Scotland.[66]

Scotland was a troubled land in the early summer of 1843: the Kirk was divided against itself, and bigotry survived in even greater measure than Cheltenham could boast. At the instigation of certain members of the general assembly—or so Southwell later claimed—the shops of two radical booksellers, Henry Robinson and his father-in-law, Thomas Finlay, were searched on 3 June 1843 for blasphemous and obscene books.[67] Finlay was arrested and released on bail; Robinson was too ill to be moved. This was clearly a case in the tradition of the radical booksellers and the English freethinkers decided to make an issue of it. Southwell, who had already announced his intention of going to Scotland, hastened North as 'Generalissimo (self-elected) of the Anti-Persecution Army On this side of the Tweed' and set up a bookshop at 46 West Register Street. Paterson also went North and established a 'Blasphemy Depôt' almost next door. Henry Jeffery and William Budge founded their own Scottish Anti-Persecution Union.[68]

The cases came before the procurator fiscal on 24 July. The charge against Robinson was that he had sold both blasphemous and obscene books. The first category included *The Bible an Improper Book for Youth* by 'Cosmopolite', which, apart from quotations from Watts and Owen on religion and statistics linking Christianity with immorality, gave biblical quotations contrasting theory with practice, examples of immoral and contradictory passages, and ended with a quotation from the *New Moral World* on the religion of love. The second category of books was much smaller and comprised works which had been specially got to order, giving the impression that 'the aim of Robinson's persecutors is to crush him for vending obnoxious opinions upon religious topics, under cover of a charge totally distinct in its character'.[69] Robinson was inescapably guilty of selling obscene books, for whatever reason, and was too ill to make a fight of it, so when the cases against him and Finlay were postponed for four months by the procurator fiscal, the English freethinkers, especially Southwell and Paterson, felt cheated and they resolved to keep the issue very much alive themselves.

Paterson's Blasphemy Depot did a brisk trade selling books to agents of the procurator fiscal. On 5 August Paterson was arrested, released on bail, re-arrested before the month was out and again released on bail. Three lads employed by him to placard the city with posters thanking the procurator fiscal for his trade, were also arrested; two of them, Hamilton and Saunderson, were bound over and a third, having pleaded contrition, returned to his work within a few hours. Paterson was apparently enjoying himself.[70]

A further opportunity presented itself to the freethinkers when the dour Scots Presbyterians discovered that Dr Robert Kalley, a native of Kilmarnock who had gone out to convert the Catholics of Madeira, had been arrested by the Portuguese authorities. With a fine sense of irony Jeffery, Southwell and Paterson tried to share in the Kirk's new-found love of toleration, while Holyoake more seriously corresponded with Kalley—each man trying to convert the other.[71] Never missing a chance to exploit the folly of others, the Edinburgh radicals then turned their attention to the case of John McNeile who kept a radical bookstall in the village of Campsie. The local minister had bought a copy of the *Oracle* from McNeile and then had had him arrested. Paterson, together with Jeffery and William Budge of the Scottish A. P. U., therefore visited the villages of Campsie and Kirkintilloch by night, placarding the streets with announcements of their intentions. Next morning they reopened the bookstall and had attracted a large crowd before the local constable arrived to take names and addresses. Jeffery then delivered a short speech, called on the Reverend Mr Lee and, finding him out, left a challenge to debate. He then returned to the stall, auctioned off the rest of the books, and next day the three men went to Stirling where Budge stood bail for McNeile. The latter then returned home to continue bookselling, the local constable deeming it wisest to ignore him. At least one outlet for the *Oracle* had successfully been kept open.[72]

The Edinburgh bookshop was then taken over by Matilda Roalfe, a young Englishwoman who was a friend of Chilton, while Paterson prepared for his trial. He appeared at the High Court in Edinburgh on 8 November 1843, 'charged with selling, or exposing for sale, a number of blasphemous publications at various periods, during the present year, in a shop in West Register Street' and he decided to conduct his own defence—or, rather, the high quality of the arguments he used seems to bear out Southwell's claim that he wrote it for him. For four hours Paterson ranged over the history of persecution and of the Church, attacking Christians with what the Bible said, and then the Bible itself with the same weapon. Volney, Drummond, Taylor, Higgins and Dupuis were summoned in the cause of comparative religion, and Pliny and Gibbon as witnesses to undermine historical Christianity. The jury was divided, but after three-quarters of an hour a majority concluded that he was guilty, since 'his sole end and object were to asperse, ridicule, vilify, and bring into contempt the Christian religion and the Holy Scriptures'. This seems a reasonable conclusion after the way Paterson had spent his time in Scotland, but the sentence he received was an unusually heavy one. He was given fifteen months' felon's treatment in Perth penitentiary, and, despite the efforts of the A.P.U., nothing was done to ease his punishment which lasted until 10 February 1845. Paterson then emerged from gaol, laughing.[73]

On the day after Paterson's trial, Robinson pleaded guilty but was still imprisoned for a year, and shortly afterwards Finlay was sentenced to sixty days in Calton gaol. As Jeffery had already been bound over to keep the peace for a year on a charge arising out of a Kalley meeting disturbance, and as Southwell had returned to England, only Matilda Roalfe was left to continue the agitation. She opened an 'Atheistical Depot' at 105 Nicolson Street and issued a manifesto declaring that she would not obey the law enacted against Robinson and Paterson, and she continued to sell books calculated to bring the Christian religion into contempt. She too was arrested a few days after the Finlay trial, and on 23 January the Sheriff's Court sentenced her to sixty days' felon's treatment for selling *A Home Thrust at the Atrocious Trinity* and other books. Her place was taken by William Baker from London.[74]

The second major centre of A.P.U. activity was Hull, where, during 1844, legal issues were raised similar to those involved in the Manchester Hall of Science cases of 1840. Emma Martin, one of the most popular freethought lecturers, had arranged to speak in Hull on 'The Crimes and Follies of Christian Missions' but the mayor had banned her lecture and had personally padlocked the lecture room. So she hired the large room of the Cross Keys Hotel which was owned by a Mr Watson. As the mayor had already prohibited the meeting, Watson was fined £1, and Richard Johnson, the local radical bookseller, was charged with taking money at the door of an unlicensed lecture room, contrary to 39 George III cap. 79, and was fined £100, or six months in prison, or distraint of goods. Johnson resolved to fight, his goods were taken, and the A.P.U. set up a committee led by Henry Hetherington to help him appeal to Queen's Bench. This appeal, conducted by J. Humphreys Parry, rested on the claim that under 2 Victoria cap. 12, prosecutions according to 39 George III cap. 79 could be initiated only by the law officers of the Crown and not, as in the Hull Case, by the local police superintendent. Lord Denman upheld the decision of the magistrates and awarded them costs.[75]

These contests in Edinburgh and Hull had every appearance of failure but both were ultimately successful. In the courts the freethinkers had lost all the way and yet they had caused so much trouble that their claims to freedom of expression were in fact granted. T. S. Duncombe managed to carry through Parliament a Bill establishing the point of law which the freethinkers had unsuccessfully claimed in 1840 and 1844, and the right of free discussion was firmly maintained in Hull by Emma Martin when in October 1844 she was able to debate the Christian evidences with the Reverend Mr Palsford in the Temperance Hall.[76] In May of the same year Arthur Trevelyan had written to Holyoake that 'The authorities in Edinburgh appear very like as if they had given up the field to our friends . . .' Roalfe and Baker were subjected to petty annoyances and were always short of money but they felt strong enough at the end of the year, with the help of W. J. Birch, to begin their own periodical, the *Plebeian, or Poor Man's Advocate and Journal of Progress*, edited by Roalfe with the intention of promoting 'Morality without religion, Politics without party'. She was not hindered in this, but the English freethinkers could not resist another sally into Scotland in 1845.[77]

Emma Martin had arranged to debate Christianity with Robert Lowery, the Chartist, at Arbroath in February of that year, but she was arrested before she could do so. Southwell immediately rushed back to Scotland to raise money for Mrs Martin, who then proceeded to take her revenge on Glasgow by placarding the Gorbals with announcements of her intention to attend the parish church and criticise the minister's sermon. A crowd of three thousand went to the church that Sunday evening, and Mr Anderson, the minister, could not even get into the pulpit. Mrs Martin was subsequently fined £3 for causing a disturbance, and Henry Jeffery, who had arrived to help her, £2.[78] One gets the impression that these occasions were not entirely serious: clergyman-baiting was a popular sport, and the fines levied were a reasonable charge for such entertainment. The authorities did not make a martyr out of Mrs Martin.

In this they were wise. The persecution started by the Bishop of Exeter in 1840 had failed, but more than just the climate of opinion had changed since 1840. The economic and political situation had also improved, and with society no longer in danger its critics could be permitted greater freedom. This meant that the freethinkers had to change their tactics. Words and actions which had been appropriate in the depression following the Napoleonic wars demanded a situation similar to that which had then existed. This is what had occurred in the early 1840s, but to have continued such tactics in the changed circumstances after 1842 would have made the conduct of the freethinkers anachronistic, if not entirely irrelevant.

Southwell realised this, and when he was released from gaol in February 1843 his actions forced the members of the A.P.U. to reconsider their aims. He refused to resume the editorship of the *Oracle*, partly because he did not want to be made responsible for the debt it had accumulated under the management of Paterson and Ryall, but mainly because he had changed his mind about the value of the tone which he had originally given to the paper and which Paterson had maintained. To the amazement of his friends, therefore, he seemed to turn his back on them and their efforts and started what looked like a rival periodical, the *Investigator*—a paper 'somewhat different in its tone, manner, and style'.[79] Temperament, however, did not readily fit Southwell for moderate leadership, and for this the freethinkers looked to Holyoake.

Holyoake was released from Gloucester gaol in February 1843, his impact was soon felt, and when he and Ryall replaced the *Oracle* in December 1843 with a new periodical, the *Movement*, the change in tone was readily apparent. The *Movement* adopted as its aim the Benthamite phrase 'to maximise morals, minimise religion'—it was to have a positive rather than negative approach—and writers for the paper included not only established Owenites and working-class radicals like Holyoake, Ryall, Chilton, Southwell, Richard Doyle, Charles Dent, Henry Jeffery, Henry Cook, William Oldham, and John Collier Farn, but also middle-class freethinkers like W. J. Birch, Arthur Trevelyan, George Gwynne, and Sophia Dobson Collet. This adoption of middle-class support and moderate aims did not represent a betrayal of the original aims of the A.P.U., for Southwell in 1841 and Paterson were neither typical of nor popular with that group of self-taught, self-improved artisans who formed the radical leadership at this time. They inspired adulation as martyrs, but not confidence as thinkers.[80]

The new mood was generally welcomed as radicals looked to Holyoake's *Movement* to create a new organisation, and some progress was made. Reports from provincial branches began to appear during 1843–1844, and the *Movement* was said to be circulating in every northern town, but communications between London and the provinces were bad, and much of the apparent organisation was very flimsy, unreliable, and short of funds. In Edinburgh, Matilda Roalfe kept the cause alive very much as a lonely and exotic outpost.[81] Only in London, where most of the leading members of the A.P.U. lived, was the position at all cheerful. Here the freethinkers were allowed to use the City Road Hall of Science and the John Street Social Institution, and among those radicals who had earlier supported Hetherington or who had heard Southwell in the 1830s a number of new radical organisations came into existence, encouraged by the Owenite dissidents and the A.P.U. Chief among these organisations was the London Atheistical Society, formed 'to establish the right of free discussion on all religious subjects—to obtain from the legislature a repeal of all Acts of Parliament interfering with the right of con-science'.[82] One of its earliest secretaries was Thomas Powell who had entered radicalism as one of Hetherington's shop-boys and had already made his mark as a leader of Welsh Chartism. He also acted as secretary of the A.P.U. when Holyoake was out of London. Other names common to both organisations included those of another secretary (J. McCullough), Thomas Brittain, Charles Dent, G. J. Holyoake, J. Tonge, M. Q. Ryall, Richard Doyle and W. W. Broom. The latter was also secretary of the Infidel Tract Society, a party of extremists whose tracts were printed by Roalfe and Baker in Edinburgh, while on a higher level the literary needs of the infidels at this time were met by William Chilton's 'Library of Reason' which he issued with the help of Birch and Hetherington.[83]

This flowering of freethought in the metropolis, coupled with hopes of better things elsewhere, prompted Holyoake to consider a more formal degree of organisation. He felt the need for some kind of focus to cater for all freethought societies, and so he began to develop his concept of an Atheon—'As the Pantheon was the place of all the Gods, the Atheon will be the place of none.' This was to be a kind of central office, presided over by Holyoake, to be used by the A.P.U., the *Movement*, the London Atheistical Society and any other organisation of similar views. It was also to have a library and reading room, and was to be a centre for 'all progressive parties in London, political or social, whether English or Foreign'.[84] Though the plan never got beyond Holyoake's head in 1845, it is important as an indication of the way in which his mind was work-ing, and in the 1850s he was to implement his idea when he opened his Fleet Street House as a headquarters for the Secularist movement.

c

The Theological Utilitarians

Radical prospects in 1845 were not good. Socialism was in rapid decline and freethought, which was still largely an outgrowth of the socialist movement, was almost brought down with it. The attack by the Central Board on the local lecturers had undermined the basis of the Rational Society and made even more certain the failure of the Queenwood community. The effect of the Central Board's decision to abandon the missionary structure was the opposite of what had been intended. Those infidel lecturers like Southwell, Holyoake, Emma Martin and Robert Cooper of Manchester who most embarrassed the capitalist friends of Owen were also among the ablest and most popular of all the socialist lecturers. Unofficially they were able to continue their work through the socialist branches and, indeed, with the failure of the community what was left of the branches became very much their own inheritance.

Southwell's first field of action was Scotland, and his adventures in Edinburgh have already been described. The Central Board noted there was no official record of his appointment at Edinburgh, but they were powerless to do anything about him. He then returned to London and in June or July 1844 began to lecture in various London halls, especially the Whitechapel Institution, and he revived the old Lambeth branch by acquiring new premises for it at 5 Charlotte Street in Blackfriars Road. Early the following year he was engaged by the Manchester branch, which had been revived by John Watts, the Coventry Owenite who since 1841 had become one of the stalwarts of Manchester socialism. In the Manchester area Southwell conducted a vigorous campaign, debating socialism with J. R. Stephens in Ashton and attracting audiences of a thousand to hear his anti-theological lectures in the Hall of Science. When his appointment ended he remained in the Manchester district, lecturing and holding dancing classes in the Hall of Science, before returning to London in June or July to take over the Charlotte Street Institution from the socialists. He re-opened it as the Paragon Hall and Coffee House, and made it a centre for his activities in London, but by this time he had travelled far from his socialist ways. He was a freelance lecturer on atheism, with scant respect for Owen or Owenism.[85]

Other missionaries were similarly occupied. Emma Martin, who, as we have seen, was active in Hull and Glasgow, was one of the most popular. She went on an extensive tour in 1844, starting in Leicester, where she addressed a crowd of five thousand in the market place after the Assembly Rooms had been closed to her, and going on to Lancashire, where she lectured in several places, including the Manchester Hall of Science, on 'Missionary Imposture' and other anti-theological subjects.[86]

Robert Cooper, though, was the most important and familiar lecturer in the north. He was a complete contrast to Southwell—a socialist prodigy who had been a schoolteacher at the Salford Social Institution at fourteen, had given his first lecture at fifteen, and had taken part in his first debate at seventeen. His lectures on 'Original Sin' had sold twelve thousand copies by the time he was eighteen, and his *Holy Scriptures Analyzed* had been quoted by the Bishop of Exeter in the Lords in 1840. While in Manchester he had been employed as a clerk, and his socialist activities had been part-time and unpaid, but in 1840 or 1841 he lost his job and so became a full-time socialist lecturer. He was employed for a short period in Hull, then in Newcastle and Sunderland, and then in Edinburgh and Glasgow, where, in 1842, he had led mass meetings held to protest against unemployment. He transferred to Derby in 1843 and to Stockport in 1844. During this time the promising youth had matured into an able and popular speaker on social and religious topics. In Edinburgh he had caused a stir with his lectures on 'The Immortality of the Soul', and, though the London-based freethought movement contains little reference to him, he had emerged as one of the leading infidels in the provinces. While in Stockport in 1844 he lectured on behalf of the Anti-Persecution Union, and in the same year he appeared at the Campfield Hall, Manchester, with a course of twelve lectures on the Bible; but, unlike Southwell, he also retained a great respect for the more traditional side of socialism and for Robert Owen himself.[87]

Cooper's career puts into perspective the infidel movement at this time. Southwell had come to socialism from the freethought movement of the early 1830s; he had never liked Robert Owen, and as a lecturer he was the least influenced by Owenite ideas and loyalties. Cooper, on the other hand, had been brought up a socialist and continued to be employed by them. In 1845 he moved back to Edinburgh and Glasgow, then went to Huddersfield for a short time, and finally came to London at the special request of Owen himself. He remained based on London until his health gave way in 1858, and during that time he was one of Owen's most consistent and loyal friends. Owen remained his leader and inspiration, and as late as 1850 he was still prepared to offer himself as an Owenite lecturer and to contribute to Owen's proposed new journal.[88] Holyoake similarly remained true to his Owenism, and this fact was to be important in ensuring that Secularism would not be just an extension of the old Paine–Carlile tradition, but that it would also contain the positive elements of Owenite socialism.

Holyoake left Gloucester gaol on 6 February 1843 and, after repeating in Cheltenham the sentiments for which he had been imprisoned, he progressed by way of the Midlands to London, where he was heartily welcomed and bombarded with invitations to lecture, suggestions for organisations and offers of posts. Already his organising and teaching abilities seem to have been recognised, and he lectured widely in London and the Midlands, taking a temporary position with the Worcester branch before finally accepting a teaching post at the Blackfriars Rotunda for 10 s. a week. He supplemented his earnings by lecturing at the Rotunda, John Street, Whitechapel and City Road Halls of Science, and by conducting an 'Improvement Class for the study of Literary Composition, Logic, and Oral Investigation' for the London Theological Association. He then went to Manchester for a time in the summer of 1844 before returning to his London base, where he attempted to reorganise freethought around the *Movement*. His plans for an 'Atheon', however, had to be abandoned when the Glasgow branch invited him to be their resident lecturer in 1845.[89]

In Scotland Holyoake did what he could to shore up the crumbling Owenite organisation, and, with Robert Cooper equally active in Edinburgh at this time, something of a revival was produced.[90] But affairs were still dominated by the fate of the official Owenite Central Board. Congress had at last in 1844 overthrown the capitalists and ejected Owen from the presidency, but working men on their own were unable to save the Queenwood community from bankruptcy, and in July 1845 a special congress assigned the property to three of its number to dispose of as seemed most advantageous for all concerned. Legal difficulties were then found to stand in the way of this course of action, and the original holders of the lease, led by John Finch, seized control. The movement was split between supporters of the latter (including most of the capitalists and Owen's friends) and supporters of the assignees (mainly ordinary members, including most of the infidel lecturers). Not until 1861, when the affairs of the community came before Chancery, was the financial chaos left by Owenism finally sorted out. Meanwhile, by April 1846 another special congress had to be called at John Street to change the rules of the Rational Society because, as no subscriptions had been paid for a year, the society was about to cease its legal existence. A new Central Board was then elected, with G. J. Holyoake as secretary, but a subsequent meeting at the community repudiated this and elected another Central Board under the old rules. Nothing came of this and, though the John Street Board survived until the Queenwood case was finally closed, for all practical purposes socialism was dead. Only 187 members paid the subscription and most of the remaining branches were disgusted, bewildered and disillusioned.[91] In 1845 the *New Moral World* was selling only 700–800 copies a week. It limped on, helped by W. H. Ashurst and Thomas Allsop, losing £2 an issue, until James Hill bought it and turned it into an anti-Owenite paper. The former editor, G. A. Fleming, continued with his own *Moral World*, whilst the John Street Central Board brought out the *Herald of Progress*, edited by John Cramp. Neither paper lasted long. The John Street A1 branch changed its constitution in 1845 to become a 'General Literary and Scientific Institution', although it continued to foster the remnant of the Rational Society under its wing. The surviving provincial branches cut themselves loose. In 1848 the Sheffield socialists 'Resolved, That until Messrs. Owen, Pare, Finch, Jones, and others have brought the affairs of Harmony to an open, honourable and satisfactory settlement, this branch cannot co-operate in any plan whatever for the public agitation of social principles.' The lecturers were scattered.[92]

'I think we may truly say with Othello our "occupation's gone",' wrote
Robert Cooper to Holyoake in March 1846. The hall in Edinburgh was
shortly to be closed, the same was expected at Glasgow, there was a
'surplus population' of lecturers in London, and no one in the old
immoral world was likely to employ a man of Cooper's reputation.
Holyoake found a similar prejudice. His immediate needs were met by
an appointment at Paisley, where he was able to repeat his Glasgow
lectures in March and April, and he was then offered an appointment in
Huddersfield; but lecturing could no longer give him the financial
security he needed to support his growing family, and he was looking for
an opportunity to return to his first love, teaching.[93]

James Watson had other ideas for Holyoake, and a very good reason
for putting them forward. He was moving his publishing business from
St Paul's Alley to Queen's Head Passage in January 1846, but found that
his trade had sadly declined. 'All the pamphlets issued against superstition or religion for years past lay on the shelves like so much waste
paper,' he told Holyoake, and attributed this to 'the want of a weekly
periodical devoted to theological investigation'. A month later he
returned to this idea, associating the decay of freethought with the lack of
a periodical. He urged upon Holyoake the need and potential demand
for 'a weekly periodical conducted in a bold but conciliatory spirit', and
shortly afterwards proposed a coalition with Cramp's *Herald of Progress*,
which had already been offered to Holyoake. This was agreed to: Cramp
was to continue the *Herald* until the socialist congress in May, after
which Holyoake was to absorb it into a new paper.[94] The outstanding
problem of finance was solved by a windfall. In 1845 Holyoake, as a
member of the Robert Burns Lodge of Glasgow, had entered for the
Manchester Unity of Oddfellows prize essays. He won all five, and in 1846
found himself in the unexpected position of having £50 to spend.[95] So,
on 3 June 1846, appeared the *Reasoner and Herald of Progress*, the
periodical around which Holyoake hoped to build a new freethought
movement.

In 1846 the *Herald of Progress* described Holyoake as 'one of our best
remaining men'.[96] That Holyoake had risen to this position was a
triumph of mind over matter. Unlike Southwell, he had not thrust himself to the front by boldness in action—he had scarcely intended or
enjoyed his six months in prison and he had no desire to go back there.
His cautious temperament and physical weakness were added to by his
awareness of his responsibilities towards his family.[97] Patience and hard
work were the qualities which made him the foremost leader of freethought in 1846: he was not the most experienced or entertaining
lecturer—he had only been a very junior social missionary—but by 1846

he was, next to G. A. Fleming, the most experienced journalist in the
socialist movement, as well as a leading member of the John Street
Central Board. His principal rivals were, and long continued to be,
Robert Cooper and Charles Southwell. Cooper was in many ways very
similar to Holyoake. He did not enjoy good health, was extremely
reluctant to push himself forward, and, despite his being noticed by the
Bishop of Exeter, no prosecution had made him a national hero among
the ultra-radicals. Cooper is one of the men who built the English
working-class movement, but he made no claims to fame, wrote no full-
length autobiography, and has found no historian to recognise his
qualities since his death. Southwell, by contrast, was the type of working-
class leader who forced himself upon his contemporaries. He appeared
as a leader but was temperamentally incapable of leading, and he rapidly
discredited himself in the eyes of his followers.[98]

The *Reasoner* was a weekly periodical of one demy sheet folded
octavo, and was sold at twopence a copy. It was printed by J. G. Hornblower, assisted by Holyoake's younger brother, Austin, and published
by James Watson. The paper promised in its first issue to be 'Com-
munistic in Social Economy—Utilitarian in Morals—Republican in
Politics—and Anti-Theological in Religion'. Its beginning was not
auspicious.

Holyoake thought that for the *Reasoner* to pay its way a weekly
circulation of 3,000 would be needed. The average number of copies sold
over the first thirteen weeks was 'little more than half that number'.
Paisley, which Holyoake had just left, sold fifty-four per week—but not
many places can have sold so many. The editor went unpaid, but still
the excess of expenditure over income was £37. 'It is evident, from the
experience of the *Reasoner*,' concluded Holyoake, 'that there are not
societies of consonant sentiments sufficiently numerous to support a
paper which chiefly supplies philosophical and metaphysical news.'
Nevertheless, he boldly assured his readers, 'the *Reasoner*, devoted to the
assailment of all speculative error *fraught with practical evil*, will be . . .
continued until the desiderated reformation is effected'. It did so, but
with only eight pages for 1½d, kept going by the generous financial aid of
W. J. Birch, W. H. Ashurst, 'Aliquis' (George Gwynne) and a few other
wealthy supporters. A 'shilling fund' was started in 1847 to guarantee an
income for the editor, but it had only three hundred contributors. The
price was again put up to twopence for a full sheet, reducing the loss on
volume II to £20, and the circulation of volume III actually improved a
little, but the paper was on a very unsure foundation and the circulation
declined again in 1849 when it fell to below a thousand.[99]

The other infidel leaders were hardly more successful. From Edin-

burgh Robert Cooper had gone to Huddersfield, but his appointment
there was only part-time and he looked forward to the time when he
might be able to find better prospects in London.[100] Charles Southwell
discovered that the Paragon Hall was damp, so he sold it to W. W. Broom
of the Infidel Tract Society and leased the Canterbury Theatre, where he
indulged his love of acting and lost his money. He then returned to
lecturing, taking premises at the South London Hall, adjacent to the
Chartist Hall at the corner of Webber Street and Blackfriars Road. Here,
in a coffee room, he formed 'The Philosophical Protestant Association',
which held discussions on Monday and Wednesday evenings, and he
also gave Sunday evening lectures at the Chartist Hall on such topics as
'Christianity in India' and 'Hell'. His downfall came when, without a
licence, he allowed alcohol to be brought in and consumed on the
premises. Faced with a demand for £150 from the Inland Revenue
Department, he decided to emigrate to America, but on the way to
Liverpool he was invited to take an appointment in Manchester; and so
in the summer of 1849 he began a new mission in the north.[101]

The activities of Holyoake, Cooper and Southwell, and the other freethought and socialist lecturers, were in no way co-ordinated. Holyoake
aimed to remedy this deficiency, and he was in the best position to do so:
his *Reasoner* was the one national organ of publicity and communication, and since his return to London in 1846 he had established himself,
despite his weak voice and ill-health, as one of the most consistent
lecturers on anti-theological topics in the London halls. He therefore
took it upon himself to announce the 'Society for the Promulgation of
Naturalism', which was to concern itself with political economy, communism, and theological, biblical, and anti-religious questions.[102]
Within a few months the title had been altered to the 'Society of
Theological Utilitarians', the members of which, according to its
founder, doubted dogma but believed in humanity and followed the rule
of Bentham, which minimised religion and maximised morals. He
further proclaimed that

> Utility is the natural resting place of morals. Upon this basis politics have
> been put—and it only remains to bring religion to this standard. We shall
> have sealed the work of intellectual reformation when we have written
> *cui bono* over the altar.[103]

The activities of this society were far less extensive than its name
suggests. Holyoake was never afraid of setting out his aims in the titles
he adopted, though sometimes, as with Robert Owen, this led him to
confuse achievement with desire. The Metropolitan Society of Theological Utilitarians—or more simply, the Utilitarian Society—met at the City
Road Hall of Science, chiefly for lectures and discussions. Its activities

were reported in an appendix to the *Reasoner*, entitled the *Utilitarian Record*, and the main value of the society seems to have been that it provided a forum for the various leading freethinkers in London and for visitors from the provinces. It is difficult to tell how large or influential the society became, but in the face of a resurgence of Chartism it probably attracted only a small number of dedicated freethinkers in London, and its hold on the provinces must have been even more tenuous than that of the *Reasoner* itself. The name 'Utilitarian Society' was adopted at a few places, such as Ipswich and Northampton, but a *Reasoner* correspondent, who suggested that a national organisation of freethinkers should be created, had never heard of it although Holyoake was optimistically claiming that it 'is increasing in numbers and usefulness'.[104] It is difficult to see that the society was playing an indispensable role even in London. Lectures were given without its assistance, and Southwell never joined in at all. Other occasions, such as the parties to celebrate Thomas Paine's birthday at the end of January each year, served to bring together much more representative gatherings of radicals, though the Utilitarian Society might have given them their focus, as on 30 January 1848 when Paine's birthday was commemorated in the Hall of Science, with Hetherington, Linton, Holyoake, Watson and Moore leading the proceedings. Southwell, typically, was not there but celebrated with his own friends in the Paragon Hall.[105]

Far more useful than a national organisation, or even a national periodical, in bringing freethinking elements throughout the country into some kind of national pattern was the personal contact made by the leaders on their extensive lecture tours. Holyoake's mind had been set on organisation, the fulfilment of his dreams of an Atheon, but in 1848 he made a new discovery:

> My previous visits to the provinces have been made in connection with existing Societies, whose influence secured me audiences. This is the first time that I have made a tour in advocacy of societarian, political and speculative principles, as recast and individualised in the *Reasoner*. The views I have hitherto explained meet with such approval, that I foresee great usefulness in making these tours *annual*. A wider sphere of action opens before me. It will be possible to collect and organise the scattered friends of progress of former days, to suggest great and *practicable* objects to them, and prepare them for communication with Mr Owen and other of his friends, who are not free as I am to travel anywhere, but who are able to do immense service if co-operating parties can be found to work with them. Many of the Halls now relinquished could be recovered, and those retained put to profitable account. I shall undertake my next tour with wider objects.[106]

Though Holyoake did not lose his love of comprehensive titles or abandon the Utilitarian Society, he now saw that the way to national

organisation, the rebuilding of Owenism, was to be through provincial
lectures, renewing the local bodies. This was to be the pattern of effective
work throughout the rest of the 1840s and 1850s, and was to continue
important even after national organisation had been achieved. In the
history of Secularism there is a continual tension between the national
leaders, pouring out their schemes in their journals and giving the
impression of activity, and the real growth and influence of the movement in the textile communities of Lancashire and elsewhere in the
north. Both head and body made their own contribution to Secularism,
and the head neglected the body at its peril.

In 1849 Charles Southwell demonstrated just how much could be
achieved in the provinces when he was invited to re-open the Manchester
Hall of Science in the cause of freethought. A combination of ability,
energy, enthusiasm and downright crudity achieved wonders, and both
the local churches and the local press was forced to take notice of his
presence. He selected two aunt sallies for special attention—the Established Church, personified by the Reverend Hugh Stowell, and the
Wesleyan conference—and started his own local periodical in which to
propagate his distinctive views.

As elsewhere, socialism in Manchester had languished after 1846, but
the soil was still fertile. A controversy was raging in the correspondence
columns of the *Manchester Examiner and Times* about some cheap
Sunday excursions to Fleetwood which had proved very popular with the
working classes, so Southwell could not resist joining the fray. The
Reverend Hugh Stowell, whom Manchester socialists had good cause to
remember without affection, called a public meeting to protest against
this abuse of the Sabbath. Southwell went along and tried to make a
speech, but he was excluded on the dubious grounds that the meeting was
a private one after all. The opportunity for revenge came on 17 September, when a meeting, chaired by the Bishop of Manchester, was called to
support an appeal on behalf of a missionary college in Hong Kong.
Southwell again attended, and Stowell, complaining that Manchester
had been in an uproar ever since Southwell had arrived, asked the police
to throw the offending infidel out. Southwell retorted by challenging the
Bishop and Stowell to debate the question, 'Are Church of England
doctrines in harmony with the *teaching*, or Church of England practises
[*sic*] in harmony with the *example*, of Jesus Christ?' The challenge does
not seem to have been taken up.[107]

Southwell's attempt to give the Wesleyans the benefits of his wisdom
met with a similar response. In 1849 the Wesleyan conference, meeting
in Manchester, had expelled three of its number over the matter of the fly
sheets which since 1844 had been lampooning Jabez Bunting and other

Methodist hierarchs. On 3 September a meeting was called in the Manchester Corn Exchange to sympathise with the expelled Wesleyans.
Southwell attended and asked permission to speak. This being refused,
he mounted the platform and was thrown out. He came back and was
again ejected.[108]

All this was excellent for publicity, but while the local press deplored
his exploits, Southwell was declaring his prowess with a more sympathetic voice in his own periodical, the *Lancashire Beacon*, in which he
asserted his belief that a radical reform of government could be accomplished only by the more radical reform of men, by which he meant the
removal of religious influences. To this end he included in the *Beacon*
a series of articles on the philosophers of freethought and extracts from
E.L. Bulwer's *The Fallen Star, or The History of a False Religion*. The
paper had no philosophical pretensions, however, and when a reader
challenged him to take up the topic of materialism he refused. His aim
was to make the *Beacon* popular and to cut out such heavy material as he
rightly felt weighed down the *Reasoner*. He therefore included a
serialised story, 'The Ghost Seer, or Apparitionist', and, most intriguing
of all, his own 'Confessions', one of the most readable items in the freethought journals of the time. The sale of No 1 of the *Beacon* in
Lancashire alone was over a thousand, and by October the first six issues
were nearly out of print. The paper lost money, though, and it closed
early in 1850 after its Wesleyan printer had refused to work on it any
more.[109]

Meanwhile Holyoake, detained in London by his teaching commit-
ments and his journalism, was passing through the depths of despair. The
Reasoner was still not paying its way, except by the generous donations
of W. J. Birch and the smaller contributions of the shilling fund, and he
did not like begging to keep going a paper which he regarded as the
responsibility of the whole freethought movement.[110] Furthermore, he
was no longer quite sure what the purpose of the *Reasoner* was to be. In
1846 it had seemed clear: to continue an official publication for Owenism
and to maintain an organ of public expression for freethought. Owenism
had, nevertheless, fallen away, the Society of Theological Utilitarians
had not grown to replace it, and the Chartist crisis of 1848, together with
the European revolutions, had made political and social issues much
more important than the theological and philosophical arguments.

In November 1848, W. H. Ashurst had acquired Alexander Campbell's
Owenite periodical the *Spirit of the Age*, and Holyoake had been
installed as editor. He used this to develop his political and social views,
but in March 1849 it failed and Holyoake was deprived of this outlet.
He therefore reorganised the *Reasoner*. On 21 March 1849 the *Reasoner*

assumed the sub-title of 'a Secular and Eclectic Journal', and from the following week the *Spirit of the Age* was included in its pages. Though he recorded in his diary for 21 March, 'issued the first *Secular* No. of the *Reasoner*' yet Holyoake refused to recognise what he was doing. Southwell saw the implication of what had happened: '*Autre temp autre moeurs*, is our admitted motto; and, doubtless, Mr Holyoake has sufficient reason to justify him in making the *Reasoner* of to-day more political, and less theological, than the *Reasoner* of two years since,' he wrote. Holyoake was furious at the suggestion of a change of policy, attributing any increase in the number of political articles to the contemporary public scene. Policy or otherwise, the new *Reasoner* was a failure. Holyoake was not popular among the Chartists—his advocacy of moderation in the *Spirit of the Age* had alienated many—and better papers were available for those radicals interested primarily in politics.[111] The circulation fell below a thousand for a time, less than the *Lancashire Beacon* was selling in the Manchester area alone. At the end of volume VII, in December 1849, Holyoake proposed to give up.

Numerically speaking, the achievement of the atheists had not been great. Up to 1850 the Theological Utilitarians, the *Reasoner*, and the individual efforts of ex-social missionaries had all failed to stem the tide which had set against Owenite rationalism with the closure of Harmony Hall in 1846. A picture of the decline can be built up from the decreasing circulation of the *Reasoner* and the reports of local branches which it contained.[112] Between 1846 and 1850 there occur each year reports of between six and thirteen metropolitan societies which were in some sense 'freethinking' in outlook, showing a steady growth in effective organisation, but in the provinces there was an overall decline in the number of societies. The *Reasoner* for 1846 contains references to twenty-three societies outside London, but in 1847, the first year of the Theological Utilitarians, the number had fallen to only nine—though activity was reported from a further forty localities. There was then a steady decline with little sign of recovery until 1852. Rational Society reports were equally bleak. Seventeen provincial Owenite societies with paid-up members still survived in 1846, and there were a further two—at Blackfriars and John Street—in London. In 1850 the two London societies still sent in subscriptions, but only Ashton, Hyde, Sheffield and Derby sent anything from the provinces.[113]

These figures cannot be regarded as being entirely accurate, as they are dependent upon the willingness of local secretaries to send in information, and not always the same societies make up the aggregate number for each year, but a few individual examples confirm the trend shown in the figures. Some societies went out of existence. At Huddersfield, for example, the socialist branch in 1845 reported itself undaunted by the failure of Harmony Hall, but in 1847 the Hall of Science was sold to the Unitarians and its library of two hundred volumes, including works by Paine, Voltaire and Owen, was dispersed. When Holyoake lectured in Huddersfield in 1848 he found that the socialists used the meeting room of the Christian Brethren, the followers of Joseph Barker, who by this time had become a deist. The town then disappears from the records, and when W. H. Johnson moved into the area in 1850 he found that 'Secularism was in a manner unknown'.[114] Other societies died, but a nucleus of supporters remained. In 1844 Holyoake had thought that 'The audiences of Oldham were the most crowded and eager of all I addressed', but a year later the members had grown apathetic. The hall was let to the Latter-Day Saints in 1846, in 'consequence of a paucity of numbers at local lectures', yet in 1848 Holyoake wrote another glowing report from Oldham.[115] There was, apparently, enthusiasm but no lasting organisation. In Sheffield there was organisation, but no enthusiasm. The local Owenites, with Isaac Ironside as their president, had kept their hall in Rockingham Street but throughout these years the *Reasoner* has no report that they did anything there. Presumably the Sheffield men were keeping to their resolution of 1848 not to involve themselves in any public agitation for socialism until the Harmony affair was cleared up. The Paisley socialists adopted a similar attitude at first, but their history is the opposite. For the Paisley branch seems not only to have maintained its existence but even to have revived during this period. Although in 1845 audiences at lectures were poor, and although the members were depressed at the failure of Harmony Hall and desired to be 'independent of any other body or Society', they nevertheless recovered. In 1846, with thirty full members, they announced their decision to reform their branch of the Rational Society, subscriptions were again sent, and in 1847 eighteen names appeared in the *Reasoner's* 'Thousand Shillings List'. The following year the trade depression hit their contributions badly but a combined meeting with the Glasgow communists was attended by two hundred people, and in 1850 the average weekly sale of the *Reasoner* was about sixty, slightly more than in 1846.[116] The explanation for this encouraging position would appear to lie in the character of the officers of the society, and particularly in that of its secretary, James Motherwell. Holyoake attributed great importance to such men. In 1846 he wrote:

> Mr Motherwell belongs to the rare genus of *living* secretaries. He is not merely a man that sits at a desk, keeps books and writes out notices—but one of the moving principles of the living machinery of the Branch. Popular freedom does not depend more on our poets than popular associ-

ations depend on secretaries. Let me choose the secretaries and I will restore your branches.[117]

Motherwell was still there ten years later, but he and Paisley were admitted exceptions to the general rule of decline.

This decline occurred for a number of reasons. Many societies were disillusioned with socialism after 1845 and were divided among themselves over the events which had led to the closure of Harmony Hall. The energies of their members were often diverted into other channels. In Glasgow, for example, several members joined the Chartist Land Scheme, and others proposed setting up a branch of the Leeds Redemption Society.[118] As Chartism revived in 1847–48, for many it replaced socialism as the major working-class issue of the day—as Holyoake himself experienced in the circulation of the *Reasoner*. Some branches lost members for other reasons. The economic difficulties of the 1840s drove large numbers of working men to seek their fortunes overseas, though the exact effect of emigration on domestic radicalism is hard to assess. What is clear is that a number of local leaders were lost to working-class movements of the 1840s and 1850s, and that some societies were decimated by emigration in the 1840s. New York had become branch 64 of the U.C.S.R.R. in 1840, and the Huddersfield socialists reported in 1843 that they had lost twenty-five members to America in the previous eighteen months. Thomas Hunt, secretary of the John Street branch, emigrated to Wisconsin in 1843, and the following year a Utilitarian Co-operative Emigration Society was formed at John Street, with a branch in Manchester, to help members go out and join him.[119] Another such body, the Tropical Emigration Society, organised in London and Glasgow by Thomas Powell of the London Atheistical Society and Anti-Persecution Union, eventually sent a party, accompanied by Powell himself, to Venezuela.[120] The Leeds socialists reported in 1845 that their society had suffered when a £25 loan had been withdrawn by a member who had emigrated to the United States, and the Northampton branch, which had adopted the name of Utilitarian Society after a visit from Holyoake in 1847, declined after its active secretary, Richard Foster, emigrated to the United States in September 1848.[121] But the major reason for the decline of the societies in the lean years between 1846 and 1850 was finance. The socialists had overstretched their resources in the early 1840s. Without large and regular audiences stimulated by first-class lecturers, not enough money could be raised to pay the mortgages on the Halls of Science, and the depression of which Paisley complained in 1847 may well have ended the feeble lives of many decaying Owenite societies. In Manchester, the centre of Owenism, the Socialists had in 1846 a hundred and fifty paying members and their weekly income exceeded current expenditure, but the Hall of Science Building Association was unable to repay the loans which had financed the erection of the Campfield Hall. A few months later they reported, 'We have no lectures in our Hall of Science now. A few of the late members and friends meet in one of the rooms on a Sunday night, and are endeavouring to form themselves into a social brotherhood.' A Society of Social Friends was formed, which in 1847 took a room and cottage at 3 Back Queen Street off Deansgate, while the Hall was let as the City Music Hall until Southwell opened it again for Socialism in 1849.[122]

At the end of the decade, therefore, Holyoake had apparently failed to halt the decline in Owenism, and he had certainly failed to rescue what he considered to be its most important characteristics. Atheism had not proved popular and the Theological Utilitarian Society was almost as moribund at the old Rational Society itself. Yet all was not lost, and with hindsight we can see that Holyoake was standing on a new threshold. Behind him lay the deistic, rationalistic intellectual tradition of enlightenment Europe, the militant radicalism of Paine and Carlile, the grand schemes and idealism of Robert Owen, and the remains of disillusioned Chartism. The 1850s were to be a time for a re-thinking of old positions and a re-shaping of old attitudes. With a decade of experience in radical freethought, Holyoake was in a position to make just such a new start. He gathered up the remnants and skilfully combined the atheistic elements of the Paine–Carlile tradition with the rationalistic elements of the Owenite tradition, and in 1851 launched a new movement which he called Secularism.

Notes

1 R. Owen, *Life*, I, p. 299.
2 'Address Delivered at the City of London Tavern on Thursday, August 21st, and Published in the London Newspapers of August 22nd, 1817', printed in Owen, *op. cit.*, IA, p. 115.
3 L. Jones, *Life of Robert Owen*, pp. 194, 203–4.
4 W. Lovett, *The Life and Struggles of William Lovett . . .* (London, 1876), p. 43.
5 *N.M.W.*, 29 November 1834.
6 W. L. Sargant, *Robert Owen and his Social Philosophy* (London, 1860), pp. 425–6; J. Gray to the secretary of the London Co-operative Society, 18 June 1831, O.C. 381.
7 F. Podmore, *op. cit.*, p. 490; *Movement*, 20 April 1844.
8 G. J. Holyoake, *History of Co-operation*, I, p. 244; *N.M.W.*, 29 May 1841, 27 June 1840.
9 L. Jones, *op. cit.*, p. 323; *Quarterly Review*, December 1839, quoted by H. Silver, *The Concept of Popular Education* (London, 1965), p. 229;

Herald of the Future, March 1840, quoted by B. Simon, *Studies in the History of Education,* p. 240. See also Thomas Frost, *Forty Years' Recollections* (London, 1880), p. 16.

10 R. B. Rose, 'John Finch, 1784–1857: a Liverpool disciple of Robert Owen', *Tr.H.S.L.C.* CIX (1957), pp. 159–84, especially pp. 173–7.

11 *N.M.W.,* 9, 23 March 1839, 14 March 1840.

12 W. H. G. Armytage, *Heavens Below,* pp. 151–2.

13 *N.M.W.,* 1 December 1838, 7 September 1839, 2 July 1840, 30 January 1841; L. Jones, *op. cit.,* pp. 360–72.

14 T. Cooper, *Life of Thomas Cooper* (London, 1873), pp. 186–96; G. J. Holyoake, *History of the Rochdale Pioneers* (London, 1893), p. 8.

15 L. Jones, *op. cit.,* p. 373.

16 J. Barker, *The Abominations of Socialism exposed . . .* (Newcastle, 1840), p. 2. For Barker, see appendix v.

17 Quoted by H. Jephson, *The Platform, its Rise and Progress* (London 1892), II, pp. 243–4.

18 *Hansard,* LI, 20 January 1840, cols. 237–8.

19 *Ibid.,* LI, LII, 24 January–17 February 1840, *passim*; *N.M.W.,* 15 August 1840.

20 *Ibid.,* 15 August 1840, 20 February 1841. W. J. Linton said the imprisonment lasted only six weeks—*James Watson* (Manchester, 1880), p. 52; see also A. G. Barker, *Henry Hetherington* (London, 1938), pp. 29–36.

21 *N.M.W.,* 17 November 1838, 13 April, 17 August, 28 December 1839. For a description of the hall see *Manchester Examiner and Times,* supplement, 4 September 1852. There is a photograph in J. F. C. Harrison, *Robert Owen and the Owenites in Britain and America* (London, 1969), facing p. 197.

22 *N.M.W.,* 26 October 1839, 9 May, 21 August 1840.

23 *Ibid.,* 20 June, 4, 11 July, 1 August 1840; *Manchester and Salford Advertiser,* 13 June, 4 July 1840; *Manchester Courier,* 27 June 1840.

24 *Hansard,* 4 February 1840, col. 1202.

25 *N.M.W.,* 11 July 1839. Owen repeated this warning early in 1840 when he heard of the Bishop of Exeter's impending attack—'Address of the Central Board', 28 January 1840, O.C. 1235.

26 L. Jones, *op. cit.,* p. 367.

27 W. Chilton to Holyoake, 26 December 1841, H.C. 22.

28 L. Jones, *op. cit.,* pp. 331, 334; H. Jeffery to Holyoake, 7 April 1842, H.C. 37; *Reasoner,* 17 February 1858. The Edinburgh socialists were largely composed of Unitarians who had broken away from their chapel in 1839— James Lindsay to R. Owen, 11 August 1839, O.C. 1140.

29 C. Southwell, *Confessions of a Freethinker* (London [1850]), pp. 36–8, 44–55. For Southwell see appendix v.

30 *Ibid.,* pp. 56–9; *N.M.W.,* 10 August, 7 September, 14 December 1839, 4, 18, 25 January 1840.

31 Southwell, *op. cit.,* pp. 56–7.

32 *N.M.W.,* 13 June, 28 November, 12 December 1840; A.A.C.A.N. minute book, 21, 24 June 1840. Whatever Southwell later claimed, he was an orthodox Owenite in 1840–see his *Socialism Made Easy* (London, 1840).

33 *Investigator,* No. 5 [29 April 1843]; Southwell, *op. cit.,* pp. 61–4; *N.M.W.,* 6 June 1841.

34 Southwell, *op. cit.*, pp. 63–4.
35 L. Jones, *op. cit.*, p. 385; *Oracle*, 26 March 1842.
36 Southwell, *op. cit.*, pp. 65–6; Chilton in *Oracle*, II [1843], preface.
37 Southwell, *op. cit.*, p. 15; but in his trial speech, quoted in *National Reformer*, 15 January 1865, he said that a gentleman near where he lived had lent him Dwight's *Theology*.
38 *National Reformer, loc. cit.*; *Investigator* [October 1843], preface; *Oracle*, 6 August 1842.
39 Log book, I, 15 June 1836–September 1840, *passim*, H. B.; E. Royle, 'Mechanics' Institutes and the working classes, 1840–60', *Historical Journal*, XIV (1971), pp. 318–20.
40 Testimonial (copy made by Holyoake), 22 July 1840, H.C. 15.
41 Id., H.C. 16.
42 W. E. Adams, *Memoirs of a Social Atom* (London, 1903), I, pp. 15–16; Hollick, *loc. cit.*
43 Log book, I, 18 August, September 1841, H.B.; Central Board to Holyoake, 15 July 1841, H.C. 20. His income was 30s. a week, less what he paid Paterson—G. J. Holyoake, *Last Trial for Alleged Atheism in England* (third edition, London, 1861), p. 3. For Paterson see appendix v.
44 Central Board to Holyoake, *loc. cit.*; *N.M.W.*, 26 February 1842, 6 November 1841; log book, I, 27 October 1841, H.B.
45 *Oracle*, 12 February 1842.
46 *Ibid.*, I [1842], preface.
47 *Ibid.*, 19 March 1842.
48 *Ibid.*, 10 September, 22, 29 October 1842.
49 *Ibid.*, 27 November 1841.
50 Chilton to Holyoake, 26 December 1841, H.C. 22; *Oracle*, II [1843], preface; 'Address of Mr Holyoake on his Release from Gloucester Goal [sic]', in *The Man Paterson . . .* (London [1843]), p. 88.
51 Ryall to Holyoake, 4 January 1842, H.C. 24; log book I, December 1841, H.B. For Ryall see appendix v.
52 G. J. Holyoake, *The Spirit of Bonner in the Disciples of Jesus . . .* (London [1842]), p. 4; *Oracle*, 18 June 1842; G. J. Holyoake, *Bygones Worth Remembering* (London, 1905), II, pp. 215–45; Holyoake to T. Cooper, 30 October 1872, H.C. 2107.
53 Handbill inside front cover, diary-cum-notebook, H.B.
54 Ryall to Holyoake, [1842], H.C. 89; *Oracle*, 30 July 1842; Jeffery to Holyoake, 23 March, 7 April 1842, H.C. 32, 37.
55 Evidence of William Henry Pierce, from the copy sent by Lear to Holyoake, 12 June 1842, H.C. 50.
56 Holyoake, *Last Trial*, pp. 4–7; Lear to Holyoake, 27 May 1842, H.C. 45.
57 Log book I, 2 June 1842, H.B.; Holyoake, *op. cit.*, pp. 8–12; *N.M.W.*, 18 June 1842; *Oracle* 25 June 1842; Galpin to Holyoake, 4 July 1842, H.C. 54; John Turnbull to Mrs Holyoake, 8 September 1842, H.C. 74; *N.M.W.*, 11 December 1841, 21 May 1842.
58 W. Lovett, *Life and Struggles*, p. 221; Graham Papers (microfilm, Cambridge University library), *passim*; *Journals of the House of Lords* (1842) and *Commons* (1842), *passim*.
59 *Reasoner*, 27 December 1848; log book I, July 1842, H.B.; Holyoake to wife, 22 July 1842, H.C. 58; J. H. Parry to Holyoake, 12 October 1842,

H.C. 78; Carlile to Holyoake, 16 October, 1 September, 25 October 1842, H.C. 79, 72, 82; Carlile to Ryall, 11 July 1842, H.C. 56; Holyoake to wife, 14 August 1842, H.C. 62.

60 Holyoake, *op. cit.*, pp. 20–65; *The Trial of G. J. Holyoake on an indictment for Blasphemy* (London, 1842); S. D. Collet to Holyoake, 4 October 1845, H.C. 62.

61 *Cheltenham Mercury*, 23 May 1891, H.C. 3302.

62 *Oracle*, 2 July 1842.

63 Ryall to Holyoake, 2 April 1842, H.C. 35; *Oracle*, 25 June, 2 July, 27 August 1842.

64 *Ibid.*, 2 July 1842.

65 Holyoake, *op. cit.*, pp. 72–3, 75; Southwell, *Confessions*, pp. 70–5; Southwell to Holyoake, [March] 1842, H.C. 28; T. Whiting, 'Necessaries supplied to Mr Chas. Southwell while in Bristol Gaol', 5 February 1843, H.C. 92.

66 *Oracle*, 24 September, 17 December 1842, 4 February 1843; *The Man Paterson, passim*.

67 *Investigator*, 22 July 1843; *Oracle*, 1 July, 16 September 1843.

68 *Investigator*, 22, 29 July 1843; *Oracle*, 8 July, 19 August 1843.

69 *Ibid.*, 26 August 1843; *Investigator*, 22 July, 19 August 1843.

70 *Oracle*, 12, 26 August, 2, 9 September, 7 October 1843; *Investigator*, 19 August, 2 September 1843.

71 *Oracle*, 16, 23 September 1843; *N.M.W.*, 30 September 1843; Kalley to Holyoake, 9 November, 28 December 1843, 6 March 1844, H.C. 101, 105, 110.

72 *Oracle*, 7 October–4 November 1843.

73 *Ibid.*, 16 September 1843; *The Scotch Trials . . .* (London and Edinburgh, 1844), pp. 14–54; *Movement*, 8 June 1844, 19 February 1845. For Matilda Roalfe see appendix v.

74 *Oracle*, 18 November, 2 December 1843; *Movement*, 3 February 1844; *The Scotch Trials*, pp. 61–80.

75 *Movement*, 16, 23 October, 27 November 1844; *Herald of Progress*, 22 November 1845. For Emma Martin see appendix v.

76 *Reasoner* 25 November 1846; J. M. Ludlow and L. Jones, *Progress of the Working Class, 1832–67* (London, 1867), p. 43; *Movement*, 16, 23 October 1844.

77 Trevelyan to Holyoake, 16 May 1844, H.C. 116; *Movement*, 10 February 1844; Roalfe to Birch, 7 November 1844, H.C. 130; *Movement*, 20 November 1844.

78 *Ibid.*, 12, 19, 26 February, 2 April 1845; *N.M.W.*, 26 July 1845.

79 *Oracle*, 11 March 1843; *Investigator* [1843], preface.

80 Harney to Holyoake, 17 November 1843, H.C. 102.

81 Roalfe to Birch, 7 November 1844, H.C. 130.

82 *Movement*, 30 March 1844.

83 A.P.U. exercise book in H.B.; *Movement*, 15, 22 June, 7 September 1844; *Circular*, August 1845; *Movement*, 20 November 1844; A. G. Barker, *Henry Hetherington*, pp. 47–9.

84 *Movement*, 1 January, 2 April 1845.

85 A.A.C.A.N. minute book, 21 June 1843; *Movement*, 21 January 1845; *N.M.W.*, 31 May 1845; Southwell, *Confessions*, p. 90.

86 *Movement*, 31 August 1844.

87 *National Reformer*, 14 June–26 July 1868; *N.M.W.*, 11 December 1841; *Movement*, 6 April, 31 August 1844.

88 R. Cooper to R. Owen, 30 September 1850, O.C. 1855.

89 Log book I, 6 February–19 June 1843, H.B.; J. Firmin to Holyoake, 28 May 1843, H.C. 97; *Oracle*, 8 July, 21 October 1843; *Movement* 27 July 1844, 5 February 1845; log book II, April 1845, H.B.

90 *Herald of Progress*, 28 February 1846.

91 See the reports of Congress, *N.M.W.*, 25 May–8 June 1844, 24 May–7 June, 26 July, 9 August 1845; *Herald of Progress*, 9 May 1846; *Reasoner*, 8, 15 July 1846.

92 *N.M.W.*, 23, 30 August 1845; Fleming to Owen, 5 October 1845, O.C. 1392; *Herald of Progress*, 25 October 1845; *Reasoner*, 17 May 1848.

93 R. Cooper to Holyoake, 21 March 1846, H.C. 162; log book II, 1 March 1846, H.B.

94 Watson to Holyoake, 27 January, 12, 27 February, 12 March 1846, H.C. 154, 156, 159, 161; *Herald of Progress*, 11 April 1846.

95 G. J. Holyoake, *Sixty Years of an Agitator's Life* (London, 1892), pp. 204–8.

96 *Herald of Progress*, 8 November 1845.

97 His third surviving child was born the day after his dismissal from Glasgow —log book II, 27 February 1846, H.B.

98 J. G. Hornblower to Holyoake, 5 March 1846, H.C. 160.

99 *Reasoner*, 13 August, 8 July, 28 October 1846, 2 June, 22 September 1847. For circulation figures see appendix III.

100 R. Cooper to R. Owen, 10 July 1847, O.C. 1480.

101 Southwell, *op. cit.*, pp. 91–4, 97–8; *Reasoner*, 20 December 1848, 21 March, 18 July, 15 August 1849.

102 *Ibid.*, 30 September, 7 October 1846.

103 *Ibid.*, 2 December 1846, 17 February 1847.

104 *Utilitarian Record*, 10 November 1847.

105 *Ibid.*, 26 January 1848; *Reasoner*, 16 February 1848.

106 *Ibid.*, 12 July 1848.

107 Lancashire Beacon, Nos. 2, 3, 4, 8, 9, 10, 11, [10, 17, 24 August, 22, 29 September, 6, 13 October 1849].

108 *Ibid.*, Nos. 6, 7 [8, 15 September 1849].

109 *Ibid.*, Nos. 1, 2, 13 [3, 10 August, 27 October 1849]; *Reasoner*, 23 January 1850.

110 *Ibid.*, VII [December 1849], introduction.

111 *Lancashire Beacon*, No. 6 [8 September 1849]; *Reasoner*, 26 September 1849; *Spirit of the Age*, 24 February, 3 March 1849.

112 See appendices I, II, III.

113 *Reasoner*, 8 July 1846, 15 May 1850.

114 *Herald of Progress*, 25 October 1845; *Huddersfield Examiner*, 4 November 1939, 20, 21 March 1946; *Reasoner*, 12 July 1848; *Yorkshire Tribune* [February 1856], pp. 116–17.

115 *Movement*, 27 July 1844; *Herald of Progress*, 6 December 1845, 25 April 1846; *Reasoner*, 5 July 1848.

116 *Herald of Progress*, 20 December 1845; *Reasoner*, 24 June, 20 August 1846; *Utilitarian Record*, 25 August 1847; *Reasoner*, 20 September 1848, 27 November 1850, 8 July 1846.

117 *Herald of Progress*, 25 April 1846.

118 *Utilitarian Record*, 1 December 1847.

119 *N.M.W.*, 3 June, 1 July 1843, 5 October, 23 November 1844.

120 *Ibid.*, 25 May, 30 November 1844; Powell to Holyoake, 24 March 1862, H.C. 1415. For Powell see a note in the A.P.U. exercise book, H.B.

121 *N.M.W.*, 31 May 1845; *Reasoner*, 17 February 1847, 20 September 1848.

122 *Herald of Progress*, 14 February 1846; *Reasoner*, 29 July, 20 August 1846; *Utilitarian Record*, 17 February 1847; *Reasoner*, 5 July 1848.

3
Old and new forms of freethought

a
Atheism

Southwell, Cooper, Holyoake, Bradlaugh and their followers were consciously a part of the Painite infidel tradition. Their thoughts and attitudes were conditioned by the literature of that tradition, which the radical booksellers kept circulating among the working classes during most of the nineteenth century. The ideas of the previous century were readily available: one pamphlet, published in 1839, contained extracts from, among others, Annet, Voltaire and Paine; Watson reissued Volney on *The Law of Nature* and Voltaire's *Important Examination of the Holy Scriptures*; and a friend tried to bring Voltaire's *Philosophical Dictionary* to Holyoake in Gloucester gaol. It is not surprising, therefore, that much of the religious and political philosophy found in the writings of the Victorian infidels is similar to that expressed in the literature of the French revolution and the Owenite movement.[1]

What the opinions were of the men and women who crowded the lecture halls, who bought the *Oracle* and who sent their sixpences to *Reasoner*, can only be a matter for conjecture since, unlike their lecturers and editors, they have left behind them no records. However, it seems reasonable to assume that, as the followers were brought up in the same surroundings as the leaders and as their views were developed by what they read and heard, the literature which does survive indicates at least some of the ideas current in the infidel movement as a whole. What cannot be discovered is how far any individual or 'typical' opinion is accurately expressed in the particular views of any one infidel leader at any one time. Especially is this true for Holyoake whose views changed considerably between 1840 and 1866. Men who grew old with him may or may not have changed their ideas with him, while young men who heard Bradlaugh lecture on the Bible in 1859 may or may not have differed from the young men who heard Cooper on the same subject twenty years earlier.

It is equally difficult to find out why men became infidels in the first place. Were they converted by the lectures or the sort of criticisms which the lecturers put forward, or were they simply 'born' infidels? Contemporaries were not afraid to guess the answers, though their conclusions tell us more about themselves than about the freethinkers. W. J. Fox, a liberal Christian, attributed unbelief to his more orthodox, fundamentalist, persecuting brethren and there was some truth in this; while John Layhe, the Manchester Domestic Missionary in 1851, thought infidelity was the product of an uncritical and exclusively intellectual education. Holyoake agreed with the latter, though without the perjorative overtones.[2]

The development of freethought confirms certain truths in all these observations. Just as Christian belief can be, and often is, founded on an emotional response in a given situation, to be confirmed later by intellectually satisfying 'evidences', so infidelity seems to have frequently been inspired by disgust with the Church and moral revulsion against Christian doctrines, and then sustained by a growing intellectual conviction of the rightness of such a rejection—a conviction perhaps hastened by an uncritical handling of the so-called facts of the matter. This is not to say that infidelity was intellectually untenable, as some contemporary clergymen thought, for the new discoveries and interpretations which attracted widespread attention during these years, whilst not perhaps creating new infidelity, certainly went far to justify the older infidel position. Mixed motives and old arguments, supplemented by new and more valid examples, seem to lie behind much of the popular infidelity of the mid-nineteenth century.[3]

A starting point for many was the Bible and the doctrines based upon it. This is not surprising, since large numbers of people, though they may never have been practising Christians, were brought up under these twin pillars of the Christian Faith. Thomas Paine's *Age of Reason* had been about the Bible; Charles Southwell had been imprisoned for criticising the 'Jew Book'; William Chilton was made an infidel, so he claimed, by the Bible. Scripture was seen as the foundation of all evil. Robert Cooper, for example, began his principal work on the Bible, *The Infidel's Text Book*, with the assertion:

> This it is, that, in all ages, and all countries, but more especially in Christendom, has blasted the hopes and labours of the patriot, the philosopher, and the philanthropist! It is, therefore, we enter upon the subject before us, believing that if the faith of the people in the Divinity of this 'tale of a tub' is one exploded, the grand corner-stone of the priestly system is shaken, and the whole fabric must speedily be razed to the ground.[4]

The most obvious way to demolish the authority of the Bible was by the simple process of internal criticism based on common sense and supplemented by the selected views of what were termed 'authorities'. Just as the fundamentalist Christians developed the art of quoting indis-

criminately selected texts to meet every situation, so the infidels substituted quotation for argument. The largest effort along these lines was
the 1180 pages of *A few Hundred Bible Contradictions, A Hunt After
the Devil, and other Odd Matters, by John P.Y., M.D.* written by Peter
Lecount, a railway engineer. The work was extensively advertised in the
freethought periodicals, and when Hetherington died in 1849 he had
more than five hundred copies in stock.[5] Briefer but covering the same
ground was Robert Cooper's *The Holy Scriptures Analyzed* which was
published in the late 1830s and became one of the most popular aids to
infidelity for a number of years. A large portion of the book comprised
lists of texts giving 'Passages Inconsistent with the Attributes generally
ascribed to the Deity by the Christian World'. For example, on
omnipotence there occur such texts as

> But Jesus beheld them and said unto them, With men this is impossible,
> but with God ALL *things are possible.—Matt. xix. 26.*
> And the Lord was with Judah, and he drove out the inhabitants of the
> mountains, but COULD NOT *drive out the inhabitants of the valley*, because
> they had chariots of iron.—*Judges i. 19.*[6]

Bradlaugh used a similar technique in his debate with the Reverend
Woodville Woodman at Ashton in 1861, and it formed one of the
principal objects of his more scholarly *The Bible: What It is*, the beginning of a commentary on the Bible which drew on Voltaire, Paine,
LeClerc and F. W. Newman, and made a liberal use of quotations in the
original Hebrew.

Inseparable from 'Passages Inconsistent' in any attack on the Bible were
'Passages Immoral and Obscene'. The presence of such passages is mentioned with more or less frequency by all the freethought writers. Holyoake, his usual moral and moderate self, thought the Bible 'a mischievous
book' and the birth of Christ 'disgraceful'. Southwell gave one of the
difficulties of Christianity as being that if the Bible be accepted as literally true then the God of Moses must be a local God 'who comes down
from heaven to take part in the miserable battles of his miserable creatures, and teaches those creatures to hate, spoil, or destroy each other'.[7]
Texts were not wanting to prove these contentions, and neither Cooper
nor Bradlaugh in particular was slow to suggest a few. A special
favourite was Genesis xix (the story of Lot), which Bradlaugh prudishly
refused to quote in his *The Bible: What It is*. Others included David, 'the
man after God's own heart',[8] and the story of the slaughter of the
Amalekites. According to Robert Cooper, only four women are named
in the genealogy of Christ:

> *Thamar, who seduced the father of her late husband: Rachel, a common
> prostitute; Ruth, who, instead of marrying one of her cousins, went to bed*

with another of them; and *Bethseba*, an *adulteress*, who espoused David, *the murderer of her first husband*:[9]

These stories and texts were useful and, it may be presumed, popular, but their purpose seems to have been theatrical rather than logical. On Paterson's placards or in the lecture hall, they stimulated a proper, if uncharacteristic, moral indignation at the wickedness of the Bible, but for arguments the infidel leaders preferred to parade those doctrines which were based on Scripture as complete proof of its immorality.

In every repertoire came the Fall and the Atonement. Holyoake cryptically summed up the problem of the doctrine of Original Sin when he posed a series of questions which had been old when Paine had asked them:

> If man fell in the garden of Eden—who placed him there? It is said, God! Who placed the temptation there? It is said, God! Who gave him an imperfect nature—a nature of which it was foreknown it would fall? It is said, God! To what does this amount?[10]

After a similar passage a decade earlier, Robert Cooper had supplied an answer which needed no geological discoveries to prompt it:

> . . . this Mosaic account of the fall of man is nothing but a mere fiction, invented by the priesthood.[11]

If man did not fall, then he did not need the Atonement, but, assuming that he did, how could the death of one man atone for all sins now and why did God wait so long? Holyoake asked further:

> If God did not require the shedding of blood for his satisfaction, how came Christ to offer it, and God to accept it? He who should require or permit the death of another, because of the offence of eating an apple, would be counted ferocious among men to this hour. . . .[12]

Christianity seemed to offer no answers to these questions, and the insistence of the Evangelicals on the literal truth of Scripture deepened rather than resolved the problem. To unprejudiced common sense, the Bible taken at face value was nonsense. The same was true of the doctrines of Providence and of Prayer. The realisation that these did not mean what they said played an important part in Holyoake's loss of faith, and the theme recurs in many of his writings. The cholera epidemic of 1849 prompted him to write one of his most successful pamphlets, the *Logic of Death*, in which he drew the conclusion:

> Man witnesses those near and dear to him perish before his eyes, and despite his supplications. He walks through no rose-water world, and no special Providence smooths his path.[13]

The doctrine of prayer was reduced to the practical question, 'I ask not have such prayer, but have they answers to their prayers?'[14]

Even more important than the rejection of Christian doctrine was the rejection of Christian practice, and it was the latter which added much bitterness to the attack. Left to itself the Bible was a foolish irrelevancy, but in the hands of the Church it became a dangerous weapon and threat to humanity. The Bible had been responsible for the quarrelings and jealousies of the early Church; each century had it heretics and its persecutions—the Crusades, the Wars of Religion, the activities of Calvin, the English Reformation legislation, Laud's persecutions, Judge Jefferys and the Puritans in England and America—and the divisive influence of Scripture was still apparent in the contemporary sectarian Church. 'I ask,' concluded Cooper, who gave this particular list, 'has not that influence been *pernicious*? Do not truth and humanity alike demand that it should be repudiated?'[15] This argument was all the more telling because many of the infidel leaders had personal experience of persecution, a fact which gave great emotional value to their use of it. 'If the dark ages had their inquisition,' Holyoake reminded his readers, 'enlightened times have their Dorchester, Bristol, and Gloucester Gaols.'[16] This approach also appealed to the political prejudices of the infidel audiences. Southwell made St Paul's injunction, 'Let every soul be subject unto the higher powers, for there is not any power but of God', responsible for Castlereagh, Sidmouth and Peterloo.[17]

Christian apologists were aware of the difficulties created for them by Church history, but they were ready to counter the infidel arguments. As John Bowes told Holyoake, 'The Christianity of the book I am prepared to defend; the Christianity of those that depart from the Scriptures I am prepared to condemn', but this attitude led to difficulties of interpretation which did not help the Christian case.[18] For example, David King tried to show that the Church of Rome was not Biblical—an obviously sectarian argument. Holyoake merely replied that the doctrines and conduct of the Catholic Church were founded on the New Testament, and he frequently lectured on this theme.[19] Another Christian who met Holyoake in debate, Brewin Grant, rightly urged that the infidel 'should judge of *them* by their fruits', but the point the infidels were arguing was that the Bible, even when judged by its own fruits, stood condemned.[20] Robert Cooper indignantly showed how Scripture-quoting clergymen had been stumbling-blocks in the way of progress:

> Talk of *social* reform, and they exclaim that poverty is a *divine* ordinance; that God made both *poor* and rich, and the people must, therefore, 'be content in the situation in which Divine Providence has placed them'. Talk of *political* reform, and they remind you that it is our duty, by com-

mand of the inspired word of heaven, to submit 'to the powers that be'. Talk of *educational* progress, and they exclaim that all education without religion, which simply means without *them*, 'would be a curse rather than a blessing'. Talk of *moral* reform in the shape of the temperance or any other kindred movement, and they caution us to quote the words of the Rev. Mr Duncan of North Shields, that 'it is an attempt to take the regeneration of man out of God's hands'. Talk of *peace* reform and we behold the mitred priest blessing the fatal emblem of human slaughter. Talk of reform in the blackest, the vilest, the meanest of all mortal abuses, the selling of human flesh, the trading in human slavery, and the man of God points his finger to the infallible page sanctioning the crime![21]

This was, of course, a one-sided argument based on selected examples of Christian conduct and selected texts, but so long as there were Christians who were prepared to justify their peculiar views in this way, the infidels had a powerful case.

A further element also appears in this kind of criticism. Infidel arguments had usually concentrated on outstandingly barbaric texts, but, although these continued to form the basis of freethought during the 1840s, the Bible was also coming under more general attack. There were inconsistencies in approach, and though Holyoake admitted that Christ 'gave utterance to many generous sayings', Cooper and Southwell only conceded that 'Do unto others, as ye would that others should do unto you' was good when they could add that it was found 'word for word in the original of Confucius'.[22] There was now less tolerance of what had been called 'genuine' Christianity, fewer attempts to rescue the Gospel from the priests, and more inclination to dismiss both as socially undesirable. It was this radical dismissal of all Christianity which separated the infidels from the various unorthodox Christian sects, such as Goodwyn Barmby's Communist Church or Joseph Barker's Christian Brethren, in the 1840s. Southwell merely sneered at Richard Carlile's attempt to prove Holyoake a Christian, and the latter, though more polite, was of the same opinion. Parts of Christ's teaching which had hitherto been regarded as harmless or even good, such as the Sermon on the Mount, were now condemned in the same way as the worst parts of the Old Testament. 'Love your enemies' was pronounced 'morally impossible' by Cooper, and 'take no thought for your life. . . .' was '*actually pernicious*'.[23] To Bradlaugh, the Beatitudes were as immoral as the conduct of Lot:

> Jesus teaches that the poor, the hungry, and the wretched shall be blessed? This is not so. The blessing only comes when they have ceased to be poor, hungry, and wretched. Contentment under poverty, hunger and misery is high treason, not to yourself alone, but to your fellows. These three, like foul diseases, spread quickly wherever humanity is stagnant and content with wrong.[24]

So the infidels set out their reasons for rejecting the Bible and the
Christian faith. All the arguments were based on, or related to, an
internal criticism of the Bible, and this was enough to convict it. Amongst
this assortment of ideas, justifications and condemnations are to be found
most of the reasons why men became infidels in the Victorian period—a
rejection of Christianity, part moral, part intellectual and part political.
But these were not the only arguments offered, and further justifications
were brought forward to reinforce the case against Christianity. These
were the external evidences, made all the more convincing by the steady
advance of knowledge and what was regarded as authoritative scholarship.

One form which such criticism took was that arising from a study of
comparative religion. The infidels shared a contemporary fascination
with the East and were well acquainted through the writings of Robert
Taylor with the possibilities which different religions offered. From the
Diegesis and other popular sources the arguments derived from a study
of mythology and comparative religion began to enter the periodicals,
lectures and pamphlets of the radical movement. The difficulties of
identifying any particular source are enormous, and the information
was often gained at many removes from the original. For example, in
1847 the Freethinkers' Discussion Committee of Aberdeen drew its
information from Hetherington's *Freethinker's Information for the
People* which published an article on a 'Comparison of the Lives,
Characters, and Actions of Jesus Christ, and the Chreeshna of the Hindoos', the substance of two lectures by Mr Charles Savage of London who
quoted from Sir William Jones's *Discourse on the Gods of Greece, Italy,
Egypt and India*.[25] But from whatever source the knowledge was derived,
it was duly pressed into service. The *Oracle* had a series of articles on
'Symbol Worship', which discussed the Brahma and the Chreeshna and
did not 'comprehend why the supernaturalism of China, or India, or of
Arabia may not have as good a claim to divine character as the supernaturalism of Europe'.[26] If miracles could prove the truth of religion, they
could prove the truth of any religion, reasoned Cooper, and Bradlaugh
drew on Sir William Hamilton's lectures for yet another comparison
between Christ and Krishna.[27]

Another way of discrediting the Bible was by a historical criticism of
its text. Again the sources are numerous and difficult to isolate, but among
the more common seem to have been Mosheim's *Ecclesiastical History*,
Milman's *History of the Jews* and *History of Christianity*, Hennell's *An
Inquiry Concerning the Origin of Christianity*, Strauss's *Life of Jesus*,
J. A. Giles's *Hebrew Records* and Robert Taylor's *Diegesis*. The ideas
contained in such books formed the substance of the first part of Cooper's
The Infidel's Text Book in which he showed, contrary to the claims of

less enlightened Christians, that the Bible was not a universal book but
had been 'revealed' to an insignificant tribe who had lost or ignored it.
The Septuagint, on which the Church relied, was compiled from various
unauthenticated Hebrew manuscripts, and the early Fathers had not
been above making their own alterations and additions. The New Testament records were equally unreliable, written long after the event,
arbitrarily selected by the contrary decisions of early Councils, and now
available only in a bad English translation protected by Act of Parliament. The so-called authors of the sacred histories were not to be
trusted, and no reliable contemporary historian confirmed what they
recorded. The books of the Bible were not written by the people whose
names they bear, nor at the time when they were said to have been
written, which was also a good reason for scepticism about their claims to
prophetic insight. Miracles were equally unacceptable, being contrary to
the natural law expounded by Voltaire and Palmer.[28]

In this way Robert Cooper built up a formidable array of arguments
against the Bible, and his work stood unrivalled as a true 'Infidel's Text
Book' until Bradlaugh's The Bible: What It is, first published in parts in
1858, provided a detailed commentary on the first part of the Old Testament. Whatever the churches taught, infidels were in no doubt that the
Bible, 'instead of being a revelation from a good God, is a revelation from
days of barbarity, of ignorance, and of cruelty, with which they now try
to bind down an enlightened people'.[29]

To reject the Bible was anti-Christian but not necessarily anti-theistic.
The positive contribution to the Painite infidel tradition of the men who
followed Southwell in calling themselves atheists was the argument
which unmistakably rejected the existence of all gods. The difference
between a Christian and a deist was often a moral one, but that between
the theist and the atheist was intellectual. It appears to have been easier
for a man to lose his Christian faith than it was for him to become an
atheist. How many of those who took the first step went on to take the
second cannot be calculated, but, considering the complexity of the
arguments offered, it is not difficult to imagine that a considerable
number did not make it. All four of the principal national leaders, Southwell, Cooper, Holyoake and Bradlaugh, called themselves atheists but
by no means all Secularists in the 1850s were atheists and Holyoake did
not require them to be so.

Atheism was founded on two arguments, one negative and one positive.
According to the first, 'The Atheist simply denies that there is reason to
believe in the existence of a First Cause, which denial is the necessary
consequence of Materialism, a philosophy which admits not the creation
or destruction of matter.'[30] This was the basis of the atheism of South-

well, Cooper and Holyoake, current in the 1840s and 1850s, and it was
no different from the atheism which Richard Carlile and his followers
had espoused in the early 1820s. For example, Humphrey Boyle of Leeds
wrote to his fellow townsman, Joseph Gill, in 1822:

> We are Materialists, because every thing of which we can form an idea is
> material. Of spirit we know nothing; we know not what it is, nor can any
> one tell us; the most illiterate being knows as much about it as the most
> learned; and before any man presumes to tell us that God is best pleased
> with this or that kind of worship, let him tell us who and what God is. I
> for my part know nothing of such a being; I can no more form an idea of
> him than I can discover where heaven and hell are situated.[31]

Logically this kind of atheism did not prove that there was no God,
though some atheists demanded this of it. On the contrary, Southwell
was typical in placing the *onus probandi* on those who affirmed the
existence of God and Holyoake regarded himself as an atheist only in his
inability to believe what the churches would have him believe. They
were content to show that the Christian concept of the supernatural was
meaningless, that the arguments in its favour were illogical, and that the
mysteries of the universe, insofar as they were explicable, could be
accounted for in material terms. 'In my opinion,' wrote Southwell, 'the
word God does not imply anything positive; and no man has any ideas
except those he found in nature, as a whole or in part, for the imagination
itself borrows all from the material world.' God, to be eternal, must be
immaterial, but if he is immaterial then man can have no conception of
him.[32] The same reasoning was applied by Robert Cooper to the
existence of the soul:

> It is certainly not astonishing that our divines should experience such
> consummate difficulty in giving an idea of the soul, for if it be a 'spirit,'
> and spirit, being the opposite of substance is a mere negation, spirit must
> imply the *absence of an idea*; Man cannot form a conception of a nonen-
> tity. Spirituality, therefore, I repeat, is the mere negation of ideas, which is
> only saying, in plain words, *it has no existence*.[33]

All ideas of God and what is called the spiritual must therefore be
material. Man created God in his own image, or, as one of Southwell's
sources, the 'German Jew', put it:

> the material world has always furnished the type of the intellectual
> world . . . it is from what man sees that he creates his opinions upon that
> which he sees not.[34]

Ideas of God have been formed like ideas of beauty and justice, out of
human knowledge and experience.

Such nominalism was not, of course, new and the sensationalist
psychology on which this atheistic materialism was based went back to

Locke. Christian apologists were well acquainted with this line of argument and many had accepted its premises, rejecting the possibility of
innate ideas and founding all knowledge on experience. Reasonable
Christianity had therefore sought to prove the existence of God from the
evidence of design in the universe. Natural theology was regarded by
some, such as Lord Brougham, as a necessary support to the otherwise
unsubstantiated claims of revelation. The atheists countered the design
argument on several fronts. First they queried the existence of design at
all. In a series of articles in the *Oracle*, entitled 'Is there a God?', Southwell wrote: 'To the Atheist, a moth in the candle's flame, or a poor fly in
the fangs of a spider, is a *proof* that the world could not have been
designed by one being, infinitely wise, infinitely good, and infinitely
powerful.'[35] This was not necessarily an atheistical argument. Thomas
Paine had used it to disprove the existence of the Christian's God, but the
atheists extended it to its logical conclusion, disproving, if not the
existence of the devil, then at least the existence of any being with the
usual attributes of a God. In three articles in the *Movement*, Southwell
deliberately reversed the argument in Paine's *Age of Reason* to prove
'The God of Nature and the God of the Bible Identifiable'.[36]

A second approach to the design argument was made by Holyoake
when he was in Gloucester gaol. Presented with Paley's *Natural
Theology*, he determined to show that, even if Paley's premises were
accepted, his conclusion did not rest upon them. The result was *Paley
Refuted in his Own Words*, containing a demolition of the design argument which occurs in nearly all the atheist writings. Briefly, the argument
is that the world exhibits marks of design and must therefore have been
designed by intelligence. Intelligence, according to the sensationalist
theory of knowledge, cannot exist without a body so the creator must
have a body. But the creator must also be superior to that which he has
created, so the creator himself must have been designed. Therefore the
creator must have been created, *ad infinitum*. The error in Paley's logic
lay in his use of analogy, for 'Creation is without an analogy. No man
ever saw the creation of any object. The watchmaker of Paley made the
watch, but he found ready-made, he did not create, the materials.' The
argument from design therefore demanded a more incredible first
principle than that which materialism required: 'A God uncaused and
existing from eternity is, to the full, as incomprehensible as a world
uncaused and existing from eternity', and one of the axioms of the Society
for the Promulgation of Naturalism was that 'The "something which
every must have been" is matter'.[37]

The materialistic interpretation of human life rested on the assumptions that, 'we have no evidence of the existence of an essence, and that

organised matter is all that is requisite to produce the multitudinous manifestations of human and brute cerebration', but these assumptions needed some verification.[38] John Bowes, for example, was able to argue against both Southwell and Holyoake that, since matter at rest cannot be moved except by mind, the material world must therefore have a prime mover.[39] This had been Berkeley's argument against eighteenth-century materialism, and the freethinkers were really avoiding the issue when they replied that motion has a physical origin and therefore an immaterial God could not possibly have given motion to a material universe. They had to go further and explain how the material universe could be self-sufficient.

The most thorough attempt to explain how matter could think, how man could function without an immaterial soul or a 'spiritual essence', was made by Robert Cooper in his lectures on *The Immortality of the Soul, Religiously and Philosophically Considered*. According to Cooper, the question was not 'Could matter think?' but 'Could organised matter think?' Matter was eternal but the specific form in which it existed at any one time was not, and thought and intelligence were simply conditions of being. These contentions he justified both philosophically and empirically. He quoted Locke and Priestley in his support—particularly the latter who had subscribed to the theory that thought is a property of matter. Experience confirmed this. 'If thought be not a function of brain, *what is?*' he asked. 'It is comparatively useless if cerebration be not its province.' The same points were made by Bradlaugh in a lecture he gave on the soul at Sheffield in 1859, and he too turned to quotations from Priestley and also d'Holbach for support.[40]

This was the standard argument for atheism, but it was not entirely satisfactory even to the atheists themselves. Southwell found that his argument in favour of atheism proved that atheism and pantheism were virtually the same. Christians maintained that the proposition, 'life implies organisation', was no more certain than the counter proposition, 'organisation implies life', and observation indicated that organisation always precedes life.[41] Above all, the rationalists' basic assumptions could be shown to lead to conclusions other than those reached by the atheists.

> We have no evidence of the existence of matter beyond what our impressions tell us—it is these, which are *within us*, that we know to exist, not objects without us, the existence of these latter being only inferred from our impressions; so we have the evidence of our internal impressions in favour of spirit and have as much right to infer its existence from these, as the existence of matter from the former.[42]

The positive argument in favour of atheism was relatively new to the infidel radicals in the 1850s, and contributed somewhat to that hardening of attitudes which was developing among them towards all kinds of theism. Its principal exponent was Charles Bradlaugh, and his use of philosophical atheism marks him out both in the Secularist movement and in the Painite tradition as the leader of a new extremism. The advent of Bradlaugh indicates the most original development in that tradition since Carlile had espoused atheism in 1822.

In debate with the Reverend Woodville Woodman, a Swedenborgian minister, Bradlaugh met the latter's arguments by distinguishing himself clearly from Holyoake

> My friend [Woodman] says, Mirabaud's or Baron D'Holbach's 'System of Nature' has formed the *pabulum* for all infidels during the past century. It is not true that noone before me repudiated this word matter. Read Priestley, in his discussion on 'Matter and Spirit'—read the works of George Berkeley, Bishop of Cloyne. I admit, frankly, that neither of these men advocate precisely the views of myself; but I do assert that they each endeavour to demonstrate but one existence: and each say, as far as I understand, that they repudiate the orthodox notion of matter, and would most certainly repudiate the views of matter put forward by my friend. But my friend says, he means by nature just what such men as myself and Mr Holyoake mean. Mr Holyoake and I do not hold the same opinions. I am an Atheist, and I say I can demonstrate one existence. Mr Holyoake does not hold this opinion; Mr Holyoake simply says to the Theist, you cannot prove your Theism. . . .[43]

Bradlaugh brought to atheism a greater philosophical understanding than is apparent in any of the other leaders. Where they had discussed materialism in a general way, justifying it by an appeal to common sense, Bradlaugh clearly grasped exactly what Priestley had meant. The language he used was the language of Spinoza, and again Bradlaugh gives the appearance of having understood what Spinoza had meant. This was not true of Southwell, for example, who had earlier quoted Spinoza's Third Proposition, 'Of things which have nothing in common, one cannot cause the other', without apparently realising that this statement was not to be taken at face value, since Spinoza was referring only to different Substances.[44] Bradlaugh's interest in Spinoza went back to at least 1856 when he edited the article on Spinoza in the *Half Hours with the Free-thinkers* series. This was largely reproduced in his published lecture, *Is there a God?* (1861), in his debate with Woodman at Wigan in the same year, and in such later works as *Heresy: its Utility and Morality* (1868). Spinoza had reduced the duality of substances expressed in Cartesian philosophy to a single Substance, a definition of which included existence and which he called God. By definition he had therefore excluded the possibility of a transcendental God, and his philosophy amounted to pantheism. At this point Bradlaugh rejected Spinoza's conclusion that

'Pantheism demonstrates one existence, but affirms for it infinite attributes'. Instead, he argued, 'Atheism denies that attributes can be infinite. Attributes are but the distinguishing characteristics of modes, and how can that be infinite which is only a quality of finity?'[45]

This was a highly philosophical way of saying what Holyoake had argued with John Bowes in 1850, namely that infinite beauty cannot exist as an attribute of God because beauty is, by our very knowledge of it, a human attribute.[46] Most of the deductions from this philosophy were in fact the same as the other atheists were already asserting, but Bradlaugh's argument was superior because it escaped the dualism implied in a loose talk about 'materialism', it provided an impressive presentation of the old conclusions, and it stated a philosophical position which denied the existence of God *a priori*. Whether many people were able to follow Bradlaugh's reasoning is another matter. Holyoake's *Reasoner* often required an intelligent reader but never approached the standards demanded by Bradlaugh. Fortunately he was an excellent performer on the platform and the sight of Woodville Woodman still groping about in his Cartesian dualism and thinking he was opposing Holyoake was probably more than sufficient for the infidel part of the audience.

The supremacy of the Bible was undermined by moral indignation and critical scholarship, but so long as some Christians held to its literal truth the weight of geological science could also be brought to bear against it. The scientific arguments did not in general create unbelief but they did supply evidence to those who were losing their faith on other grounds. Great progress had been made between 1815, when J. B. Sumner in his Burnet Essay on 'The Records of Creation' had believed that the story of the Creation had probably been given to Adam and had been handed down to posterity by him, and 1836 when Buckland in his Bridgewater Treatise had said that Genesis recorded who made the world but not in what manner. Yet many people were still far from convinced and in 1857, when Baden Powell wrote that 'nothing in geology bears the smallest semblance to any part of the Mosaic cosmogony, torture the interpretation to what extent we may', he was still giving expression to an alarmingly new idea.[47] The infidels rejoiced to quote the more liberal scientific authorities and were confident that, as each new discovery made the last Christian position more untenable, the day would come when scientific truth would prevail in total confirmation of their own philosophy. They rejected 'the science of accounting for a beginning, of which we know nothing, by referring it to an intelligent God, of which we know less', in favour of materialism, ' . . . the search after *calculable causes—that progress may no longer be a vague, or capricious aspiration*

—but a serious scientific pursuit in which the steps shall be definite, measured, and reliable'.[48]

Both Buckland and Lyell, representing the catastrophic and uniformitarian schools of geological thought respectively, had rejected the Mosaic time-scale. 'The six thousand year-old story won't do for this generation,' declared Southwell, but modifications to the traditional belief—such as 'The six days are not employed in the work of creation, but of formation' which Brewin Grant offered in a debate with Bradlaugh in 1858—were acceptable neither on the grounds of biblical scholarship nor geology. Buckland's attempt to interpret the six days as six eras was silly, thought Robert Cooper, because the Jews had obviously developed the idea of the Sabbath as a conventional day. The story of the creation of man was equally absurd. Not only did geology show that man had existed long before the time permitted by the biblical time scale, but comparative anatomy proved that not all men could have come from the same pair.[49]

Next to the story of Creation, the Deluge was a favourite with the infidels. It was physically impossible, said Cooper, since the Andes were 20,000 feet high, and the story of the ark went against all ornithology, entomology, natural history, chemistry, physiology and zoology: not only were there millions of species, but how could the fishes have drowned anyway? Brewin Grant offered the explanation that the flood was universal in the sense that it drowned all but eight people, rather than that it covered the earth, but if so, Bradlaugh replied, why did Noah bother to save the birds, and how did eight people manage to look after all the animals? Cooper raised another numerical problem: how could the population have multiplied in the hundred and fifty years after the flood sufficient to build the tower of Babel?[50]

Scientific arguments in the early nineteenth century were sufficiently confused and offered so wide a variety of interpretations that Christians were able to refute fact with fact. John Bowes quoted the *Edinburgh Review*, the *North British Review*, J. Pye Smith, and even the *Vestiges of Creation* to oppose the view that mankind had a unitary origin. On the origin of the universe he quoted Humboldt's *Cosmos*, and on geology both Lyell and Sedgewick.[51] As more evidence became available, however, the uniformitarian position became clearer and the atheists continued to press its conclusions beyond those held by Lyell towards an acceptance of the eternity of matter. This led to a new interpretation of the nature of life.

Geology and common sense could be set against Genesis, but more important to the atheists were those scientific discoveries which supported materialism. Geology proved merely that the Bible—or, rather, one interpretation of the Bible—was wrong, whereas the mental sciences threatened to undermine the whole spiritual concept. Sir Charles Morgan, in his preface to his *Philosophy of Morals*, had warned that 'To place the credibility of a future state of existence upon a physiological necessity, is to take up a weak and a dangerous position. It is a mere *argumentum ab ignorantia*, liable to be affected by any change in the state of science . . .', and the sciences of anatomy and physiology were beginning to offer some evidence to show how the mind could be interpreted as no more than a bodily attribute.[52] Morgan himself defined life as the sum total of functions of organs of the body, and Sir Astley Cooper in his *Lectures on Surgery and Anatomy* demonstrated how excitement of the mind uniformly accompanies excitement of the brain. '*Casual injury of the brain*', for example '*infallibly produces a corresponding derangement of thought*'; material influences affect mental phenomena by way of dreams; inebriation affects the brain, causing disorder of the mind. Professor Lawrence had drily remarked, '. . . they who talk of and believe in, diseases of the mind, are too *wise* to put their trust in *mental* remedies. Arguments, syllogisms, discourses, sermons, have never *yet* restored *any* patient. . . .' With this evidence in view, Robert Cooper felt justified in concluding that

> Mind is developed as brain is developed. Mind is mature as brain is mature. Mind is decrepid as the brain is decrepid. Mind is *defunct* as brain is defunct.[53]

Many people, who might have been able to accept this argument for animals, were unable to agree that man should be placed in the same category. Of such Cooper asked, 'Why, in jumping from the sagacious monkey to man, are we to have recourse to the stimulus of an *essence* for explaining the superior cerebration he manifests?' According to Paley's argument, the nest of birds, the cell of the bee, the spider's web, the mound of the ant, the dam of the beaver and the hills of the termites all exhibited marks of contrivance and therefore of intelligence. Morgan had stated his opinion 'that reason is nothing but a more highly developed instinct', and a few years later, in his *Principles of Psychology*, Herbert Spencer was to agree that 'When regarded under its fundamental aspect, the highest reasoning is seen to be one with all the lower forms of thought, and one with instinct and reflex action even in their simplest manifestations.'[54]

Reception of these scientific theories and conclusions was made easier by the widespread acceptance of phrenology, one of the most popular pseudo-sciences of the nineteenth century. The phrenological system had first been suggested by Franz Joseph Gall (1758–1828), and for this he had been charged with being dangerous to religion and forced to leave his native Austria. He went to Paris and was there charged with being an atheist. His ideas were developed with minor differences by Dr J. G. Spurzheim, and the latter when lecturing in Edinburgh in 1815 converted George Combe (1788–1858) to the system.[55]

Led by Combe, the phrenological movement made astonishing progress in Britain and North America. In 1836 he gave up his profession in the Law and devoted himself full-time to phrenological missionary work, and already by 1837 he had over ninety societies throughout the United Kingdom devoted to a study of phrenology. His textbook for the movement, the *Constitution of Man*, first published in 1828, had sold 70,000 copies in England alone by 1840. It was, according to John Morley, 'seen on shelves where there was nothing else save the Bible and Pilgrim's Progress'.[56] Richard Cobden, Dr Richard Whateley and Sir Walter Trevelyan were amongst the more eminent people who showed interest in the subject; George Jacob Holyoake and Robert Cooper were among the lesser.

Combe's doctrine sums up much of the eighteenth-century inheritance which underlay nineteenth-century thought. He believed in the overriding powers of the laws of nature, physical, intellectual and moral: 'that Man cannot alter or evade their action, nor avert the consequences of them; and that hence his well-being is greatly influenced by the extent of his knowledge of and compliance with, the laws of their operation'. Moreover, he held the theory that 'The brain is the organ of the mind. It is subject to the general laws of the organism, and is strengthened by the same means as the other organs . . . Thought and feeling are to the brain what bodily exercise is to the muscles.' In common with the freethinkers, Combe was brought by this doctrine to a firm faith in the necessity and efficacy of education: 'The first step, therefore, towards establishing the regular exercise of the brain is to educate and train the mental faculties in youth; and the second is to place the individual habitually in circumstances demanding the discharge of useful and important duties.'[57]

Such views, which many Owenites could have and often did hold for themselves, naturally aroused suspicions as to Combe's theological soundness. He certainly was not an orthodox Christian, but like Owen he was a firmly convinced deist. The laws of nature had their origin in God and the mental organ of veneration proved the existence of such a God. A natural religion, harmony and a natural morality, the key concepts of the eighteenth century, were the foundation of the phrenological creed, but some of Combe's followers were not so old-fashioned in their beliefs. The idea that brain was the organ of mind was interpreted as materialism

by Dr W. C. Engledue and Dr John Elliotson, the founder of the Phrenological Association, and an address given by Engledue to that association
in 1842, published as *Cerebral Physiology and Materialism, with the
result of the application of Animal Magnetism to the Cerebral Organs*,
was widely circulated among the freethinkers.

Like phrenology, mesmerism could be interpreted both religiously and
atheistically. Combe accepted the basic ideas of this allied cult and added
a chapter on 'Mesmeric Phrenology' to the fifth edition of his *System of
Phrenology*, published in 1843, but in the same year Elliotson produced
his *Numerous Cases of Surgical Operations without Pain, in the
Mesmeric State*. Though one could take this as proving the power of
mind over matter, so far as the materialists were concerned it demonstrated the very opposite—that the mind could be controlled by purely
physical means—and the freethinkers found satisfying and widely
accepted 'scientific' proofs of materialism in the articles written by
Elliotson and Engledue in the *Zoist* and by Spencer T. Hall in the
Phreno-Magnet.[58]

So, just as geology was abolishing the traditionally accepted catastrophic developments in the history of the earth, the mental sciences
were blurring the distinctions between mind and matter, between the
animate and inanimate, between man and the lesser creatures. The way
was being cleared for a comprehensive 'Theory of Regular Gradation'.

This was to be the special contribution to freethought of William
Chilton, the Bristol compositor who in 1841 had helped Southwell establish the *Oracle of Reason*. Until his early death in 1855 Chilton was the
principal writer on the biological sciences for the various freethought
journals and his basic ideas were set out in a series which Southwell had
started in the *Oracle*, entitled 'The Theory of Regular Gradation'.[59] In
these articles Chilton showed a familiarity with most of the readily available writings on the subject, concerning both the discoveries of the nineteenth century and the theories of the eighteenth: Buckland, Lyell,
Cuvier and Lamarck are among the names quoted, though he seems
mainly to have met their ideas at second hand in *Chambers's
Information*.

Developments in palaeontology from Cuvier onwards had ensured
that 'it is now almost universally admitted by naturalists that there has
been a regular gradation or succession of organised forms upon the
earth, and no facts in support of the opinion still maintained by many,
that all the animals, plants etc., were created at *one* time, the earth being
at that time fit for their habitation. . . .' The principal point of dispute
between Chilton and many Christian writers concerned 'whether there
have been *successive creations*, or whether all is not merely results from

the different conditions of matter—consequent upon the never-ceasing change of position of its particles'.[60] The object, therefore, of Chilton's theory was 'to prove the capabilities of unassisted, unacted upon, uncontrolled, undirected matter for the production of all the varied, complicated, and beautiful phenomena of the universe', unassisted matter being defined as 'matter acting of itself, by virtue of its own inherent *properties*'. That is, the theory advocated transmutation of species rather than special creation, and the process by which the species developed was to be explained purely in material terms. In describing this process, Chilton did not progress beyond the vague suggestion of Lamarck, that 'animals were originally produced from the earth in consequence of a favourable condition of matter at the time, and that their lives were subsequently sustained from the same reason; but that whenever any material alteration of the locality in which certain animals resided took place, they either accommodated themselves to the different circumstances, or became extinct'.[61]

This theory raised several critical objections. The first was purely scientific. The fossil record showed that simple and complex creatures had existed together in every stratum, and Lyell used this fact to attack the notion of regular gradation. Chilton therefore qualified his statement to show that by gradation he simply meant that a highly complex organisation should have been preceded by a simple or less complex organisation.[62] Then there were critical questions about what constituted living matter and what distinguished man from the lower animals. On both these points the theory asserted that there was no significant break or difference. The problem of where the supposed 'immaterial principle' entered into man did not exist for Chilton because he did not believe there was any immaterial principle.[63] This was what shocked the Christian about the theory.

Nevertheless what Chilton argued was not new. The development hypothesis is to be found in Erasmus Darwin, Buffon, Laplace and Lamarck, and in 1851 Herbert Spencer came across Von Baer's formula of 1828 that 'the development of every organism is a change from homogeneity to heterogeneity', which led Spencer himself in 1852 to write an article on 'The Development Hypothesis'.[64] The first step in the argument, the nebular hypothesis of the creation of the universe, goes back to Kant, though Chilton found it in Sir John Herschel's *Astronomy*, as given in an article in *Chambers's Information*, and the best known exposition of the theory of regular gradation, the *Vestiges of Creation* which appeared anonymously in 1844, was virtually known to Chilton in 1842, for, as one speculator pointed out in 1848, it drew so heavily on material which had appeared in *Chambers's Information* that either it had been written by Chambers, or had been 'most seriously plagiarised from Mr Chambers'.[65]

But despite appearances and the critical comments of reviewers, the development hypothesis as used by Chambers or Erasmus Darwin was not atheistical—though, as Chilton pointed out in his review of the *Vestiges*, it could be used by atheists.[66] Robert Chambers was no more an atheist than George Combe, whom many thought to be the author of the *Vestiges*. Chilton was aware of this, and wrote in the *Reasoner*:

> The author of the 'Vestiges' . . . sees in every thing predetermination and design, for though he disbelieves the personal superintendence of the deity in the creation of animal and vegetable life and in the conduct of the material universe, he yet believes all to be the result of preordained law, having its origin in the divine mind. . . .[67]

The theory of regular gradation was therefore of use to atheists only, as 'Aliquis' realised in a more general context in 1854, 'through shewing mankind at large that there is no "sufficient reason" to believe in the existence of a "First Great Cause" '. It did not prove that there was no God, and, as Major Evans Bell, another of Holyoake's patrons, had pointed out in the previous year, it provided a very unsatisfactory and incomplete theory of the universe. Bell was only being logically sound when he refused 'to accept a nicely-compacted and neatly-finished theory of development, which after all requires either a creative power to compound its fire-mist, or a plastic power to originate its symmetrical evolutions'.[68]

The atheists tried to meet these requirements by putting the argument from design into reverse. The existence of 'a creative power' was, they thought, implausible because it was absurd to imagine that the most complex beings, which had had to pass through all the simpler stages of evolution, could possibly have been the work of a creative intelligence: 'we do not find a coach-maker, when he has to build a nobleman's carriage, begin by making a mud cart or pair of trucks,' observed the *Oracle*. But analogy could not rescue Chilton from the basic weakness of the development hypothesis, for materialism gave no answer to the problem of origins—it merely asserted that there was no origin.[69] Pure materialism could not explain the mechanism by which the theory operated. The importance of Darwin's *Origin of Species*, published in 1859, was that for the first time a mechanism was suggested which was at least plausible in scientific terms. The theory of evolution through random variation and the survival of the fittest at last provided a purely secular view of the world in which there was no necessity for man to seek the hand of God and the marks of intelligent design.

b
Rationalism

'Rationalism may be defined as the mental attitude which unreservedly accepts the supremacy of reason and aims at establishing a system of philosophy and ethics verifiable by experience and independent of all arbitrary assumptions or authority.'[70] This was the positive side of atheism. *Douglas Jerrold's Shilling Magazine* traced it back to Rousseau and French philosophy, and Holyoake assumed that the readers of his pamphlet on the subject would be familiar with the main features of the system. But the word itself had a distinct meaning for him; it meant in particular that philosophy which had been systematised by Robert Owen.[71] When Owenism was declining in 1845 Holyoake determined to rescue the basic philosophy of the movement from the ruins of the community experiment and to put it forward as a philosophy for individuals as well as for society. This was Rationalism, and more than any other Owenite Holyoake was responsible for teaching those positive doctrines which were an integral part of the freethought movement.

Following Thomas Chalmers, the *Oracle* had distinguished between the knowable and the unknowable.[72] Atheism depended upon a demonstration of this division. The supernatural was unknowable by the five senses and therefore presumed not to exist, whereas Rationalism was the scientific quest for the knowable. It was, according to Holyoake,

> the science of *material* circumstances. Rationalism advises what is useful to society without asking whether it is religious or not. It makes morality the sole business of life, and declares that from the cradle to the grave man should be guided by reason and regulated by science. It looks on man, to all practical purposes, as a purely material being—other systems have chiefly spiritualised him.[73]

The rationalist, proclaimed the *Oracle* in its first issue, 'takes nothing for granted, save his own existence, as also the existence of that universe of which he forms a part'.[74]

The most distinctive feature of Rationalism as taught by Owen was that a man's character is formed for and not by him, and this raised a number of controversial issues about the place of moral responsibility and freedom of the will, the nature of belief, the possibility of improvement, the purpose of education, and the aims of punishment.

The most complicated of these issues concerned free will, because often Christians and atheists were unable to accept a common definition of the term. For example, in his discussion with Holyoake, J. H. Rutherford claimed that moral choice could exist only where there was freedom of the will. Holyoake replied that if a man's will were not determined by circumstances it would be unreliable and therefore immoral.[75] This confusion was possible because the doctrine of circumstances was necessitarian, not deterministic. The difference between these two concepts becomes apparent in the different definitions given to the word 'will'. Holyoake defined it in the usual way adopted by necessitarian thinkers since Hobbes:

> The term WILL misleads us. We think it an ethereal personality sitting within us, on a little throne, deciding cases, when, in fact, the cases are deciding us. When a number of conflicting reasons equally influence us, we naturally hesitate. But when the argument appears to us to be chiefly, or altogether on one side, our feelings are at once inclined there. We acquiesce—acquiescence is will. Will may be defined—susceptibility entirely harmonising with an impression—consciousness stimulated to action. Thus all men are guided to their decisions. No man can be said to have a *free* will but he who is without human susceptibilities and incapable of distinguishing the weight of evidence.[76]

This was not determinism, first because it did not claim that all men were born the same but that each had susceptibilities, and secondly because it recognised that not all circumstances affect all men alike. This distinction meant that a man could master his fate: 'in proportion as you understand your natures and your own abilities, you see where your weakness lies, and guard against it, and you do it by virtue of the conviction of your being truly the creature of circumstances'. This was, therefore, a progressive philosophy. By understanding his circumstances, a man could master them.[77] Science, the study of the material world, could be the true redeemer. Lecturing on 'Original Sin' in 1838, Robert Cooper had made this same point:

> It is man's ignorance of the laws of his own nature, of the laws of the external world in general, and the true principles upon which society ought to be based, and by which it ought to be governed, that is the cause of his depravity, and not, as assumed by the religionists, his inherent corruption or innate sinfulness.[78]

Out of this belief in the importance of understanding the material world grew most of the principles and practical results of Rationalism. That 'Science is the Providence of man' was one of Holyoake's favourite assertions. It meant that the physical needs of man could be met only by that knowledge which comes from an understanding of the material world. In fire-damp, Davy was of more use than Deity. The life of man was to be protected by 'science, art, courage, and industry', not by a spiritual Providence and prayer. The God who had fed four thousand persons with five loaves and a few small fishes had neglected to prevent the failure of the Irish potato crop.[79]

The doctrine of philosophical necessity meant self-help. Holyoake told
John Bowes in 1850:

> It is in proportion as you see that men are creatures of circumstances,
> subjected to human influences, and human exhortation and reproof that
> you see the element of *improvability* which is in every human nature. From
> this point of view you command your own nature, your own destiny; you
> control fate; for there is no condition so bad which may not be improved;
> if a man can but find out the conditions and circumstances for his
> improvement.[80]

This gave the gospel of Rationalism an intense tone of moral earnestness.
In his lecture on C. R. Pemberton in 1844 Holyoake urged individual
purity, self-reliance, courage and wisdom; Rationalism imposed 'high
personal duties on the individual'; it was the foundation of 'moral
elevation'. In a pamphlet entitled the *Logic of Life*, written in 1861,
Holyoake set out the sort of person he expected the freethinker to be.
He was to be devoted to the pursuit of Truth and courageous in holding
to his own opinions, even to the point of eccentricity. He was to be
independent, for government existed to help only those who were given
over to injustice, disorder or excess. The just man was to be capable of
self-control. 'A true freeman will not be the slave of dress, of stimulants,
or of diet, or doctors, or custom, or opinion, any more than the slave of
priests or kings.'[81]

This self-help invariably meant mutual improvement. Education was
to be the great emancipator; it was the primary concern of the Owenites
and it was always held by Holyoake to be of the greatest importance. In
the 1840s he produced a series of text-books to help artisans educate themselves. In the first of these he wrote: 'Intellectual bondage is worse than
physical, because the physical chain is riveted by others, the mental by
ourselves. The ignorant man is at the mercy of educated opinion,' and
he compared grammar with the right of self-defence laid down in Magna
Carta.[82] With knowledge based on experience, the Rationalist was in a
position to challenge all pre-conceived ideas; he was able to justify himself to the world, independent and free.

Beyond what the individual could do for himself, Holyoake was willing to grant the State a small but important role in the regulation of
affairs. This was to be mainly indirect. Because a man is affected by
circumstances, then the state must improve circumstances. He did not
believe that the government could improve the general character of the
people if there were not also individual improvement, but he was too
close to reality and to his Owenite upbringing to neglect the influence of
external circumstances in the formation of character. The best example
of this comes in Holyoake's attitude to the temperance question. He was

opposed to direct intervention in the form of the Maine Law, but equally he urged against those who sought improvement by individual moral effort alone that

> It is not enough to point from the gin palace to the pump, the world will not go to the pump: it requires discipline, self-denial, education and careful instruction to sustain conviction, to go to the pump, and keep to the pump,—for this no adequate preparation is made. There are causes of intemperance in bad air, bad food, in over-working, in excitement, in over-eating, in animal food, in the want of recreation, in the want of art in life, in the want of credit for abstinence, in the want of self-reliance which is never encouraged, better homes, better prospects for the working classes.[83]

This realisation had been Owen's achievement at New Lanark and, like that experiment, Holyoake's ideas on temperance bring a refreshing air of reality into the otherwise stultifying atmosphere of rationality. The danger with the moral doubters was that they frequently overestimated the ability of the majority of the people to exercise the same moral restraint and indefatigable will-power which they themselves displayed. On this issue Holyoake was at one with Charles Kingsley who, in *Alton Locke*, had made the point that whereas alcohol killed slowly water from the pump killed quickly.

This attitude towards the temperance question clearly shows the liberal conclusions which could be drawn from Rationalism, and demonstrates why most freethinkers adhered to the Liberal Party. The same ideas are to be found in the writings of Holyoake as in that gospel of liberalism, J. S. Mill's essay *On Liberty*. Holyoake perceived that the Maine Law advocates meant well but did not see '*the evil of the method*': 'Force is a present evil. It is saving drunkards and making tyrants.' The same principle was at issue in the struggle for freedom of opinion. If every individual were to be allowed to force his opinions on other people Urquhart would be allowed to put everyone in a Turkish bath and make them read Blue books, and freethinkers would be able to legislate against religion.[84] The state was therefore assigned only a small and negative role in the freethinkers' scheme of affairs. Richard Carlile had announced in 1829:

> We want in this country the abolition of great masses of our laws. We have too many laws by a thousand-fold. . . . There should not exist any law in relation to currency, except as to forgery or base coining; no law in relation to trade, to exports or imports; no custom-house, no excise laws—no laws about religion. Life, liberty, and property, are the only things which require legislative protection; and let a necessary revenue be raised in the least expensive and least injurious mode that can be devised.[85]

This theory of government had much in common with the more widely accepted radical programmes of the Benthamites and the Manchester

School, but the freethinkers had a special reason for valuing freedom
from restraint. They had bitter experience of the powers of the laws of
England, and knew only too well that the Georgian and Victorian state
had wide and often unwelcome powers. Their liberalism was based on
the conviction that 'Society has not, never had, never can have any right,
founded on justice, to dictate to individuals what they shall believe or
disbelieve', and this conviction was upheld by their typically Liberal
faith in the powers of reason.[86] Laws were not only wrong, Holyoake
argued with Owenite confidence, they were also inappropriate: 'I shall
contend,' he told G. E. Lomax, 'for the doctrine that the world is too much
governed—that laws are the expedients of government who, not knowing
the conditions of nature, are obliged to substitute those of art, to substitute those of force, to accomplish what reason ought to accomplish.'[87]
Punishment was wrong because man was not responsible for his beliefs
and actions; society had 'no moral right to do more than *protect* itself'.[88]

Such enlightened views were not peculiar to freethinkers, but the
theological conclusions drawn from them were. 'The Christian doctrine,'
said Holyoake in his debate with Rutherford, 'is reformation by afflic-
tion; we want reformation by instruction, and a wise application of the
principles of causation.'[89] The Last Judgment had evidently not kept
pace with the latest developments in penal theory. On this issue, the
atheists were brought face to face with one of the fundamental doctrines
taught by the Evangelical clergy—justification by faith.

The freethinkers maintained that a man could not help what he
believed because what he believed rested upon evidence which he was
unable to control. Bradlaugh told Rutherford in 1861, 'We cannot now
believe in that which is opposed to our present consciousness. New
consciousness of facts develop new thinkings; no man can believe in
opposition to the fact as he knows it. Yet your Bible says, 'He that
believeth not shall be damned''.'[90] Such a doctrine was especially
immoral if a man were also asked to accept that God was responsible for
his nature and circumstances. Holyoake found it inconceivable that a
man should be judged according to what he believed, when the nature
of that belief was purely arbitrary. And yet the Church had a great hold
over even loyal freethinkers because it could threaten them that they
might be judged according to their opinions if there were an after-life.
To allay this fear, therefore, Holyoake expounded his doctrine of justification by sincerity.

'A man's creed,' he argued, 'can be nothing in the eyes of God compared with the integrity of his intentions and the earnestness of his
endeavours after moral improvement.' Freethought was a primary condition of the quest for Truth, and he who held what he believed to be a true

opinion was sincere.[91] Christianity was the negation of this because it accepted an *a priori* truth not necessarily based on scientific observation and experiment. This did not mean that a Christian could not be a sincere believer, for Holyoake was logical enough to admit to others the toleration he demanded for himself. He was also consistent enough to admit that a sincere belief need not be a true one, and he did not judge the man who might cling to error with sincerity. The way to change such opinions was by rational argument.[92] The Christian doctrine of justification was also wrong because it discouraged good works and exalted 'the mere act of faith over the nobler act of doing'.[93] The Reverend J. A. James, for example, had urged his congregation to concentrate exclusively on the question, 'What shall I do to be saved?', and, as James Martineau had pointed out, ' . . . no inquirer can fix a direct and clear-sighted gaze towards truth who is casting side-glances at the same time as to the prospects of his soul. . . .'[94]

Holyoake's treatment of this doctrine of justification by faith was a distortion—as the clergymen with whom the atheists debated were quick to point out—but there was a great deal of truth in what Holyoake said. Rutherford quite correctly showed that 'faith', as discussed by Paul and James, was not divorced from good works, but at the same time he contended that the notion of the judgement of God was essential to the moral government of the universe.[95] The Evangelicals in particular found the fires of hell indispensable to their theological world view.

The question of morality was reached sooner or later in most of the writings, lectures and discussions of the atheists, and one of the oldest charges against infidelity was that it encouraged immorality. The doctrine of circumstances denied moral responsibility, whereas in contrast Christianity claimed to supply the motives for and sanctions of moral conduct. The atheists countered these charges and claims by asserting that Christianity was not a moral system at all. In his lectures on the *Immortality of the Soul*, Robert Cooper stated that 'The *moral* man esteems excellence not for its value in the world to come, but its practical worth in *this* life. That man can never be purely or permanently virtuous who is *frightened* into it. He must *love* it to be secure.' Christian morality had clearly broken down: no Christian sufficiently believed the Sermon on the Mount to put it into practice, and Christianity was no inducement to morality. In Lancashire and Yorkshire, where, according to Cooper, 'psalm-singing, spirit-moving, soul-saving Methodism is most rampant', one child in thirteen was illegitimate.[96] The Rationalists, therefore, more moral than the moralists, sought to create a new system of ethics based on a scientific interpretation of life. One of the objects of the Society for the Promulgation of Naturalism was 'The promulgation of Systematic

Morality, founded on the nature of man and his harmonious relation to external things—a Morality independent of religion, and which, instead of showing men to heaven shows them to themselves, and deduces their course of life and behaviour from that which their real natures point out....' The basis of this naturalistic ethic was utility, 'the natural resting place of morals'. Morality was to be that code of useful practices which could be induced from a careful observation of society.[97]

Such a definition raised several problems, and Holyoake was not entirely logical in working out his system. One charge he was not guilty of: the doctrine of philosophical necessity did not make the concept of morality meaningless, because it did not exclude choice—it merely stated that all choice is predetermined by motive. But Utilitarianism had its weaknesses. The orthodox teaching of the Utilitarians was that self interest is always the predominant motive and, therefore, the first guarantee of morality. Holyoake, like J. S. Mill, realised that this was not true as a simple statement of fact, and so he introduced other elements into the system which were not a logical part of Utilitarianism. In the first of his three lectures at Heywood in 1852 Holyoake argued that 'their [sic] exists guarantees of morality in human nature, utility, and intelligence; and that morality has independent sanctions in the relations of social life'.[98] The meaning of this was explained on the third evening of the discussion with Brewin Grant in 1853. Human nature meant 'the sum of those passions and natural qualities manifested by men and women, chiefly before, and often after, artificial treatment and demoralising circumstances have perverted their spontaneous impulses'.[99] In other words, Holyoake was appealing to a moral sense, partly the product of circumstances but preferably innate, a doctrine more to be expected of a follower of Rousseau or Godwin than of Bentham. Despite its superficial Utilitarianism, Holyoake's ethical theory was, like the rest of his philosophy, based primarily on Owenite Rationalism. In reply to a questioner at the Heywood lecture quoted above, he defined conscience as 'A man's habituated sense of right and wrong'.[100] The same confusion is to be found in Bradlaugh's mind. Debating with Woodman at Ashton in 1861, he asserted:

> That is right which tends to make mankind happier; that is right which tends to make mankind purer; that is right which tends to make men nobler; that is right which tends to make men wiser.... That is right which tells you to practice [sic] wisdom, truth, honesty, and virtue; not because God says it, or the devil waits on you if you don't; but because it is good and right to do it.[101]

Here Bradlaugh begins with the greatest happiness principle, but ends with the moral maxim that it is right to do right.

The second foundation of morality which Holyoake offered was the intellect. He assumed that the rational man would observe society, see what was good, and do it because it was rational. The third foundation was utility. Holyoake assumed that the useful, the rational and the dictates of conscience would all reach the same conclusion, but that, as a psychological fact, the sanctions of utility would not usually be consciously operant but could be held in reserve for those who were not good by nature and not capable of being taught to perceive the rational good:

> If any one will not pursue right conduct for its own sake, it is still worth his while to do it for his interest sake: if any one will not live uprightly because of the intellectual beauty and harmony of the thing, we say it is worth his while pursuing it as a matter of calculation.[102]

If Holyoake had gone no further, he would have remained a mere Utilitarian but like J. S. Mill he sometimes confused the greatest happiness of the greatest number with the greatest good of the greatest number. Secularist morality therefore aspired to be something which Bentham could never have claimed for Utilitarianism: 'a feeling higher than the multitude, leading us to something greater' which appealed to utility and 'to the artistic sense'.[103]

These contradictions are inherent in Utilitarianism, and any writer influenced by Owen inevitably had to consider the part played by circumstance and education in the formation of a social morality. The advantage of the standard of utility was its practicality as a measure. To write *cui bono* over the altar was the aim of the Theological Utilitarians, but Holyoake, more than any other of the atheist leaders, was well aware of the inadequacies of this crude rule as a complete system of morality. In his old age he wrote, 'I differ with diffidence from Mr Mill as to the propriety of carrying the Utilitarian doctrine into the domain of morals. Truth is higher than utility, and goes before it. Truth is a measure of utility, and not utility the measure of truth. Conscience is higher than consequence. We are bound first to consider what is right.'[104] He was not alone in this dilemma. Like so many of his contemporary doubters, he had rejected a metaphysical system but was left with a metaphysical ethic unexplained but real. F. W. Newman was in a similar position when his quest for a universal morality grounded in human nature brought him to the belief

> that the human mind is a moral existence, having within itself moral tendencies, and a moral law, which is developed by culture; and that in the long past of mankind numerous great moral truths have established themselves in the conscience of nations, and especially of the most unbiased and most cultivated individuals.[105]

Holyoake accepted this as his own. In his Glasgow discussion with Brewin Grant in 1854 he spoke of Secularism as appealing to the law of the heart and moral sentiments. 'Conscience illustrated by common sense' was to be the arbiter of conduct.[106] The importance of his trying to reconcile this doctrine with Utilitarianism was that each checked the other. A belief in the good elevated crude utility; a demand for the greatest happiness controlled the elitist implications of 'the most un-biased and most cultivated individuals'.

The Rationalists were not philosophers; they were not system-builders. The aim of Rationalism was, according to Holyoake, 'to *fit* men to work out their improvement, not to *fetter* them as to the mode of doing it'.[107] The strength of the atheists' reasoning, then, lay not in its philosophical infallibility but in its concern with the limited and the practical. The freethinking radicals derived from their axioms, their experiences and their prejudices, a common set of attitudes towards the social and politi-cal problems of the day. These attitudes were not peculiar to them but they felt able to justify their activities in contemporary affairs in terms of their Rationalism.

The political programme of the freethinkers was that which Carlile had championed. He defined his two major points as follows:

> By Republicanism, I mean a Representative Legislature, and a Magistracy founded upon equal election; and by Deism I mean the abolition of all religion, and all sorts of priesthood, and a turning of our churches and chapels into schools for teaching the arts and sciences, and such of our priests as are qualified into schoolmasters, lecturers and professors.[108]

The infidels were, therefore, theoretical Chartists, but their heritage kept them apart from the Chartist movement: they had learned from both Carlile and Owen that to win political reform without accomplish-ing a moral reform would constitute a very shallow victory indeed.

Southwell expressed his doubts in his *Investigator* in 1843: 'There cannot be any useful organic change in the constitution of human society, so long as the humbler members of it remain in bondage to religion.' The *Oracle* was uttering similar comments in the same year, denouncing religion as 'a kind of mother tyranny'.[109] The Owenites took this argument one step further. True to their Rationalism, they held that reform was to be accomplished only by moral means, and a leading article in the *New Moral World* distinguished those two schools of political thought which go by the names of 'moral force' and 'physical force':

> The Socialist relies on reason, intelligence, and moral power, as the means for the establishment of his plans. The Radical looks to the concentration of the physical force of the people, as a means of overawing the privileged classes and carrying his views.[110]

When the Owenites did become involved in Chartism, therefore, they were frequently among the leaders of the moderate, moral force wing.

This division, though, was not quite so clearly cut. Some Chartists— perhaps the great majority of the rank and file—felt that political change would probably be the best prelude to social change, and this was the course William Lovett had followed when he had turned from socialism to the Charter. As Lawrence Pitkethly, the Huddersfield Owenite and former follower of Carlile, explained in the *New Moral World*:

> He advocated Chartism that he might ultimately obtain the innumerable and solid advantages of Socialism with perfect political security; and it was upon this point only that he and many other Chartists differed from Mr Owen, who thought that the advantages of Socialism could be obtained and secured sooner than the political objects sought for by the Chartists could be obtained.[111]

This view brought some moderate socialists close to the position held by extremists like G. J. Harney, who looked beyond the Charter to social revolution, and after the failure of direct socialism in the early 1830s and again in the mid-1840s there was a marked swing towards political action among many radicals who still adhered to the ultimate Owenite goal.

The question of religion also confused relationships between the Chartists and the socialists. Some Chartist leaders, including Henry Vincent and J. R. Stephens, were unable to share the religious opinions of the followers of Carlile and Owen—Vincent said openly that Southwell had deserved his imprisonment, and the editor of the *Northern Star* called Owen's infidelity 'a national evil'.[112] The strength of Bible Chartism among the rank and file suggests that Vincent's view had some support, but many other men took the opposite line. The unstamped press of the 1830s had been markedly anticlerical in tone, and had lost no opportunity to exploit the unpopularity of the Church. The same was true of the *Northern Star* in the 1840s. Joshua Hobson, whose *Voice of the West Riding* had screamed abuse at the clergy and the Whigs in 1833–1834, was scarcely less moderate when he edited the *Northern Star* during 1843–1844. G. J. Harney, who was Hobson's sub-editor, needed no prompting to continue the policy when he became editor. Even O'Connor himself, who in his political and social views had little in common with Harney, Hobson and the Socialists, won the praise of the *Oracle* when he 'repeatedly declared he *never knew any good come of bible chartism*'.[113]

The Socialists were also cut off from the Chartists by their political theory. It is remarkable to find Southwell of all people pedantically criticising the Chartists for demanding their natural rights. In the first number of the *Oracle* he declared 'the question of actual rights resolves itself into that of *actual powers*', and in the *Investigator* he returned to this point with a quotation from Thomas Hobbes to the effect that if everyone had his natural rights, then no-one would have any rights at all. He ended by attacking the Chartists for their belief in 'the inherent, indubitable, and constitutional right' to the franchise.[114] This may have been political realism, but it was not a message which was likely to endear Southwell and his associates to the Chartist leaders.

Nevertheless, despite these differences of theory, there was co-operation between the two groups. William Chilton urged Holyoake in 1841 that 'The Chartists should be our friends', and Holyoake needed no such prompting. He was already on close terms with G. J. Harney in Sheffield, and when he was arrested Harney took collections on his behalf among both Chartists and socialists, although many were 'too poor to give a penny'. The Cheltenham lecture for which Holyoake was prosecuted was given on Chartist premises, and the Chartists refused to be intimidated when he returned there to lecture on free speech immediately before his arrest.[115] Other examples of local co-operation might be given to underline the point that, whatever the differences at the top level of leadership, radicalism at the grass-roots could be surprisingly unsectarian in its organisational relationships. The Chartists of Huddersfield started a co-operative store, and those at Ashton met in one when they were deprived of their ordinary meeting place. The Birmingham Chartists used the Lawrence Street Hall of Science for a meeting in 1841, and O'Connor lectured at the Campfield Hall, Manchester, in 1842. Two years later the Huddersfield Chartists and socialists reached agreement whereby the Chartists were to have the use of the Hall of Science on occasional weekdays and alternate Sundays.[116] The *Northern Star*, especially when edited by Hobson in Leeds, was one of the best and friendliest non-Owenite local papers to report the progress of socialism and radical freethought. In 1842 Harney had appealed for funds for Holyoake in the *Northern Star*, and he continually gave high praise in his notices of Holyoake's publications. 'This is an excellent little publication,' is how the *Movement* was greeted, and in 1846 he recommended the first number of the *Reasoner* 'to all who dare to reason, who proving all things, will hold only to that which is good'.[117] Harney's influence is again apparent in the sympathetic coverage given to the Scottish persecutions of 1843 and the escapades of Thomas Paterson.[118] No Chartist who read his *Northern Star* can have been unaware of the activities of the freethinking radicals, and, if the Chartists took their opinions from their paper, they must also have approved of what they read.

Yet, before 1848, the two movements remained distinct, and, despite the friendliness shown in particular by Harney, Chartism was not, and never became, involved with organised freethought.[119] Similarly, the freethought leaders were too busy with their own concerns to take an active part in Chartism. Paterson perhaps summed up a prevalent attitude towards political reform when he cynically 'looked upon political reform, more as a thing to be desired than expected, while the people were the slaves of creeds, and the dupes of priestly knaves'.[120] Holyoake was one of the few freethought leaders—and the only one of national stature—to dabble seriously in political agitations in the 1840s, but he did not join the Chartists. In 1846 he was on the committee of the Birmingham Parliamentary Society, a moderate debating club of which George Dawson was president, and in 1847 he assisted the Liberal cause in the Westminster and Middlesex parliamentary elections.[121] Only in March 1848 did he allow himself to be drawn into the latter-day Chartism of the People's Charter Union, and then when another member of the Union, W. J. Linton, suggested to him that they should bring out a new Chartist paper, he agreed, but the *Cause of the People*, which came out on 20 May, lasted for only ten weeks. Linton later claimed that Holyoake 'did nothing' for the paper, but it did introduce him to purely political journalism for the first time and doubtless gave him the experience which he later used to bring out the first numbers of Harney's *Friend of the People*.[122]

All this occurred after 10 April. On that fateful day the People's Charter Union symbolically sat on the side-lines, sending Holyoake and others out with notebooks to watch the police for signs of violence. Only after the Kennington Common failure, when both socialism and Chartism had felt the frustration of defeat, was the political scene ready for the moderates to take the lead. The sense of urgency which the failures of 1848 produced was caught by Southwell when he wrote in 1849,

> Our political house is on fire and he is little better than a fool who is very particular as to the way in which we are to escape from it. Animated by a spirit superior to mere partizanship we see good in Chartism, in Socialism, and, last not least, in Financial Reform. This kind of reform is no less loudly demanded than any other.[123]

This was to be the most fruitful way forward in the 1850s.

The atheists may not always have been enthusiastic Chartists but they were dedicated republicans and this was a far stronger element in the Painite socialist legacy. Throne and altar, especially in Continental Europe, were two aspects of the same repressive system, and socialism and communism were international terms linking the aims and even the organisations of the British radicals with those of their opposite numbers overseas. This spirit of international co-operation was pro-

K

moted by the fact that Britain in the nineteenth century was a recognised
political sanctuary for refugees of all persuasions.

The pattern had been set by Carlile. In 1822 his *Republican* had
appeared under such dates as '46th Year of American Independence' and
'1822 of Jesus the Jew, and 46th of the Independence of the United States
Republic in North America' and 'Year 3 of the Spanish Revolution, and
last, or last but one, of the Holy Alliance', and in 1831 the *Prompter* had
reported the progress of the revolutionary movements in Poland, Italy,
Belgium, France, Spain and Portugal, while at the Rotunda Taylor
produced his anti-monarchical play *Swing, or Who are the Incendiaries?*
Southwell had fought in the Spanish revolution for a time in 1835, and
in 1836 the *New Moral World* published the address of the London
Working Men's Association "To the working Classes of Belgium' which
urged an eventual federation of the working classes in Belgium, Holland
and the Rhineland provinces.[124] When the German revolutionary Weit-
ling came to England in 1844, he was given a warm welcome by an
assembly of English and foreign socialists at John Street, and among
those who made speeches on this occasion were G. A. Fleming, Maltus
Ryall and Holyoake. The following day, 23 September, a democratic
banquet was held in Islington, attended by republicans from England,
France, Germany, Spain, Italy, Switzerland and Poland, at which Hetherington, partly at the suggestion of Holyoake, proposed that an international committee be set up, comprising one delegate from each
'democratic section' to promote national fraternisation. This new committee was known as the 'Democratic Friends of All Nations', one of the
first of a number of moderate republican organisations which flourished
in the 1840s. In 1846 came the 'Democratic Committee for the Regeneration of Poland' and the following year Holyoake received a circular from
Linton proposing the formation of an 'Association for spreading the
principles of National Liberty and Progress.' This association became
the People's International League in October 1847, when Linton sought
Holyoake's help in securing a good attendance at its first public meeting.[125] It was this common interest which drew the two men into partnership in the *Cause of the People* in 1848.

Holyoake's participation in republican societies in the 1840s was of
the same kind as his participation in the affairs of Chartism. He was
closely associated only with moderate groups, and, despite his friendship
with Harney, he had no inclination to become involved with the
Fraternal Democrats and the extremist refugee groups. Only after 1848,
when the two sides began to draw together in foreign affairs as they did
in home affairs, did the implicit republicanism of freethought become
explicit. Italy was the issue which helped Holyoake and his followers to

express their creed most clearly. In the 1840s there was little beyond the anti-Hanoverian growls of Paterson to justify their claims to be active supporters of the republican ideal.[126]

This isolation from the mainstream of working-class activity is no better exemplified than by the attitude of the freethought leaders towards trade unions. Here again their outlook was shaped by Owenism and reinforced by the writings of Carlile. The latter had declared in 1834 that 'Political Unions, Trades' Unions, all unions are nonsense, until we have union of mind on the subject of religion.' Holyoake viewed trade unions with the same suspicion which he showed towards government. They were for him a necessary evil, and with a typically Owenite argument he claimed that they had failed to increase wages because they had not appreciated the root cause of the industrial problem that there was too much labour on the market. The solution was for unions not to waste money on strikes but to build communities to plant the surplus labour force on the land.[127] This was attractive advice to many, and the persistence of this characteristic of Owenite socialism is a tribute to its impact on the working population. It even survived into the 'new unionism' of the 1850s, when John Finch offered his Windsor Foundry in Liverpool to William Newton's Amalgamated Society of Engineers in 1851. Cooperative production had been favoured as an alternative to strike action in 1846 by the National United Trades Association for the Employment of Labour, an offspring of the National Association of United Trades for the Protection of Labour; and after the employers had locked out the A.S.E. men in 1852, association was again considered as an alternative to industrial action.[128] But, despite the persistence of these co-operative ideas, Holyoake's Owenism was outdated. He never really appreciated the new class language of Ernest Jones. When he was appointed with Jones as one of the Society of Arts' mediators in the Preston Strike of 1853, he attributed the strike and lock-out not to the low wages of the workers but to the impossible demands made by the workers through their ignorance of foreign market conditions.[129]

This inability to understand the real attitudes of labour is seen in the approach of Holyoake and Bradlaugh to Political Economy. They naturally had no sympathy with the extreme views of Harriet Martineau —typified by her comment that the only hope for factory children was that the race would die out 'in two or three generations'—and Holyoake once condemned a political economy which 'has no higher consolation than the assurance that society is a scientific scramble, where it happens that Intellect and Capital get all the kernels, and Ignorance and Poverty all the husks', but his verdict on the Preston strike was doing just this. Bradlaugh shared this ambivalent attitude. 'An acquaintance with political economy,' he wrote in 1861, 'is as necessary to the working man as is a knowledge of navigation to the master of a ship.' It was not a 'dismal science'—on the contrary, the writings of the economists contained 'descriptions of the people's wrongs, written in glowing and eloquent language, full of earnest sympathy'. By learning the cause of a thing, a man could prevent the recurrence of the effect. This was the old theme that knowledge was power, and Holyoake even advocated a simple test, based on Mill's *Political Economy*, as a qualification for the franchise.[130]

These attitudes suggest that the early Secularists had not really moved far from the older analysis of society which had prevailed in the 1820s, and that their Owenism, far from contributing to a deeper understanding of economics and society such as J. B. O'Brien had offered in the *Poor Man's Guardian* in the 1830s, had actually reinforced their conservatism. Holyoake or Bradlaugh could well have written in 1860 the article with which Carlile opened his *Lion* in 1828. He wrote:

> There is no cure for pauperism, for vagabondage, for the present growth of crime, but in teaching the labouring-man the great advantages which accrue from the accumulation of capital, so as to make each aspire to an accumulation to some degree.[131]

The gospel of self-help was known and accepted by working-class leaders long before Samuel Smiles wrote about it.

The political arrangement which Holyoake seems to have envisaged was that of a meritocracy. In traditional terms this was to be a classless society, though this does not mean he was against all class distinctions. The complexity of his views is illustrated by a passage in his little book on *Rationalism*: 'I here raise no voice against capital. I have no antipathy to rich men. I wish we were all rich. But capital has influence, it ought to have it, but its influence, however just, commercially, is incompatible with equality.' The same views recur in his discussion with Grant in 1854:

> The government of the people by the people, is far more just than government of the people by a class. So far from destroying the nobility, I should be glad to see a real nobility set up. We want a nobility of genius, instead of a nobility of ribbons and garters. We have never made war upon the rich. We have always held that riches are the glory of the state, the first element of civilisation. We have only demanded, and shall never cease to demand, that arrangement of society in which the worthy shall attain to wealth and the industrious to competence.[132]

Only in matters concerning education did the freethinkers get the chance to match their theoretical assertions with practical applications, and appropriately so, since the use of a trained and independent reason was the basic assumption of their philosophy. Education was a great national question in the 1840s. Church disputed with Dissent, State-educator with Voluntaryist, while the lower classes received what education they could on an *ad hoc* basis. 'We live in an age,' wrote the Vicar of Leeds in 1846, 'when the question is not *whether* but *how* the poor are to be educated.' He was, of course, concerned about the quality of religious education, but he was also bold in advocating compulsory secular education by the state.[133] The atheists shared this latter view, the main opponents of which were the Dissenters and certain Evangelicals in the Established Church. In 1843 the education clauses of Lord Ashley's Factory Bill, which gave the Church of England an influence in a rudimentary form of compulsory education, aroused a storm of protest from the Dissenters. This was an opportunity not to be missed by Southwell: he first—and ironically—took the side of Church against Dissent; then rejecting both sectarian education and the non-sectarian education proposed by J. A. Roebuck, he made an outright demand for secular education. At Worcester, a meeting of Dissenters was held in the Baptist chapel on 14 April to oppose the Factory Bill. Holyoake and Paterson attended, but when Holyoake asked leave to insert a new clause in their petition, he was threatened with the police. Paterson then tried to say something, and the two men only just escaped before the police arrived. They had their revenge four days later when, at a public meeting called at the Hall of Science, their own petition for secular education was carried by a large and popular majority.[134]

Until the Secular Education movement grew in the late 1840s, the socialists could do little more than shout from the side-lines on the issue. Their own positive contribution was made on a much smaller scale. First they used the Mechanics' Institutes. It is a mistake to ignore the Institutes because of the restrictions placed upon them by local clergymen and others, for the situation varied widely from place to place. In Coventry, for example, 'some sixty or seventy Socialists' seceded from the Institution in 1840 because of the restrictions placed upon learning by the clergy; but, as the *New Moral World* pointed out, the men only realised the existence of this restriction because of the education already received there: 'far from the Socialists opposing such Institutions, they regard them with favour, as half-way-houses to the attainment of sound knowledge. . . .' The truth of this assertion is illustrated by the Birmingham Mechanics' Institution, in which Holyoake was educated and in which he taught. When the Finsbury branch of the Rational Society became a Mechanics' Institute in 1846, the opening ceremony was presided over by W. Devonshire Saull, the John Street Owenite, and Holyoake was among those on the platform. Holyoake himself taught grammar, logic and rhetoric at the City Mechanics' Institute, Gould Square, during 1846 and 1847.[135]

Like the Chartists, the socialists also conducted their own schools. The *Oracle* urged that 'Halls of Science and Social institutions should be schools for the adult population; through them should be diffused every species of useful knowledge; every plan supported that has a tendency to do good, either in or out of community'. Holyoake taught grammar and logic at the Lambeth branch in 1844, while J. B. Lear of Cheltenham appeared as a teacher of Latin at Walworth on Sunday mornings. The newsroom of the Sheffield Rationalists in 1846 supplied the *Daily News*, the *Sheffield Independent* and *Sheffield Times* alternately, the *Family Herald*, the *Reasoner*, the *Regenerator*, the *Peoples' Journal* and *Chambers's Journal*.[136] Nor were the children neglected. In 1840–42 there were Socialist Sunday schools at Honley, Oldham, Rochdale, Bradford, Hyde, Failsworth, Congleton, Ashton, Padiham, London, Sheffield and Leicester. The school at Honley, near Huddersfield, had at one time between seventy and eighty scholars, although there were only eleven hundred houses in the village.[137] In London the education movement did not lose its impetus with the decline of socialism and the socialist schools were incorporated in the new secular schools of the metropolis. The Secular Education League was founded at the Gould Square Mechanics' Institute in 1847 and, though its activities are not fully explained in the *Reasoner*, it may well have been responsible for the opening of a number of secular schools in London during the next few years. In 1849 the *Reasoner* was able to list eight such places.[138] Holyoake himself was becoming prominent in working-class educational circles. Over fifty pupils came to his class at the City Mechanics' Institute; when the South London Oddfellows opened a Literary Institute, it was Holyoake who delivered one of the opening speeches; by 1847 his *Practical Grammar* was in its fifth edition and was to be reprinted a further five times by 1852.[139]

The sort of person the Rationalists hoped to produce was an independent thinker, even to the point of eccentricity. In this they did not fail, and among the movements which Rationalists favoured or supported were some of the more radical and unusual campaigns of the age, some of which have since prospered, others of which are now forgotten, and most of which were justified as a natural consequence of the philosophy of Rationalism.

One issue discussed in the radical periodicals was neo-Malthusianism —a difficult subject for moral Victorians. The radical movement had long been identified with the advocacy of birth control which was usually linked with a discussion of low wages and unemployment. The merits and de-merits of birth control had been aired by Carlile in the *Republican*, and when Cobbett put forward a plan in 1824 for the equal distribution of land as a solution to the problem of poverty, Carlile replied that the real remedy was not to give everyone the means of production but rather to give them the means of consumption. He considered whether this could be achieved by birth control, but admitted he did not like the idea and instead proposed a land tax, a thorough reform in Church and State, and national education. Shortly afterwards he seems to have changed his mind, and in 1825 he started using the *Republican* to advocate a method of artificial contraception of which Robert Owen had recently learned in Paris. Cobbett attacked Carlile for his views, but in the *Republican* Richard Hassall wrote an article condemning the Poor Laws and advocating smaller families instead.[140] Carlile devoted his pen to telling women how this could be done, and contraceptive advice appeared both in the *Lion* and in a pamphlet entitled *Every Woman's Book*. Similar works came on the market from other sources. In 1830 Robert Dale Owen published his *Moral Physiology*, a highly popular work on the subject, and two years later came Dr Charles Knowlton's *The Fruits of Philosophy*, of which Holyoake bought a copy in 1836. Both these works, together with *Notes on the Population Question* by 'Anti-Marcus', appear in the list of James Watson's books sold by Holyoake in 1855, and the booklets by Owen and 'Anti-Marcus' were brought into Holyoake's discussions with Brewin Grant in 1853 and 1854. Holyoake preferred to keep his personal views out of the matter; he said he had not even read the 'Anti-Marcus' and he thought the Owen book to be a moderate and moral work.[141] Neo-Malthusianism was a delicate issue which divided the radicals. It touched not only a moral nerve, but also raised controversial matters of economic theory, and so did not become an important issue among freethinkers until Bradlaugh began to advocate it in the *National Reformer* after 1860.

Almost as dangerous in the eyes of the public was the socialist teaching about marriage. The most extreme position is to be found in a pamphlet by John Ellis, the former Social Missionary:

> We oppose the marriage system of the priesthood because it is founded in error, and error can never benefit mankind. It is founded on the supposition that man forms his convictions and feelings by his will. This is not the case: animated beings are compelled to love that which to them appears lovely and to hate that which to them appears hateful.

Holyoake shared these views but put them more tactfully. Divorce was advocated only as a moral solution to an infrequent problem.[142]

The readiness of freethinkers to consider the questions of birth control and divorce was a part of their wider concern for the place of women in

society. It would perhaps be too strong to call ultra-radicalism one of the
first feminist movements, but it did not neglect the rights of women in
its campaign for the rights of all. Women were not social inferiors in
working-class movements to the same extent that they were in more
respectable organisations. Richard Carlile had been supported in his
campaign by women as well as by men, and Manchester had even had
a female committee which sent sixty-six subscriptions from Manchester
and Bolton to Mrs Carlile in 1822.[143] Carlile's womenfolk and Mrs
Susannah Wright had been among the leading martyrs to the cause, and
their counterparts were to be found in the later agitations: Eliza Sharples
at the Rotunda, Emma Martin and Margaret Reynolds in the socialist
halls, Matilda Roalfe in the Edinburgh bookshop, and Frances Wright,
the indefatigable campaigner for the rights of women and slaves on
both sides of the Atlantic, were among the most formidable; and a later
generation still saw two worthy champions of their fathers' causes and
reputations in Emilie Holyoake Marsh and Hypatia Bradlaugh Bonner.
The freethinking radicals, with their keen sense of equality, were alert
to the part which women could play in society. Holyoake advocated the
independent right of women to property and earnings as part of his 1857
election address at Tower Hamlets, and he even went so far as to chide
other radicals with advocating manhood instead of universal suffrage.[144]

The Rationalist was, above all, a believer in freedom, and this included
freedom from addiction to such undesirable commodities as alcohol,
tobacco, and even meat. Richard Carlile told the readers of his
Republican:

> Drunkenness I abominate, and would not look at the man, calling himself
> a Reformer, who could intoxicate himself, or waste his means in an ale-
> house, or spirit-shop, or tavern,

and he admitted he was favourably inclined towards vegetarianism.[145] In
this we can see an element of extremism, and there does seem to have been
a type of radical who was attracted to extremism of all kinds—in religion
and politics as well as in matters of diet. Individuality often shaded over
into eccentricity. Rowland Detrosier, of whom Carlile and the Lancashire Zetetics had such high hopes, had been brought up by the
'Manchester Benevolent Vegetarian Institution', and he preached for a
time at the 'Beefsteak Chapel' in Ashton—so called because of the
vegetarian views of its members. The Ham Common concordium, with
which a number of leading Owenites were associated, practised vegetarianism and its inhabitants were active in forming the 'British and Foreign
Society for the Promotion of the Abstinence from Animal Foods'.[146]
Holyoake was abstaining from animal foods during the early months of

1837 and was 'inclined to vegetarianism' during the time of his imprisonment, though he later refused the post of teacher at Ham Common
because he did not think he could keep to the diet. In 1849 during the
cholera we find him once more 'Trying more carefully an experiment
in vegetable diet' and at the same time he 'Began to abstain from cigars',
though not for long. He occasionally attended the vegetarian meetings
advertised in the *Reasoner* by Messrs Turley and Harrison of Aurora
Villa in Hampstead. Bradlaugh also was a vegetarian for a while.[147]

Temperance in the use of alcohol or even total abstinence was, however, the major restraint which many freethinkers felt obliged to practise.
Southwell, who sometimes had great difficulty in being temperate about
anything and who was certainly no abstainer, was firm on this point: 'No
drunkard can enter our political heaven.'[148] The self-help and mutual
improvement radicalism of the mid-century working-class movement
had little time for the waste and irrationality of alcohol, at least when
taken in excess, and some were even prepared to go further in the 1850s
and demand a Maine Law forbidding the sale of all intoxicating drinks.

These were the principal attitudes of the people whom Holyoake was
beginning to organise in the late 1840s. Taking their religious, political
and social views from either Carlile, or Owen, or both, they had a varied
but roughly coherent outlook on life. With this material, Holyoake was
to attempt to create a new form of freethought.

c
Secularism

The conditions which had generated the radical infidel tradition of
Paine, Carlile and Owen were passing away by the middle of the century.
Not only was the separation of theology and socialism being achieved
by the new co-operative movement based on Rochdale, but also the
secular education movement was indicating a growing concern with the
purely secular among people of all classes and opinions. The Church was,
in the form of Christian Socialism, responding to the needs of the times,
and some clergymen were even prepared to tolerate and listen to Holyoake. New and humane religious ideas were being promulgated by F. W.
Newman, Leigh Hunt, W. R. Greg and James Martineau. New philosophical ideas were becoming known in the writings of Auguste Comte,
Harriet Martineau and John Stuart Mill. Biblical scholars, geologists and
biologists were beginning to convince Christian opinion that the views
of the atheists were respectable. The pressures which had created a lower-
class radical tradition in religion and politics were being relaxed.

Co-operation between the classes had never entirely broken down, but at times, especially during the years of economic hardship in the late 1830s and early 1840s, the situation had been critical. Holyoake, unlike some Owenites, had never opposed the Anti-Corn Law League and he had advocated free trade in his little book on Rationalism, but his offers of help to the Leaguers in Glasgow in 1845 had, perhaps understandably, been refused.[149] Partnership between the classes became easier after 1848. The first meeting of the People's League, which represented the followers of William Lovett and the moderate Chartists, was chaired by Colonel Thompson, and among the speakers were, Sharman Crawford, M.P., J. Humphreys Parry, Joseph Sturge and Edward Miall.[150] The League did not last long, but it was the first of a series of reform organisations and movements in which middle- and lower-class radicals attempted to work together for common objectives. The People's Charter Union continued in this spirit of co-operation when it met in 1849 to consider Richard Cobden's national budget and to petition him to include in it the abolition of the newspaper stamp. Financial reform in general, and the taxes on knowledge in particular, brought the leaders of the former Anti-Corn Law League and the Chartists together in a common cause. The Association for the Repeal of the Taxes on Knowledge, formed in 1851, included such diverse men as T. Milner Gibson, president, John Bright, Richard Cobden, Joseph Hume and William Ewart (all members of the House); Passmore Edwards, E. R. Larken, William Addiscot, Thomas Donatty and G. J. Holyoake. When the secretary, C. Dobson Collet, went on a missionary tour of the north, Cobden told him to call on Bright and George Wilson, and a public meeting was actually held at the League's headquarters in Newall's Buildings, Manchester. In this way the new radicalism of the 1850s was built up, and none of this activity had anything to do with religion.[151]

The same point was made in an even more impressive way by the movement for secular education which gathered momentum after 1847. The leaders in this agitation were again Richard Cobden and the Lancashire radicals. In 1847 these men launched the Lancashire Public Schools Association in an effort to avoid the bitter sectarian rivalry which was delaying educational developments throughout the country. The Association proposed a plan for national, unsectarian education paid for out of the rates and controlled by a board of elected ratepayers. The idea spread. In 1849 William Biggs, the mayor of Leicester, made a speech in favour of the plan, and the following year an educational conference was called at Manchester, attended by delegates from the surrounding districts, including Holyoake, who represented the Miles Platting Mechanics' Institute. At this conference, held on 30 October, the

Lancashire Public Schools Association, the London Working Men's Association for National Secular Education, and similar bodies in Birmingham, Leeds, Leicester, Sheffield, Huddersfield, Halifax, Coventry and other places were united as the 'National Public Schools Association'.[152]

A campaign then began in Parliament. W. J. Fox introduced a Bill which, on the suggestion of J. S. Mill, proposed purely secular education —a thing which Holyoake had advocated at the Manchester conference. It was overwhelmingly defeated, but in 1851 Lord Melgund's bill for secular education in Scotland was defeated by only thirteen votes. Manchester, however, remained at the heart of the agitation. The National Public Schools Association put forward a Secular Education Bill which would have excluded religious education from schools but allowed times at which schools were to be closed, when parents, guardians, and religious teachers could impart what information they liked. In opposition to this, the Reverend Hugh Stowell and a Mr Entwistle put forward a Manchester and Salford Borough Education Bill to provide for a similar scheme but which would include religious instruction. This in turn provoked protests from other Evangelicals, notably Francis Close and J. H. Hinton. They argued that secular education promoted atheism and was therefore out of the question, but that a comprehensive system of religious education would be doctrinally impossible and a free system would raise the issue of an education rate for Church purposes.[153] So deadlock remained.

The importance of this movement for Holyoake is twofold. First, it was yet more evidence that compromise between two hitherto opposed groups was possible: Christian and non-Christian were able to join in a common agitation. Cobden's work in political and religious affairs symbolises an end to the isolation of the Painite tradition; he was the bridge between early nineteenth-century radicalism and Gladstonian Liberalism. Secondly, the education movement drew Holyoake's attention to the possibilities of purely secular reform, and may even have given him the word which he was to apply to his new movement of Secularism.

These new developments can be seen at work in the history of socialism during these years. The religious issue had divided socialism since 1828 if not before. How the movement responded to the changed times is, therefore, the best pointer to the difficulties of and opportunities for secular progress in the 1850s. Socialism in the late 1840s can be divided into four streams. First there was the old Rational Society, which in 1850 had six branches and a total income of £2 5s 3d.[154] Secondly there were the local revivals based on the Rochdale store system, which were yearly becoming increasingly important. Thirdly there were the various schemes projected by the old Owenite leaders, including Owen himself. And lastly came the new ventures of the Christian Socialists.

The Rochdale Equitable Pioneers Society, formed in 1844, was not original in its ideas. The Pioneers aimed to use the store to raise funds for a community, as had been done at many places in the earlier co-operative movement of the late 1820s, and even their principle of the division of profits was not a new one. What was new and important about Rochdale was that it set an example which was followed on a large scale. The co-operative movement grew rapidly, and in 1851 forty-four societies were represented at a congress held in Bury. Religious differences played little part in all this and, although the stigma of infidelity was still attached to co-operation, the movement had at last broken away from the overwhelming influence of Owen's personality and the members were determined that future growth should not be imperilled by sectarianism. The stores were open to all: a 'Cookite' Methodist, two Swedenborgians and a local preacher, as well as a nucleus of Owenites, were among the original Pioneers.[155]

The old Owenite leaders also found new life. A Society of Social Friends was formed at John Street in 1847 to apply the principles of Robert Owen, and in the same year Owen himself stood for Parliament at Marylebone, though he did not go to the poll. More effective steps were taken in 1848 when hopes were high for the socialists in France. In the spring James Rigby called a meeting in Williams Pare's office to further the cause, and plans were made to establish a Labour League and a magazine to be called the *Communist*. Nothing happened immediately, but in July Alexander Campbell brought out the *Spirit of the Age*, which remained a socialist paper until November, when Ashurst bought it for Holyoake, who advised its closure in the following February. Meanwhile, also in November, a new Owenite League of Social Progress had been formed in clear imitation of the old Rational Society. Indeed, a *Reasoner* correspondent failed to see why the new League was necessary at all. On its Central Board were many old figures—Lloyd Jones, Henry Hetherington, G. A. Fleming, Robert Buchanan, Henry Ivory, James Rigby and Holyoake among them—and hence many of the old theological problems were present as well.[156]

The difficulties encountered by these men working together once again were further complicated by the rise of the Christian Socialists. This group, inspired by F. D. Maurice and Charles Kingsley, had reacted to the Chartist demonstration of 10 April 1848 by determining to educate the middle classes in the needs of the working classes and to serve the latter. Their socialist thought came largely from the third leader, the French-bred J. M. Ludlow. At the suggestion of Walter Cooper, whom they had attracted to their ranks, regular conferences were held with working men at the Cranbourne Coffee Tavern in 1848, and among those who came were Lloyd Jones, Hetherington and Holyoake. The principal contributions made by Christian Socialism to co-operation during these years were in the organisation of co-operative producer associations and in the propagation of the objects and principles of co-operation in general. Cooper and Jones were closely involved in both, Cooper as manager of the Working Association for Tailors and Jones as manager of the London Co-operative Store. Both were also in great demand as lecturers in the north, which enabled the Christian Socialists to draw on the support of the stores which had already been founded there. Jones was a particularly valuable acquisition. In 1848, with unusual modesty, Holyoake had described him as 'the Champion of Socialism'.[157]

The League of Social Progress does not seem to have survived, but at a meeting with Owen at Anderton's Hotel in October 1849 it was virtually reconstituted as the Social Reform League, and at a social congress held by the League and chaired by Jones in May 1850 the issue of the theological opinions of the socialists was again raised. Delegates comprised Christians and non-Christians, including the Reverend E. R. Larken and Thornton Hunt of the *Leader*, George Dawson of Birmingham, and Robert Cooper and Holyoake representing Manchester. The sixth rule of the League made clear that it eschewed all identification with theological creeds but at the same time allowed individuals to express and advocate their personal views. Holyoake wished to make this latter part less positive, and thought the League should permit an individual to defend his views only when called upon publicly to do so. This distinction was a nice one, though perfectly valid, but when his amendment had been defeated matters were made worse by the entire omission of the offending clause. Holyoake was now more dissatisfied than ever, and Robert Cooper agreed with him. They both felt that an organisation which was not religious in any way did not need a rule saying that it was not religious. But in fact the two men reached this same opinion for opposite reasons. Holyoake wished the League to be completely neutral in theological affairs, and he feared that a rule which drew attention to past disputes might harm the future of the League, whereas Cooper did not believe that neutrality was at all possible or even desirable.[158]

Holyoake tried to put his belief in neutrality into effect in his relations with the Christian Socialists. Although he was sceptical that Christians could ever be real socialists, he urged freethinkers to co-operate with them on the grounds that 'When doctrinal error is allied to excellent practice, such as that presented in the Co-operative exertions of the Christian Socialists, we will leave their doctrinal error alone till we can find an opportunity of disproving it, without appearing at the same time as the opponents of their good works.'[159] When the Christian Socialists established their Central Co-operative Agency, trading as Lechevalier, Woodin, Jones & Co., Holyoake therefore offered himself in their service. He was accepted by them, and on his lecture tours he did all he could to advertise their agency and to urge secular co-operative stores to trade with it. There were difficulties. Holyoake objected to Christian Socialist tracts being available at the London Co-operative Store and urged the promoters to 'keep the proselytism of the Church distinct from social or political reform'. In their turn Lechevalier, Woodin, E. V. Neale and Thomas Hughes expressed concern at Holyoake's championing their cause, lest he should give the impression that they were not theologically sound.[160] Nevertheless this was the beginning of a joint effort in the work of promoting co-operation, which for Holyoake, Neale and Hughes was to be lifelong. The old thesis that no reform could take place without religious reform was plainly not true.

'Secularism is the province of the real, the known, the useful, and the affirmative. It is the practical side of scepticism,' announced the *Reasoner* in January 1853. It was a development of what Holyoake had previously called Naturalism, Rationalism, or Cosmism, and its basic doctrines and assumptions were the same: justification by conduct and sincerity, study of the order rather than the origin of Nature, trust in science as the providence of man, and belief in a morality guaranteed by human nature, utility and intelligence. It included both the positive and negative sides of freethought: the negative in that it attacked what Holyoake called 'speculative error', and the positive in its attempt to discover a new system of moral truth.[161]

Secularism did not attack Christianity as such. Its sphere of controversy was 'the criticism of Sacred Books and existing Religions only in those respects in which they seem to contradict ascertained Moral Truths, and are impediments to a Rational progress'. Christian teaching was therefore to be judged by the dual standards of morality and utility, and this latter was to replace the standard of traditional Christianity. In his debate with J. H. Rutherford in 1853, Holyoake concluded that 'tried by the morality of common men, the instincts of the human heart, and the judgment of mankind, Christ is not a model for our instruction—an absolute example of moral perfection'.[162] In other words, human nature, utility and intelligence found Christianity lacking. But Holyoake was almost equally dissatisfied with the old atheism, and in Secularism he hoped to offer a philosophy which would combine the best of both worlds. The atheists had emphasised the distinction between the knowable and the unknowable, and had argued that a philosophy of the unknowable was meaningless and therefore a root cause of a misunderstanding and underestimation of the knowable, but Secularism no longer implied a negation of all philosophical and religious systems built on the unknowable. Holyoake was now prepared to say that religion was an interesting, if irrelevant, speculation. Provided it did not interfere with the secular to the detriment of the latter, he was quite ready to ignore it, and where Christianity or any other religion was useful in the world, he wished to co-operate with its adherents.[163] In an early article on Secularism he wrote:

> We do not say every man ought to give an *exclusive* attention to this world, because that would be to commit the old sin of dogmatism, and exclude the possibility of another man walking by a different light than that by which alone we are able to walk. But, as our *knowledge* is confined to this life, and testimony, conjecture, and probability are all that can be set forth with respect to another life, we think we are justified in giving the *precedence* to the duties of this state, and in attaching *primary* importance to the morality of man to man.[164]

This was an emphasis new to Secularism as expounded by Holyoake.

The public education question more than any other had drawn to Holyoake's attention the way religious differences could be a barrier to progress. This had been the point of Owen's denunciation of religion in 1817, and Holyoake's bitterness in 1842 had been prompted by a belief that religion had robbed the new moral world of principle. Secularism therefore proposed a code of conduct relating exclusively to the requirements of the here and now and offered a philosophy which, neutral in matters of belief, would be concerned solely with the requirements of the present age. He assumed that a suitable moral code would be easy to find. Christian morality had failed 'because the Christian constantly holds up the Bible as the only source of morals, and that, consequently, all who do not believe in the Bible as a divine book are without morality'.[165] Holyoake, on the contrary, could see that all men had a common morality grounded in the moral sense, namely that system which he had put forward as Rationalism. Given this practical, rational, secular morality, all creeds could be abandoned and human energies diverted to the welfare and improvement of the present life.

Casting aside the exclusive claims of Christianity also meant casting aside the exclusive claims of atheism. Holyoake therefore wished to abandon the old terminology. He no longer wished to be called an atheist, 'since the public understand by that one who is without God and also without morality, and who wishes to be without both'; and he

wanted to abandon the term 'infidel', 'since Christians understand by
that term one who is unfaithful or treacherous to the truth'.[166] Instead
of these divisive labels he hoped to establish common cause with theists
who shared the same morality. The purpose of Secularism was, therefore,
fourfold: to attack obstructive error; to ignore all other speculation; to
advance an alternative philosophy; and to encourage secular improve-
ments, unhindered by theological labels.

The reasons why Holyoake propagated this philosophy of Secularism
were numerous. His opponents were in no doubt. Brewin Grant charged
him with expediency, and W. J. Linton accused him of wishing to please
his respectable friends.[167] There is something in both these charges. The
Theological Utilitarians had not been a success, and some of Holyoake's
statements give the impression that he was quite prepared to sacrifice
the means to the end. For example, in his first discussion with Grant he
admitted that 'To keep back the truth when it can be serviceable is indeed
a serious fault: yet to suffer it to be dragged forward to be destroyed is to
betray the truth.'[168] Moderation and an emphasis on the positive had
long been characteristic of Holyoake's outlook. In 1845 he had told the
despairing Owenites, 'The conditions of success require that our early
steps shall not only be determined, but *sedate*', a view echoed a few
months later by the *Herald of Progress* when it stated 'that our business
now is constructive, and that we should aim rather to exhibit the work-
ings of our own principles than at the refutation or destruction of
others'.[169] Holyoake pressed this theme time after time in the *Reasoner*:
'Infidelity has been too long a *mere* negation. It has reached a new point
—it interests itself with a practical system of morality. Its negative theory
must assert its positive influence, or the apathy of its present friends will
be eternal.' In the same issue he wrote that whilst religion was 'a serious
practical error', theology was 'entitled to respectful consideration', and
a week later he was willing to concede that 'Religion is a thing of degree,
and to elevate it, may be serviceable with those whose convictions cannot
be successfully changed'. A correspondent inquired whether Holyoake
had taken holy orders yet![170] In the next issue an unperturbed Holyoake
was 'anxious to convince our government that we are disposed to avail
ourselves of this season of comparative peace and liberty, to place our
views on the broad foundation of general usefulness. . . .' Southwell was
outraged: 'It is the theory of conciliation, and nothing but conciliation,
which, like the congenial theory of non-resistance, is so repugnant to
practical good sense, that even its advocates seldom act upon it. . . .
No man *can*, under all circumstances, unless he be servile and hypo-
critical.'[171] But still Holyoake went on. In 1847 he was criticising the
way the anti-theological war was being conducted in an 'indiscriminate'

manner and urged freethinkers to rescue morality from the ruins of theological argument. In 1849 he admitted that Utilitarianism was stationary and, acknowledging that he might be thought a 'trimmer', he urged atheists to avoid antagonising Christians with their zeal.[172]

Holyoake was not alone in his desire for moderation, though he went further than most were prepared to go. In 1843 Southwell had abandoned the *Oracle* in favour of the more moderate *Investigator*, and in the same year the editors of *The Man Paterson* (W. J. Birch and M. Q. Ryall) had maintained that the *Oracle* was never intended as a merely negative 'manufactory of atheism', but was also meant to establish 'the right of private judgment'. A contributor to *Cooper's Journal* in 1850 urged free-thinkers to 'respect the feelings of others, and make due allowances for the prejudices of early education. . . . We *must endeavour to construct* as well as to pull down. We must not only seek to detect error, but to discover truth. We must conserve whatever is excellent, as well as destroy all that is injurious. We must labour to find out agreements as well as differences.'[173] It was almost inevitable that a system which set up for itself the standard of utility, should, in consistency with its own principles, be open to the charge of expediency.

Although Holyoake had long been disposed towards moderation, yet there is some truth in the charge that he did change his ideas in the early 1850s from older to newer forms of freethought. In 1842 he had held the traditional socialist view that '*truth only can regenerate the world*' and that therefore 'it is a first *duty* to break down all the dams that obstruct its progress'; and even at the same time as he was speaking moderately about religion in 1846 he was still able to say that '. . . it does not appear to us that religion is 'rational' or 'natural', since it is shown to be *unreasonable* and *useless*, and infidelity being 'unpopular' is of little consequence, so long as it appears to be *right*. Believing religion to be an error, we cannot consent merely to 'reform' what we ought to eradi-cate.'[174] Holyoake indeed admitted in 1853 that he had changed his mind since those days. He had once thought that all he had to do was to cut through the tree of religious evil and all would be demolished but experience had taught him differently, and he even made a virtue of this inconsistency. 'Perpetual consistency with *past* opinions,' he told South-well, 'would exclude a man from growing wiser.'[175] New evidence had led him to new convictions, and in this new evidence lie the origins of Holyoake's Secularism.

A prominent feature of Holyoake's mentality was his respect for men of a higher social rank. He admired men of learning and was happy to bask in the reflected glory of their friendship. Like Kingsley's Alton Locke he would have liked to have been a scholar or a literary man, and

L

he never gave up trying to become one. In 1847 and again in 1849 he even attended classes at London University, encouraged by Arthur Trevelyan, W. J. Fox, J. S. Mill, W. H. Ashurst and other middle-class patrons of the British radical movement.[176]

Holyoake's breakthrough into the literary world of London came in 1849 when his review of G. H. Lewes's *Robespierre* was favourably noticed by its author. Lewes invited Holyoake round for a cigar and to meet Thornton Hunt, a rising young journalist and the son of the radical poet, Leigh Hunt. Hunt was particularly keen to organise a society of literary men whose theological and political opinions were more radical than those they openly expressed, and he wanted Holyoake to help him in the matter. His idea was for a 'Political Exchange' where men of all viewpoints could co-operate together as they were already doing in the Lancashire Public Schools Association.[177]

Hunt's private scheme never made much headway, though the idea was embodied by Holyoake in the Secularist movement. In public his plan was more nearly realised in the *Leader* newspaper, which became the organ of the literary radicals in the 1850s. Among the founders of this paper were a number of middle-class figures who had been prominent in the radical cause—the Reverend E. R. Larken, George Dawson and Thornton Hunt, who was the editor—as well as leading religious free-thinkers like Lewes himself and Richard Congreve. W. J. Linton, the extreme republican, was also involved for a time. Holyoake, the only atheist, officiated as Hunt's general assistant and contributed articles over the pseudonym of 'Ion'.[178] His justification of this involvement illustrates the degree to which he was now prepared to compromise in the pursuit of the secular. He told his critics on the *Weekly Tribune*, 'I can *work* with all men, though I cannot *agree* with all. That is, I am free to co-operate with as much as leads in what I think the right direction, although there may be much else not to my taste.'[179] To Holyoake's work as 'Ion' we can attribute most of the unpopularity which he later incurred with 'genuine' radicals, but at the time the companionship he found on the *Leader* was a major factor in the development of his ideas.

In addition to the *Leader* group one of the most important single influences on Holyoake's career was W. H. Ashurst, Owen's lawyer and adviser to a generation of radical leaders. Ashurst was not an atheist himself, but he continued to give to Holyoake the encouragement he had given to Owen and the other socialists, and to Ashurst can be traced the use of the word 'secular' to describe those ideas which were developing in Holyoake's mind under the above-mentioned influences. In April 1848 the *Reasoner* had adopted the sub-title of 'Secular and Eclectic Journal', though this was shortly followed in April 1850 by a vigorously anti-theological volume. Ashurst was a keen supporter of the *Reasoner*, and in November 1849 he had banked £100 to finance the new *Reasoner* which Holyoake was proposing to start. He must have been sadly disappointed by the anti-Catholic illustrations with which volume VIII commenced, but he continued his support, urged a course of moderation, and in June 1851 suggested to Holyoake that he should adopt the name of 'Secularist'. Holyoake replied that he had been considering this step in a lecture on the Martineau-Atkinson *Letters*, and thereafter the word was gradually introduced. It was used in a letter from 'S' in August 1851, but was still sufficiently new in January 1852 for Holyoake to explain that secular, in the words of George Combe, referred to that 'which pertains to this world—"the issues of which can be tested in this life" '.[180]

While these personal connections were gradually helping Holyoake to reconsider the organisation of freethought, two other sources were providing further 'new evidence' which was to determine the future nature and content of Secularism. Francis W. Newman, brother of the more famous Cardinal, represented a respectable school of religious thought which came very close to Holyoake's own position, while the ideas of Auguste Comte provided a parallel movement to his own on the continent.

'Nothing is destroyed until it is replaced' was probably Holyoake's favourite justification of Secularism.[181] It was a quotation from the writings of Comte. Nevertheless much of Holyoake's intellectual inheritance was independent of the direct influence of Comte. This is not surprising. Comte himself was not an entirely original thinker—his ideas go back to Bacon, Hobbes, Gassendi, Bayle and Locke; they had been developed by the Philosophes from Fontonelle to Condillac and Condorcet, and by the British Empiricists, James Mill, Bentham and Hume; they had been anticipated by Turgot, Condorcet, Kant and Saint-Simon.[182] This was the same tradition on which Holyoake drew, and Hobbes, Locke, Bentham and Hume can be shown to have had an important influence on the ideas expressed in the *Reasoner*: a quotation from Bentham had appeared on the front pages beneath the headings of the *Movement* and the *Reasoner* long before the quotation from Comte. But Comte's ideas were important in the shaping of Secularism. Before the publication of *The Positive Philosophy of Auguste Comte, Freely Translated and Condensed by Harriet Martineau*, which in 1853 made Comte really familiar to British readers, the ideas expressed in it were already current among those intellectuals with whom Holyoake was developing his connections. G. H. Lewes's article on Comte in his *Biographical History of Philosophy* was first published in 1846, and this influenced Harriet Martineau and Henry Atkinson in their *Letters on* the *Laws of Man's Nature and Development* of 1851. Comte's *Philosophy of the Sciences*, in a translation by Lewes, had appeared in the *Leader* from April to August 1852, though it was not published as a volume till 1853. Holyoake is therefore likely to have known of Comte through Lewes and the *Leader*, and through the Martineau–Atkinson *Letters* which had prompted him to consider adopting the word 'Secularist' in the first place. Moreover, Harriet Martineau had discussed with Holyoake as early as October 1851 the translation of Comte which she was preparing, and in Comte he found the justification for the new step which he was taking.[183] If Comte did not create Secularism, then he did give Holyoake the courage to go ahead and develop Secularism himself. When Martineau's *Comte* finally appeared in 1853, Holyoake welcomed it wholeheartedly:

> No man who masters this work need ever again feel that painful shame that many of us have felt at being unable to give a clear, convincing account of his disbelief of popular superstition. . . . In it we have a body of positive doctrine, substantial, affirmative, impregnable, in a comparison with which the doctrines of theology and metaphysics are cloud pictures in a rising wind.[184]

This eulogy is not surprising. Comte, like Holyoake, had abandoned belief in the Absolute for a scientific understanding of nature. 'He is not an Atheist, simply because he does not *know* there is *not* a God; he is not a Deist, because he does not know that there *is*', is how the *Weekly Dispatch*, approvingly quoted by the *Reasoner*, summed up the Comte of Martineau's translation, and Holyoake immediately became a devotee of Comte. In 1854 he even suggested that Comte's birthday should be celebrated, like Paine's, by 'the friends of positive philosophy in England', and the following year he visited Comte in Paris, obtaining permission to publish a letter which Comte had addressed to him as head of the English Secularists. He also considered translating Comte's *Philosophy of History* but never did. In 1860, however, he was obliged to distingush between Comte's positive philosophy and his later religious views.[185]

Like Comte's Positivism, Secularism itself as interpreted by Holyoake had many of the trappings of a religion. In his oration at Hetherington's grave in 1849 Holyoake had stated, 'It seems to me that, in point of solemnity and decorum, the Church Service is perfect; and in every substitution of ours, the qualities of propriety and earnestness should be most anxiously and effectually preserved.'[186] This religious outlook was, in part, natural to atheists as most of them came from a Christian and evangelical background and could not easily shake this off. Victorian doubt was heavily moral and no exponent of it more so than Holyoake.

Indeed, John Stuart Mill felt compelled to write to him in 1848, accusing him of accepting 'the present constitution of the family & the whole of the priestly morality founded on & connected with it—which morality in my opinion thoroughly deserves the epithets of "intolerant, slavish & selfish" '.[187] Secularism as developed by Holyoake after 1851 clearly went beyond an atheism with religious trappings though, and the reasons for this are to be found partly in Holyoake's personality and partly in the change which was taking place in public opinion.

In the early 1850s a number of religious books were published which marked a new and humane development in religious thought. This is what Holyoake had in mind in 1853 when he wrote in the *Reasoner* of

> Men of reputation, genius and attainments [who would] shape this age and rule the next. Thomas Carlyle, Francis William Newman, Leigh Hunt, G. H. Lewes, Charles Mackay, Harriet Martineau, Rathbone Greg, W. J. Fox, M.P., Rev. Frederick Foxton, Rev. Thomas Wilson, Rev. Newenham Travers, Theodore Parker, Ralph Waldo Emerson . . . bring lustrious contributions to the truths of the future.[188]

The *Clerical Journal* in 1854 saw where all this was leading. It perceived that infidelity 'clothes itself now in social respectability; it affects to have the welfare of the masses at heart, and proclaims a religion of its own. From the pages of the elegant and amiable Leigh Hunt, to the more openly destructive volumes of Newman and Parker, we may see the same spirit at work.'[189] The development of Holyoake's Secularism can be interpreted as a part of this general mood and Holyoake welcomed the efforts of these fellow-writers. When Leigh Hunt published his *Religion of the Heart* in 1853, Holyoake wrote to him asking him to 'Accept the thanks of a stranger for the publication of so brave and wise a book as the "Religion of the Heart". Its letter I may not accept—its spirit I do . . .', and he quoted from the work in his second debate with Brewin Grant. Holyoake was probably already acquainted with Hunt's views in 1851 through his son, Thornton, and another of these writers whom Holyoake was later to know through his son was W. R. Greg, whose *Creed of Christendom* Holyoake quoted in his first debate with Grant in 1853, along with an extract from another of these authors of liberal theology, James Martineau.[190] Joseph Barker later characterised such men as those who, 'though they still retain their faith, no longer rest it on the old foundations. They seem to substitute feeling or instinct for reason and argument, as the general ground of their faith.'[191] This was, of course, unacceptable to the atheists, though it demanded more refined refutations from them. Robert Cooper in his *Immortality of the Soul* and Holyoake in his *The Philosophic Type of Religion* and *Trial of Theism* attempted to provide these, but the liberal theists did not leave the atheists completely untouched. Holyoake was a sentimentalist, and he recognised the irrational appeal of the religion of the heart.

The most influential of all these writers on religion was F. W. Newman, whose *Soul, its Sorrows and Aspirations* was first published in 1849. Holyoake reviewed this book in the summer of 1851, and in it he found two features which appealed to him and which are to be found in Secularism.[192] The first was the power of the feelings, the moral sense; and the second, a belief in the growth of a universal morality. He welcomed the *Soul* as 'the first *religious* book I have been able to read for years' and he admitted that 'The analysis of feeling, and of the presumptive evidence on the side of human estimate of Deity, has long appeared to me as the only ground on which the believer could ever win the ear of the world.' Sentiment provided Holyoake with the basis of his system of morality. He agreed with Newman that conscience, by which he meant a 'sense of justice or duty', was supreme, 'a subject of growth, and amenable to reason'.[193] The effect of this book was to hasten Holyoake along the path he was already taking both in his ethical theory and in his rejection of crude atheism. The existence of God was 'a hypothesis of the heart, not in our present state of knowledge to be dogmatically asserted, nor—having in view the deep feeling connected with it—to be irreverently rejected'. A future life he admitted to be 'undoubtedly desirable'. The extent to which Holyoake had gone by 1854 is shown in his last speech in the discussion with Grant. Quoting Newman he said, 'We regard God, when we realise the idea of his possible existence, as the infinite enlargement of man's purest nature and highest faculties,' and he concluded, 'For, if Secularism does not proceed upon knowledge of a God *Actual*, it moves towards a God *Possible*.'[194]

Newman's second contribution towards Secularism was in its organisation. Suggestions had been made to Holyoake by Thornton Hunt for an organisation in which men of different views could come together, and also by the pantheist, William Maccall, but Newman was one of the most persistent advocates of the idea. In 1853 he wrote to Holyoake urging a Moral Union of which Secularism was to be a part.[195] All these influences cannot be directly related to Secularism, but these were the ideas which were being put to Holyoake at the time when he was working his own ideas out, and it seems likely that Newman's insistence on a common morality prior to theology did have some influence on the Holyoake who at the same time was striving to create in Secularism a philosophy which would unite theists and atheists in a common morality for the common good.

The development which Holyoake's ideas underwent between 1850 and 1854 met with a mixed reception. Charles Southwell had himself also been affected by the changing circumstances. In 1849 he began to have doubts about the philosophical possibility of atheism, since the very word implied the existence of something which did not exist. The atheist, he felt, was being driven to accept his terminology from the theist to the detriment of his cause, and so the true and effective freethinker would do better not to accept any such label as 'atheist' at all. Carlyle, Bulwer, Dickens and Jerrold were, he thought, far more effective as freethinkers than any of the so-called atheists. At first glance this looks like Secularism. In place of atheism Southwell was advocating a 'New Mind Church' based on Truth, so that 'men will see the glorious sight of a dead and buried church, full of corruption, rising again in all purity and strength of truth, phoenix-like, from its own ashes', and, incredibly, he stated that he believed in 'the God of Saint Paul, that unfathomable Deity in which we live, move, and have our being'. 'We do not deny the "truth of Christianity" though our conception of that truth may be different', he told a member of the Manchester Y.M.C.A. who had challenged him to debate.[196] This took Southwell very close to that interpretation of Christianity with which Richard Carlile had ended his days. In 1852 he was claiming to be an eclectic and founded in that year a Society of Eclectics in Glasgow, probably built on the foundations of the old Glasgow Zetetic Society.[197] But as with Carlile, Southwell had not changed so radically as might be thought from some of the things he said. He still maintained that the task of the person who was opposed to Christianity was to 'Bring the Priest to book'; he still was not satisfied with Holyoake's arguments in his discussion with Brewin Grant in 1853, and wrote in a very critical review of the debate that Holyoake 'argued throughout as if prepared to accept Christianity in part—as if Christians could believe their own theory—as if supernaturalism might be something more than assent without ideas, and as if the scheme of his opponent might be overthrown without disturbing its fundamental assumptions'. Holyoake had stated that Secularism was concerned solely with the affairs of this life, but he had failed to show that there was nothing else for man to be concerned with.[198] Southwell here observed the weak point in Holyoake's new position: he saw that Holyoake had changed because he no longer felt able to demolish the theist's point of view in a manner convincing to himself.

Robert Cooper reacted differently. In his lectures on 'The Soul' he totally rejected Newman's explanation of religion, and by dismissing entirely the existence of the soul, he felt able also to ignore 'the religion of the heart'. He could accept no compromise with the theists: 'Secularism need not shroud itself in refined obscurities', he told a joint meeting of Secularists and William Maccall's Pantheists in 1854. 'Its object is a plain

one, and must be plainly stated, or it will fall, and deservedly, into
inanity. Broadly emphatically, irrevocably, is Secularism at issue with
theology.' He had equally firmly rejected compromise with the Christian
Socialists. He could not ignore Christianity, because it was a hindrance to
progress: 'Priestcraft is *essentially* obstructive. It is in its element when
arresting, not premating [sic] human improvement.' There were, he
admitted, exceptions to this general rule but only a few. Cooper was,
however, a moderate man and he did not oppose Holyoake's Secularism
outright. 'I do not wish to return to the tactics of Southwell and Patterson
[sic]', he told Holyoake in a letter in which he attempted to clear up
differences of opinion. Cooper was prepared to accept the label of
Secularist and he played an important part in the development of the
movement.[199]

These different reactions to changes in public opinion and in the
nature of freethought, can be related to two differing kinds of personality
among both followers and leaders. Some people believed that religion
could be abolished only by a frontal attack on its teachings, institutions
and influence, whereas others thought that religion could be dealt with
only when a substitute had been found. These positions can be related
roughly to the psychological make-up of the individual leaders. A man
like Holyoake, who found the religious impulse necessary but Christianity morally and intellectually repulsive, was likely to turn to a substitute religion—Deism, Positivism or Theosophy—or at least he was
likely to want his freethought to serve the function of a substitute religion;
whereas a man like Cooper, Southwell or Charles Bradlaugh, who found
the whole experience of religion foreign to his nature, was inclined to
regard it as simply something to be eradicated.[200]

Holyoake's new move, therefore, did not appeal equally to all freethinkers, and, although he was in the ascendant throughout the 1850s,
men of his viewpoint were probably in a minority in the movement as
a whole. He was able to lead just so long as he was the most effective
leader and many of his quarrels with the other principal freethinkers,
which superficially appeared to take abolitionist/substitutionist lines,
were in fact occasioned by purely practical or personal issues. But with
the emergence of Charles Bradlaugh as an effective abolitionist leader
towards the end of the decade the whole concept of Secularism in Holyoake's sense was challenged. The attempt he had made to remodel freethought as Secularism was then rejected by a considerable part of the
movement.

Critics of Holyoake's efforts often described his Secularism as sectarian,
but a closer analysis suggests that, in fact, what he was doing was just the
opposite. The infidel organisations had always been sectarian to a greater

or lesser extent, but as Holyoake warmed to the praise and influence of men like W. H. Ashurst and F. W. Newman he began to abandon many of the sectarian characteristics and to turn freethought into a denomination. The evolution of the British freethought movement and the course it took in the 1850s can usefully be examined in this light.[201]

Freethought, particularly in the period 1815–50, was similar to many of the other millenarian sects of early industrial society. A 'sense of blockage' and a 'sense of a social order which cannot be reconstituted to yield the satisfactions desired' have been seen as the motivation behind the millennial sect.[202] These were present, to some extent, in the early freethought movements. The men who made up the radical movements of the first half of the nineteenth century had faced seemingly insuperable barriers and they had frequently turned in on themselves, giving rise to a variety of millennial or quasi-millennial sects. The embattled feeling which the freethinkers sensed so acutely at times was a part of this. The reader of the *Republican*, the *Poor Man's Guardian*, or the *Northern Star* had to face a hostile world and a rigid social order, or so he thought. But Holyoake's new move was helped by changing circumstances. By the middle of the century signs of hope were beginning to appear, and with them came an appreciation of realistic gradualism instead of the millennial leap of faith. In politics and in religion things were changing, and Holyoake's Secularism reflected this change. He was not a millennial prophet in the sense that Owen had been, and his teachings were rarely sectarian. Under his leadership denominational characteristics became much more pronounced. The distinct line between the sect and the world began to be blurred; inclusiveness was encouraged instead of exclusiveness; breadth and toleration were advocated; formality and hierarchy began to appear in the organisation, meetings became more like services, and Holyoake was sometimes referred to, albeit by his enemies, as the high priest. The values of the outside world—Broad Church theology and orthodox political economy —were being accepted. Above all there was a move towards respectability.

This was a key word in the development of mid-Victorian society. The leadership of most popular movements was markedly respectable, despite Feargus O'Connor's repeated appeals to 'the Fustian Jackets, the Blistered Hands, and Unshorn Chins' of *Northern Star* readers. The leadership of the Secularist movement in particular was recruited largely from that 'middling' group of superior artisans, tradesmen and shopkeepers, who occupied the lowest rung on the ladder of respectability and who in different circumstances would have been called *sansculottes*.[203] Holyoake belonged to this group. He had begun at the very bottom, as an artisan during the depression of 1837–1842 when the

most respectable and skilled workmen could be plunged into the depths
of poverty. During the 1850s he was rapidly emerging as a respected
author, journalist and lecturer—respected, that is, by his own social
group. He had achieved recognition from his equals, and he came to take
this for granted, even to despise it, as he went on to seek a higher recognition from his betters. To reach true middle-class respectability was his
ambition for the rest of his life but, like many other working-class leaders
in a similar position, he was to fail. This cult of respectability depended
upon the reality of social mobility, the removal of the personal sense of
blockage. Without prospects of advancement, bitterness and class-
conscious hostility could result, as in the 1830s and 1840s. In the 1850s
this was on the wane. Individuals and organisations alike, united for
self-help and mutual improvement, could make their way forward in
the world. So freethought, like the political reform movement, like the
trade unions and the Co-operative movement, abandoned the millen-
narian, sectarian past for a moderate, progressive, realistic, respectable
future. Just as the larger religious groups—the Congregationalists,
Baptists, Quakers and Roman Catholics—experienced a 'coming out' in
the mid-century as they moved from sectarianism to denominationalism,
so Holyoake's Secularism emerged in the 1850s as a new phase of freethought.[204]

Yet like the Society of Friends, Secularism did not experience a single,
natural progression from sect to denomination, and the conflicts between
Holyoake and the other sections of the movement can be seen in terms of
a conflict between the two aspects of the movement. Holyoake was
abandoning the tradition of the Fathers—Paine and Carlile—and he was
fiercely attacked for it, while Charles Bradlaugh was able to reintroduce
a number of sectarian characteristics. At the end of the 1850s he
re-emphasised the exclusiveness of Secularism as atheism; he drew again
the dividing line between those who belonged and those who did not;
his militancy stirred up renewed opposition, and with it the sense of
blockage returned. The struggle between the two men and their two
interpretations of Secularism was to be enacted for the rest of the century.
How far the nature of their support differed is hard to tell without much
more research into the later history of Secularism. One suspects that a
reason for the widespread support Holyoake received from the leaders
of the movement in the north, even after 1861, is that they, like him,
were becoming respectable and achieving positions of importance in
civic life. In the end, the times were against the sectarian approach.
When the world was rubbing out the dividing line, when religious men
could sponsor 'rational' and 'secular' reforms, and when even doubt
could become respectable, exclusiveness had lost its meaning.

Secularism was, therefore, very much a product of its age, and the new developments and the persistence of old arguments, the aims of Holyoake and his failure in 1861, can all be interpreted within the general context of social development in the 1850s.

Notes

1 'List of James Watson's books and pamphlets . . .', H.C. 778; Manchester P. L. tracts, 335.1 B26; 211 R31; *Oracle*, 25 June 1842.

2 *Movement*, 29 June 1844; *Seventeenth Report of the Ministry to the Poor* (Manchester, 1851), pp. 40–1; Holyoake, *Bygones*, 1, pp. 86–7.

3 H. R. Murphy, 'The ethical revolt against Christian orthodoxy in early Victorian England', *A.H.R.*, LX (1955), pp. 800–17; S. Budd, 'The loss of faith: reasons for unbelief among members of the Secular movement in England, 1850–1950', *Past and Present*, XXXVI (April 1967), pp. 106–125.

4 R. Cooper, *The Infidel's Text Book . . .* (Hull, 1846), p. 6.

5 P. Lecount to [?], 9 September 1849, H.C. 319.

6 R. Cooper, *The Holy Scriptures Analyzed . . .* (third edition, London, 1843), p. 15.

7 *A Report of the Public Discussion Between George J. Holyoake and David King . . .* (London [1850]), pp. 24, 27; C. Southwell, *The Difficulties of Christianity . . .* (London [1843]), pp. 53–4.

8 The title of a book attributed to Peter Annet–see E. Twynam, *Peter Annet*, pp. 5–8.

9 Cooper, *Infidel's Text Book*, p. 142; also *Oracle*, 22 April 1843.

10 G. J. Holyoake, *The Logic of Death* (London, 1852), p. 6.

11 R. Cooper, *A Lecture on Original Sin . . .* (second editon, Hulme, 1838), p. 10.

12 *Discussion on Secularism . . . between the Rev. Brewin Grant . . . and George Jacob Holyoake . . .* (Glasgow, 1854), p. 48.

13 Holyoake, *Logic of Death*, p. 8.

14 *Holyoake–King Discussion*, p. 21.

15 Cooper, *Infidel's Text Book*, pp. 167–82.

16 G. J. Holyoake, *A Short and Easy Method with the Saints* (London [1843]), p. 24.

17 *A Report of the Public Discussion, between Mr John Bowes . . . and Mr Charles Southwell . . .* (Newcastle, 1850), p. 92.

18 *The Report on the . . . Public Discussion . . . between George J. Holyoake . . . and John Bowes . . .* (London, 1850), p. 7.

19 *Holyoake–King Discussion*, pp. 38–43.

20 *Holyoake–Grant Discussion, 1854*, p. 123.

21 R. Cooper, *The Immortality of the Soul . . .* (London, 1852), pp. 99–100.

22 *Holyoake–Bowes Discussion*, p. 86; Cooper, *Infidel's Text Book*, pp. 135–6; *Southwell–Bowes Discussion*, pp. 65–6; see also *Oracle*, 1 April 1843.

23 Cooper, *op. cit.*, p. 137.

24 C. Bradlaugh, *What did Jesus Teach?* (London [1861]), pp. 1–3.

25 *Reasoner*, 6 October 1847.

26 *Oracle*, 20 November 1841 and 1 [1842] preface.

27 Cooper, *op. cit.*, p. 108; *Is the Bible a Divine Revelation? A Discussion between Rev. Woodville Woodman . . . and 'Iconoclast' . . . at Ashton . . .* (London [1861]), p. 70; Cooper had attended Hamilton's lectures at Edinburgh University in 1841–2.

28 Cooper, *op. cit., passim.*

29 *Bradlaugh–Woodman Discussion at Ashton,* p. 55.

30 C. Southwell, *Reply to a 'Discourse on the Subject of Deity' by a Philosophical Inquirer . . .* (London, 1842), p. 10.

31 *Republican,* 23 August 1822.

32 *Oracle,* 23, 30 July 1842; *Southwell–Bowes Discussion,* pp. 19–20.

33 Cooper, *Immortality of the Soul,* p. 5.

34 Southwell, *Difficulties of Christianity,* p. 18.

35 *Oracle,* 19 March 1842.

36 *Movement,* 18 May, 6, 13 July 1844.

37 G. J. Holyoake, *Paley Refuted in his Own Words* (London [1843]), *passim,* especially pp. 32–3; *Holyoake–Bowes Discussion,* p. 35; *Reasoner,* 7 October 1846.

38 Southwell, *An Apology for Atheism . . .* (London 1846), p. 46 and Cooper, *op. cit.,* p. 49.

39 *Holyoake–Bowes Discussion,* pp. 10–13; *Southwell–Bowes Discussion,* p. 60.

40 Cooper, op. cit., pp. 45–58, especially p. 48; C. Bradlaugh, *Has Man a Soul?* (London, 1859), pp. 7, 10–11.

41 Woodville Woodman, *The Doctrine of the Supreme Being Vindicated . . .* (1852), pp. 6–7.

42 *Ibid.,* p. 10.

43 *The Existence of God: A Discussion between Rev. Woodville Woodman . . . and 'Iconoclast' . . . held at Wigan . . .* (London, 1861), pp. 31–2.

44 Southwell, *op. cit.,* pp. 35–6, and Bradlaugh's comments on this in *Half Hours with the Freethinkers* (1856–7), pp. 53–4.

45 *Half Hours,* p. 54; *Is there a God?,* p. 6; *Bradlaugh–Woodman Discussion at Wigan,* p. 17. The *Half Hours* article was taken from the 'Library of Reason' series, no. 5, which in turn was taken from the *Westminster Review.*

46 *Holyoake–Bowes Discussion,* p. 41.

47 J. Hunt, *Religious Thought in England in the Nineteenth Century,* pp. 51–2; J. M. Robertson, *History of Freethought,* I, p. 116.

48 *Reasoner,* 11 September 1850; 10 June 1855.

49 Southwell, *Difficulties of Christianity,* p. 11; *A Full Report of the Discussion between the Rev. Brewin Grant . . . and 'Iconoclast' . . .* (London and Sheffield, 1858), pp. 18–33, especially pp. 20, 23; R. Cooper, *Infidel's Text Book,* pp. 157–9; *Holyoake–Bowes Discussion,* pp. 61, 87.

50 Cooper, *op. cit.,* pp. 160–1, 163; *Bradlaugh–Grant Discussion,* pp. 33–50, especially pp. 38, 40.

51 *Holyoake–Bowes Discussion,* pp. 80–1.

52 Cooper, *Immortality of the Soul,* p. 46.

53 *Ibid.,* pp. 9–10, 61, 65–9.

54 J. M. Robertson, *op. cit.,* II, p. 371.

55 *Ibid.,* I, pp. 123–7.

56 *Ibid.,* p. 70.

57 G. Combe, *Constitution of Man . . .* (Edinburgh, 1893), pp. 8, 86–7.

58 C. Gibbon, *The Life of George Combe* ... , 2 vols (London, 1878), II, p. 158.
59 Southwell wrote nos. 1–6–*Oracle* 28 May 1842; Chilton began with no. 7 on 19 February 1842 and continued throughout the existence of the *Oracle*.
60 *Oracle*, 2 July 1842; see also *Movement*, 6 November 1844.
61 *Oracle*, 28 May, 11 June 1842.
62 *Ibid.*, 30 April 1842.
63 *Ibid.*, 6, 20 November 1841, 19 February 1842.
64 J. M. Robertson, *op. cit.*, II, pp. 316–18.
65 *Reasoner*, 22 November 1848. Chilton knew who the author of the *Vestiges* was—Chilton to Holyoake, 1 February 1846, H.C. 155.
66 *Movement*, 8 January 1845.
67 *Reasoner*, 3 June 1846.
68 'Aliquis' to Holyoake [1854], H.C. 683; *Reasoner*, 26 April 1853.
69 *Oracle*, 11 June 1842; *Reasoner*, 10 July 1859.
70 Discussions on the formation of the Rationalist Press Association, 1899, quoted by F. J. Gould, *The Pioneers of Johnson's Court* ... (London, 1929), p. 23.
71 G. J. Holyoake, *Rationalism* ... (London, 1845), front cover, preface and p. 6.
72 *Oracle*, 1 [1842], preface.
73 Holyoake, *op. cit.*, p. 31.
74 *Oracle*, 6 November 1841.
75 *Christianity versus Secularism. A Public Discussion* ... *between the Rev. J. H. Rutherford and Mr G. J. Holyoake* ... *1853* (London, 1854), pp. 17–20.
76 Holyoake, *op. cit.*, pp. 15–16.
77 *Holyoake—Bowes Discussion*, p. 117; Holyoake acknowledged his debt to Priestley in *Reasoner*, 29 July 1846.
78 Cooper, *Original Sin*, p. 11; see also *Holyoake—Bowes Discussion*, pp. 45–7.
79 Holyoake, *Logic of Death*, p. 9; see also *Christianity and Secularism. Report of a Public Discussion between the Rev. Brewin Grant* ... *and George Jacob Holyoake* ... *1853* ... (London, 1853), p. 65.
80 *Holyoake—Bowes Discussion*, p. 143.
81 Holyoake, *op. cit.*, p. 21; *Logic of Life* (London, 1861), pp. 8, 12.
82 G. J. Holyoake, *Practical Grammar* (eighth edition, London, 1870), p. 7.
83 *Report of a Discussion on the Maine Law, between Mr G. J. Holyoake* ... *and Mr G. E. Lomax* ... (second edition, Blackburn, 1858), second night, pp. 28–9.
84 *Ibid.*, pp. 9–11.
85 *Lion*, 4 December 1829.
86 Southwell in *Oracle*, 6 November 1841.
87 *Holyoake—Lomax Discussion*, first night, p. 6; see also *Public Discussion on teetotalism and the Maine Law between George Jacob Holyoake, Esq., and Dr Frederic R. Lees* (reprinted in *The Works of F. R. Lees*, III), pp. cxci, cc.
88 Holyoake, *Rationalism*, p. 37.
89 *Holyoake—Rutherford Discussion*, pp. 91–2.
90 ... *Report of the* ... *Debate at Liverpool between 'Iconoclast' and the Rev. J. H. Rutherford* (London [1861]), p. 37.

91 *Holyoake—Rutherford Discussion*, p. 41; Holyoake, *Logic of Life*, p. 4.
92 *Holyoake—Bowes Discussion*, pp. 42–3.
93 *Holyoake—Rutherford Discussion*, p. 8.
94 *Holyoake—Grant Discussion, 1853*, p. 24.
95 *Holyoake—Rutherford Discussion*, pp. 12–13, 79–80.
96 Cooper, *Immortality of the Soul*, pp. 83, 79–80.
97 *Reasoner*, 7 October, 2 December 1846.
98 *Mr Geo. J. Holyoake's Three Lectures, in Heywood* . . . (Manchester and London [1852]), I, p. 6.
99 *Holyoake—Grant Discussion 1853*, p. 105.
100 *Three Lectures in Heywood*, I, p. 10.
101 *Bradlaugh—Woodman Discussion at Ashton*, pp. 88–9.
102 *Holyoake—Grant Discussion, 1853*, p. 108.
103 *Ibid.*, pp. 110, 124.
104 Holyoake, *Bygones*, I, pp. 31–2.
105 *Reasoner*, 12 October 1853.
106 *Holyoake—Grant Discussion, 1854*, pp. 203–5, 165.
107 Holyoake, *Rationalism*, p. 30.
108 *Republican*, 27 September 1822.
109 *Investigator* [1843], preface; *Oracle*, 25 February 1843.
110 *N.M.W.*, 24 June 1837.
111 *Ibid.*, 21 December 1839.
112 *Oracle*, 23 July 1843; *Investigator*, no. 7 [13 May 1843].
113 *Oracle*, 21 January 1843; *Northern Star*, 3 April 1841.
114 *Oracle*, 6 November 1841; *Investigator*, no. 6 [6 May 1843].
115 Chilton to Holyoake, 26 December 1841, H.C. 22; Holyoake, *Last Trial*, p. 8.
116 *Northern Star*, 10 October 1840, 15 May, 13 February 1841, 12 March 1842, 3 February 1844.
117 *Ibid.*, 18 June 1842, 30 December 1843, 13 June 1846.
118 *Ibid.*, 23 September, 25 November, 2, 23, 30 December 1843.
119 *Ibid.*, 12 February 1848.
120 *Oracle*, 22 April 1843.
121 *Utilitarian Record*, 30 December 1846, and see items in H.C. 228, 229.
122 *Cause of the People*, 20 May 1848; W. J. Linton, *Memories* (London, 1895), p. 106; Harney to Holyoake, 9 December 1850, H.C. 394.
123 *Lancashire Beacon*, no. 7 [15 September 1849].
124 *Prompter*, 9 April 1831; *N.M.W.*, 26 November 1836.
125 *Movement*, 14, 21 September, 2 October 1844; circular from Linton, 22 April 1847, H.C. 202; *Utilitarian Record*, 13 October 1847; Linton to Holyoake, 12 November 1847, H.C. 234.
126 E.g. *Oracle*, 6 May 1843.
127 *Gauntlet*, 30 March 1834; G. J. Holyoake, *The Advantages and Disadvantages of Trade Unions* (Sheffield, 1841), pp. 3, 5–8, 11.
128 G. D. H. Cole, *A Century of Co-operation* (Manchester [1945]), pp. 99–100; T. Christensen, *Origin and History of Christian Socialism* (Aarhus, 1962), pp. 242–69.
129 H. Ashworth, *The Preston Strike* . . . (Manchester, 1854), p. 64; [Holyoake] to [John Bright], [1869], H.C. 1863.
130 G. J. Holyoake, *Secularism, the Practical Philosophy of the People* (Lon-

don, 1854), p. 3; C. Bradlaugh, *Jesus, Shelley and Malthus* (London, 1861), pp. 11, 14, 16; *Reasoner*, 12 December 1858.

131 *Lion*, 4 January 1828.

132 Holyoake, *Rationalism*, p. 36; *Holyoake—Grant Discussion, 1854*, p. 106.

133 W. F. Hook, *On the Means of Rendering More Efficient the Education of the People* . . . (eighth edition, London, 1846), p. 5.

134 *Investigator*, nos. 8, 10, 12, 15 [20 May, 3, 17 June, 8 July 1843]; *Oracle*, 22 April 1843; *Northern Star*, 22 April 1843.

135 *N.M.W.*, 18 July 1840; *Reasoner*, 29 July, 3 June 1846; *Utilitarian Record*, 13 October 1847.

136 *Oracle*, 5 May 1842; *Movement*, 2, 30 October, 27 November, 18 December 1844; *Reasoner*, 1 July 1846.

137 *Investigator*, 1 January 1859.

138 *Utilitarian Record*, 19 May 1847; *Reasoner*, 3, 17 October 1849.

139 *Utilitarian Record*, 13 October 1847; *Reasoner*, 5 January 1848.

140 *Republican*, 22 October, 17 December 1824, 6 May 1825, 21 April, 4 August 1826.

141 *Holyoake—Grant Discussion, 1853*, pp. 192–3; *ibid., 1854*, pp. 137–8, 147–50, 153–4.

142 J. Ellis, *Marriage* . . . (London [1845]), pp. 5–6; Holyoake, *Rationalism*, pp. 40–1.

143 *Republican*, 10 May 1822.

144 *Reasoner*, 26 May 1858.

145 *Republican*, 13 December 1822.

146 G. A. Williams, *Rowland Detrosier, passim*; W. H. G. Armytage, *Heavens Below*, pp. 180–1.

147 Log Book 1, 23 May 1837, H.B.; Holyoake, *Sixty Years*, I, p. 172; *Reasoner*, 19 September 1849; A. H. Nethercote, *The First Five Lives of Annie Besant* (London, 1961), p. 98.

148 *Lancashire Beacon*, no. 7 [17 September 1849].

149 Holyoake, *Rationalism*, pp. 44–5; J. McCabe, *Life and Letters of George Jacob Holyoake*, 2 vols. (London, 1908), I, p. 111.

150 *Cause of the People*, 3 June 1848.

151 *Reasoner*, 24 January 1849, 12 March 1851; C. D. Collet, *History of the Taxes on Knowledge* . . . 2 vols (London, 1899), I, pp. 150–1.

152 C. Gibbon, *George Combe*, II, pp. 10–11, 238, 296–7; B. Simon, *Studies in the History of Education*, pp. 340–1; *Reasoner*, 30 October 1850; *Northern Star*, 2 November 1850.

153 See the following pamphlets in Manchester P.L.: *The Scheme of Secular Education proposed by the National Public Schools Association Compared with the Manchester and Salford Borough's Education Bill* (London 1851); *Report of the Conversazione of Friends and Supporters (of the Manchester and Salford Bill), 28 August 1851*; *The Secular System, the Manchester Bill, and the Government Scheme Contrasted* (London, 1852); *A Few Plain Words on the Two Education Bills now before the Country* (London, 1852).

154 *Reasoner*, 15 May 1850.

155 T. Christensen, *Christian Socialism*, p. 177; G. D. H. Cole, *Century of Co-operation*, pp. 103, 72.

156 *Reasoner*, 10 March, 4 August 1847, 22 March 1848; *Utilitarian Record*

5 April 1848; *Reasoner*, 21 June 1848; McCabe, *op. cit.*, I, pp. 144–6; *Reasoner*, 30 May 1849; Christensen, *op. cit.*, pp. 102–3.

157 *Ibid., passim,* especially pp. 99, 103; *Reasoner*, 19 April 1848.

158 *Ibid.*, 31 October 1849, 22 May, 5 June 1850.

159 *Ibid.*, 15 January 1851; see also the letter in *ibid.*, 5 February 1851.

160 Holyoake to Lechevalier, etc, 9 December 1851, H.C. 449; *Reasoner*, 15 January 1851; Lechevalier, etc, to Holyoake, 16 December 1851, H.C. 450.

161 *Reasoner*, 19 January 1853; Holyoake, *Secularism*, pp. 5—6.

162 *Ibid.*, p. 6; *Holyoake—Rutherford Discussion*, p. 157.

163 Holyoake, *ibid.*, p. 4.

164 *Reasoner*, 19 January 1853

165 *Holyoake—Grant Discussion, 1854*, p. 132.

166 *Ibid., 1853*, p. 4.

167 *Ibid.*, p. 14; W. J. Linton, *Memories*, pp. 162–4.

168 *Holyoake—Grant Discussion, 1853*, p. 6.

169 *Herald of Progress*, 25 October 1845, 25 April 1846.

170 *Reasoner*, 15, 22, 29 July 1846.

171 *Ibid.*, 6 August, 2 September 1846.

172 *Ibid.*, 30 June 1847, 13 June 1849.

173 *Oracle*, 11 March 1843; *The Man Paterson,* preface; *Cooper's Journal*, 19 January 1850.

174 *Oracle*, 13 August 1842; *Reasoner*, 6 August 1846.

175 *Holyoake—Grant Discussion, 1853*, p. 9; *Reasoner*, 4 August 1852.

176 George Hooper to Holyoake, 23 November 1847, H.C. 237; Holyoake to Daniel Baker, 6 June 1849, H.C. 310; diary-cum-notebook, April–June 1849, *passim*, H.B.

177 G. H. Lewes to Holyoake, 8 August 1849, H.C. 316; Hunt to Holyoake, 22 November, 16 December 1849, H.C. 331, 333; pocket diary, 6 October 1849, H.B.; Holyoake and Hunt to Hooper, 17 April 1850, H.B.; Hunt to Henry Travis (printed), 24 October 1850, H.B.

178 'Leader Newspaper Co.—Copy of Deed', H.B.; Hunt to Holyoake, 19 February 1850, H.C. 359; W. B. Jerrold to G. H. Lewes, 1 April 1850, H.C. 367.

179 *Reasoner Tract* No. 8 [29 May 1850], p. 3.

180 *Reasoner*, 25 June, 13 August 1851, 14 January 1852. J. P. Adams later said G. H. Lewes gave Holyoake the name 'Secularist' when the latter went to see him to discuss the *Robespierre—National Reformer*, 27 August 1865.

181 E.g. *Reasoner*, 31 December 1854.

182 D. G. Charlton, *Secular Religions in France, 1815–70* (Oxford, 1963), pp. 43–4.

183 R. K. Webb, *Harriet Martineau*, pp. 299–309; H. Martineau to Holyoake, 6 October [1851], 7 April [?1852], B.M. Add. Mss. 42,726.

184 *Reasoner*, 25 May 1853.

185 *Ibid.*, 1 January 1854; J. K. Ingram to Holyoake, 29 August 1899, H.C. 3763; *Reasoner*, 30 September 1860.

186 *Ibid.*, 12 September 1849.

187 J. S. Mill to Holyoake, 7 December 1848, H.C. 287.

188 *Reasoner*, 2 November 1853.

189 *Ibid.*, 15 October 1854.

190 Holyoake to Leigh Hunt, 28 October 1853, B.M. Add. Mss. 38,111; *Holyoake—Grant Discussion, 1854*, p. 178; *ibid., 1853*, pp. 24–5. For Percy Greg see appendix v.

191 J. Barker, *Confessions of Joseph Barker* . . . (London, 1858), p. 4.

192 'The philosophic type of religion', *Reasoner*, 18 June–2 July 1851, later issued as a pamphlet (London, 1852). Quotations are taken from the *Reasoner*.

193 *Ibid., loc. cit.*

194 *Holyoake—Grant Discussion, 1854*, pp. 15–16, 215.

195 W. Maccall to Holyoake, 6, 27 July 1853, H.C. 577, 581; F. W. Newman to Holyoake, 11 October, 19 November 1853, H.C. 601, 611.

196 C. Southwell, *The Impossibility of Atheism Demonstrated* (London [1852]), p. 20; *Lancashire Beacon*, nos. 6–10 [8 September–6 October 1849].

197 C. Southwell, *Another 'Fourpenny Wilderness'* . . . (London, 1852), p. 17; *Reasoner*, 21 November 1858.

198 C. Southwell, *Review of a Controversy* . . . (London, 1853), pp. 39, 21.

199 *Investigator*, April 1854; *Reasoner*, 5 June 1850; R. Cooper to Holyoake, 19 January 1852, H.C. 460.

200 C. B. Campbell, *Sociology of Irreligion*, pp. 37–8, 53–5; S. Budd, 'Militancy and expediency . . .' (unpublished *Past and Present* Conference Paper, 1966).

201 C. B. Campbell, 'The pattern of religious denominationalism in England' (unpublished Conference Paper, Los Angeles, 1972); B. R. Wilson, 'Sect development', in B. R. Wilson (ed.), *Patterns of Sectarianism* (London, 1967), pp. 23–5.

202 D. F. Aberle, 'A note on relative deprivation theory . . .', in S. L. Thrupp (ed.), *Millennial Dreams in Action* (The Hague, 1962), p. 214.

203 See below, pp. 237–44; also appendix iv.

204 E. Isichei, 'From sect to denomination among English Quakers', in B. R. Wilson (ed.), *op. cit.*, pp. 161–81.

M

4
Holyoake and the first decade of Secularism

a
International freethought

Freethought in the first half of the nineteenth century was very much the product of Enlightenment rationalism, and, as such, it was a Europe-wide phenomenon.[1] Many of the forces which went into the making of Secularism are recognisable in different forms throughout the continent. There were differences, but these are attributable more to the individual political, social and economic circumstances of each country, rather than to a fundamental difference in ideology. For example, anti-clericalism was a potent force throughout Europe, but in the Catholic countries of southern Europe—in Spain and Italy it was especially strong —the usual form which organised freethought took was freemasonry, which, by its secretive nature, was well adapted to the political require-ments of those countries but not suited to the propagation of popular freethought on a wide scale. In France the same was true to a lesser extent, and not until after 1871 was the situation such that freethought could flourish openly. Fourierism, which might have developed as Owenism had in England, was markedly less irreligious than its English counterpart, and in the United States was even regarded as being 'Christian' as opposed to the 'infidelity' of Owenism.[2] The same might be said of Saint-Simonism and Comtism, which were offered as post-Catholic religions and which failed to draw on the widespread anti-clericalism of the Parisian sansculottes.

In Germany the scene was somewhat different, though national organisation was hindered by the political and religious fragmentation of the country. Carl Scholl's 'Church of Humanity' was strong in the Catholic south and east—a congregation of four thousand in Vienna, and ten thousand at Breslau in Silesia—but his churches in Saxony and Prussia were mostly small. Freethought was strong in the Protestant universities, but this very liberalism blunted the edges of popular free-thought's most effective weapons. Yet militant freethought was wide-spread among Germans, as can be seen from its success among the emigrant communities of North America. The principal weaknesses in

Germany itself appear to have lain in the political situation. Where radicals were organised they had immediate political objects to contemplate, and the development of Marxist socialism later in the century was inimicable to old-fashioned 'utopian' freethought. Particularly after 1848, popular societies were repressed and, as in France, could not operate openly. The German organisation *Der Bund*, established by Dr A. Stamm, was largely a federation of refugee committees, optimistically embracing the whole world. London, not Berlin, was its headquarters.[3] The weakness of popular German societies was underlined by Rudolph Hirzel, a German Swiss who had been secretary of the Leeds Secular Society in 1861. He was in Nuremberg in 1865, where he was president of the local Working Men's Society, and he seems to have been making a conscious effort to transplant his British experience to Germany. He started a 'Feuerbach Society' to look after that aged philosopher, and also a 'People's Society', modelled on the London debating societies, to agitate for secular reform. It was, he claimed, 'the first corporation who declared positively for Secular schools, for abolition of the oath, for separation of Church and State, and for the abolition of standing armies'. One should not, perhaps, take the whole of this claim too seriously, but Hirzel's impression is a useful indication of the comparative positions of Britain and Germany at this time. The primacy of the British movement was also apparent in Holland, where R. C. Meijer looked to Holyoake to give leadership to freethought in Europe.[4]

Militant popular freethought, then, was a peculiarly British phenomenon, and it thrived best beyond the seas in those areas where the cultural impact of Britain was greatest. In India, for example, Secularism was a tiny part of that cross-section of British life and thought which was taken to the sub-continent by Anglo-Indians and anglophile natives educated in England. So, in 1846, the first number of the *Reasoner* was able to announce that the weekly publication of infidel tracts had been commenced in Calcutta, the centre of British influence, and that a young man had published his 'General reflections on Christianity containing a brief and philosophic exposition of the folly of believing in the divine origin of Christianity, and relying on it for human salvation'. The *Reasoner* itself appears to have had some circulation in India. A report comes from Bombay that a group of freethinkers, led by a government official, had been formed after the members had read some of Holyoake's works, and in 1860 the *Bombay Guardian* reported that 'as many as 100 copies of Holyoake's paper, the *Reasoner*, are received in Bombay, and read by Parsees and Hindoos with the greatest gusto'. A young Bengali, Rakhal Das Haldar, who had been educated in London, corresponded regularly with Holyoake. In 1863 he was trying, in vain, to raise money for Holyoake's affirmation fund, and was eagerly discussing the Colenso controversy and the situation in Poland and the United States.[5]

The complete mirror of British freethought, though, is to be found even further away still, in Australia and New Zealand. The Auckland Secular Society was founded in 1855, apparently as an *emigré* offshoot of the Paisley society, by Archibald Campbell and his friends. The rules were based on those of the London Secular Society. Times appear to have been hard as the membership crept slowly upwards from ten to fifteen, but these were scattered over a wide area, and in 1859 the society was reported to be 'dormant'. Charles Southwell, who had also emigrated to Auckland, seems to have had little to do with Campbell and his society.[6] Things were somewhat livelier in Australia, where a small group of freethinkers met in Sydney for the first time in 1859 to celebrate Paine's birthday. By 1863 they reported that there were numerous freethinkers in Sydney, and discussions were held with Home Missionaries in the public park on Sundays. In 1861 another society was founded further north at Newcastle, and this organisation illustrates the close connection between the colonial societies and those at home. Between 1856 and 1861 the drive for regional organisation in English West Midlands appears to have come from D. Wallwork, a locksmith of Dudley. Then, shortly after the formation of the Midland Secular Union of which Wallwork was secretary, in 1861, his reports ceased and the Union disappeared; but in 1864 a familiar report came in from Wallwork once more, only this time from Newcastle, New South Wales, where he had opened a Secular Library and was busy distributing Secularist tracts. A year later he had become the secretary of the Newcastle Secular Society and was at the centre of an active movement in the north of the state. The Midlands' loss had been New South Wales' gain.[7]

Most emigrants, though, made their way to the United States, and it is here that we find the largest freethought organisation outside Britain. North America was a cultural extension of Europe, and its freethought was intellectually and socially the same as that found in England. Popular organisations had flourished in the 1790s, as in England, and were revived in the 1820s in the same manner. The initiative came from England as, after 1819, immigrants began to pour into the new country— among them Robert Owen, Robert Dale Owen, Frances Wright, Gilbert Vale, Benjamin Offen, and many other future leaders of American freethought. Dale Owen and Frances Wright were among the most effective propagandists, and their paper, the *Free Enquirer* (1829–36), published in New York, was a thoroughgoing radical and freethought weekly which attracted the same sort of opprobrium as Richard Carlile was meeting in England at the same time. The similarity between the course of freethought in the two countries was evident. Halls of Science and other similar institutions were opened in New York, Boston, Rochester, Pittsburgh and elsewhere in the north-eastern states. Inland, freethought flourished, often in association with Owenism and the communities of the frontier. St Louis had a Society of Free Inquirers in 1829, and a Society of Rational Religionists in 1845. Small groups flourished on the frontier in Illinois and Wisconsin. The works of Carlile were circulated and other rituals of British freethought were faithfully imported. In 1825 the New York emigrés introduced the celebration of Paine's birthday, which, as in England, rapidly became the focal point for popular freethought organisations. Albany and New Hartford, Boston, Nantucket, Paterson and Philadelphia, Providence and Pittsburgh, Cincinnati and St Louis quickly followed suit in the next few years.[8] England received in exchange the works of Elihu Palmer and of Dr Charles Knowlton (on birth-control), while the trial of Abner Kneeland of Boston for blasphemy (1834-38) entered into the popular tradition on both sides of the Atlantic. In the 1850s popular freethought suffered a temporary setback in the United States as the abolitionist issue came to dominate all others. Societies continued though, and the *Boston Investigator*, the longest-lasting freethought periodical of the nineteenth century—1831-1904—was a continual example and reproach to the British Secularists.[9] The most important of all the links between Britain and the United States in the 1850s was Joseph Barker. He had gone to the United States in 1851 and had been converted to freethought by the radical abolitionists, for the Bible upheld slavery. In 1854 he was elected president at the Hartford Bible Convention, a radical freethought gathering; and in 1857 he was engaged in Philadelphia as a lecturer on theological, moral, scientific and general subjects. He appears to have been the leading freethinker in the city, but was unable to attend the next Convention, held there in 1857. He returned to Britain in 1860, a mine of critical information about life across the Atlantic.[10]

Secularism as a particular form of freethought can, therefore, be said to have flourished only in a particular sort of environment—that in which men like Joseph Barker could live and breathe and speak. These were the conditions to be found *par excellence* in mid-nineteenth-century Britain.

The first prerequisite for freethought was freedom. Though by modern standards, and by the ideals of the freethinkers themselves, Britain was oppressively ruled by an authoritarian, class-biased government and clergy, by contemporary standards nineteenth-century Britain was a liberal country. The continental refugees who poured into London and Liverpool and Newcastle certainly thought so. The organisation of Secularism demanded freedom of speech and publication, and the number of prosecutions for blasphemous and seditious libel, though considerable, was almost negligible compared with the thousands of infidel and republican works which circulated freely, and the millions of words which thrilled the faithful followers each year. The campaign for a liberal society needed a liberal society in which to operate.[11]

b
National organisation

'Let our watchwords, then, be "Union and Organisation". Separated, we are mere inorganic elements. United, we shall be a living body, with a circulation of good works from the centre to the circumference, and back again to the heart; and with a brain and nerves insuring harmony of action in the whole living machine.' This extract from the Principles of the Philadelphian Freethinkers, printed in the *Reasoner* in 1858, sums up a deep-felt need on the part of all freethinking groups. Disunity was seen as the bane of all working-class affairs. The *Cause of the People* expressed a common feeling when in 1848 it urged Chartists to seek understanding, energy and organisation, 'that power may not be scattered, but concentrated,—that we may not be beaten in detail, nor lose time or opportunity for want of combined action'.[12]

Chartism had left a dual and contradictory legacy: on the one hand, it had shown the need for unity, but on the other it had demonstrated the danger of trusting all to one powerful leader. Early working-class politics were charismatic, and this was both their strength and weakness. O'Connor had risen to such power because he was needed. His decline appeared to leave Chartism both leaderless and disorientated. Lecturing on the failure of 1848, Holyoake demanded that 'a great political movement' should have a common object, a power of uniting and a leader to direct, for 'Party has been cried down till no one will belong to a party, and yet we affect to wonder and to mourn that there is no large party'. The tensions created between the need for organisation and the natural independence and suspicion of leadership which freethinkers felt lie behind all attempts at Secularist organisation during the decade. 'Differences of views, of tastes, of aims; differences of manners, of temper and of character, unite, with personal enmities, to render the thing impossible,' concluded Joseph Barker in 1861.[13]

The first attempts at organisation arose out of a series of 'Free Discussion Festivals' held at the City Road Hall of Science. The object of these festivals was partly social—a gathering of freethinkers for mutual enjoyment and instruction—and partly an exercise in the right of free discussion. At the first of these festivals, chaired by W. J. Birch on 29 December 1851, Holyoake gave an address on 'The Organisation of Freethinkers' in which he urged the 'intellectually independent' opponents of Christianity to unite to promote those objects which have been described above as Secularism. He saw this as a continuation of the work of the 1840s. The Utilitarian Society he now called the Secular Society, a Central Federation of local societies. The local societies were to be small cells of activists, each of which was to meet every week in a private house to organise its work and to train its members for propagandism. The Central Secular Society was to give general directions. One of the other speakers at the festival, Thomas Evans Bell, also spoke of the need for organisation. It was necessary, he said, so that freethinkers could make themselves known, for mutual protection against the law and public opinion, and for mutual instruction. He even looked forward to the time when Secularism might become a radical political party.[14] Little was done to bring this about, though, and while Holyoake settled down in London to create his Central Secular Society and a centre of propaganda, the real initiative passed to the provinces.

In the spring of 1852 Robert Cooper set out from London on a provincial lecture tour. Everywhere he saw the need for organisation. After visiting Northampton and Nottingham he urged, 'Freethinkers, look to union and to action. *Organisation* is, at this moment, our urgent necessity.' In Bradford he observed, 'Their want is *organisation*. Everywhere this is the cry.' In Heckmondwike he reported that 'the intelligent operatives' had their own room in which they held a secular Sunday school—'a further proof that the materials of an organisation exist'. When he reached his native Manchester he waxed eloquent. His audience was gathered from all the surrounding towns; many of the faces he recognised as belonging to the audiences of his youth; everywhere men desired to see and hear Robert Owen. For Cooper, Secularism meant the socialism of 1840; organisation meant the revival of the Owenites. To him the new moral world was as close as ever: 'Though the vulture of oppression, lay and clerical, is at this moment soaring in brutal ascendancy over Europe, it only needs *organisation* on the part of the peoples themselves to bring it down to the dust. The power of the millions is in their *unity*—their success, in their *perseverance*.'[15]

The first moves towards organisation came in Lancashire, probably in response to Cooper's lecture tour, when James Butterworth of Heywood appealed to freethinking friends in some eighty localities in Lancashire to write to him. A series of regional conferences were then held in Manchester at which a district committee was set up by the representatives of seventeen Lancashire localities, with John Matthews of Heywood as

chairman and Wilkinson Burslam of Manchester as secretary The Lancashire Secularists then convened the first national conference which was
held in the Manchester Secular (formerly Social) Hall on 3 October.[16]
No lasting organisation, regional or national, resulted from these conferences, but the efforts of 1852 did encourage the creation of local
secular societies, marking the beginning of the first period of Secularist
expansion.

Almost all the representatives at the first national conference were
from Lancashire, the neighbouring parts of Cheshire, and the West
Riding, though Holyoake was asked to take the Chair. 'The First Secular
Conference for the Organisation of Freethinkers' was, therefore, little
more than the Lancashire district organisation out of which it sprang.
Nevertheless, Holyoake succeeded in imposing his stamp firmly upon it
and created the basis for a possible national organisation. The Manchester Conference marks the beginning of Holyoake's ten-year rule of
Secularism.[17] Robert Cooper was unable to attend the conference, but
even if he had done so the result would probably not have been much
different. Cooper had urged organisation, but he does not seem to have
worked out how it was to be accomplished. Holyoake, on the contrary,
had been concerned with the problems of organisation ever since the days
of the Anti-Persecution Union. To the Manchester delegates he was the
renowned figure from London, a martyr in the cause of free speech, the
editor of their *Reasoner*. It is not surprising that he was able to assert his
authority.

Holyoake was extremely sceptical about the success of any organisation, and he had thought Cooper's proposals premature. His own plan,
as approved by the conference, was for a loose federation of local societies
controlled by a strong Central Board, not unlike the early structure of
Owenism before the adoption of those autocratic measures associated
with the Queenwood project. He had told the Sheffield Rational Society
that 'The name of an association is of no consequence. Not only names,
but all local constitutions and management, will be left free as much as
possible. The intention is to leave individual activity unfettered, while
securing a common co-operation.'[18] This local freedom was written into
the 'Constitution and Objects of Secular Societies' agreed to by the
conference, but with certain important limitations: Holyoake's own
definition of the nature of Secularism was accepted; the officers of any
local society had to be of good moral character, which meant Holyoake
was determined to avoid the difficulties men like Paterson had caused in
the Anti-Persecution Union; 'the old spirit of indiscriminate disparage-
ment of bodies or antagonism of persons' was declared to be futile; and
a weekly contribution of one halfpenny per member was imposed to

finance a Central Council. The Federation was to be governed by the Central Council which was to be elected annually at a conference of delegates meeting in the provinces every October, and this council was to elect its own central director and secretary. For the first year, until the local societies could be organised, the Council was to be Holyoake, James Watson and W. J. Birch, with Arthur Trevelyan, William Chilton and others as corresponding members. The *Reasoner* was to be the organisation's official paper.[19] In one day Holyoake had outlined an organisation for Secularism, imposed his own doctrine upon it and a levy for the support of his work, and he had nominated himself and his friends as directors. That he was able to come to Lancashire and do this is an indication of his great influence among the former socialists, but he did not command the overwhelming respect accorded to Owen himself, and his supremacy was not to remain unchallenged for long.

After this promising start nothing happened for some time. The next effective step was taken by the most prominent of the London societies, the London Secular Society. This body was formed after a meeting at the City Road Hall of Science, chaired by James Watson, on 1 May 1853, and included many prominent London freethinkers, among them Holyoake and Robert Le Blond, a London businessman who had put at the society's disposal his library of over three thousand books and periodicals. The society decided to send out missionaries to spread the gospel of Secularism, and in the autumn of 1853 Holyoake and Le Blond visited the North East and Scotland. Outside London, however, the society was unable to establish any lasting organisations.[20]

Meanwhile the Lancashire district continued to progress slowly, and a conference was called at Stockport on 2 July 1854 to coincide with a visit from Holyoake. Robert Cooper had been urging the calling of such a general conference since April and, although he was unable to be present at Stockport, he sent a letter of support. His brother, James R. Cooper, proposed that arrangements should be made for calling a full national conference and a provisional committee was appointed to meet in Stockport to consider the matter. This committee, chaired by Joseph Barker and containing representatives from Manchester, Bolton, Huddersfield and Slaithwaite, Oldham, Stockport, Staleybridge [*sic*], Bury and Hyde, decided, on the motion of James Cooper and J. Bamford, the Yorkshire delegate, to call a national conference at Leeds, the object of which should be to create a National Secular Society. Unfortunately there was some confusion over dates and when a joint meeting of Lancashire and Yorkshire societies was finally held at Bradford over Christmas it was attended only by delegates from the Yorkshire societies, though Stalybridge sent a letter.[21]

The next move came from Holyoake, when, at the very end of 1854, he announced that a board of directors, comprising the committee of the London Secular Society and the board of the Manchester conference of 1852, with himself as president, had been formed at his premises at 147 Fleet Street. The committee of the L.S.S. in 1854 included most of the leading London Secularists, with James Watson, president, John Maughan, vice-president, and J. P. Adams, secretary. Holyoake replaced Watson as president in 1855, and was thereafter in a dominant position as leading member of the Manchester committee of 1852, president of the L.S.S. and head of the new Fleet Street board of directors. In the name of 'the Council of Directors appointed at the Secular Conference, Manchester, 1852' he then called a conference at 147 Fleet Street for 16 May 1855. This was a Wednesday and so attendance was small, London men being delegated to represent some of the provincial societies. Robert Cooper, Henry Tyrrell, Holyoake, Le Blond, Maughan and Frederick Farrah, the last four all of the L.S.S., then formed themselves into a 'Preliminary Committee' to organise a general conference to secure unity of action and to act as a Central Board for the societies.[22] Maughan was appointed secretary and he appears to have made strenuous efforts to establish contact with the numerous local provincial societies. He issued a circular, stressing the need for organisation, to which he received replies from all over the country and especially from the north, though, like other attempts at organisation, this effort then seems to have petered out. Holyoake was curiously indifferent. He frequently said he wanted local societies to be unfettered, and praised the local initiative taken by individual districts, but he then announced himself opposed to their schemes and reminded the districts that the action of the Stockport conference of 1854 in calling a national conference was invalid. A conference could be called only by the Manchester committee of 1852.[23]

It is hard to escape the conclusion that Holyoake was satisfied with organisation only when he was at the centre of it. This is what the 1852 plan allowed. During the mid-1850s he was preoccupied in London, especially with the affairs of his publishing establishment in Fleet Street. He would neither call a conference nor permit others to do so. He may have been right. A district-level organisation was perhaps preferable, for it was easier to administer, it preserved local autonomy, and the intermediary authority of the districts could be seen as a bulwark against too much centralised power as it had been in the early days of Owenism. But Holyoake was always skilful at rationalising his own prejudices and he may simply have been too busy to bother. For whatever reason, it is certainly true that the success of Secularism in the 1850s and early 1860s was entirely provincial. The London Secularists were unable to represent truly the aspirations of Lancashire, but without London leadership no organisation could be accepted by the other regions as being truly national.

c

Provincial organisations

The southern parts of England, with the exception of London and its vicinity, do not figure largely in the early history of the Secularist movement. Like other forms of predominantly working-class organisation, Secularism was in the main an urban movement, and the south was largely rural. As Ludlow and Jones said in their *Progress of the Working Class*, 'Ideas of social reform do not easily penetrate, or rapidly spread, among the solitary workers in the fields. They are not given to association.'[24] Secularist groups are therefore to be found only in the towns, and even here they were often very weak. Reports in the Secularist press are few and far between and our whole picture is at best sketchy.

In Norwich, for example, a Discussion Association was formed in 1853, but no further reports occur in the *Reasoner* until 1860 when the following rather apologetic notice was sent in:

> you may be somewhat doubtful of the existence of a Norwich Secular Society, judging by its published proceedings. There is such a Society, nevertheless. . . .[25]

It was probably of recent origin, organised by Lot Hill, a local radical bookseller. On 14 October when the society opened a new hall, eighty people were present and speeches were delivered by Hill, Edward Moulton Adams (the secretary), and a man called Weavers. This was almost certainly Daniel Weavers who had been secretary of the Owenite Branch 51 at Norwich in 1840. The inspiration for this revival may have come from Charles Bradlaugh who had visited Norwich in June, and with Bradlaugh's help the Norwich men then set about organising a similar society in Great Yarmouth.[26] Not until this date was Secularism of any real importance in East Anglia. Elsewhere it had either been confined to the exertions of one man, as at Peterborough where a shoemaker named Edward Scoley sold the *Age of Reason*, the *Reasoner* and the *Logic of Death*;[27] or it was confined to short-lived societies often dependent upon one leader, as at Ipswich where John Cook, a journeyman shoemaker and Chartist, opened the Ipswich Infidel Repository in 1844 and took two copies of the *Movement*. He persevered and in 1848 formed a branch of the Theological Utilitarians which the following year had nineteen

members and the beginning of a small library. But there are no further
reports after 1850, and F. R. Young, who was at Ransome's Agricultural
Works in Ipswich before he became a Secularist lecturer in 1853, makes
no mention of Cook or of his society.[28]

The same sort of pattern could be traced in any number of places in
the rural south. In Brighton a branch of the London Secular Institute
was formed in 1855 which the following January became the Brighton
Secular Society, but then no more is heard of it.[29] Much local organisation
must have been on an *ad hoc* basis. The Isle of Sheppy [*sic*] or Sheerness
Discussion Society met next door to a tavern on a weekday night; when
Holyoake was invited to Gravesend, his host conducted a freethought
publicity campaign for the occasion but did nothing permanent.[30] When
Holyoake visited the railway workers of Swindon in 1847 a society was
formed of 'some twenty or thirty of the more intelligent mechanics who
meet together on Sunday evenings to discuss general questions'.[31] There
is no evidence that they met for long or that they were a specifically freethinking organisation. In Oxford in 1848 a discussion class existed with
eighty members, but scarcely half ever attended and they discussed 'any
subject except positive theology'.[32]

Even in those towns where Owenism had been strong, the Secularists
had singularly little success. Worcester, where Holyoake had held his
first socialist appointment, was disappointing. The Worcester Owenites
were, he noted in 1843, 'believers in a barren god', and their secretary,
Timothy Allen, transferred his energies from Owenism to the Leeds
Redemption Society before his death in 1850.[33] Bristol infidelity was
scarcely more promising. In the 1840s the local leader was H. Cook, a
bookseller and newsagent in Broadmead near the old Hall of Science, but
no society was organised in the city until after Holyoake's visit in 1857.[34]

Only in Devonport was the story slightly different, and this can be
attributed to the heterogeneous nature of the population attracted to this
garrison port, though the Bishop of Exeter was inclined to blame the
weakness of organised religion in the town. There seems to have been
some sort of freethought organisation here throughout the 1850s. A
Secular Society was founded in 1855 with forty members, and when
opposition to their activities mounted a Mr John built a hall in Plymouth 'for the least orthodox of this populous neighbourhood', which
was opened by Holyoake in 1860. The Plymouth, Devonport and Stone-
house Secular Improvement Society was then announced.[35]

This lack of successful organisations in the south was, perhaps, predict-
able, but the cities of the East Midlands with their long-established
crafts and independent workmen might well have been expected to
have formed the basis for a thriving Secularist movement. This was not

the case. Organisation in Northampton, Leicester, Nottingham and Derby was more frequently attempted than further south, but with scarcely more success. In each place, though, the Owenite legacy was strong and individuals seem to have kept the tradition alive. In Northampton, where the continuous history of Secularism begins in 1854, Joseph Gurney, the first president, had been the local secretary in 1840 and 1841. There was continuity of personalities throughout the period. Gurney had been succeeded in 1842 by Richard Foster, the secretary of the Northampton branch of the Theological Utilitarians until his emigration in 1848. Foster's successor, George Corby, was on the committee in 1854. John Bates, the secretary of the 1854 society, and Edward Pebody, its treasurer, held the same offices in a revival of the society in 1860.[36] Gurney remained the backbone both of Secularism and of radical politics. He and Bates were partly responsible for bringing forward Charles Gilpin as the extreme Liberal candidate in the 1857 election; he was elected himself on to the town council in 1858; and it was Gurney who brought Bradlaugh forward as a parliamentary candidate in 1868 and supported him right through the parliamentary struggle.[37]

Secularism in Leicester, Derby and Nottingham followed the same pattern as in Northampton, only in pale imitation of it. The continuity in Leicester was provided by W. H. Holyoak, a local radical bookseller. In 1844 he was secretary of a branch of the Anti-Persecution Union which met in the Social Institution, and in 1853, 1861 and 1867 it was he who called and organised the meetings which founded a Secular Society. Only the last one succeeded, and its president was Josiah Gimson, head of an engineering firm, who in 1845 had been president of the socialist branch. Like Gurney, Gimson became a town councillor and he was responsible for Holyoake's offering himself as Liberal candidate for Leicester in 1884.[38] The Nottingham Secularists, based on Radford's Temperance Hotel in the 1850s, had the same lack of success in their quest for permanency, and in Derby the movement was confined almost entirely to the efforts of Benjamin Hagen who was an ex-Quaker, a socialist, and retired brewer.[39]

The West Midlands showed a little more strength, but even here the freethought organisations were weaker in the 1850s than might have been supposed from the fertile nature of artisan radicalism in Coventry and Birmingham. 'Infidelity in Coventry,' noted Holyoake in 1843, 'is not a ricketty, but a fine-grown boy. More is done than is recorded, and liberal views extend farther than is supposed.' He was presumably referring to the one-time mayor, Abram Herbert, who had helped the Owenites, and in 1848 there was still an active Socialist group in the town. During the 1850s there was no formal Secular Society, but a mutual improvement society, founded in 1851 by C. Shufflebotham, kept the flag flying. It was secular in all but name and, though its membership fell as low as ten at one time, in 1858 it had sixty members, with meetings twice a week and a library of two hundred and fifty volumes. J. C. Farn, the former social missionary, seems to have been involved also, but Shufflebotham must be given most of the credit for the success of the society.[40] Birmingham freethought took a little longer to re-organise. Not till 1854, when 'Christopher Charles' Cattell opened his Eclectic Institute, was there any formal organisation, and only in 1860 did he and Thomas Ranford, the local bookseller, really begin 'to take steps to ensure more united action through the Midland districts'. The real inspiration for organisation in the West Midlands, in 1856 and again in 1861, came from the Black Country which looked to Birmingham to create a regional union.[41]

The characteristics of Secular Societies throughout the industrial districts of Great Britain were very similar to those of the Midland towns. In Newcastle and Liverpool, Glasgow and Sheffield, societies grew and declined, afforded hope and then withered away, were reorganised and suffered neglect, adopted new names and made new resolutions. The same people, by and large, figured in all of them. The histories of no two societies were exactly the same, but they all shared in at least two of the main features of Secularism: they were rooted in Owenism, and they were most successful in the growing industrial districts where regional collaboration was most easily achieved.

First, Secularism was rooted in Owenism. Where Owenism had been strong, it also was strong. This is partly because the thickly populated industrial areas were hotbeds for all such movements, and partly because Secularism was a development of, and principal heir to, socialism. The continuous history of the Paisley society under James Motherwell is the best example of this, but the transition from the one to the other is most clearly illustrated by the development of the Sheffield branch. The Sheffield Owenites, dominated by their president, Isaac Ironside, never lost control of their Hall of Science, but they did fail to keep pace with the times. William Lawton, secretary of the branch in 1847, represented the society at the Manchester conference in 1852. There he reported only thirty-two members, but said that Sheffield had 'a large population of freethinkers'. The number was certainly in excess of those who attended meetings of the organisation at the Hall of Science. Holyoake was invited to Sheffield in 1851 'by an unknown party'—unknown, that is, to Isaac Ironside and his followers. In October 1852 there were two letters from Sheffield in the *Reasoner*, one advocating the formation of a Secular Society in the town, the other saying the writer had never heard of the Sheffield Rational Society. When Joseph Barker and Holyoake lectured there in 1854, 'The oldest freethinkers in the town were astonished at the great number of people who crowded the theatre, and sympathised with the views enunciated'. The final breach between the old and the new came in 1855 when Ironside was converted to Urquhartism. A new Secular Association was formed which met at Heald's Temperance Hotel in Arundel Street and which was much more outward looking than the old Rational Society. The leading figure from 1857 was Henry Turner, a warehouseman and sometime lecturer at the Mechanics' Institute. After a discussion between Bradlaugh and Brewin Grant in 1858, the society expanded and moved into the North Street schoolroom. The membership continued to grow, and in October, when it had reached sixty-three, the secularists moved back into the Hall of Science where they proposed in 1860 to open a Sunday School.[42]

Such continuity is more typically illustrated by events in Manchester, because here the society did not manage to retain its Hall of Science, which was finally relinquished by the socialists in 1850. In that year they moved to St Patrick's Hall in Garratt's Road where they opened a co-operative store, and in this state Robert Cooper found them when he urged the 'old guard' to reorganise themselves in 1852. This they did and, calling themselves a Secular Society and their hall a Secular Institution, they acted as hosts to the 1852 conferences and began to plan a new hall of their own. They never achieved this aim. In 1853 their landlord cancelled the tenancy, they were made homeless, and until 1856 they had only a small committee room in George Street. Lectures had to be given in the People's Institute in Heywood Street. Then they obtained the St John's Temperance Hall in Hewitt Street until 1859, when they transferred to the former premises of the New Co-operative Store in Queen Street, Hulme. There had been no break in organisation, but not until 1867 did they acquire permanent premises.[43]

A second general feature of the development of provincial Secularism was its social nature. Individual societies did not usually have a long life, but where several such societies were situated closely together they appear to have gained strength from each other. Being a member of a tiny society in a large town must have seemed a pointless activity when there was no persecution or visiting lecturer to lend excitement, but where friends in neighbouring societies could be visited and rallies planned in different places Secularism as a social organisation seems to have thrived, and the clearest evidence of Secularist progress is in the development of regional unions.

Unions were attempted in the West Midlands in 1856 and 1861; the Central Valley of Scotland in 1854, following visits from Cooper, Holyoake and Southwell, and in 1861 following the opening of new premises in Glasgow by Holyoake;[44] on Tyneside; and in Lancashire and the West Riding. The example of the north-east illustrates the nature and strength of regional—as opposed to local or national—organisation at this time. As with Birmingham in the Midlands, Newcastle provided the regional centre but not the initial inspiration—that came in 1856 from E. Thompson of Bishop's Wearmouth. Prompted by the creation of local societies at South Shields in 1855 and in Durham the following year after lectures by Cooper, he called upon Secularists from Newcastle, Shields, Darlington, and 'also many important villages' to form a 'Northern Union of Secular Societies'. Some of the village debating societies could be quite strong. In County Durham, for example, there was a flourishing little society at Cockfield, which was started on New Year's Day 1856 and lasted for several years, drawing in Secularists from the neighbouring villages of Wolsingham and Hamsterley.[45] The strength of regional Secularism lay in its ability to link such small groups in a worthwhile organisation. Its development depended very often not on the large towns themselves but on the exertions of individual men, perhaps from small communities, assisted by occasional visits from the national leaders. Nowhere was this more true than in the textile areas of Lancashire and Yorkshire. Nearly half of the regular societies recorded in the provinces during the period 1837–1866 were in these two areas, which give an epitome of all the forces creating the provincial Secularist movement.

There was a very strong Owenite tradition. Again, nearly half the Owenite societies had been in this area, which was also the cradle of the co-operative movement. The population was thickly spread. A circle with a radius of twenty-five miles drawn around Manchester, thought Lloyd Jones, 'would hold within it a greater number of large busy towns than perhaps could be found within the same space on any other portion of the globe'. Such a population would be larger than that of London, thought the translator of Léon Faucher's description of Manchester.[46] When one local society failed here the tradition could be maintained in the neighbourhood by other societies. Ashton and Stalybridge, for example, had both shared Branch 29 of the Rational Society and they were to share much Secularist organisation as well. With so many groups there was no shortage of local talent, which meant that the progress of Secularist development was never dependent upon the accident of personalities. Indeed there was a surplus of good local leaders, and Lancashire and the West Riding even exported lecturers to other parts of the country as they had in the days of Owenism: when the Scottish Secularists joined forces in 1856 they engaged as their lecturer Joseph Bowker of Huddersfield.[47] During the 1850s attempts at regional organisation outside Lancashire and the West Riding failed, though more successful unions were to be created in the later 1860s; in Lancashire and Yorkshire the attempts were successful at a comparatively early date, and the two counties set the pace for elsewhere in the country, both regionally and nationally.

Secularism was based primarily on Owenism, but it also drew on the Chartist tradition. Holyoake was not only one of the last members of the Owenite Central Board; he was also one of the last members of the last executive of the National Charter Association. The new organisations of the 1850s can therefore be seen as embodying Holyoake's followers in both movements. This is particularly well illustrated by developments in the West Riding. A Chartist delegate meeting had been held at Mitchell's Temperance Hotel, Bradford, on 9 May 1852, at which Thomas Wilcock had spoken up in defence of Holyoake's conduct as a member of the National Charter Association executive. A month later we find Wilcock calling a meeting of West Riding Secularists, also at Mitchell's, to consider the decisions of the first Lancashire district conference. As a result of this meeting a West Riding Secular Alliance (W.R.S.A.) was formed with Wilcock as secretary. Just at the moment when Chartism was breaking up Secularism seems to have provided a substitute. Shortly afterwards a Bradford Secular Society was announced under the presidency of Wilcock. We can presume that this body too recruited its members largely from Bradford Chartism, for not only did the Secularists continue to use Mitchell's, which was the Chartist meeting-place, but one of their first acts as a society was to debate the suffrage and to plan a traditional Chartist camp meeting at Shipley Glen. In the personality of Wilcock, the constitution of the West Riding Secular Alliance, and the activities of the Bradford Secular Society we can see direct continuity at the local level between one wing of local Chartism and Holyoake's Secularism.[48]

The Lancashire and Yorkshire attempts at organisation did not at first prosper. Lancashire concentrated on its plans for a national conference, while in Yorkshire the foundations of the district organisation were laid at quarterly district meetings.[49] A new impetus came in 1854 when 'Atheos' of Huddersfield wrote to the *Investigator*, pointing out that groups of Secularists existed 'in nearly every town' and urging

> a number of societies in contiguous towns and villages to unite together and form a union, like the Wesleyan Methodists and Sunday-school Union, say, for instance, Leeds, Bradford, Wakefield, Huddersfield, Keighley, Todmorden &c., to have district meetings; and every *three* months let a *'plan' be issued*, stating where meetings will be held, and the names of local advocates . . . After a district is formed, let there be a central council and secretary, for the purpose of engaging lecturers to lecture throughout the districts.

N

Robert Cooper agreed with this proposal and suggested it should be applied to the whole country, with districts based on Manchester, Blackburn, Nottingham, Stoke, Glasgow and Dundee.[50]

'Atheos' may well have been W. H. Johnson, who was rapidly emerging as one of the most vigorous Secularists in Yorkshire. He wrote again to the *Investigator* in December 1854, urging the formation of a West Riding District with a full-time district missionary, and after several meetings of the W.R.S.A. arrangements were completed in April 1855 for a new West Riding Secular Union (W.R.S.U.—still sometimes referred to as the Alliance) to implement such a scheme. The December quarterly meeting divided the county into seven districts, based on the towns of Huddersfield, Leeds, Halifax, Bradford, Keighley, Todmorden and Stalybridge—the inclusion of the latter being the only tribute to the attempts of the Lancashire Secularists to create a national organisation in 1855.[51] The Stalybridge Secularists, in fact, furnish the best example of how these districts were meant to operate.

The original lead in Stalybridge seems to have come from the secularists and friends of Tintwistle who began meeting together during the autumn of 1855 in the house of Joseph Blunt, a tailor from Tintwistle who had been an active Owenite for nearly twenty years. Then, following the decision of the W.R.S.U., they came together with their neighbouring Secularists in 1856 to form the most comprehensive organisation to be found anywhere at the local level during the 1850s. Four societies were originally represented: at Stalybridge, led by Mr Norris, a bookseller; at Hyde, led by Willis Knowles, another bookseller; at Ashton, led by Charles Greenwood; and at Tintwistle, led by Joseph Blunt. The latter was president, J. Williamson was treasurer, and J. Andrew, secretary. The first quarterly meeting, held at Tintwistle on 21 September, was attended by between thirty and forty members from Ashton, Dukinfield, Hyde, Stalybridge and Tintwistle, and the next, at Newton in March 1857, showed no diminution in strength. The following winter more elaborate arrangements were made and a plan was issued. Meetings were to be held on Sundays at 2 p.m.: the first Sunday in each month at J. Andrew's in Stalybridge; the second at W. Knowles's in Hyde; the third at J. Blunt's in Tintwistle; the fourth at C. Greenwood's in Ashton; and the fifth, when there was one, at J. Biltcliffe's, Mill Brook, near Stalybridge. The organisation does not, however, appear to have survived for a third full winter. In January 1859 the *Reasoner* contained a notice from Stalybridge that the Secular work had fallen out of regular order and that the plan of lectures had not been kept to.[52]

During 1856 and 1857 the main body of the W.R.S.U. also continued to prosper. The first lecture of the new Union was given by W. H. Johnson on 20 May 1856 at High Barton, on the appropriate subject of 'The Life and Philosophy of Robert Owen', after which those present decided to form 'the Barton Secular Society for the Suppression of Infidelity among Christians'. About the same time Joseph Bowker was appointed District Missionary, and David Woffenden of Lockwood opened a Saturday-night market stall in Huddersfield, which he called the 'West Riding Secular Establishment'. The W.R.S.U. was now at its peak, extending its activities over a wide area and involving men from many of the various local communities. The Committee of the Union in 1856 represented Halifax, Bradford, Huddersfield, Slaithwaite, Northowram, Queenshead, Holmfirth, Sowerby Bridge, Bradshaw, Greetland, Elland, Mountain, Wike, Thornton, Ossett and Dewsbury, with Jeremiah Olive of Halifax as president and Thomas Oates of Northowram as secretary.[53] The aims of the West Riding Secularists, which were set out at the June quarterly meeting and in a circular issued in August 1856, were to hold a series of camp meetings and to visit various towns and villages to explain the objects of the Union; to promote lectures and the distribution of tracts; and to establish a West Riding Sick and Benefit Society. In 1857 Jeremiah Olive was able to claim that these objects had been partly achieved, but, even as he wrote, decline was setting in.[54]

In the mid-1850s Secularism in the West Riding was sufficiently strong to support its own monthly periodical, the *Yorkshire Tribune*, which is the earliest example of sustained local initiative independent of the London leadership. This paper is particularly interesting because, although its editor, William Mitchell of Stanningley near Leeds, used his publication to express views not necessarily those of the official W.R.S.U., the contents can give us some idea of the real concerns of provincial Secularists at the grass-roots level. The *Tribune*, subtitled 'a monthly Journal of Democracy and Secularism for the People', was first and foremost a Chartist paper and was concerned to perpetuate the Chartist cause in the West Riding. Theological Secularism was only a small part, and atheism an even smaller part, of the West Riding movement. The aims of the *Yorkshire Tribune* were, in order of priority, universal suffrage; the rights of labour; secular education by the state; nationalisation of land; Home Colonisation; Maine Law; Rights of Women; and freedom of opinion. Mitchell wished to see an alliance of atheists, Christian Brethren ('Barkerites') and Unitarians, of Secularists and Chartists, to preach the gospel of Democracy and Secularism. He considered Secularism on its own to be too weak and so urged united action, just as Tory, Whig and Peelite factions in Parliament had united under Lord Aberdeen. For Mitchell, and probably for many northern Secularists, Secularism was really seen as a revival of the mass movement for

social and political reform which had been so strong in the 1840s. 'Is it
forgotten how many have met at Blackstone-Edge, at Skirtcoat Moor, or
at Shipley Glen?' he asked his readers. 'It will be so again when we give
the call.'[55]

When W. H. Johnson went to live in Blackburn in 1855, he took with
him into Lancashire the same passion and desire for organisation which
he had shown in Yorkshire, and he seems to have been responsible for
calling a delegate meeting at Manchester 'to consider the organisation'
of the district. The meeting was chaired by James Robertson of Manchester and attended by W. H. Johnson, Austin Holyoake, James and
Robert Cooper, and delegates from Stockport, Rochdale, Bury, Ashton,
Oldham, Bolton, Stalybridge and Hyde. A District Board of six members
was appointed with objects similar to those of the West Riding Secular
Union. The Ashton and Stalybridge Union was reported to be working
'uncommonly well', and prospects were encouraging in Rochdale,
Bolton, Bury and Blackburn.[56]

The result of these organisations, now existing on both sides of the
Pennines, was a greater co-ordination of activities throughout the north.
Camp meetings were very popular. Joseph Jagger of Honley suggested
that the Honley and Holmfirth Secularists should walk to Dunford
Bridge on 5 July 1857, and the Huddersfield Secularists, led by David
Woffenden, and the Stalybridge Secularists asked to join them. In the
end many Secularists from all over the Huddersfield and Ashton districts
gathered at Dunford Bridge in response to this initiative from one of the
smallest village societies. The occasion was such a success that a further
meeting was held at Bills o'Jacks on Saddleworth Moor on 6 September,
at which the Lancashire District Board issued an address to all the
Secularists in the North of England, appealing for union and regularly
subscribed funds.[57]

Camp meetings now became a regular feature of Secularism in the
north. In June 1858, two thousand Secularists from fifteen societies, all
within a radius of twelve miles of Hollingworth Lake, gathered at that
favourite Lancashire excursion ground to hear open-air speeches from
Holyoake, Johnson and James Cooper. The latter referred to 'the dis-
organisation and falling off of the Secular cause', but was refuted by
James Robertson. The meeting then discussed organisation to agitate
for the Jew Bill, Sunday recreation and boats on Hollingworth Lake.
This meeting was the most impressive Secularist gathering so far held
and although the histories of the individual societies bear out Cooper's
complaint, there was little sign of decline at Hollingworth Lake. The
numbers may have been exaggerated, but not grossly so. The *Reasoner*'s
estimate of two thousand was deliberately low and the *Manchester*

Examiner and Times estimated more than twice that number. The Yorkshire Secularists held three more camp meetings that summer. One of them, called by the Sheffield Secularists at Saltersbrook on the Yorkshire–Cheshire–Derbyshire border, launched a testimonial fund for Charles Bradlaugh, who was rapidly emerging as a popular lecturer, especially in the north, at this time and who had been largely responsible for reviving the Sheffield society. The Bradford part of the union meanwhile organised its usual Shipley Feast camp meeting in Shipley Glen with Holyoake as principal speaker. Then, at the end of the same month, the Holmfirth Secular Society, complete with Holmfirth Temperance Brass Band, proceeded to Bills o'Jacks where they hoped to meet contingents from Hyde, Ashton, Oldham, Stalybridge, Rochdale, Honley and Huddersfield.[58]

All was not so well as this Sunday recreational activity suggests. 'A Looker On' who had attended the Shipley Glen meeting asked whether the Secularists were making the best use of their materials. He claimed 'that there is scarcely a Secularist meeting-room in the West Riding open at present', and asked what had become of the West Riding Secular Alliance. To judge solely from the reports in the *Reasoner*, the Alliance (or Union) was still flourishing. Meetings were held at Huddersfield in October and November. Joseph Jagger of Honley was president and Jeremiah Olive of Halifax secretary. The following year several hundred attended a camp meeting at Bills o'Jacks in June, and a thousand one at Saltersbrook in July. Yet the organisation had become hollow and the camp meetings were mere froth. They show that Secularism as a popular movement had succeeded, at least temporarily, and that it was filling the void left by Chartism and was providing an alternative to Sunday School outings and the social activities of the Chapel, but earnest Secularists like the Cooper brothers and Bradlaugh looked for something more. They wanted committed Secularist groups, for without commitment interest would soon wane or be diverted into other channels. Bradlaugh had helped create such a committed society at Sheffield. In 1859 he spoke to the Bradford Secularists about the need to renew their organisation and he held up before them the example of Sheffield; and Henry Turner, the Sheffield secretary, was not slow to urge others to follow the example of his own society.[59]

The rebuilding which went on at the local level in 1859 and 1860 gave new power and meaning to the mass meetings, and the summer programme for 1860 was planned to lead up to a grand climax with a camp meeting for the whole north of England on Castle Hill, near Huddersfield, on 3 June. The meeting was washed out by rain and another was called for 29 July.[60] Meanwhile more local rallies were held, and on 11 June Halifax, Huddersfield, Oldham, Bolton, Rochdale and Todmorden Secularists made their way to Hollingworth Lake where a meeting of over two thousand people, chaired by James Cooper, was addressed by Robert Cooper, Bradlaugh and Johnson.[61] This number was dwarfed by the size of the second Castle Hill meeting at the end of the month. Over five thousand people attended, which is not an implausible figure if the gathering be regarded as a recreational activity, similar to a modern football match. Over one thousand came by special train. Holyoake presided, and John Watts, Austin Holyoake, J. H. Gordon, J. Barker and Bradlaugh were all present. Indeed, every major Secularist leader, except Robert Cooper who was ill and J. B. Bebbington, attended. This meeting was the greatest single demonstration of Secularist strength. Henry Turner thought that as a demonstration this one united mass meeting had achieved more than all the separate meetings could have done alone, and as a result of this new-found solidarity arrangements were made for a convention to meet at Halifax in October to create a new national organisation.[62]

More local rallies were held throughout the summer. The usual Shipley Glen meeting was held by the Bradford society in August and, also in August, the Oldham Secularists arranged a Lancashire meeting on Tandle Hill, which was addressed by Holyoake and attended by two thousand people.[63] The Halifax Conference, however, revealed the same lack of basic organisation of which Cooper and Bradlaugh had long been aware. In April Bradlaugh had found societies organised to his satisfaction only at Sheffield, Halifax, Bradford, Oldham, Bolton and Rochdale.[64]

The balance was corrected in 1861, and this time the meetings did lead to more lasting regional organisations. Another Castle Hill meeting was arranged for 21 July and, though bad weather halved the morning attendance, some five to six thousand came in the afternoon. Then the Lancashire Secularists held a meeting at Oldham, 'to arrange for an outdoor demonstration' which took place on Boardman's Edge on 11 August with Royton Brass Band in attendance. Bradlaugh was the chief speaker to a crowd of over two thousand people which the police tried to move on in vain. Out of this gathering came a determination to organise the Lancashire District. Further meetings were held, and in December a new Lancashire Secular Union was announced. A similar event occurred across the Pennines where the newly formed Leeds Society announced a Yorkshire Secular Association to replace the by-now moribund W.R.S.U., and, also in December, a delegate meeting was called to discuss the promotion of Secularism in Yorkshire.[65]

d
London freethought

While Secularism in the north, led by Bradlaugh, was taking the initiative in creating a vigorous basis for a new provincial—and eventually national—organisation, Secularism in London was developing along its own individual lines.[66] London had a long radical tradition, a large and concentrated population, and was the centre of working-class journalism and leadership. Lecturers were readily available, rooms and audiences were easily obtained, and the leaders of Secularism lived in London. A study of London Secularism therefore presents problems which are either absent or of less importance in the provinces. Radical groups were so plentiful in London that it is hard to distinguish between Secularist organisations and other organisations which co-operated with, and often shared premises, membership and even leadership with the Secularists. Furthermore, to a greater extent than in the provinces, coffee house discussion clubs of indeterminate structure could easily be formed. As M. Q. Ryall wrote in 1843 in an article on the 'Progress of Free discussion', there were in the metropolis a number of 'well-conducted places' —public coffee houses and social institutions—'in which much good temper, spirit, and freedom are preserved', and continued to be preserved throughout the Victorian period.[67]

It is therefore difficult to pin-point Secularism in London, and any examination of it from the reports which appear in the periodicals of the movement must necessarily be even more inadequate than an application of the same method to the provinces. Nevertheless some picture can be built up. First there were those societies which were more than ordinary local organisations; secondly there were those which can, more or less, be called Secular societies—though they were often merely groups existing in definable geographical areas but without permanent meeting places; and thirdly there were those organisations which, whilst not being specifically Secularist, were sympathetic to some of the views of the Secularists.

The Central Secular Society, which was to have been at the heart of a federation of local societies, became, at a meeting held at the Hall of Science on 1 May 1853, the London Secular Society. It quickly enrolled over a hundred members and had branches in Paddington, at John Street and in Woolwich. Samuel Pooley was employed as full-time missionary, and Holyoake and Le Blond were sent on a tour of the provinces. James Watson, the first president, was replaced by Holyoake in 1855 and the L.S.S. reached its peak shortly afterwards. It then declined to the level of a local organisation, partly because of internal disputes between Holyoake and Bradlaugh, who became president in 1858, but mainly because it lost its permanent premises in 1857 when Thomas Cooper, newly reconverted to Christianity, temporarily acquired the Hall of Science as the City Road Chapel. With the general revival of Secularism in 1860 the General Secular Benevolent Society, an offspring of the L.S.S., took over its functions and acted in many ways as a link organisation rather like the provincial unions in the north. It organised excursions on Sundays, but these were normally on a much smaller scale than the northern camp meetings—the annual excursion to Rosherville Gardens, near Gravesend, on Sunday 18 August 1861 was attended by two hundred and forty 'ladies and gentlemen'. Again as in the north, a desire for greater unity arose out of this recreational activity, and a meeting was held on 28 August to consider 'the present position of the Secularist Party in England; and the advisability of renewing the activity of the London Secular Society, and the employment of its funds either in Propagandist efforts or otherwise'. Those present then announced a new body, called the 'General Secular Reformers' Society'. The man behind this move was John Maughan, former vice-President of the L.S.S., secretary to the Secular Provisional Committee and secretary of the Benevolent Society.[68]

Yet Secularism was not strong in London, considering the size of the population. Apart from the two major centres—the City Road Hall of Science and the John Street Institution—there were only seven societies which met at all regularly between 1851 and 1861: the North East London Secular Society (Euston or King's Cross), the West London Secular Society (Marylebone or Paddington), the South London Secular Society (Blackfriars), the London Secular Society (principally at the City Road Hall of Science), the City Forum (Barbican), a Clerkenwell group, and the East London Secular Society (Philpot Street). Even these societies did not always meet every year or throughout the year. The group which used the Commercial Hall, Philpot Street, usually led by J. P. Adams, had good and bad periods, and was fairly typical. Reports of meetings at Philpot Street occur during every year between 1851 and 1860, but during 1858 there are indications that a new start had to be made. The hall was finally closed down in 1860 after a riot, and Adams seems to have transferred his efforts to the City Road Hall of Science.[69] Another example of tenuous continuity was to be found south of the river in the Blackfriars area. This part of London had a long infidel tradition, going back to the days when Carlile had held the Rotunda and when the Lambeth Branch of the Rational Society had included Southwell and Holyoake amongst its members. The socialists left the Rotunda in 1844, and Holyoake launched a fund to turn it into a Philosophical Institute for Emma Martin, but the landlord refused to let it for atheistical purposes. Meanwhile the Owenites moved temporarily to St George's Temperance Hall, Webber Street, and then to the Social Institution at 5 Charlotte Street, Blackfriars Road. Southwell acquired these latter premises in October 1844 and opened them as the 'Paragon Hall and Coffee House', where Socialists and atheists met until he gave up the premises in 1848. They then took another hall in Blackfriars Road until, in 1849, they acquired the Chartist Hall at the corner of Webber Street and Blackfriars Road. Southwell continued to dominate the area on his return from the provinces, and in 1853 he obtained the Providence Chapel in St George's Road, near the Elephant and Castle, which he converted into St George's Hall. When he left for Glasgow in 1854, Henry Tyrrell continued to manage the hall until September 1856, when it became the Birkbeck School Rooms. The freethinkers moved out to the Newington Hall, Francis Street, Walworth, where a South London Freethought, Literary, and Scientific Society was started 'for the promotion of Free Inquiry, Intellectual Improvement and Secular Progress', but the following year premises were again acquired in Blackfriars Road, with John Watts as the manager. The Society settled there until 1862 and, after a brief period in Waterloo Road, returned in 1866. Despite fluctuations and set-backs, the freethinkers of Blackfriars had maintained a continuous tradition from the days of Carlile to the foundation of the National Secular Society.[70]

Not all places were so fortunate. The Hackney/Hoxton area was strong in 1850, but appears to have faded during the course of the next few years. Mrs E. Sharples Carlile's Warner Street Temperance Hall was a centre of activity when the young Charles Bradlaugh first attended and conducted Secularist meetings there in 1850, and J. P. Adams used it as a base for his Victoria Park missions. In 1852 a new Secular Hall was built in Goldsmith's Row, but this had to be pulled down again when the landlord objected to it. The initiative in the mid-1850s seems to have passed across the Kingsland Road to Isaac Sparkhall, a 'fashionable silk and felt hat maker' who was secretary of the Hoxton Secular School Rooms in 1855 and who took part in the campaign to prevent the enclosure of part of Victoria Park in that year. John Maughan's name is associated with the work in Hoxton in 1856, but thereafter organisation seems to have been sporadic: during 1861 discussions were held on Monday and Thursday evenings in a Harvey Street lecture hall, but in May these were discontinued and no further announcements concerning the area appear in the *National Reformer* until the Freethought Propagandist Society moved there for a few months in 1865.[71]

Small, scattered and short-lived societies made up the rest of Secularism
in northern, eastern and southern London in the 1850s: the Tower
Hamlets Literary Institution, opened in 1853 in the former Morpeth
Street Baptist Chapel; the Stepney Secularists, who held lectures and
discussions in 1855; the King's Cross Secular Society, which held Sunday
lectures in 1856; the North London Secular Institute, which acquired
'a large Hall for Sunday evening lectures, and discussions during the
week' in Weston Street, Somers Town; William Worseldine's group at
no. 8 Clerkenwell Green; the Woolwich friends who met at Langham's
Coffee House in 1854, and were called together again in 1856 by a local
newsagent who wanted them 'to adopt measures for the extension of
Freethought and discussion'.[72] Secularism in London consisted largely
of such groups, which were local and limited, their strength often coming
from outside leaders like J. P. Adams and John Maughan. Further
organisation was not really necessary. As long as halls were available for
lectures, the national leaders were near enough at hand to maintain the
freethought tradition without such formal organisations as were to be
found in the provinces.

In the West End, apart from the Paddington Society, there were no
long-lasting Secularist groups which belonged exclusively to the Secularists. Even the John Street Institution was not wholly under their control.
In 1859 it was at a low ebb, and audiences at lectures had fallen to between twenty and eighty. 'They had aimed at conventional respectability
that they never can reach, and lost the respect of earnest and thoughtful
reformers,' said Austin Holyoake, and W. Turley pointed out that
neither Bradlaugh nor G. J. Holyoake was on the committee. Revival
came in 1861 when the long-planned Cleveland Street Hall and Jenkins
Institution was at last opened, but even then the meetings did not always
appeal to the more rugged freethinkers who frequented the Hall of
Science: Charles Bradlaugh complained that it was 'half way between
a methodist chapel and a Quaker's meeting house'.[73]

There were a number of 'half-way' societies in London in which the
Secularists played a part. One of the most important was the Free
Inquirers' Society, of which Holyoake was president in 1849; and
J. P. Adams's Society of Materialists, founded in 1857 in opposition to
Holyoake, was never an official Secular society though it was Secularist
in all but name.[74] There were also foreign societies: the Humanistic
Society, founded by Johannes Ronge, the German religious radical; and
Dr A. Stamm's German Alliance which met at 147 Fleet Street.[75] On
a more respectable level came the Society of Independent Religious
Reformers, or Free Church, which met in Newman Street off Oxford
Street under the leadership of P. W. Perfitt; William Maccall's pan-

theistic Brotherhood of the Religious Life which met at John Street; and, above all, the liberal-Unitarian South Place Chapel with its notable preachers, W. J. Fox, Newenham Travers, Henry Ierson, H. N. Barnett, and P. W. Perfitt.[76]

London therefore presents a complex, colourful and diverse pattern of freethought. It is easy to see how, under these circumstances, the rougher edges could be worn off Secularism. As in the case of Chartism, London provided a leadership more sophisticated than the provincial body, and this created a number of difficulties for the leaders since the real heart of the movement lay outside the metropolis.

Notes

1 See J. M. Robertson, *A Short History of Freethought*, pp. 385–92, and the same author's *History of Freethought in the Nineteenth Century*; also S. P. Putnam, *400 Years of Freethought* (New York, 1894), and A. Post, *Popular Freethought in America 1825–1850* (New York, 1943).

2 *Ibid.*, pp. 184–5.

3 *Reasoner*, 10 September 1851; A. Post, *op. cit.*, pp. 118–21, 197–8; S. P. Putnam, *op. cit.*, p. 639; *Reasoner*, 14 May 1854.

4 *Ibid.*, 1 July 1865; R. C. Meijer to W. J. Birch, 18 May 1860, Letter Book consulted privately in I.I.S.H., Amsterdam.

5 *Reasoner*, 3 June 1846, 3 March 1858, 10 June 1860; *National Reformer*, 8 March 1862; Rakhal Das Haldar to Holyoake, 21 August 1863, H.C. 1509.

6 *Reasoner*, 29 April, 30 September 1855, 16 March 1856, 8 May 1859.

7 *Ibid.*, 15 May 1859; *Investigator*, 1 June 1859; *National Reformer*, 17 October 1863, 7 May 1864, 6 August 1865, 13, 20 May 1866.

8 A. Post, *op. cit.*, pp. 32–44, 74–118, 155–8; also J. F. C. Harrison, *Robert Owen and the Owenites*, pp. 54–5.

9 A. Post, *op. cit.*, pp. 71, 52–7

10 J. T. Barker (ed.), *The Life of Joseph Barker* . . . (London, 1880), pp. 311–315, 338–41; S. P. Putnam, *op. cit.*, pp. 520–1.

11 See H. Weisser, 'Chartist internationalism, 1845–48', *Historical Journal*, XIV (1971), p. 52.

12 *Reasoner*, 3 February 1858; *Cause of the People*, 17 June 1848.

13 *Reasoner*, 4 July 1849; *National Reformer*, 22 June 1861.

14 *Reasoner*, 14 January 1852.

15 *Ibid.*, 7, 28 April, 26 May 1852.

16 *Ibid.*, 4, 19 May, 14, 28 July, 8, 29 September 1852. According to Brewin Grant, Cooper originated the Secular Conference—*Holyoake–Grant Discussion, 1853*, p. 422.

17 *Reasoner*, 20, 27 October 1852, and supplement, 10 November 1852.

18 *Ibid.*, 20 October, 22 September 1852.

19 *Ibid.*, supplement, 10 November 1852.

20 *Ibid.*, 18 May, 1, 8 June, 7 September, 5 October 1853.

21 *Investigator*, April 1854; *Reasoner*, 23 July, 6 August 1854; *Investigator*, December 1854; *Reasoner*, 24 December 1854, 14 January 1855.

22 *Reasoner*, 31 December, 4 June 1854, 15 April, 27 May 1855; *Investigator*, June 1855.

23 *Reasoner*, 17 June, 23 December 1855, 28 June 1857.

24 Ludlow and Jones, *Progress of the Working Class*, p. 5. For the distribution of societies see appendix 1.

25 *Reasoner*, 26 October 1853; *Reasoner Gazette*, 12 August 1860.

26 *Ibid.*, 4 November, 2 December 1860. For Weavers see *National Reformer*, 5 May 1867.

27 *Reasoner*, 13 August 1851.

28 *Movement*, 13 April 1844; *Reasoner*, 1 November 1848, 3 January 1849; *Northern Star*, 2 February 1850. For Young see appendix v.

29 *Reasoner*, 9 December 1855, 20 January 1856.

30 *Ibid.*, 7 September 1856; E. Cathels to Holyoake, 8 February 1856, H.C. 834.

31 *Reasoner*, 4 August 1847.

32 G. Hooper to Holyoake, 3 January 1848, H.C. 249.

33 *Oracle*, 3 June 1843; *Reasoner*, 7 August 1850.

34 *Herald of Progress*, 9 May 1846; *Reasoner*, 29 August 1849, 10 April 1850, 23 September, 11 November 1857.

35 *Hansard*, xcv, 13 December 1847, cols. 963–5; *Reasoner*, 16 December 1855, 1 May 1859, 22 January 1860.

36 *Ibid.*, 25 August 1847, 20 September 1848, 26 March 1854; *Reasoner Gazette*, 9 September 1860. For Gurney see appendix v.

37 *Reasoner*, 19 April 1857, 14 November 1858; D. Tribe, *President Charles Bradlaugh, M.P.* (London, 1971), pp. 105, 111,

38 *Movement*, 13 January 1844; *Reasoner*, 9 March 1853; *National Reformer*, 19 January 1861; F. J. Gould, *The History of the Leicester Secular Society* (Leicester, 1900), pp. 9–11. For Gimson see appendix v.

39 *Reasoner*, 9 February 1853, 5 September 1858; *Reasoner Gazette*, 15 April 1860; *National Reformer*, 2 February 1861 (Nottingham); *Reasoner*, 23 March 1853, 3 September 1854, 23 November 1856, 9 October 1859 (Derby).

40 *Oracle*, 3 June 1843; *Utilitarian Record*, 2 February 1848; *Reasoner*, 27 December 1848, 11 August, 21 November 1858.

41 *Ibid.*, 26 February 1845; *Reasoner Gazette*, 30 September 1860; *Reasoner*, 27 January 1856; *Investigator*, February 1856; *National Reformer*, 10, 17, 31 August 1861.

42 *Utilitarian Record*, 24 February 1847; *Reasoner*, 27 October 1852, 23 April 1851, 13, 20 October 1852, 24 September 1854, 29 April 1855, 14 October 1857, 12 December 1858, 20 March, 10 July 1859; *Reasoner Gazette* 7 October 1860.

43 *Reasoner*, 30 October 1850; handbill, 2 October 1852, O.C. 2078; *Reasoner*, 17 November, 1 December 1852, 15 June 1853, 23 July, 3, 17 September 1854, 2 March, 1 June 1856, 11 September 1859; *National Reformer*, 21 April 1867.

44 *Reasoner*, 4, 25 November 1855, 9 June 1861; *National Reformer*, 7 December 1861.

45 *Reasoner*, 18 February 1855, 20 July, 12 October 1856, 31 May, 23 September 1857, 23 January 1859.

46 Ludlow and Jones, *op. cit.*, p. 6; L. Faucher, *Manchester in 1844 . . .* (London and Manchester, 1844), note on p. 15.

47 *Reasoner*, 13 April 1856.
48 *Northern Star*, 21 December 1850; *Star of Freedom*, 15 May 1852; *Reasoner*, 2 June, 7 July 1852; *Star of Freedom*, 31 July 1852. For further links see *ibid.*, 15, 22 May, 14 August 1852.
49 *Reasoner*, 21 July, 1 September, 29 December 1852, 10 August 1853.
50 *Investigator*, June 1854.
51 *Ibid.*, December 1854; *Reasoner*, 14 January 1855
52 *Ibid.*, 8 June 1856; *Investigator*, August 1856; *Reasoner*, 5 October 1856, 22 March, 30 September 1857, 30 January 1859.
53 *Ibid.*, 10 June, 4 November 1855, 18, 25 May, 2 November 1856.
54 *Ibid.*, 27 July 1856, 11 November 1857.
55 *Yorkshire Tribune* [July 1855], pp. 2–10. For the dating of the issues see *Reasoner*, 17 June 1855.
56 *Investigator*, April, June, August 1857; *Reasoner*, 12, 19 April, 14 June, 1, 8 July 1857.
57 *Ibid.*, 31 May, 14, 21 June, 15 July, 19 August 1857; 'Address of the District Board to the Secularists and Friends of Freethought in the North of England' (1857), H.C. 983.
58 *Reasoner*, 7, 21, 28 July, 11, 22, 29 August 1858.
59 *Investigator*, 1 September 1858; *Reasoner*, 3 October, 21 November 1858, 3, 17, July, 25 September, 27 November 1859.
60 *Reasoner Gazette*, 25 March, 15, 29 April, 6, 20, 27 May, 3, 24 June 1860.
61 *Reasoner*, 8 April 1860; *National Reformer*, 9 June 1860.
62 *Reasoner*, 12, 26 August 1860. The Tory *Huddersfield Chronicle*, 4 August 1860, thought 5,000–6,000 were present at Castle Hill; the Liberal *Huddersfield Examiner*, 4 August 1860, thought 6,000–7,000.
63 *National Reformer*, 25 August, 8 September; *Reasoner*, 26 August 1860.
64 *National Reformer*, 14 April 1860; *Reasoner*, 21 October 1860.
65 *National Reformer*, 13, 20 July, 3, 10, 17 August, 14 December 1861; *Counsellor* November 1861.
66 See appendix ix ii.
67 *Oracle*, 6 May 1843.
68 *Reasoner*, 20 April, 18 May, 1, 8 June 1853, 25 June 1854; *Investigator*, October 1856; *National Reformer*, 2 June 1860; *Reasoner*, 18 December 1859; *Reasoner Gazette*, 29 April, 20 May, 18 November, 16 December 1860; *National Reformer*, 24 August, 7 September 1861.
69 *Reasoner*, 20 January 1858; *Reasoner Gazette*, 2 December 1860.
70 *Movement*, 3 February, 20 April, 31 August, 9 October 1844; *Herald of Progress*, 25 October 1845; *Reasoner*, 3 June 1846, 6 July 1853; *Investigator*, October 1854, October 1856; *Reasoner*, 28 September 1856, 2 September, 9 December 1857, 8 April 1860; *National Reformer*, 16 September 1866; see also above, p. 89.
71 *Reasoner*, 3 April, 28 August 1850, 27 October 1852; D. Tribe, *op. cit.*, pp. 41–2; *Reasoner*, 17 June, 30 September, 14 October 1855, 30 November 8 June 1856; 3 March. 19 May 1861; *National Reformer*, 1865, *passim*.
72 *Reasoner*, 12 January 1853, 1 April 1855, 28 September, 2 November 1856, 18 November 1857, 12 February, 23 July 1854, 10 August 1856.
73 *Ibid.*, 30 October 1859, 3 March, 16 June 1861; *Counsellor*, August 1861; *National Reformer*, 18 June 1865. The original John Street buildings had

been relinquished in 1858, when temporary premises had been taken in
nearby Cleveland Street until the new hall was ready.

74 *Reasoner*, 29 August 1849, 5 August, 9 September 1857
75 *Ibid.*, 19 February 1854, 5 September 1858, 22 July 1860, 14 May 1854.
76 *National Reformer*, 10 August 1861; *Reasoner*, 5 February 1854, 26 September 1858.

5
Propagation

a
Leadership

The character of most, if not all, radical movements in the nineteenth
century was largely determined by the quality and nature of their leadership. Most men naturally preferred the backbenches and had neither
the time nor the ability to involve themselves in arduous administration
and constant exhortation. Yet radicalism was never short of leaders.
Indeed, very often there were too many national leaders, and this was a
constant source of trouble, for men who were willing to make the sacri-
fices necessary to become leaders were often not willing to subordinate
themselves to their equally ambitious colleagues. Owenism is perhaps
the major exception to this generalisation, chiefly because of Owen's
unique position at the head of the movement. Some men may be born
leaders but others have leadership thrust upon them by circumstances.
One suspects that G. J. Holyoake, Robert Cooper, and even Richard
Carlile fall into the latter category. Carlile was not a radical when he
first came to London in search of work, and he became deeply involved
only when Sherwin wanted someone to take over his shop, and events
led on from there. Similarly, Holyoake was rather naïve about his rise
to fame. In other circumstances he might well have continued as a
popular teacher, perhaps eventually securing a post in the state system,
but the events of late 1841 created an unexpected situation, and the
course of his life was changed. After 1841 Holyoake achieved as much as
he did mainly by hard work against considerable natural disadvantages.
In Robert Cooper's career there was no such turning-point. He learned
his radicalism at his father's knee, and his career was one of steady
growth, but he never sought leadership and for that reason perhaps he
never became so important as he might otherwise have been. Southwell
on the other hand could be nothing but a leader, for he was incapable
of following anyone. His vigorous platform style and boldness in action
marked him out by temperament, though, lacking any sense of proportion, he did not survive for long. Charles Bradlaugh had all Southwell's
better points and few of his worse ones. He too was a born leader, a man

of oustanding intellect, and when he resumed platform advocacy in the
1850s after a spell in the army, he showed he also had the necessary
physique for the primitive conditions of Victorian back-street halls—
powerful lungs and tall stature.

Whatever their natural advantages or disadvantages as leaders, all
were motivated by one thing—a burning sense of righteousness. This is
probably the one quality shared by all radicals. A man has to be convinced that something is badly wrong and needs putting right before he
is willing to embark on a radical career, pushing against the innate conservatism of institutions and vested interests, and risking health, liberty
and even life in the process. Cooper and Carlile, Southwell, Holyoake
and Bradlaugh, however different their temperaments, all had this sense
of mission. It was to some extent an experience common to many auto-
didacts. When a man discovers for himself that something is false which he
had previously believed to be true and which most other men still believe
to be true, then he feels compelled to draw the blinds from the eyes of
his comrades. Whether this takes place within a specifically religious
context or not, it is, in a sense, conversion. Since Plato pictured the
philosopher rushing into the cave to tell men that the reality they
thought they saw was only a shadow of the truth, those to whom the
revelation is given have sought to communicate it to others, and have
often been made more insistent by the refusal of others to listen. Carlile
read Paine and was impelled to reprint his works; Southwell became a
radical and went out to preach the good news; Owen had the secret of
circumstances revealed to him and he had to proclaim the message;
Cooper and Holyoake inherited the same drive to teach the implications
of Owen's moral revolution; and Bradlaugh was stung with indignation
at the treatment he had received and the wrongs of others, and his
mission became to heal the wounds by cutting out the cancer of religion.
Like Mr Gladstone and Oliver Cromwell, St Paul and St Ignatius Loyola,
these were men of mission, and outside the ranks of formal religion they
were stirred by the same impulses which have made saints and martyrs
in every faith.

Yet though only an extreme cynic would deny this, there were other
motives besides, and just as critics have pointed them out in Mr Gladstone and the rest, so we can detect them in the freethought leaders.
Significantly, Owen is the only one whose motives approached purity.
He really did believe he was right and that was all there was to it.
With normal mortals there was also the challenge. Carlile fought for
the sake of the challenge thrown down to him. The greatest mistake his
opponents made was to prosecute him, and the same is true of Holyoake.
He had no love of fighting or controversy, except in a purely academic

sense. He could wield a pen, but had not the strength to lift a sword. He was kept going by his determination not to lose face once he had been made a martyr, and by the prestige which his position gave him. He liked being at the centre of things, and he enjoyed the sense of importance which leadership gave him and the respectable company into which it brought him. But once he found his organisation stood in the way of further prestige and respectable company, it ceased to be so important for him and the campaigns of his later life were to be comparatively solitary affairs. This is not to say that he had no integrity. Respectability was important to him, but it was only one of many motives and he never took the ultimate step which would have assured him great prestige—reconversion to Christianity.[1] Inside his frail body was a dogged persistence and streak of intellectual honesty which never failed him. He also had that remarkable itch, common to many radical leaders, to be always expressing himself in a plethora of literature. A major reason for this was that, because a leader dominated his own periodical and movement, anyone else who wanted to get a word in had to have his own rival periodical and movement. So that excessive individualism which was almost a necessary quality of being a leader naturally led to a vast output of pamphlets and periodicals and a multiplicity of organisations. Southwell never had the energy to say much in print, but he more than compensated for this on the platform. He was an actor first and foremost. He loved the limelight and had to appear before people and hear their applause. Because of his convictions he became a radical orator, but he might just as well have been a preacher or a serious actor if his convictions or talents had been in that direction. The same was true of Joseph Barker. He had to preach, no matter what his convictions. As with Mr Gladstone, speech was part of the fibre of his being. Charles Bradlaugh similarly was an immensely gifted orator and gained great emotional satisfaction from his performances on the platform. His became a rather lonely life and he needed the warmth of an audience. Like most of the other leaders he was undoubtedly an egotist, but he differed from the others in deserving his own high opinion of himself. He was one of the best public speakers of the nineteenth century, and made his mark alike on the popular platform and in Parliament. With such a light he would have had difficulty finding a bushel under which to hide it.

The leaders of early nineteenth-century radicalism could reach their followers in two major ways: by means of the written word in pamphlets and periodicals, and by means of the spoken word in lectures, public meetings and debates. Before the building of a national railway network in Britain these methods were slow and expensive at the best of times but whenever the authorities wished to restrict radicalism these forms of propaganda were especially vulnerable. Hence the readiness with which the government taxed the press, forbade public meetings, and applied the laws of blasphemous and seditious libel in years of discontent, particularly in the Six Acts after Peterloo. Even after the mid-1840s, when means of communication had become easier, Britain still remained an intensely regional country. Unity of organisation could only be maintained by hard work and frequent lecture missions. The radicals' constant aim was therefore to remove those last restrictions on the press and against liberty of expression which prevented a free propagation of their views.

b
Lectures

The successful organisation of Secularism was largely dependent upon the quality and availability of lecturers. This the fate of Owenism had made clear, and another lesson was that militancy provoked opposition which ensured success. Apathy was a major threat to the spread of any radical movement. Regular visits from lecturers were indispensable to any real progress, and the pattern of the growth of Secularism was linked to the lecture tours. Revival came to Manchester in 1849 when Southwell was active there. In 1850 Holyoake returned to the provincial lecture field with ten secular and eight religious topics which he delivered in Lancashire, the north-east and East Anglia during the summer, and whilst in Manchester he attended the opening of the new and more modest hall in Garratt's Road.[2] In the same year he also held his first two important public debates—with John Bowes in Bradford, 22 April for four nights, on 'The Truth of Christianity and the Folly of Infidelity'; and with David King at John Street on the questions, 'What is the Christian System?', 'What are its legitimate effects?'. Meanwhile, Robert Cooper was active in Scotland, based on Paisley where he had opened a new room, and in his own manner he spread infidelity and Owenism to Dundee and Denny, Kilmarnock and Kirkaldy.[3] This pressure was kept up the following year, and in 1852 the first signs of positive organisation followed upon Robert Cooper's lecture tour through the provinces. Wherever reports of local organisation appear in the *Reasoner* the visit of a lecturer appears to have provided the stimulus. The lecturer was also able to maintain continuity where little organisation existed. Newcastle upon Tyne gives a good example of this. There is no record of an infidel organisation in Newcastle after the decline of Owenism, and the Society for the Overthrow of Superstition which existed in 1843 was opposed to both the *Oracle* and the Anti-Persecution Union. But Newcastle was on the lecture route to Scotland and so was not neglected by the national leaders. Speakers were always able to attract large audiences to the Nelson Street Music Hall. In September 1850 Newcastle was inundated with radicals: Southwell was debating 'God and Christianity' with John Bowes; Walter Cooper was advocating Christian Socialism; and Robert Cooper was lecturing at the Joiners' Hall on Theology. Holyoake, Thomas Cooper and Emma Martin all appeared at the Nelson Street Music Hall that same year, and not surprisingly the magistrates announced a ban on itinerant lecturers. Not till 1852, when a Secular Society was announced, was there any organised freethought in the city.[4]

The importance of the lecturer's contribution and his ability to stimulate interest is illustrated by the fluctuating fortunes of Secularism in the 1850s. The success which greeted the lectures of 1852 greatly concerned the autumnal meeting of the Congregational Union when it assembled in Bradford in October 1852. Particularly anxious was the Reverend Brewin Grant, who had contested with the Socialists a decade earlier and who had kept a wary eye on them ever since. He and the Reverend Andrew Reed delivered lectures at the beginning of the four-day session in Bradford 'to the working classes of the town', which prompted William Logan of Bradford to write to the *British Banner* suggesting that Grant should commence a general mission against the infidels. The Reverend John Angell James, Holyoake's childhood minister, supported the idea as did the editor of the *Banner* and other correspondents. So was begun a campaign which can only be compared to that organised by John Brindley against Socialism in 1840, and it had similar results.[5]

The accepted way for opposing lecturers to air their differences was in debate. This had been a standard Owenite practice, and both Holyoake and Southwell had already debated with John Bowes in 1850. It was therefore almost inevitable that Holyoake should eventually meet Grant on the platform, and on six successive Thursday evenings, 20 January to 24 February, at the Cowper Street schoolroom in the City Road, London, the two men met to discuss: 'What Advantages would Accrue to Mankind Generally, and the Working Classes in Particular, by the removal of Christianity, and the Substitution of Secularism in its Place?' This debate illustrates the way in which most such confrontations were conducted. First there was always a long and involved correspondence over the phrasing of the motion and the conduct of the debate, negotiations usually being conducted by committees representing each party.[6] The challenge to Grant had been issued as early as June 1852, before the beginning of his mission, and the arrangements had taken six months to complete. Each side had a chairman who conducted the meeting for his respective speaker and there was also an umpire to settle disputes between the chairmen. Holyoake's committee was James Watson, Richard Moore and Austin Holyoake, with Ebenezer Syme, a former Unitarian minister from Sunderland, acting as chairman. Grant's committee was the Reverends J. Campbell and Robert Ashton, and Messrs Samuel Priestley and J. S. Crisp, with Samuel Morley acting as chairman. The umpire was the Reverend J. Howard Hinton. Each night each speaker was allowed to speak for two half-hour and one quarter-hour periods, alternating with his opponent. Admission was threepence per evening or a shilling for the course, and income from the sale of tickets indicates that well over a thousand people attended each evening. In addition, 45,000 copies of the printed report of the debate were sold.[7]

Holyoake was not a good public speaker and debater, and his effort was a triumph of will over nature. A hostile observer saw him as 'a sickly-looking, sallow-complexioned man', and everyone noticed his peculiar and inappropriate voice which was 'much against him when addressing a large audience; it was a shrill treble, thin and wiry, but clear'. Contemporaries were also agreed, however, in passing on from the feebleness of his voice to the powerfulness of his intellect: 'it was remarkable to see him rise, and, himself cool almost to iciness, toss right and left his bolts of invective hissing hot, or tipped with insidious poison, rousing into turbulent discord the vast mass before him—a raging sea of many thousands!' Although Holyoake might have repudiated this melodramatic description of his impact, it certainly contains an important element of truth. The emotional power of the spoken word was enormous, and crowd hysteria often provided that excitement and entertainment which was so often lacking in working-class lives. As his 'shrill and plaintive voice echoed round that vast assembly, it carried with it the feelings of the audience . . . his great reasoning powers far excel his personal appearance, and astonished all present, and by all classes he is pronounced a clever man . . .', wrote a more friendly observer of another occasion in 1859.[8]

Grant was a complete contrast. He was physically robust, with a loud and quick voice. As a debater he probably got the better of Holyoake, but the latter left a better impression on those in the audience who were not wholly partisan. The Unitarian *Inquirer* was openly contemptuous of Grant, and Henry N. Barnett, then a Unitarian minister and later a lecturer at the South Place Chapel, wrote to Holyoake, 'many Christians thoroughly sympathise with *you* though they have no sympathy with your opinions'.[9] Grant was an excellent performer but an embarrassment to those Christians who were sensitive to the integrity of Holyoake's position.

Who won this debate is really an irrelevant question. Neither side could hope to convince the other or his followers. In debating points Grant was probably the more successful, but in publicity given to his views Holyoake benefited most, though some supporters were disappointed at his general performance. The way to deal with Grant, Syme had warned, was to 'open a battery upon him out of Scripture . . . draw him into a bog and let him flounder in the demoralising passages . . . Considerate treatment would be thrown away upon Grant—I mean—sparing his feelings or his cloth. He will appreciate *facts* better than *arguments* . . . Bedaub him with orthodox dirt and he will keep out of your way for the next half century.'[10] This advice Holyoake was temperamentally unsuited to accept, and so he was unable to give that powerful vindication of Secularism which Charles Bradlaugh was later all too ready to offer to his audiences. 'Only a few of the Secularists seem thoroughly satisfied,' wrote Southwell in a review which was remarkably fair in its conclusions. 'They all admit the ability of their champion—they admire the cool dignity of his bearing—but very many dispute the wisdom of his tactics, and consider that though the discussion will have a decidedly rationalistic and humanising tendency Secularism is still an enigma to the general public; the Secularist leader so much dislikes denunciation that he cannot but associate therewith pettiness of aim and vulgarity of thought. According to his theory men of genius are always polite.' Southwell recognised the teacher from whom Holyoake had acquired his style: he 'had taken a leaf from the book of his friend Owen, and throughout this controversy lectured rather than debated'. Thomas Cooper was to make a similar comment in 1858 when he asked Holyoake to debate, 'that is to say, contest argument with argument from your own mind—and not read written matter of stale age, or prosy extracts from poor Francis Newman, or other slender-witted people'.[11]

Despite these defects, the discussion between Grant and Holyoake made Secularism well known if not well understood. The circulation of the *Reasoner* rose in the first six months of 1853 from 3,000 to 4,500 per issue, the highest it had been to date. Secularism was busily denounced in the religious press, dwelt on from pulpits, and declaimed against on the platform. It entered into the currency of everyday language, so as to need no explanation when used by Horace Mann in his Religious Census Report of 1854.[12]

The moment the last evening of the discussion was over, the nationwide debate began. The umpire of the discussion, Howard Hinton, announced what he hoped would be an antidote of a speech before the audience could even leave the hall, but when his promised lecture took place Southwell was there to reply—greatly to the entertainment of the audience.[13] In Yorkshire the Reverend J. Gregory of Thornton made his own contribution to the defence of Christianity, stirring local Secularists A. Robinson and C. Shackleton to give four lectures in reply. Mr Gregory, helped by his neighbouring clergymen, G. W. Conder of Leeds, J. A. Savage of Wilsden and E. Mellor of Halifax, countered these with four more lectures which were published. So the controversy spread. Grant himself went on tour. Robert Cooper, Southwell and Holyoake went in pursuit. The report of the Cowper Street discussion was read and discussed at public meetings in Leicester. Clergymen prepared to debate further.[14]

Cooper followed closest on Grant's heels. In April he was in Bradford, Keighley, Bingley, Farnhill, Silsden, Blackburn, Bolton, Sheffield, Nottingham and Rotherham. At Middlesbrough in July he was refused the use of the town hall which Grant had recently used, but this did not stop him. Then, in spite of ill-health, he went on to Newcastle, Glasgow and Paisley, then back to Lancashire, the Midlands and the North-East again.[15] Southwell lectured in Manchester at the end of March, and then followed Grant elsewhere in Lancashire. In Rochdale he attended one of Grant's lectures and replied from the floor. Then in June he met Grant in a three nights' debate in Nottingham, and at the end of September did the same with the Reverend Woodville Woodman, a Swedenborgian minister, at Bolton.[16] Holyoake followed a similar path —though he was busy at the same time in fitting out his new Fleet Street establishment—and he was in Nottingham the week after Southwell. In August he met the Reverend J. H. Rutherford in Newcastle upon Tyne for a three nights' discussion on 'Christianity versus Secularism', and in September he returned to the North East with Le Blond on the London Secular Society mission.[17] By the most conservative estimate, sales of the *Reasoner* reached the 5,000 mark, their highest ever.

Holyoake's reputation was also at a peak. His mild manner had impressed clergymen and made an important impact on public opinion. Despite the exertions of Cooper and Southwell, Grant's name was inextricably linked with Holyoake's, and the reports of all the events reached the Secularist public only through the tinted spectacles of Holyoake's *Reasoner*. John Wright, secretary of the Glasgow Eclectic Association, when writing to the Reverend Dr Anderson in July 1853 to persuade him to debate with Holyoake, described the latter 'as a man of unblemished moral reputation, and held in high esteem by many persons in every sphere of life . . . who are altogether opposed to his doctrines'. Such a man was the Reverend Dr Joseph Parker, later one of the most

eminent ministers in the country, who debated with Holyoake at Banbury in 1854 and had nothing but praise for him. As Robert Cooper later
wrote of Grant's mission, 'A more pitiable failure is not on record. More
unbelievers were made during this Mission than at any known period.'[18]

Apart from Holyoake, Southwell and Cooper, there were a considerable number of men in the early 1850s who appeared on radical
platforms up and down the country as lecturers on Secularism and allied
topics. Former Chartist orators like Thomas Cooper, S. M. Kydd, Gerald
Massey, Bronterre O'Brien and Ernest Jones, mixed with unorthodox
Christians such as Ebenezer Syme, Henry Ierson and Henry Barnett, and
local Socialists such as James Wilkie of Glasgow, Joseph Smith of Leeds
and James Campbell of Manchester. To the ranks of full-time lecturers
were added in 1853 F. R. Young, a Unitarian who did not long remain a
Secularist, and in 1854 Joseph Barker, who had emigrated to America
but who was home on a brief visit. The topics such men offered were
many and various, encompassing a wide range of radical ideas. In 1852
Holyoake listed eight subjects of a political and social nature, five
educational topics and nine theological ones. He ranged from lectures
on Mazzini, the Middle Classes, Socialism, and the Suffrage, through
Aesop, Logic, and the Taxes on Knowledge, to Christ, Confucius,
Miracles and Emma Martin.[19] Such a catholicity of choice was not unusual. In 1860 Joseph Barker announced fifty-two topics, often more
than one lecture on each. Most of them were connected with religion,
but others were upon such subjects as the French Revolution, Human
Progress, the Maine Law, Buckle, Brougham, Money, the English Constitution, John Brown, the Use of the Pen, Books, Self-Culture, Economy,
the Press, and Emigration.[20] He was unusual only in the number of
American topics he was prepared to lecture about, and many of his and
Holyoake's subjects would have graced the most respectable mechanics'
institution. Some other Secularists were a little more down to earth.
J. H. Gordon in 1860 was offering thirteen subjects on such miscellaneous
topics as 'The Bible God, the Sin-tempter and Sin-author', 'Priestcraft,
the Science of Ignorance' and 'The Book of Mormon from God. An
Application of the Arguments Used to Prove the Same of the Bible'.[21]

With such a range of subjects, varying according to the temperament
of the lecturer, the appropriateness of the occasion, and the nature of
the audience, the lecturers kept up the pressure of propaganda in 1854.
Holyoake, Robert Cooper, Southwell and Barker, together with local
men like W. H. Johnson and W. W. Broom in the north, continued to
extend their influence. The by-now well-established lecture routes were
followed, through the midland cities, the textile areas of Lancashire and
Yorkshire, and Tyneside to the Central Valley of Scotland and back

again. Occasional visits were also paid to more out-of-the-way places, and
in 1854 both Cooper and Holyoake lectured in Devonport. Formal and
informal debates were again held, many of them involving Robert
Cooper who met both Grant and John Bowes in that year, but the most
important occasion was again the meeting of Grant and Holyoake.
This second encounter between the two men, held on Mondays and
Thursdays from 2 to 19 October in the City Hall, Glasgow, was clearly
an attempt at a repeat performance. The subject was 'Is Secularism
inconsistent with Reason and the Moral Sense, and condemned by
Experience?', and Holyoake claimed that over three thousand persons
were present on the opening night, the 'most numerous' gathering he
had ever addressed. As might have been expected of a conscious
repeat, it was something of an anti-climax. Those who were not wholly
prejudiced in favour of their particular champions were disappointed.
As in 1853 Grant was too violent and Holyoake too timid. According to
the *Glasgow Constitutional*, both men missed the point: 'We fear the
only result has been, that one of its [Christianity's] bitterest and ablest
opponents has, instead of venting his scepticism to some hundred or
two of his own disciples in some obscure corner of the city, been raised
to a rostrum where he has had an opportunity of pouring his infidelity
into the ears of some three thousand of our unsuspecting youth.'[22]

The aftermath of the Glasgow debate was similar to, though not so
sustained as, that of the debate at Cowper Street. Sales of the *Reasoner*,
which had begun to fall off, rose by a hundred per week during the
debate, but interest was not sufficient to overcome the rise in price to
$1\frac{1}{2}d$ in September 1853 and to $2d$ in March 1854. Southwell kept the fires
burning in Glasgow for a few weeks but there was no general campaign
as after the first debate.[23]

There are several reasons for this, but the most important one seems
to have been the prolongation of the Crimean War. First the war put up
the price of paper and, consequently, of the *Reasoner* and increased
Holyoake's financial worries about the Fleet Street House.[24] Secondly the
war increasingly attracted public attention, and with the crisis of the
winter of 1854–5 and the accompanying political upheaval, the Secularist
lecturers could not hope to maintain public attention at the level it had
reached after the first debate. As the novelty and shock of Secularism
began to wear off men turned to other things. David Urquhart's Foreign
Affairs Committees were reorganised in 1854 and nearly a hundred and
fifty were established throughout the country. Isaac Ironside of Sheffield
was only the most prominent of the Secularists who was diverted into
Urquhartism. The consequences of the Foreign Affairs agitation, for
example, were disastrous for the Preston Secular Society when the

secretary, William Singleton, became an Urquhartite and took five other members with him.[25] The issues raised by Urquhart divided the radicals. He denounced Kossuth and Mazzini. 'Every Englishman, republican and liberal, is bound to speak out' against Urquhart, said Holyoake in 1855, yet among Urquhart's followers were John Buxton, last governor of Harmony Hall, C. D. Collet, secretary of the Association for the Repeal of the Taxes on Knowledge, and William Hilton of the Bolton Secular Society, in addition to those mentioned above, together with disillusioned Chartists such as J. R. Stephens, John Frost, and even Karl Marx.[26] Thomas Cooper's most successful tour of 1855–6 was on the Crimean War, illustrated by a model of Sebastopol. In the Manchester area for 'a period of nine or ten weeks he succeeded in drawing large audiences together two and three times in the day' and he was equally successful elsewhere in the north.[27]

With these counter attractions, the Secularist leaders in the localities could not hope to maintain widespread interest. The number of societies stagnated, increased again with the spread of regional unions at the end of the war, and then stagnated again in the depression which followed the financial crisis of late 1857. But the depression was not entirely to blame for the weakness of Secularism in the late 1850s. Although lectures continued to be given, the lecturing force was depleted for other reasons and operations had to be conducted on a reduced scale in comparison with the hectic years of 1853 and 1854. Southwell emigrated in 1855; Joseph Barker, after a mammoth ten nights' debate with Grant in Halifax in January and February 1855, returned to America; Robert Cooper suffered repeated ill-health which greatly restricted his lecturing activities, and he retired to his native Manchester in 1858.[28] Holyoake remained the most prodigious lecturer but not always on Secularist subjects. After the publication of his *History of Co-operation in Rochdale* in 1858, he was increasingly asked to lecture on this topic. His principal debates, with F. R. Lees in 1856 and G. E. Lomax in 1858, were on the Maine Law Question. In 1858 he suggested that the Temple Secular Society should investigate the probable effect of Bright's rating franchise proposals on the number of electors in St Bride's. The President, J. B. Bebbington, queried whether this was really the legitimate province of a Secular Society, but Holyoake's mind was clearly moving in the direction of politics and in 1859 he announced, 'I shall confine myself north of York to *political* and Co-operative subjects— or Literary', to avoid prejudicing his work with the Northern Reform Union. Not only the subjects, but also the character of his lectures was changing. He wrote to Joseph Cowen about his N.R.U. lectures: '1400 at my lecture on Monday at Nott[ingham]. 1000 at doors shut out. Two

Councillors in the Chair. Don't speak now with less than a Councillor
or an Alderman in Chair. Growing so respectable that I suspect myself.'[29]

The problem of Secularism during these years was a combination of
general radical weakness and a lack of leadership from Holyoake. The
defeat which radicals of both middle and working classes suffered at the
time of the Crimean War is the background to the decline of Secularism.
There was no issue around which support could revive. In 1840–2 and
1852–3 the infidels had thrived on hostility. Once Brewin Grant had
ended his mission, opposition diminished and Holyoake's mild 'Fabian'
leadership was not likely to provoke it again. All this was changed at
the end of the decade. The radical political movement at last revived
and with it the Secularist movement. New leadership was given to
Secularism, narrower, fiercer, and therefore provoking more hostility,
martyrdom and success. Charles Bradlaugh came on the scene.

Bradlaugh had first entered the freethought movement in 1849 at the
age of sixteen. In that year he began attending open-air lectures in
Victoria Park, East London, where Bishop Bonner had centuries before
burnt Protestant heretics. Here all manner of radical speakers used to
harangue audiences from the East End on Sundays during the summer.
City missionaries jostled with infidels in their efforts to proclaim their
rival truths, and young Bradlaugh was drawn from his home in Hackney
to enjoy the fun. He had been a Sunday School teacher at St Peter's,
Hackney Road, until the Reverend J. G. Packer had upset him by treat-
ing as incipient atheism a query about discrepancies in the Thirty-Nine
Articles. After this Bradlaugh gradually slipped out of the orthodox
fold and though at first he tried to answer the infidel lecturers their
arguments and their kindness towards him won him over. He left home
and went to lodge with Mrs Eliza Sharples Carlile and her family, who
had been installed to look after the Warner Street Temperance Hall
where the infidels held some of their indoor meetings. Just as Holyoake
had received the blessing of Carlile himself and become his heir, now
Bradlaugh too had received the blessing of Carlile's second widow and
had entered into the tradition.[30]

In the company of East End Secularists like J. P. Adams and James
Savage, Bradlaugh now began to play an active part in freethought. In
1850 he declared himself in public by addressing the crowds in the park,
and a *British Banner* correspondent gives us a hostile, but probably not
too inaccurate, picture of one of Bradlaugh's earliest performances. At
this time Bradlaugh was

> an overgrown boy of seventeen, with such an uninformed mind, that it is
> really amusing to see him sometimes stammering and spluttering on in
> his own ignorant eloquence, making the most ludicrous mistakes, making

all history to suit his private convenience, and often calling yea nay and nay yea, when it will serve his purpose.[31]

Yet with discipline and experience this raw youth was to become one of the greatest popular orators of the nineteenth century.

The Secularists welcomed his talents, and Austin Holyoake introduced him to his famous brother who did Bradlaugh the honour of chairing his first public lecture, which was delivered on 10 October at the Philpot Street Hall, on the subject 'The Past, Present, and Future of Theology'. Freethought did Bradlaugh's finances little good, though, and religious prejudice ruined his attempt to earn a living as a coal merchant. By the end of the year he was in debt, and so took the Queen's Shilling as an honourable way out. Three years in the army made a man of him, and when he returned to civilian life he was a force to be reckoned with. Thereafter he divided his time between Charles Bradlaugh the solicitor's clerk, and 'Iconoclast' the atheist lecturer.[32] Though he tried to keep the two separate, the legal knowledge he picked up at his work was to prove invaluable to him as an agitator for freethought, and he was always ready—perhaps overready—to fight every inch of the way through the courts of the land in order to establish what he considered to be his rights. In this respect his style was to be quite different from that of Holyoake, whose closest knowledge of the inside of a courtroom had come from the dock.

To begin with, Bradlaugh was just another of the local London leaders who kept freethought bubbling in the East End, but gradually his reputation spread, and in 1858 he made his first major provincial lecture tour and achieved national recognition when he held his own in public debates with Thomas Cooper at the City Road Hall of Science and with Brewin Grant at Sheffield. His style was still very primitive, but was none the less very effective. His lecture 'Has Man a Soul?', delivered at the Sheffield Temperance Hall in March 1859, consisted merely of a series of rhetorical questions, far below the intellectual standard of Robert Cooper's lectures on the same subject from which Bradlaugh probably drew most of his ideas, but what he had to say must have been very effective *viva voce*. Henry Turner, the Sheffield secretary, gives us a description of his impact:

> he stands 6 feet 1 is about 25 years of age & has done terrible execution with both the Bible & the Saints Ministers of Religion Battersby & Giles & Laymen Adam Wood Blake Wolstenholm Watson & Liddell have been so many play things in his hands he takes no notes & the Sledge Hammer falls heavy sharpened with wit & tempered by eloquence [sic].[33]

He added, 'we are all well satisfied and shall have him again'. Unlike Holyoake, Bradlaugh was a big man with a loud voice and sufficient

courage, enthusiasm and ability to give the Secularists the encouragement and positive leadership which they wanted.

He set about rebuilding Secularism in the north, lecturing, exhorting,
organising through 1858 and 1859. He debated with John Bowes in
Northampton, and T. D. Matthias, a Welsh Baptist, in Halifax, both in
1859, and with Woodville Woodman at Ashton and Wigan and with
J. H. Rutherford in 1861. The reaction could not have been better
from Bradlaugh's point of view. Militant atheism was met by militant
Christianity which was experiencing a similar revival in 1859. About
1600 people attended Bradlaugh's lectures at the Eclectic Institute,
Glasgow, on Sunday 9 October 1859 on the 'Creation' and the 'Deluge',
and over 4,000 were said to have heard his mid-week lecture at the City
Hall on 'Revivals'.[34] Far from having a councillor on his platform,
Bradlaugh had difficulty in securing a hall. Contracts were broken at
Bolton in September 1859, Doncaster in October and Glasgow in
November. In the Bolton case Bradlaugh sued the Town Hall Company;
in Doncaster he spoke from a wagon in the market place and so doubled
his audience; in Glasgow the threat of prosecution for blasphemy
resulted in very crowded lectures.[35] Everywhere Bradlaugh went he
recreated Secularism in his own image. In 1860 and 1861 he ventured
into the radical deserts of East Anglia, creating the society at Great
Yarmouth, encouraging the new society at Norwich, and urging the
formation of an East Anglia Secular Union. In June 1861 he met John
Brindley, again active in the Faith, in debate at Norwich.[36] The Oldham
Secularists reported in 1859, ' "Iconoclast" had done an immense deal
of good by the lectures he has recently delivered to large and attentive
audiences in this borough. For a considerable length of time, the orthodox "gentlemen in black" have had it all their own way. . . .' Holyoake, confined to London by other duties and a severe illness, noted
approvingly, 'In the very useful tour "Iconoclast" is making, a good
deal of wholesome discontent is manifested in clerical quarters.' When
Holyoake came to Oldham in 1860 he was agreeably surprised at the
transformation. 'After so long an absence from the platform,' he wrote,
'it was a new sensation to deliver a provincial lecture; and after a yet
longer absence from Oldham, the immediate friends with whom I
communicated were all new to me.'[37]

The total Secularist lecture force in 1860 was the strongest it had
ever been. Joseph Barker had again returned from America, offering his
fifty-two topics on which he lectured throughout the north, and he also
held debates with Brindley and Thomas Cooper; Holyoake renewed his
efforts as well, though he was not so prominent as formerly; John Watts
and J. B. Bebbington set out on a mission tour of the provinces in May

1860; J. H. Gordon was engaged as a full-time lecturer in Yorkshire; and a newcomer, Mrs Harriet Law, delivered her first lecture at the City Road Hall of Science on 24 June. All these, in addition to Bradlaugh who was the most active, carried the revival of Secularism through the land, promoting new organisations and regional unions and stimulating activity in the hitherto neglected rural areas.[38]

c
Publications

The lecturers made the primary impact. There was an immediacy about the presence of a leader on the platform, declaring the truth, routing the clergy and inspiring the faithful. But as the lecturer gazed down at the rows of eager faces he was often given a misleading impression of the movement. The hundreds and even thousands of working men whom he saw before him would melt away into the night, not to reappear until the next important lecturer came. Those who had the responsibility for maintaining the local organisations knew all too well that consistent supporters were to be counted only in tens. Bradlaugh realised this as he talked with such men in the north at the end of the decade, while in London Holyoake mistook the size of the camp meetings for signs of strength. He should have known better, though, since the best temperature chart of all which measures the health of Secularism in the 1850s is the circulation of the *Reasoner*. This was the only weekly periodical in the movement between 1846 and 1860, and so gives a good indication both of Holyoake's personal popularity and the strength of his organisation.[39]

The printed word was as important as the spoken word in propagating ideas and encouraging organisation. Unlike the lecturer, the pamphlet or periodical could be mulled over for weeks or even months after its first appearance, and it could be handed on to others. It could be everywhere at once and new every weekend. The press was, as Richard Carlile had appreciated, all powerful. For ten years Holyoake was supreme because he was the leading propagandist in the Secularist movement. For weekly persistence the *Reasoner* far outstripped the *Republican*, the *Poor Man's Guardian* and the *New Moral World*; it compares only with Cobbett's *Weekly Register* and the *Northern Star*. The pen was Holyoake's most powerful weapon, and his training had been in its use since his earliest days as a radical. By 1851 he had a considerable number of books and periodicals to his name, he had been an editor for most of the previous ten years, and his brother Austin was a printer, trained by his brother-in-law, John Griffin Hornblower. So the two Holyoake brothers complemented each other in their propagandist skills and in 1851 entered into a formal partnership as printers. They were still, however, left dependent upon outside agencies and publishers for the distribution of their works. Their next step, therefore, was for them to become publishers themselves and to enter the agency business.[40] This object was achieved in 1853 when, with £250 presented to him as a testimonial, G. J. Holyoake took over James Watson's publishing business at 3 Queen's Head Passage and transferred it to better premises at 147 Fleet Street. Holyoake wanted these premises for several reasons: 'Fleet Street is one of the highways of the world—perhaps the best known highway in it,' he wrote. It was a matter of pride and prestige that the headquarters of Secularism should be in this street which evoked memories of Richard Carlile and that earlier Fleet Street House.[41] The establishment at '147' therefore was to be more than just another printing and publishing house. The *History of the Fleet Street House* which Holyoake wrote in 1856 was subtitled 'A Report of Sixteen years'. The place was, in this view, to continue the radical campaign which had been waged since the days of the *Oracle of Reason*, and the establishment was to be the final realisation of Holyoake's plans of 1844 for an Atheon. The Fleet Street House was to have all that a progressive movement could desire—a 'Political Exchange' with a reading room, such as Thornton Hunt had advocated; a meeting place for radical reformers of all views and nationalities; a centre for metropolitan freethought and political activity; and a haven for visitors from the provinces and abroad.[42]

All this cost money. The £250 was soon spent: the lease alone cost £570 and fitting out the place another £150. In addition Holyoake had promised Watson £350 for the publishing business, and a further £600 went on stock. Holyoake incurred this debt in the expectation that Le Blond would give him £1,000, but the latter went bankrupt, leaving Holyoake with a huge debt which was not paid off till 1861.[43] The man who had been so caustic about the debt and extravagance of the Harmony Hall venture might have paused to wonder if he were not about to repeat the folly.

The work of the Fleet Street House was divided into three business departments. In 1856 these were Publishing, under Frederick Farrah; the News Agency, under Thomas Wilks; and Printing, under John Watts. Holyoake was the Director, and his brother Austin, secretary and general assistant. The three departments were semi-independent and run on co-operative lines—that is, beyond a minimum salary, those conducting the business were paid a proportion of the profits. The principal duty of the Director was the production of the *Reasoner*.[44]

Despite the debt with which the House was loaded and the energies which were required to reduce it, the establishment at 147 made an invaluable contribution to freethought during the ten years of its existence, 1853–62. First, it continued the work of the radical publishers. Among the stock which Watson supplied through Holyoake were works by Volney, Mirabaud, Annet, Paine, Palmer and Hume, as well as by more recent authors, such as Robert Owen and Robert Dale Owen, Hetherington, Thomas Cooper, Bronterre O'Brien, W. J. Linton and Holyoake himself.[45] During the 1850s this list was maintained and added to. The freethought heritage was supplemented in 1856 and 1857 by *Half Hours with the Freethinkers,* a fortnightly periodical edited by Bradlaugh, Watts and Johnson, which gave brief lives of and extracts from the leading freethinkers of earlier generations. Holyoake himself remained a prolific writer and he published a great many pamphlets, some of which had already been printed in the *Reasoner* and which appear to have been in great demand. These miscellaneous works were published in a comprehensive volume, entitled the *Trial of Theism,* in 1857. According to a report from Halifax in 1861, at least one society used this work as a text book for discussion.[46]

Secondly, the House trained new freethought leaders: Farrah and Watts both set up as publishers and booksellers in their own right, and Watts was also editor of the *National Reformer* for a time. The printing and publishing business was taken over by Austin in 1859, lapsed in 1862 when the Fleet Street House was sold, but was revived as 'Austin & Co.' at 17 Johnson's Court in 1864. This business then passed successively to Charles Watts, Charles Albert Watts and the Rationalist Press Association. Provincial copies of '147' were also created: at Northampton, for example, by John Bates, and by Thomas Ranford in Birmingham.[47]

The third facility which the House offered to the freethought movement was an organisational headquarters: its committee room was the first home of the London Secular Society and the central office of Dr Stamm's German Alliance; indeed, it became—as Holyoake had always intended it to become—a centre for all kinds of radical and republican, British and foreign, activity.

The larger aims of the House, though, were never realised: the idea of a 'college of propagandism' never caught on; the British Secular Institute, which Holyoake announced in 1857, was no more than a new name for the old establishment.[48] But the closure of the House in 1862 does not detract from the value of the work done there in the 1850s. Without it, Secularism would have been a less coherent and well-directed movement.

The most important contribution of Holyoake's publishing work for

Secularism was the *Reasoner* and, although the paper long preceded the creation of the Fleet Street House, he always regarded it as a central part of the work. A periodical gave its editor a powerful instrument in the world of nineteenth-century working-class affairs. He alone governed its contents and chose whether or not to print material detrimental to his own views, and, as Charles Kingsley made Alton Locke realise, the editor of a popular journal could not be touched by replies in other journals which his own readers would not see.[49] It was the *Reasoner* which made Holyoake the leader of British Secularism.

The revival in freethought began in 1850 with a marked turn in the fortunes of the *Reasoner*. In that year W. H. Ashurst started a new monthly, the *People's Review of Literature and Politics*, which enabled Holyoake to reverse the disastrous policy of the previous year when he had tried to ape the political press. Now, instead of emphasising social and political matters in the *Reasoner*, he banished them to the *People's Review*, making the *Reasoner* purely theological. Ashurst had already offered the paper £100 and W. J. Birch promised ten shillings a week. The new *Reasoner* began, reduced in size, at one penny and the venture was immediately successful.[50] Six hundred new subscribers were found in the first ten weeks, partly owing to the reduction in price and partly because of the change in emphasis. The truth was that Holyoake had not the skill of a Thomas Cooper or a Joseph Barker to make a general periodical popular. Unlike Southwell, Holyoake rarely modified his style to suit his readers and his treatment of politics was way off the mark; but what he had to say in theology was popular. In the *Reasoner* for 6 February 1850 he wrote a long article on *The Logic of Death* in which he set down some theological thoughts on the cholera. The issue sold an extra five hundred and fifty copies and marks the turning point in the paper's fortunes. The volume was cut short at the end of the quarter and a new one, volume IX, was begun in April with double the number of pages for the same price. The sale of this was even better. The first number contained the promise of a series of articles on Hell, accompanied by an eye-catching figure of Satan sketched by W. J. Linton. The first imprint sold out immediately and three days later an extra edition of a thousand had gone also.[51] The next eight issues contained pictures of Hell, illustrating comments on a book of Catholic doctrine by Father Pinamonti, together with a criticism of this work. Anti-Catholicism paid off and the pictures drew a warm response. J. W. T. of Osmotherley wrote:

> I receive your *Reasoner* regularly. The horrible plates that have appeared in it of late, have done good service to the cause of free-thought in this village. I have taken them from the book and pasted them in rows on my

window panes, and have watched with intense interest their effect upon the passers by . . . Mr. Holyoake, these plates force people to think: my young men thank you for them, I thank you for them.[52]

When the series ended it was replaced by a relatively tame weekly article of educational interest for children with illustrations of flowers by Linton, but the circulation still kept rising rapidly. Volumes IX and X made a surplus of over £48, excluding editorial expenses. Though still dependent on the Shilling Fund for the latter, Holyoake and his paper were at last in a relatively healthy position.[53]

Encouraging though this was, the circulation of the *Reasoner* was dwarfed by those of its contemporaries. In January 1849 Thomas Cooper had started a new weekly, the *Plain Speaker*; by the end of the first week it had sold 3,000 and by the end of the first month the sales of the first number had gone up to 7,000. *Cooper's Journal* in 1850 sold 5,000 in the first week (9,000 eventually) and although average sales dropped to around 3,600 in June, this was still well above anything the *Reasoner* had achieved up to that time.[54] According to one estimate, the circulation of Joseph Barker's *People* reached 20,000 at the height of its popularity and the *Northern Star* claimed between 35,000 and 60,000.[55] Holyoake's efforts seem even smaller when compared with the output of the religious press. In the second half of 1850 alone, the Religious Tract Society put into circulation some 15,000 tracts, and none of the free-thinkers could match that.[56] The *Reasoner* maintained itself amid this mass of literature solely by the consistent efforts of its editor and the loyalty of its financial backers, and the peak of its success owed much to the notoriety given to it by the efforts of Brewin Grant. The circulation, which had soared from about three thousand at the beginning of 1852 to around five thousand a year later, was back to around three thousand by late 1854.

The mid-50s were a critical time for all periodical literature. The financial stability of the *Reasoner* and the *Investigator* was precarious at the best of times, but in 1854 paper costs were rising by three to four shillings a ream, and not until the repeal of the Paper Duties in 1861 was this burden removed. At the same time, the repeal of the Stamp Duty in 1855 meant that periodicals, which had hitherto dominated the cheap press, were for the first time being subjected to the fierce competition of popular cheap newspapers. The periodicals had to adapt themselves if they were to survive, and this Holyoake attempted to do with his *Reasoner*. In March 1855 he took over the *Tyne* (or *Northern*) *Tribune*, which had been started by Joseph Cowen and G. J. Harney in New-castle, and issued the '*Reasoner* and *London Tribune*, a Weekly and Secular Newspaper', printed at twopence in anticipation of the removal

P

of the Stamp.[57] From the commencement of volume xix on 1 April, the paper was issued on foolscap folio instead of octavo, but although it tried to look like a newspaper it was never a good one. Holyoake was later to become a successful journalist with the popular Liberal press, but before 1861 he had little experience in the new medium. Although he had contributed occasional articles to the newspaper press, his *English Leader* (1864–6) was his first real venture into popular journalism.

The style of the *Reasoner* was that of the *New Moral World* and the papers of an earlier generation. Its format could easily have been mistaken for that of the *Republican*. The contents resembled those of the *Oracle* or the *Movement* and the other papers on which Holyoake had learned his trade. In 1856 the *Reasoner* described itself as containing

> . . . weekly articles by the Editor; occasional papers by distinguished writers; controversial letters from clergymen and ministers; communications from leaders of Freethought in Great Britain, Germany, India, America, and other countries; reports of discussions, lectures, and of the progress of organisations for advancing positive philosophy; reviews of leading books which elucidate or bear upon Freethought principles; incidental communications from the leaders of the European democracy; discussion, earnest and relevant, in Secularism, Theology, Sociology, Communism, Physiology—denied utterance in the general press may have a 'Free Platform' in the *Reasoner*.[58]

This was all very old-fashioned. Like much of the literature which Holyoake published in the 1850s, its purpose was supposed to be educational and its aim was to promote free thinking, but in fact, no less than the religious literature of the period, it assumed the conclusions which it sought to prove. The man who bought his Secularist newspaper did not read it for its news but for its Secularism, and the *Reasoner* continued to exist on the unsuccessful fringe of the thriving market for religious literature. It appealed to philosophically inclined working men, who must have been few, and to liberal clergymen who wished to keep in touch with the latest developments in popular infidelity.[59] The similarity between the *Reasoner* and Evangelical papers such as the *Record* was noticed by the *Saturday Review* when in 1856 it turned its critical eye to Holyoake's paper:

> Perhaps an even more curious characteristic than logical deficiency is the narrow sectarianism in which the journal before us so closely resembles the religious newspapers of the day. . . . Both of them [the *Reasoner* and the *Record*] attach infinite importance to a certain set of opinions—both of them believe that their respective views are indispensable conditions of all human progress and happiness—and each of them goes on gyrating in its own small circle, grinding its own small assortment of tunes on the same barrel, over and over again, and never showing the smallest result. . . .[60]

This was, of course, an exaggeration of the truth and ignored the fact that a doctrinal paper has of its nature to be didactic rather than informative, but the weekly *Reasoner* is clearly recognisable in this criticism. It was at times a tedious publication in the true Owenite tradition, substituting repetition for argument, and confusing quantity with quality. The new cheap press was to leave it and its like behind. Holyoake persisted but in 1859 his frail health broke down completely. A final effort was made in 1860 to take the financial burden off his shoulders and a '*Reasoner* Company' was launched, but before this had properly got underway Holyoake had decided to give up the struggle and he ceased weekly publication on 30 June 1861.[61]

The *Investigator* was no better than the *Reasoner* in this respect. Started as the *London Investigator* by Robert Cooper in April 1854, it was an old-fashioned monthly periodical and like the *Reasoner* it provided sixteen octavo pages for twopence. Although its editorial line was opposed to Holyoake's moderate Secularism and although most of its contributors were, at one time or another, in disputes with Holyoake, it was not really a rival to the older paper. It made no impression on the circulation of the *Reasoner* and was even published by Holyoake at 147 Fleet Street. Cooper was as set in his ways as Holyoake. As a monthly the *Investigator* was not liable to the newspaper stamp, but it still contained no news and even after the abolition of the stamp, when suggestions were made that the paper should become a penny weekly, Cooper (who also was in ill-health) was not inclined to abandon his periodical and to turn it into a true newspaper. In 1857 he retired, Edward Truelove took over the publication, and W. H. Johnson as the new editor tried to change the paper but with little success. The *London* part of the title was dropped, and in October 1857 the price and size were cut by half, but little else was altered. The last two volumes, commencing March 1858, were issued in fortnightly numbers but when Charles Bradlaugh took over the paper at the end of that year its appearance and problems were still those of the *Reasoner*. Crippled by lack of funds, it reverted to monthly publication in June 1859 and ended altogether in August.[62]

The third Secularist paper, the *National Reformer*, was entirely different. It began as a real newspaper and it grew out of the popular movement in the north on the initiative of the Sheffield Secularists in 1860. Bradlaugh and Barker were chosen as its first editors and both were well suited for the task. Barker, who had been a prominent West Riding Chartist in 1848, already had a considerable reputation in the north as a political and religious radical. Bradlaugh had learned his trade with the *Investigator* and was intimately involved in the revival of Secularism in the north. The paper was given a commercial basis from the start, a 'National Reformer Company' being formed to raise £2,000 in ten-shilling shares. The president of the company, James Dodworth, was president of the Sheffield Secularists, and the secretary, Henry Turner, was secretary of the Sheffield society. Holyoake did not at first see the new paper as a threat to his own position, and he acted as the London agent for it. The beginning of the new paper seems to have made no difference, for better or worse, to the gradual decline of the Reasoner, but Holyoake may have misread the signs.[63] The National Reformer was founded at a time when the expansion of Secularism could have satisfied the circulation of two papers as in 1854, but in 1860 the Reasoner did not greatly benefit from this second revival, which was, like the National Reformer, provincial and Bradlaugh orientated. Holyoake and his Reasoner had little part in it.

d
Finance

This propaganda had to be paid for. Like all radical campaigns, Secularism needed finance, and like all predominantly working-class organisations, the Secularists were always short of money. Holyoake's work was never self-supporting, the Reasoner and the Investigator could seldom meet their expenses and rarely paid anything to their editors, the Fleet Street House was chronically insolvent, and the radical agitations lived from hand to mouth.

The first source of money came from what could be earned, and this was never enough. In 1853 volume xv of the Reasoner, which reached its maximum circulation of 5,000, cost over £337 to produce but the income from sales was only a little over £312, and only in 1860 was a profit made when the format and size were reduced while the price remained at 2d. The National Reformer in its first year sold nearly twice as many copies as the Reasoner did in its last year, but at 2d a copy it only just paid its way, and it went into deficit the following year. The periodicals therefore had to be subsidised, and the necessary balances were usually raised by other means.[64]

The classic form of working-class finance was the 'propagandist fund'. An appeal was issued, and then each week lists of names were published in the periodicals as the pitifully small sums amounted up. Carlile had been maintained in this way between 1819 and 1826; in 1829 he and Taylor had collected their 'Infidel Rent'; the Anti-Persecution Union had relied upon small subscriptions; and the Owenites had fallen back on them in the 1840s. The *Reasoner* could not have existed without the 'Shilling List', as it was hopefully called, which raised between £50 and £100 a year. In addition to its own propagandist fund, a radical periodical was also likely to have at least one other similar appeal in its pages at the same time, collecting pennies and sixpences for foreign refugees, the reform effort, the repeal of the Taxes on Knowledge, or Italian Liberation. Only at the end of the decade were joint stock companies formed to provide more efficient finance for the periodicals, and neither the '*Reasoner* Company' nor the '*National Reformer* Company' lasted long. The editors were too individualistic to submit to the control of a board of directors. Earlier, other and more desperate remedies had been tried. In the late 1850s Secular bazaars were organised at Fleet Street, to which goods as well as money were contributed by local Secularists, but very little profit was made on these occasions. In 1859 Bradlaugh too had to resort to the same sort of function in his attempt to save the *Investigator*.[65]

Though small subscriptions from working men were predominant in the subscription lists, most of the money usually came from wealthy patrons. Richard Carlile had been supported by Julian Hibbert, and the Owenites had relied upon the Home Colonisation Society. Like the Reform League in the 1860s, Secularism in the 1850s was unable to attract sufficient working-class funds to remain independent of external aid, and so it was tied to the middle-class radicals.[66] Holyoake, no less than George Howell after him, was compelled by financial necessity to tread the path towards respectability which appealed to him for other reasons.[67] The 'Shilling Fund' contained many sums of less than a shilling, but not a few of more than £1, and the Fleet Street House was practically paid for by a handful of well-known radical supporters. W. J. Birch and W. H. Ashurst had been the principal sponsors of the Anti-Persecution Union and the Theological Utilitarians; Trevelyan, Ashurst and J. S. Mill had financed Holyoake's university studies in 1849; Mill had sent a further £35 in 1856 to help Holyoake after he had raised a loan on his life assurance policy in an effort to save the bankrupt Le Blond; Ashurst, junior, (£150), J. G. Crawford (£100), W. Shaen (£20), J. S. Mill (£30), Colonel Henry Clinton (£150), Percy Greg (£30), Sarah Lewin (£20) and the Rochdale Pioneers (£10) all loaned money to the Fleet Street House between 1858 and 1861. Considerable gifts were also made by such people. In 1858 £651 was raised in a special appeal, but London contributed £451 of this, chiefly in sums of over £1. 'A Friend of Free Thought' gave the bulk, £350, and other names mentioned include those of Crawford, one of the sponsors (£5), and P. T[aylor (?)] (£10). Well-known names from elsewhere were those of

Evans Bell (£25), Joseph Cowen, junior (£25), Harriet Martineau (£1), Samuel Ingham of Manchester (£10) and James Dodworth of Sheffield (£5). A second subscription, opened in 1861 to clear the rest of Holyoake's debts, was sponsored by Arthur Trevelyan, Henry Clinton, Joseph Cowen, William Shaen and J. G. Crawford.[68]

The local societies also had to be self-financing, and this was one of their greatest weaknesses. Their only source of income, apart from rare gifts from wealthy friends, were subscriptions, admission charges and social events. The West Riding Secular Alliance asked for a penny a week from all its members to finance a missionary organisation. It is unlikely that much money was raised in this way, as the scheme for a network of paid agents was never implemented.[69] The general level of subscriptions was low. The Blackburn Secular newsroom in 1853 charged 1s 6d a quarter; Leicester in 1861 asked 1s a quarter; Paisley in 1851 charged only 1s a year; Glasgow relied upon voluntary collections on Sundays, and lecture charges of 1d or 2d during the week.[70] These seem to have been about the usual level, so after the cost of hiring a hall and paying for a lecturer had been met, there cannot have been much profit left for the societies' own funds. Yet this was the income on which they relied. Admission to soirées and tea meetings was higher—perhaps 1s or more—but these efforts were of social rather than of financial importance. Like the Chapel, the local Secularists seem to have valued their bazaars and teas and musical evenings as much for their own sake as for any financial advantage.

It the movement was built on a flimsy financial basis, then the leaders fared no better. Despite frequent charges to the contrary, Holyoake does not appear to have profited from his business though he was dependent upon it for a living.[71] Bradlaugh survived only by remaining in full-time employment as an attorney's clerk and company promoter, and until 1870 he supported his propaganda efforts and his family mainly out of his own slender income.[72] Robert Cooper had no regular source of income. He had taken a job as a clerk with a Huddersfield chemical manufacturer in 1846 to support himself as a socialist lecturer at the local Hall of Science, and in 1851 he was employed in London as a travelling salesman, but he did not relish such employments and regarded them merely as means to the end of propagandism. In 1856 he was left as sole executor and residual legatee in the will of a rich friend, Samuel Fletcher, but as Fletcher's wealth was largely in the form of a government annuity, the liabilities of the bequest exceeded the assets.[73] Holyoake relied upon lecturing and journalism for an income, and Edward Truelove, the Owenite freethought bookseller, built his business largely on the antiquarian trade.[74]

In theory, a popular lecturer could make a considerable sum of money —J. B. Langley in 1849 estimated between £500 and £1,000 a year—but Holyoake never reached these heights. In 1851 he was charging an average of two guineas a lecture, but his travelling expenses must have consumed most of this.[75] 'I am sorry I can only send you £4 as I have not earned much and am obliged to keep some to carry me about with,' he wrote to his wife from Stockport in 1851. 'I shall send you 10/- to make up your £2–10–0 weekly,' he added later from Sheffield.[76] The rest of the money presumably came from the *Reasoner* fund and the sale of publications in London, but even such money was often ploughed back. In 1853 Holyoake was presented with £250, all of which went into the Fleet Street House. In 1856 Holyoake estimated his income from lectures to be £42 19s, and he made almost another £50 from his writings.[77] These sums were adequate for the support of himself and his wife and children, but scarcely more than he could have earned as a skilled artisan back in Birmingham, and he was constantly troubled by his lack of security. Burdened with debt on account of the Fleet Street House, he looked forward to a regular salary but he was never to achieve one.[78]

This was the dismal future which faced many, perhaps most, popular working-class leaders. They were dependent upon their movements to support their propagandist efforts, and 'payment by results' was even more real to these self-appointed 'teachers of the people' than it was to teachers in the state-financed educational system under the Revised Code. Without capital they could not make their organisations permanent, and without a regular income they could offer themselves and their families none of that security and independence which was so much a part of their moral, self-help creed. All the leaders had to be rescued by at least one special appeal: G. J. Holyoake (1853, 1858, 1861), Robert Cooper (1856), Charles Bradlaugh (1858) and Austin Holyoake (1864); and without the additional sums brought in on these occasions it is doubtful whether they could have carried on at all. They looked to their followers and they looked to their patrons. Holyoake in particular relied upon the latter, and though there is no evidence of his deliberately moderating his policy to attract funds as the Owenites had done in the early 1840s, one suspects that at some level of consciousness Holyoake realised that he who pays the piper must call the tune. In this respect, Secularism followed Owenism and was one of the many attempts at working-class organisation in the second half of the nineteenth century to be torn apart between the expectations of its followers and the needs of finance.

e
Meeting places

When one of the national lecturers visited a known centre of Secularism,
he usually delivered his lectures in some public hall. Rarely did a local
secular society have premises of its own adequate to accommodate the
large audiences which were likely to be attracted by a Bradlaugh or a
Holyoake. Most of the large halls built by the Owenites had passed into
other hands, and even those societies which had endured the storms of
1846 had had their problems. Stockport was lucky enough to keep its
original hall until 1854, but then William Coltman, who had provided
the mortgage, died and the hall had to be sold to repay the executors.[79]
Very few societies could echo the sentiments of James Motherwell of
Paisley, who in 1857 was able to refer to

> the twentieth anniversary of our society, being formerly erected one of the
> Branches of the 'Association of All Classes of All Nations'. Our Charter,
> signed by the hand of the venerable Robert Owen, bears the date the 18th
> day of October, 1837, exactly twenty years ago. And it is something to be
> proud of, that for this lengthened period we have never been without a
> place of meeting. We have passed through many vicissitudes, have achieved
> great success and experience. But our labours, and the labours of a
> Fleming, a Lloyd Jones, a Jefferey [sic], a Watts, a Farn, a Spiers, a
> Buchanan, and last, though not least, a Holyoake, have not been in
> vain. . . .[80]

Most societies had had to begin again in a small way. The Newcastle
Secularists at first had no premises of their own at all: they continued to
use the Nelson Street Music Hall for lectures and their committee met
in the Nun Street Reading Room which belonged to the Chartists. The
Bolton Secular Society was formed at a meeting in July 1852 at the
Conqueror Lodge of Oddfellows in Bowkers' Row and they continued
to meet there until they acquired their own premises in 1857. The
Preston Secularists met in the Weavers' Committee Room, and the men
of Lancaster in the Unitarian schoolroom. The Leeds Secularists were
more fortunate in acquiring the 'Progressionist Hall' in Cheapside,
which would hold 350 people, but they seem to have lost this place some
time during the mid-1850s.[81] The attraction of the open air very often
was that it was free and spacious. Only a few societies were ever to obtain
their own premises, and the impetus in this direction often came when
no adequate hall was available or, more likely, when no landlord would
let his premises for Secularist purposes. Not all places were as fortunate
as Burnley, where Messrs L. Ashworth and B. Holdsworth put up a
public hall costing £2,500 which was 'to be free for all parties'. Holyoake

opened this hall in 1862 with a lecture on Mill's *Liberty*.[82] Leeds was more typical: in 1862 the Secularists were saving up for their own hall, but they were still saving in 1865. Indoor meetings had to be held in an overcrowded room in the Bazaar, whilst really large gatherings had to take place in the open air at Vicar's Croft—both former Chartist meeting places.[83] In the early history of provincial Secularism, Bradford was one of the few places to raise sufficient funds in small subscriptions for a Secular Hall. Every public room in Bradford, it was claimed, was closed to the Secularists, so in 1863 a Secular Hall Company was launched to raise £700 in £1 shares. Edward Kirkbride had purchased the Teetotal Hall in Southgate for £660, and the aim was to purchase the hall from him. The project seems to have been successful.[84] But most societies, if they had halls at all, had to be content with renting them, and the typical society was never really big enough to justify its having its own premises. The reading room, the public house and the Temperance Hotel were the usual kind of meeting place.

Public houses were important in the development of British radicalism. They were natural centres of working-class society and friendly landlords could usually be found in all but the smallest communities. The Oldham Social Society, an early attempt to revive Socialism in the town, used to meet each first Sunday in the month in 1851 at Edward Rye's 'Red Lion' at Bottom-of-Moor. In 1853 Rye was again trying to revive interest by summoning the 'friends of Secularism' to his inn. The Isle of Sheppy [*sic*] Discussion Society used to meet in a public room adjoining the 'Shipwright's Arms', and Secularism was revived in the area in 1861 at the 'Russell Tavern'. When the friends of Secularism in Northampton wanted to celebrate Paine's birthday in 1864, the only room they could obtain was a small one in the 'Admiral Nelson' on the Green, owned by their old friend Edward Pebody, and when the Northampton Secular Society was revived in 1866, the monthly meetings also took place at the 'Admiral Nelson'.[85] Generally speaking, though, the Secularists shared the abhorrence with which many radical groups viewed the institution of the public house. It was seen as the place where the working man drank away his wages, and it provided an unwholesome environment for organisations which emphasised the virtues of self-help, mutual improvement, sobriety and thrift. The Norwich Secularists had to meet at the 'Pigeons Inn', but they were very apologetic about this, admitted it was a drawback, and assured the readers of the *National Reformer* that the room was engaged on the understanding that members would not be expected to buy drink.[86]

The coffee house therefore became the working-class institution *par excellence*, and the rapid spread of this social phenomenon in the mid-century indicates both the growth of the temperance movement and the development of that sort of working-class Liberalism which Mr Gladstone so much admired. John Doherty had retired from Trade Unionism in the mid-1830s to become a bookseller and coffee house keeper, and he provided ninety-six newspapers and periodicals which working men could read for a penny. William Lovett had opened 'Lovett's Coffee and Conversation Rooms' in 1834, with a library of several hundred volumes and twenty-eight journals. Lovett himself estimated in 1849 that there had been a fivefold increase in the number of coffee houses in the country during the previous seventeen or eighteen years, and he thought that there were about two thousand such places in London, a quarter of them with libraries.[87] Such places were centres of radicalism where Secularists and others could freely mix and discuss their ideas. For example, after the Whitechapel Social Institution had closed in 1848, the freethinkers started discussion groups in the coffee rooms of various public houses, and when the teetotallers opened a hall in the neighbourhood, they began to meet there as well. In 1851 they acquired their own 'Areopagus Coffee and Reading Room', where lectures and discussions were held and a large variety of newspapers were taken, including the *Times, Sun, Express, Leader, Reynolds', Dispatch, Illustrated News, Bell's Life, Punch, Reasoner, Owen's Journal, Operative, Friend of the People, Chambers's Journal, Family Herald* and *Railway Guide.*[88] This sort of meeting place, with good healthy refreshment for mind and body, was to be found in many parts of London and other large towns and cities.

In the provinces, the coffee room or Temperance Hotel was vitally important for the early development of Secularism and other radical movements. The preliminary step to be taken before Secularism could be effectively propagated in a community was very often the opening of a reading room and coffee house. At Banbury in 1855, a Mr Bunton was discovered by Holyoake to have opened 'a good bookseller's shop, news-room, and coffee-room where friends meet weekly'.[89] At Nottingham, according to the *Reasoner* in 1851, Smith's Coffee House on the Pavement was a place where 'a triple coterie of Chartists, Socialists, and Theologians are nurtured on ginger beer, coffee, and lemonades'.[90] In Leeds, the local leader was John Smith, for twenty years a Methodist, a class leader and a preacher, who in 1852 took over the Temperance Star Hotel in Swan Street, Briggate.[91] Smith's and Dawson's Temperance Hotels and Shaw's Coffee House were the principal meeting places of the Leeds Secularists throughout the 1850s. In 1855 the Halifax Secularists held Sunday evening lectures and discussions at the Gibbet Street Temperance Hotel and the Sheffield Secular Association met at Heald's

Temperance Hotel. The Bradford Secularists met at either Mitchell's or Greenwood's, while their camp meetings could find refreshment at Whitehead's in Shipley Glen.

One of the most famous of all the West Riding Temperance Hotels was Thornton's in Huddersfield. Situated over a hatter's shop in New Street, the principal thoroughfare, it was 'The Centre of Light and Knowledge' to generations of radicals. The hotel was started in 1850 by Henry Wimpenny, a tailor, and was taken over the following year by Joseph Thornton who was a cloth-finisher by trade. When the Secularists lost the use of the Christian Brethren's rooms in Albion Street in about 1855, they moved to the hospitable Thornton's, and Holyoake stayed there when he lectured at the Philosophical Hall in 1860. Joseph Thornton and his establishment sum up much that was important in the structure of nineteenth-century radicalism. He was 'a man of exceptional intelligence, great good humour, sound judgment, broad and advanced political and religious views, a keen follower of the immortal Shakespeare, a total abstainer . . .'. Under his auspices all kinds of radicalism thrived, and his hotel 'was thought by more timorous townsmen to be the resort of wicked conspirators and schemers plotting against religion and the throne'. Inside the hotel was a large room with a raised platform at one end where Thornton often sat to chair discussions, a commercial room where meals were provided, and a small room for draughts and chess. All manner of topics were open to discussion, and one favourite was always Joseph Barker's latest change of faith. All were welcome to take part; it was frequented by 'all the local intellectuals—real and would be—who gathered in its rooms to discuss political and religious topics over coffee cups'. In this kind of atmosphere Secularism thrived.[92]

The same sort of social function was also provided by a much more unlikely institution—the Turkish bath. The public bath was a working-class institution closely associated with the ideal of self-improvement and respectability. Ordinary public baths had spread rapidly since their first introduction in London in 1846, and in 1856 the Stalybridge Secular Society was meeting 'in Mr. Wagstaff's new room, the Baths'. According to the Field, quoted by the Reasoner in 1860, the Turkish bath had been introduced by David Urquhart in 1856 and following his opening of an establishment in Manchester in 1857 the idea spread rapidly.[93] The Turkish bath can be seen as an aspect of the Foreign Affairs agitation which Urquhart was popularising at the same time, and the fact that a number of leading Secularists seem to have been closely involved, suggests, among other things, the impact which Urquhartism was making on Secularism at this time. Thomas Wilcock, founder secretary of the West Riding Secular Alliance, established a 'Turkish Bath and Foreign Affairs Association' in Bradford in 1858. Holyoake was fired with enthusiasm: 'Mr. Wilcock wishes to see a Turkish Bath in every district of every town, and wishes the attention of Secularists called to the possibility of it,' he wrote in the *Reasoner*. Other Secularists were busy trying to accomplish this. Charles Hindle opened a bath at Stockport in 1859, John Maxfield one in Huddersfield, and Joseph Jagger one in Rochdale. Joseph Barker and Charles Bradlaugh were no less enthusiastic about the new idea, which was spread rapidly by Secularists. Wilcock opened baths in Sheffield, Stockport and Liverpool; Maxwell and Jagger opened baths in London; and other premises were advertised by Secularists in the Edgware Road and in Golden Square, London. Jagger also wrote a tract on Turkish baths, and a United Turkish Baths Association was formed in October 1860, with John Maxfield as chairman, Thomas Wilcock as secretary, and Abel Andrew of Stalybridge as treasurer.[94] The source of this enthusiasm for Turkish baths was to be found in Lancashire and the West Riding where Secularism too was at its strongest, and the relationship between the two movements was close. During the winter of 1858–9 the Bradford Secular Improvement Society gathered at Thornton's Turkish Bath Establishment, while the Leeds Secular Society used John Shaw's Coffee House and Turkish Bath Establishment, and in 1861 the committee of the Leeds Secular Society and the Members' Instruction Class met at Mr Rawnsley's Turkish bath. There can be little doubt that this new enthusiasm for Turkish baths among Secularists, particularly among the leaders, was a major reason for the weakening of the W.R.S.U. in the late 1850s. John Shaw, F. S. Rawnsley and A. Robinson, who were all Secularists, had been prominent members of Urquhart's Foreign Affairs Committees in the West Riding during the Crimean War, and the continuing appeal of Urquhart through the Turkish bath movement was a constant threat to Secularism, even though the baths often gave Secularism a home.[95]

The appeal of the Turkish bath to men of a Secularist outlook is not hard to explain. Cleanliness was next to godliness, but it was very difficult for the Victorian working man to keep clean or warm. The Turkish bath promised to satisfy both these needs, and, according to Holyoake, Urquhart intended the baths to 'supply the place of public inns, and be adapted for social assemblies of health and recreation'. This was a secular improvement which appealed to the working man who was trying to better himself and his class by means of self-help and mutual improvement.[96]

The radical goal of improvement, and the way in which some Secularists trod that path from perdition to success which was so beloved by middle-class moralists, is perhaps best illustrated by a consecutive list of the sorts of places at which successive Secularist groups met during the 1850s. In Oldham, for example, the Secularists started, as has already been noted, in a public house. They then went on to the school room of the Mutual Instruction Society in Henshaw Street, Leonard Haslop's Temperance Hotel in the Market Place, Samuel Taylor's Secular Bookshop in Yorkshire Street, and finally, in 1861, to a room belonging to the Oldham Co-operative Society.[97] The Manchester Secularists had followed an almost similar course from public house to Co-operative store, and one might apply to some of the Secular societies in the late 1850s the tag which Ernest Jones had fastened to the Co-operative movement—'an attempt of a small knot among the aristocracy of labour to creep on to the platform of the middle class'.[98] With Holyoake, the movement was becoming respectable.

f
Activities

The sort of meetings to be held on Secularist premises varied a great deal according to local circumstances. Lectures were especially important in the larger halls, such as the City Road Hall of Science or the Cleveland Street Institution (formerly, the John Street Institution) in London, but such places were not typical and the kind of performance put on by Holyoake or Bradlaugh was even less typical of the weekly fare tasted by most Secularists. The lecture tours of the leaders naturally dominate the accounts given in the periodicals but much else went on within individual societies. The relative scale of proceedings is indicated in a report from Huddersfield in 1862: Bradlaugh's lecture on 24 August was attended by a thousand people, but the actual membership of the local society was eighty, and there were only sixteen members in the mutual improvement class.[99] Some societies were little more than mutual improvement classes.

The 'atmosphere' of Secularist meetings therefore depended largely on the location, the occasion and the scale of the event. We are sometimes left with the impression that every Sunday evening was like an evening of the Holyoake–Brewin Grant debate, described above.[100] This was not so, and there are occasional hints in the reports that even the most prominent societies could not always secure full halls. When Robert Cooper addressed the London Secular Society in 1855, for example, he was 'listened to with interest by a fuller audience than usual'. Weekly meetings in obscure, greasy, back-street halls and

public houses must have been far different from those conducted in
the best rooms of Temperance Hotels or smart Halls of Science left over
from the days of Owenism. Grand-sounding names can mislead us.
W. E. Adams recalled that the Temple Forum in Fleet Street was 'held
in a back room of the Green Dragon, small and ill-ventilated', and we
may presume that this was true of many such societies.[101]

Secularism in the 1850s shared in the working-class cultural heritage.
The men and women who had met in the Chartist clubs or Social Institutes ten years earlier, or who had formerly been a part of the active
social life of some Little Bethel, carried over into Secularism their
expectations and aspirations and leisure-time activities.[102] Sunday was
the most important day—the day of rest and rational recreation. Only
the larger branches had two or more lectures on that day; some had
lectures only once a month, or even less frequently, and most seem
to have abandoned a formal indoor programme during the summer
months. Each local society had its own preferences. Colne, for example,
had a Secular Society in 1852: meetings were held Saturday evenings
when news readings and political information were shared; on Sunday
afternoons and evenings general and philosophical works were read,
followed by discussions. On Sunday mornings the local leader used to
distribute the *Reasoner* around the town. Only the largest societies
might manage meetings on Sunday mornings–Manchester, for example;
whilst the smallest, as at Redditch, had to be satisfied with Monday
evenings only.[103] A description of the Pantheistic Society which met in
London suggests what might have happened at such small meetings:

> [The Pantheists were] a small society of thirteen working men, who agreed
> to hold a periodical meeting at a public-house in Broad Street, Golden
> Square, for the purpose of improving each other. They got together a
> library, and arranged for the composition of essays on different subjects,
> the chairman to read to them, and the meeting to judge of their merits.
> It was open to the public, and several persons attended. The first essay
> was on the subject, 'What is God?' Several were written in prose and verse,
> but the one which was adjudged best only contained these four words,
> 'God is the universe'. The man who wrote this was the secretary of the
> society.[104]

Reports of serious lectures and philosophical discussions, though, give a
misleading impression of what life in a Secular Society could be like.
The Woolwich friends were only being honest when they admitted
that shopkeepers were too tired to attend lectures during the week, and
that lectures should really be regarded as an amusement. Rather, their
report went on,

> We all feel our propagandism has been unsuited to the mass, that it
> appeared to savour more of passion than of principle, but we hope our

friends will meet and cultivate those qualities necessary to give stability and attraction to any community.

This was the limited ideal of many Secularists, who wanted the local society to provide a suitable environment in which life could be improved and enjoyed, and character developed in a wholesome and rational way.[105]

When Holyoake went to Nottingham in 1859 to deliver a course of lectures in the Assembly Rooms, Low Pavement, the ordinary member of the public who read the bill announcing the meetings would have learned that the doors opened at 7.30 p.m., that the lectures started at 8 p.m. and that the admission charge was a penny (threepence for a front seat); but if he had been a Secularist he would have read further, learned that for a shilling he could buy a Sunday tea-ticket, and he would then have met the great man in person over a cup of tea in Radford's Temperance Hotel.[106] The tea meeting was an important institution: when the Bolton Secularists opened their premises over a shop in Cheapside in 1857, fifty people sat down to tea and sang social hymns; the Todmorden and Rochdale Secularists met over tea; the Glasgow and Paisley friends exchanged hospitality.[107] Soirées, concerts and dancing helped fill leisure hours and brighten dull working-class lives. Robert Cooper experienced this when he attended a Good Friday soirée at Newcastle in 1855:

> The diligence of our purveyors had early caused the tables to groan under the superabundance of eatables, whilst under the superintendence of a lady friend . . . the tea would have done justice to the critical palate of Hazlitt himself. . . . Mr. James Charlton was called upon to preside, and in an excellent manner introduced the objects of the meeting [in honour of Cooper and the *Investigator*]. . . . A selection of songs and recitations now followed, continued at intervals during the evening. They were alike varied, amusing, and appropriate.[108]

Special occasions demanded special treatment. Paine's and Owen's birthdays called for parties in honour of those worthy benefactors of mankind; and celebrations enjoyed by Christians were not denied to atheists. The Secular Sunday Schools had their Whitsun outings: on Whit-Tuesday 1861 a hundred and thirty scholars and teachers in Halifax went in procession to the local museum; on Good Friday 1865 a hundred and eighty scholars, teachers and friends in Failsworth went on the traditional Whit Walk, singing secular hymns from the old *Social Hymn Book*. In Huddersfield, the Secularists even held a Sunday School Anniversary and Prize Giving each year, when hymns were sung from a new collection of nearly two hundred *Secular Hymns for Sunday School and Secular Gatherings*, compiled by Henry Fielding, a local printer.[109] The life of the local chapel was faithfully reproduced—and more besides. On 24 October 1849, when the churches of Manchester were holding their Cholera Fast, the unbelievers at the Hall of Science celebrated with a quadrille party. Music was an important part of any Secularist gathering, however inappropriate the occasion. At the Halifax Convention of 1860, serious business gave way to song and the meeting degenerated into an impromptu concert, with James Dodworth of Sheffield rendering 'John Brown' and 'When is a Man less than a Man?' and other popular numbers.[110]

The most important aspect of Secularist conviviality, though, was the camp meeting. One object of the West Riding Secular Alliance was 'to hold weekly Sunday camp meetings, and expound Pentecostal truths, combining the acquisition of knowledge with health and exercise', and, as we have seen, this object was largely carried out. With the help of a local brass band, secular hymns from the *Social Hymn Book*, and solos such as 'There's a good time coming, boys' by Charles Mackay, rang across the lonely Pennine moors. One of the earliest reports of Secularist activity in Wales is of 'hundreds' who, led by Mr E. Davies from Pontypridd, made their way up to a natural pulpit on the mountaintop at Mathmalewg.[111] The importance of the camp meeting in the development of Secularism cannot be overemphasised. It gave the lecturers a far wider audience than they could have reached in their inadequate halls, and it lent greater attraction to the activities of the Secularists themselves. A report from Sheffield is typical:

> On Sunday, May 18, the members and friends of the Sheffield Secular Society had their first ramble this season. Happily for the people of Sheffield, we are within a short distance of some of the most delightful spots that the mind can imagine. The place we went to was the Riverlin Hotel. After regaling ourselves of a cup of tea, we went out to climb the rough, rugged, rocky road, until we reached the highest point, and there we pitched our tent. Those who remained at the top were instructed and amused by a short address, followed by songs, recitations, &c., from our friends. Others rambled about the rocks gathering wild flowers, getting health, and receiving instruction as they went along. In fact we were one of the happiest gatherings that were out that day. It was the most numerous out-door meeting we have had. We consisted of all ages, from one year old to seventy. About eight o'clock we returned home, joyful and happy, after our well-spent day. Next Sunday, May 25, we propose going to Chatsworth.[112]

This is an authentic glimpse at working-class culture—of the attempt of humanity to grapple with the problems of urbanisation and industrialisation, and to triumph over them. On an earlier occasion, the Sheffield Secularists had spent Whit-Sunday in Derbyshire, reading Shakespeare

in the Winnatts Pass, high above Castleton.[113] Culture—a widening of
the human experience through music, drama, reading and entertainment of all kinds—was what the Secularists sought and found in their
little societies. This was a way of life which they shared with the chapels
and temperance societies, but which was far removed from the atmosphere of the beer-house and other such dens of iniquity. Secularism
was appealing, but only to a certain sort of person.

g
Appeal

'Secularism was embraced by thousands and tens of thousands of the
working classes. The success which attended the attempts made to propagate it was due partly to the fact that great masses of the working
classes, especially in the large manufacturing towns, were already lost to
Christianity, and had, in many cases, almost unconsciously adopted the
ideas which Mr. Holyoake fixed, and shaped into distinct doctrines . . . ,'
wrote W. N. Molesworth in his *History of England*.[114] This interpretation of the importance of Secularism, eagerly off-printed by a flattered
Holyoake, makes two fundamental assumptions: first that the Secularist
movement had a very wide appeal, and secondly that this appeal was to
the working classes.

A favourite starting point for a discussion of these issues is the *Report
of the Religious Census*, published by Horace Mann in 1854:

> This is the creed which probably with most exactness indicates the faith
> which, virtually though not professedly, is entertained by the masses of
> our working population; by the skilled and unskilled labourer alike—
> by hosts of minor shopkeepers and Sunday traders—and by *miserable
> denizens of courts and crowded alleys*. They are *unconscious Secularists*.[115]

What is not usually noticed is that in reviewing this report, Holyoake
explicitly denied a direct relationship between the Secularist movement
and mass infidelity. Far from being 'unconscious', the Secularist was 'one
who inquires, takes sides, and endeavours to act out his convictions'. As
the Holbeck Domestic Missionary pointed out, the most prevalent form
of unbelief was non-belief—neglect of religion rather than opposition
to it. Indeed, if the vague residual beliefs of the masses be taken into
consideration, 'unconscious Christians' would be as accurate a description of them as 'unconscious Secularists'.[116]

The Secularists freely admitted that they were a small minority movement, and sought consolation in the reason why. 'It is because infidelity
addresses itself more to the intellect than to the imagination and feelings,

Q

that it has never exhibited the union, zeal, enthusiasm and influence, that religion has displayed in all ages and countries,' wrote 'Inquirer' in the *Reasoner* in 1846. The same was still felt to be true at the end of the decade. 'The masses *cannot* become Secularists until they have opportunities of developing their intellectual and moral faculties, or until those whose faculties are developed become the social and political leaders of mankind.' The masses therefore do not enter into a discussion of organised Secularism, or of any other organised working-class movement for that matter. Southwell in 1843 announced that his *Investigator* was 'calculated to interest only the intelligent and reasoning portion of the community'. Even a quick glance at any of the freethought periodicals will confirm this aim.[117]

How large was this group? Contemporary estimates varied widely. On the one extreme there is W. N. Molesworth or Horace Mann, quoted above. On the other there are the views of the Christian missionaries who often lamented the prevalence of infidelity, but who were honest enough observers to see the problem in perspective. In 1858 Francis Bishop, the Manchester domestic missionary, thought that if the term 'unbelievers' were understood 'as designating persons who have bent their minds seriously to the subject of religion, and deliberately rejected its claims, I should say, judging from my own observations, that in this sense there are comparatively few unbelievers'. The Manchester city missionary shared this observation. In one of his reports, he wrote: 'Besides a good many sceptics, who are practically infidel, I have discovered four or five avowed rejecters of the whole of Divine Revelation.' Secularism was the concern of these four or five, and, in some places, the numbers may not have risen above this.[118]

Even where reasonably accurate figures do exist, as for the sales of the *Reasoner* and attendances at lectures and public meetings, there is no more real certainty about the size of the Secularist movement. A Manchester Domestic Missionary in 1854 observed the increase in the circulation of the *Reasoner* and in the attendance at meetings, but thought, perhaps rightly, that 'Many persons like to hear or read discussions on any topic, not for the sake of arriving at definite conclusions, or satisfying their doubts, but simply to gratify their curiosity'.[119]

The circulation figures for the *Reasoner* are inadequate for two reasons. On the one hand some copies of the *Reasoner* would be read by several Secularists, while on the other some purchasers of the *Reasoner* were not Secularists at all. As David Glassford, president of the Paisley socialists, wrote in 1849, 'The readers of the *Reasoner*, in this part of the country, consist of two classes, viz., the Socialists, and the liberal and intelligent among the Christians. The latter class read it for the sake only of the theological questions and discussions that it contains.' Holyoake himself estimated on another occasion that 'more than a third of the *Reasoner's* supporters are of the middle and educated class'. The other two-thirds would be working class in a very general sense, and here sales give no really accurate measure of circulation. A paper which was kept in a public reading room would go through many hands, and when men like William Taylor of Birmingham were prepared to buy ten copies and then give them 'to the Birmingham Parliamentary Society, Discussion Classes, to Co-operative Leagues and to Coffee Shops' one can only presume that considerable propagandist work was done in this way. As James Motherwell wrote from Paisley in 1848, 'The directors of the Mechanics' Institution here have the *Reasoner* regularly supplied to the periodical table of their news room, which enables many parties to peruse it that would not otherwise have an opportunity.'[120]

The size of the audiences at lectures or at public meetings is really no better indication of the numbers involved, for there is no clear way of distinguishing between adherents and spectators. The Reverend A. Burdett of Long Buckley estimated in 1847 that one of Holyoake's lectures was attended by a hundred people: 'Perhaps one third of the number may have sympathised with the views of the lecturer, but did not admire his advocacy of them.' This was a rural audience. In Manchester a Secularist lecturer might get an audience of a thousand or more, and most of these would be favourable.[121] The huge northern camp meetings, though, were more than ordinary gatherings of Secularists. Most of the meetings were held at well-known beauty spots to which many people frequently went for purely recreational reasons. The presence of a Secularist rally must have attracted folk rather like a wakes' week fair. The Castle Hill meetings of 1860 and 1861, for example, are put into perspective if one remembers not only that the same site was used for Chartist camp meetings in 1843, 1847 and 1848, and for a weavers' strike protest meeting in 1883, but that crowds also gathered on the hill to watch a dog fight in 1855, and prize fights in 1863 and 1865.[122]

The outdoor meetings illustrate the way in which Secularism could appeal to men who were not Secularists. The lecturer was an entertainer, and the spirit which today is associated with Hyde Park Corner was then commonly found in many outdoor places in London and other large towns and cities. The use the East End Secularists made of Victoria Park has already been mentioned.[123] Another such place was Smithfield. The Sunday preachers here in 1850 were described in the *British Banner*:

> One man had an old book, from which he endeavoured to convince his hearers that the Prophets were a set of drunkards. Another of these holders forth said,—'I do not want anything you have; no, not a crust of bread.

If you want a ready-money devil, you will find one stuck up in any of the Churches or chapels in the city.' A third orator said, 'If you wish to have heaven for ready money, or hell made easy, you have but to go to one of the chapels and pay your money.' A fourth said,—'I am a Christian and a Red Republican. My religion is this—fill the stomach first and the soul afterwards.' This young man drew from his pocket what he called the first number of the 'Red Republican newspaper,' and expounded portions of it to the people. The most earnest and clever fellows present were stern advocates of the Church of Rome. My opinion is that some of these were young priests clad in such garments as are usually worn by mechanics.[124]

Though this latter comment may have been produced by the prevailing anti-Catholicism of the year 1850, this picture seems to be broadly representative. The infidel lecturers were skilful in exploiting the curiosity and general sympathies of the crowd. Wherever working men met, the infidels seemed always to be there and were commented upon by the Christian missionaries who were always there. This frequently led the latter to exaggerate the importance of the former.

Any numerical estimates of Secularist influence must therefore be highly speculative. In the 1850s there were only about a hundred and twenty localities reported, all told, in the periodicals, and certainly not more than about seventy appear in any one year. Branch attendance figures appear to have varied between a handful and a hundred or more. If the higher figures are taken all round, then total Secularist numbers could not have exceeded 12,000 and the committed membership may well have been only a quarter of this. *Reasoner* circulation figures suggest a similar figure. The average circulation throughout the decade was just over three thousand. It seems plausible that the two thousand of these which were bought for or by working men may each have reached half a dozen interested readers as well as countless casual browsers in the coffee shop reading rooms. What is clear is that beyond these people there was a tremendous potential following which was occasionally excited into active participation in the movement. The circulation of Southwell's *Lancashire Beacon* in 1849, for example, shows support out of all proportion to the actual size of the movement, even in Lancashire, during the next ten years. Similarly, the peak of the *Reasoner's* circulation in 1853–4, capped by the *National Reformer* in 1861, suggests that support, at least in those years, might have been double that suggested for the average. These very tentative figures give approximately the same picture as Holyoake himself once suggested. He was quoted by a correspondent to the *Christian Spectator* in 1852 as having 'said that his (i.e. infidel—not exclusively atheistic) views, have a hundred thousand sympathisers in the United Kingdom, and are held, as deliberate convictions, by twenty or thirty thousand'. The correspondent thought this estimate was moderate. It was probably generous but not excessively so. Certainly, when the Reverend F. Meyrick was told by a Secularist in 1856 that there were five hundred Secularists in London and as many again in the provinces, the London estimate was rather on the low side and the provincial one so inaccurate as to indicate that the ordinary Secularist in the London street had no idea of the strength of the movement in the north.[125]

The safest description of Secularist membership, therefore, is probably as follows. In the widest possible sense there may have been a hundred thousand sympathisers, and this figure would include many Chartists and others who were not really interested in the organisation of Secularism. The most optimistic estimate we can make of the number who were, at some time or other, more closely associated with Secularism cannot be more than twenty thousand, and in poor years this figure may well have been halved. When we look closer still, at the public meetings (other than lectures by national figures), we might conclude that the committed hard core was as small as two or three thousand. Even in 1880, when the movement was reaching its peak, the National Secular Society could claim an affiliated membership of only six thousand. Hence, when a local commentator chose to descend from generalities about mass infidelity and to concentrate on real infidelity, he often found he was dealing with a very small group of men, a cell rather than a mass movement.[126]

The second generalisation about Secularism is that it was a working-class movement. This is true, but only within certain limiting definitions. Few, if any, nineteenth-century working-class movements really penetrated to the lowest of the lower orders, and Secularism was no exception to this. Feargus O'Connor may have liked to appeal 'To the Fustian Jackets, the Blistered Hands, and Unshorn Chins' but Charles Southwell was proud to quote from the *Glasgow Sentinel* in 1852 that his audiences in the Communist Hall had been 'not of the mob, not the mere rabble, the unwashed, the unshaven, and unshorn, but for the most part, nay almost entirely of respectable, well dressed, intelligent looking trades-men—the very life-blood of our country'.[127] Contemporary observers were in agreement about this point even when they differed on many others. Audiences at the 'Infidel Halls' in 1849, according to a *Reasoner* correspondent, were 'from the mechanical classes'. Socialist doctrines were, thought Lord Shaftesbury, to be 'found principally among the artisans and skilled workmen, and especially in the metropolis'. W. R. Greg thought that 'total unbelievers' were 'the best of the skilled workmen', and *Reasoner* articles were intended for 'an intelligent mechanic', a man who belonged to 'the class of artizans in our manufacturing towns'.[128] Nineteenth-century freethought did not appeal to the lowest social groups, and, indeed, the artisan leaders did not even appreciate the problems of the poor. For example, when Holyoake urged poor men to become temperate and build coffee houses, he completely missed the point and earned an instructive rebuke from F. W. Newman,

> the poor of whom I speak are not the frequenters of the coffee-shops which you plan, but the builders of them. You call out to men who have no building funds, and ask them why they do not build. *This* is what I say is a virtual insult to the poor. The supporters of the Alliance, and of the Teetotal Societies, are prevailing poor; I think, much poorer than you are. The frequenters of superior coffee-houses would be the comparatively rich.[129]

This was a crucial distinction. The radical leaders, with their self-help ideals and political Liberalism, set the tone of the Secularist and other movements and they did not appreciate how unrepresentative they were. The lower orders had no voice, they were not organised, and were rarely conscious of anything beyond the instincts of the crowd—against the clergy and particularly the Roman Catholics, against dear bread and unemployment, against any attack on their basically conservative outlook. Not until the end of the nineteenth century were these people to articulate their own views through the new Socialist leaders, and then the old radicals were to find how much out of touch they were.

The residuum was therefore as much neglected by the radicals as it was by the middle-class Liberals. A bond of morality, reliability and rationality united the two latter groups and excluded the former. In 1851 Holyoake doubled admission charges at his lectures 'in order to reduce the numbers to the limits of order, hearing, and health'. This was no individual snobbery. He was following the excellent precedents set by no less a person than Richard Carlile who had similarly used admission charges to keep out the rabble. Secularism, like Owenism and the co-operative movement, was beyond the poor man's purse. Its organisation and propaganda were designed for an educated, financial and social elite among the working classes.[130]

The nature of the appeal of Secularism is suggested in the pattern and distribution of Secularist growth. The rise and fall of Secularism does not seem to have been closely linked to the trade cycle in the same way that the political reform movement was. There was a general correspondence, especially in 1858 when the Secularist decline coincided with what has been called 'one of the worst [years] for the working classes in the nineteenth century', yet even in that year, considerable funds were collected for Holyoake's 'Secular Institute' at the Fleet Street House.[131] In 1861, when Henry Turner feared that the depression in Sheffield would harm propagandist efforts, it seems to have made little difference for better or worse.[132] So Secularism does not appear to have been a movement of social and economic protest; it was not 'a knife and fork question'. At the same time, though, many of its followers were very sensitive to a rise in the cost of the periodicals, as the circulation of the *Reasoner* shows.[133]

The geographical distribution of Secularism gives a useful indication of the sort of people who probably made up the membership and audiences. There were not many agricultural labourers; there were a great many artisans. In London some specifically trade-orientated groups were reported—the West End shoemakers who met at John Street in 1851, and the Clerkenwell watchmakers. Shoemakers throughout the country make up about a quarter of all identifiable artisan names in the periodicals. Weavers appear to have been another influential group. This might suggest that Secularism was a protest movement of the dying trades, but the strength of the following in Lancashire and Yorkshire, and the comparative weakness of organised Secularism in the midland towns, indicates that the association between Secularism and certain occupational groups is not a simple one.[134]

The artisan traditionally had time to think. 'The workshop depraves,' wrote Léon Faucher in 1844, 'but it throws open to the minds of the operatives a whole world of ideas.' Samuel Kydd wrote of Ayrshire in 1847, 'The inhabitants of the weaving villages are the most intelligent men with whom I ever conversed; they are readers and thinkers.' The same picture of artisan life is given by Lloyd Jones in a description of Manchester, and finds a place in the novels of Mrs Gaskell. The artisan therefore—particularly in those trades such as shoemaking and weaving into which there was easy entry—was likely to be radical not because he was discontented, but because he was educated and politically conscious.[135]

The prevalence of Secularism in a given locality can be better related to the nature of that locality than to any nationwide generalisations about class or occupational groups, and historical reasons are as important as economic ones. London was a strong centre because Holyoake could build on the artisan-radicals who had made up the Painite tradition since the days of the London Corresponding Society. It would have been surprising if Secularist groups had not flourished in the fertile soil of Bethnal Green and Blackfriars. More instructive is the appeal in the north of England where the historical tradition from Owen onwards was stronger than in London, and where all manner of radical organisations flourished. The limits of the spread of northern Secularism would appear to exclude certain occupational groups. Fishermen and miners seem to have remained loyal to their Methodist creeds, and, although the miners of Durham were later to support Bradlaugh, in the 1850s they are conspicuously absent from the records. In Durham the Cockfield Debating Society flourished, but it was to the west of Bishop Auckland and away from the coalfield. John Tennant, a collier from Seghill in Northumberland, appears almost as a voice in the wilderness.[136] It is harder to generalise about the Lancashire and Yorkshire coalfields, since mining took place alongside the manufacturing industry which it served. What is important is that mining alone, which was a rural pursuit, was not a significant basis for Secularist organisation. The same comments might be made of handloom weaving. The Barnsley weavers, for example, who had been a backbone of Chartism, seem to have made no impact on Secularism, and Barnsley was not on the usual lecture route through Yorkshire. Wigan was similarly beyond the range of East Lancashire Secularism, and the small weaving towns and villages of the Ribble valley were not so prominent in the movement as the larger spinning and weaving towns nearer Manchester. Though the weavers of Preston let the Secularists use their committee room, they do not seem to have contributed much to the survival of Secularism in the town, and they did not noticeably turn to Secularism as a means of social protest during the prolonged strike and lock out of 1853.[137] The best map of Secularist distribution, in fact, might be that illustrating the distribution of occupations prepared at the 1851 census. The areas selected for enlargement on that map are Glasgow and district; Newcastle and district; Birmingham, Wolverhampton and districts; and—by far the biggest—Lancashire and the West Riding. The latter itself breaks down into two smaller areas, centred on Liverpool and Sheffield, and two larger areas, centred on Manchester and Bradford–Leeds. Secularism is almost entirely confined to those areas shaded as being 'the chief manufacturing districts of Great Britain'.[138]

Within these areas further tentative observations can be made. In general, villages were weaker than towns, but the largest towns were not always the strongest. A marked feature of the Lancashire Secular Union in the early 1860s, for example, is the weakness of Manchester. The towns in Lancashire and Cheshire where Secularism was strongest—Ashton, Stockport, Stalybridge, Hyde, Oldham—were the towns in which the factory system had made its greatest impact. Léon Faucher quoted in his description of Manchester in 1844 the findings of a survey conducted in 1836 concerning the social composition of the East Lancashire towns. Operatives composed 64 per cent of the populations of Manchester, 74 per cent of Salford, 71 per cent of Bury, 81 per cent of Ashton, 90 per cent of Stalybridge and nearly 95 per cent of Dukinfield.[139] Here Owenism had been rooted partly as a constructive movement of social protest and here Secularism continued, but not as a social protest in the same sense because Secularism was an intellectual movement, and offered little which could be grasped in popular terms. Protest movements needed the positive grievance—the lack of employment, the demand for political reform—and Owenism and Chartism had offered something positive in return—the Community, the Charter. Secularism in contrast was rather vague. It offered freedom, an intellectual ideal. Secularism therefore has the appearance of an Owenite holding-operation, remaining strong in the Owenite areas for historical and not economic reasons.

This was made possible by the transformation of the textile industry between 1840 and 1860. In the earlier days the economic position of the cotton industry had seemed precarious, with fluctuating markets, over-production and periodical unemployment. By 1860 the economy had become much more stable, the cotton industry had expanded rapidly, wages were rising, and a new class of skilled and semi-skilled workpeople was joining and in some cases replacing the older skilled workmen. Although the distinction between the elite and the residuum was as pronounced as ever, the factory and the workshop were drawing closer together. The Secularist movement appears to have drawn support, without discrimination, from all trades which offered regular employment and a degree of social security.[140]

The broad basis of Secularist support is illustrated by a comparison of Lancashire and Yorkshire. Ashton may be taken as representing the new style of factory-monopolised textile community. Huddersfield presents a complete contrast. In the 1850s the handloom weaver still thrived in the fancy woollen trade, domestic clothiers were still taking their products to the Cloth Hall for disposal, and where mills existed they were comparatively small in size. By contrast again, the worsted industry of Bradford was organised more like the cotton industry. Yet all three types of textile community were strongholds of Secularism, and there is no reference anywhere in the periodicals to the support coming from untypical groups within these various communities.[141]

Indeed, there is some evidence—albeit of a rather negative kind—that Secularism thrived best in a heterogeneous community. This is suggested by a comparison between Chartism and Secularism in the Huddersfield district. In December 1842 nine weavers were nominated to the general council of the National Charter Association from the village of Almond-bury, two miles out of Huddersfield. The village had once been the senior partner of the two, but was now in decline, overshadowed by its near neighbour. Huddersfield, by contrast, nominated two tailors, two packers, a weaver, a shopkeeper, a printer, a clothier, a gentleman, an

iron moulder and a newsagent (Joshua Hobson). The diversity of occupation is striking, and this same diversity is to be found in the Secularist
leadership in the town, which included in 1864 a grocer, a newsagent, a
printer and a temperance hotel keeper. Almondbury, by contrast, though
it had given support to Carlile, played no significant part in the early
history of Secularism.[142] We can therefore suggest that the Secularist
movement was not generated by any one social or economic group, but
rather by an attitude, and it was an attitude which was fostered in the
industrial communities of the north. Lloyd Jones wrote of the towns
round Manchester:

> All are more or less engaged in similar industries, all contain a vigorous,
> active, intelligent population; men who *will* busy themselves with public
> questions, will *not* confine themselves to the routine of their daily duties
> in workshop or factory; men who feel, and in many ways already have been
> able to prove, that they are not mere implements of production, but
> citizens of a great empire, connected by a thousand links with all other
> classes of that empire, and therefore concerned in the discussion and settle-
> ment of every question that can interest any. It is in such a district as this
> therefore (though the West Riding of Yorkshire, for instance, might
> furnish just such another) that the true character of the working men of
> Great Britain can be appreciated, their power estimated, their progress
> realised....Without disparagement to the London working men, who have
> qualities of their own, it is certain that almost, if not quite, all great
> movements affecting the class have had their origins in the provinces.[143]

So in these northern textile districts were to be found Methodism and the
temperance movement, the Poor Law Agitation and the Ten Hours'
movement, socialism and Chartism, Mechanics' Institutes and the co-
operative movement—and, last and least, Secularism. The north was, in
the words of one historian, 'a land of chapels and clubs, of co-operative
and friendly societies . . . of small but energetic social and religious
groups, of intense and variegated loyalties'. This was the land of those
self-help communities which shaped the nature of mid nineteenth-
century radicalism.[144]

The diversity of Secularist membership, and the similarity between
the Secularist movement and other mid-century radical organisations, is
borne out by what detailed figures are available. Names appear in the
periodicals, but only very occasionally are occupations given or addresses
which would permit a more detailed investigation in the census returns.
But of some six hundred names which occur in the periodicals of the
fifties, a third can be identified in the local trade directories and more
can be located with less certainty. Further, one can reasonably surmise
that at least half of the names which cannot be traced belong to men who
were of too low a social position to be mentioned in the directories. The

figures which can be so obtained, together with the general picture
inferred above, give a likely if not definite description of who the
Secularists were in the 1850s.[145]

Less than ten per cent of the names are those of men from the higher
social classes—men like Josiah Gimson, the head of a Leicester engineering firm; Benjamin Hagen of Derby, a retired brewer; or Thomas
Wilcock of Bradford, founder of the West Riding Secular Alliance, who
is listed in one directory as a private resident. Approximately one-third
of the names are from that class which was responsible for much of
organised Secularism—newsagents and booksellers like W. H. Holyoak
of Leicester or Willis Knowles of Hyde; publicans, like Samuel Ingham
of Manchester or James Mellor of Oldham; coffee-house keepers like
James Spurr of Liverpool or Joseph Mitchell of Bradford; shopkeepers,
like Joseph Firth of Keighley or Joshua Goddard of Huddersfield. A
slightly smaller proportion, about a quarter, may be classed as artisans:
that is, cobblers, tailors, joiners, plumbers, hatters, hairdressers and the
like. The rest are semi-skilled and unskilled, and here we cross the
border between what we can know, and what is beyond recall. Individual
examples suggest the sort of men who might have made up this group:
Henry Turner, a warehouseman but also a lecturer at the Sheffield
Mechanics' Institute; James Campbell, a weaver but also principal
lecturer for the Manchester Secular Society; Watts Balmforth, also a
weaver, whose son Owen, named after the Social Father, was educated
at the Secular School in Huddersfield and grew up to be mayor of the
town; Joseph Jagger, leader of the W.R.S.U., who was born into a
clothier's family and brought up a teazer of wool, but who became the
proprietor of the Turkish Baths in Rochdale.[146]

Obituary notices are one of the best guides in the quest for the
'typical' Secularist. Thomas Barker of Todmorden died in 1864, aged 34.
He was a 'working man' (a bookseller and stationer), an outspoken
radical who had first introduced Holyoake to the town. When a local
Board of Health was established for the township of Langfield, he had
been elected to it at the top of the poll, and he was re-elected shortly
before his death. William Mallalieu, also of Todmorden, held 'a lucra-
tive position' at Fielden Bros. Before coming to the town he had lived
in Rochdale where he was one of the famous Pioneers and president of
the local branch of the Rational Society. John Hampson of Heywood,
who died in 1862 aged eighty, was an admirer of Paine who had dis-
tributed the publications of Carlile and Hetherington. Rebecca Brook
of Huddersfield died in 1865, aged twenty-seven. Her parents had
attended the Rational Society and she had been sent to the Rational
school. When the society came to an end, she looked first to Holyoake

and then to Bradlaugh. John Wilding of Lamberhead Green, near Wigan, was more solitary. He was the only sceptic in his village. By trade he was a handloom weaver who had raised himself to provision dealing. He was fond of music and favoured Malthusian ideas.[147] The characteristics of many such people might be summed up in an obituary sent to the *Secular World* in 1863, describing Thomas Holt of Barrowford:

> In intellectual attainments he was above average of his class. Though but a working man he possessed a vast amount of general knowledge, and I believe, excelled in some branches of science. At the age of 24 he embraced Secular views, and for 25 years cherished them with the ardour of youth.[148]

These were exceptional men, full of intelligence, energy and enthusiasm. By outlook as well as by social position they had much in common with the lower-middle classes. Secularism as a movement belonged to no single occupational group, and though we may still call it a working-class movement it was never class-conscious in any meaningful sense. It remained ultra-radical by repute, but it posed little threat to society in the 1850s, and Holyoake's avowed aim was to make Secularism as respectable as possible.

This can be seen as part of a general move in working-class politics in the 1850s and 1860s. The members of trade unions and co-operatives were no less concerned to find a place in society, rather than to remake society according to their own lights. The status group which provided the leadership and the bulk of the membership of such organisations claimed to speak in the name of the whole working class, but in fact it spoke only for itself and its policies were adapted to its own social opportunities and political experience. Secularism started at a disadvantage, since atheism was very hard to make socially 'safe', but Holyoake did his best and a study of the political agitations in which he involved his movement in the 1850s can therefore be used to illustrate in miniature the social and political basis of what one recent historian has called the liberal consensus.[149]

Notes

1 See W. J. Linton to Holyoake, 16 June 1849, H.C. 313.
2 *Reasoner*, 24 April, 30 October 1850.
3 *Ibid.*, 3 July 1850; R. Cooper to R. Owen, 17 July 1850, O.C. 1828.
4 *Oracle*, 26 August 1843; *Reasoner*, 18, 25 September 1850, 8 September 1852.
5 *British Banner*, 27 October, 3, 10, 17 November, 1 December 1852.
6 This correspondence appears in *ibid.*, 13 October 1852, and in *Reasoner* 3, 17, 24 November, 8, 22, 29 December 1852.

7 *Holyoake—Grant Discussion, 1853*, p. vii; *Reasoner*, 12 January, 13 April 1853; Holyoake, *Origin and Nature of Secularism*, p. 55.

8 *Reasoner*, 31 August 1853, 30 January 1859.

9 *Inquirer*, 27 August 1853, quoted in *Reasoner* supplement 16 November 1853; H. N. Barnett to Holyoake, 10 August 1853, H.C. 584; see also S. D. Collet to Holyoake, 1 February 1853, H.C. 561.

10 E. Syme to Holyoake, 10 November 1852, H.C. 541.

11 C. Southwell, *Review of a Controversy*, pp. 5, 17, 39; T. Cooper to Holyoake, 9 July 1858, H.C. 1029.

12 See *Reasoner*, 9 April 1854.

13 *Ibid.*, 9, 16 March 1853; J. H. Hinton, *A Lecture Delivered . . . on the Conclusion of the Discussion . . .* (London, 1853).

14 J. Gregory and others, *Modern Atheism . . .* (London, 1853), preface; *Reasoner*, 18 May 1853.

15 *Ibid.*, 23 March, 4, 11 May, 13 July, 17 August, 14, 28 September, 19 October, 2 November 1853.

16 *Ibid.*, 20 April, 4 May, 29 June 1853.

17 *Ibid.*, 13 July, 10, 17, 31 August, 12 October 1853.

18 *Holyoake—Grant Discussion, 1854*, p. iii; J. Parker, *Six Chapters on Secularism . . .* (London, 1854), p. i; *National Reformer*, 12 July 1868.

19 *Reasoner*, 28 April 1852.

20 *Ibid.*, 19 February 1860. He offered a different list of sixty topics in *National Reformer*, 29 December 1860.

21 'John Henry Gordon's Lecture-Subjects, 1860', printed on the cover of J. H. Gordon, *The Exodus of the Priests: a Secularist's Dream of Better Times* (London, 1860).

22 Quoted in *Reasoner*, 12 November 1854.

23 *Investigator*, December 1854.

24 *Reasoner*, 3 September 1854. Holyoake estimated his costs to be £100 p.a. higher because of this.

25 A. Briggs, 'David Urquhart and the Foreign Affairs Committees', *Bradford Antiquary*, x (1962), pp. 197–207; G. Robinson, *David Urquhart . . .* (Oxford, 1920), pp. 124–5, 131–2, 136.

26 *Reasoner*, 14 October 1855. Robinson, *op. cit.*, pp. 130–2, 160, 171, 270.

27 *Reasoner*, 20 January 1856.

28 *Ibid.*, 14 January, 17 June 1855; *Investigator*, July, October 1857; *Reasoner Gazette*, 22 January 1860; *National Reformer*, 19 July 1868.

29 *Reasoner*, 14 November 1858. Holyoake to R. B. Reed, 26 February 1859, C.N. C.540; Holyoake to Cowen, 21 October 1858, C.N. C.464.

30 D. Tribe, *Charles Bradlaugh*, pp. 17–22.

31 *British Banner*, 31 July 1850.

32 *Reasoner*, 16 October 1850; D. Tribe, *op. cit.*, pp. 24–7, 38–117.

33 H. Turner to W. Hilton [?1858], B.L. 67.

34 *Reasoner*, 30 October, 6, 13 November 1859. For the religious revival, see *ibid.*, 25 September, 20, 27 November 1859, 15 January 1860.

35 *Ibid.*, 9, 16, 30 October, 6, 20 November 1859.

36 *National Reformer*, 29 June 1861.

37 *Reasoner*, 20 November, 23 October 1859, 5 August 1860.

38 *Ibid.*, 19 February, 6 May 1860; *Reasoner Gazette*, 1 July 1860.

39 See appendix III.

40 *Reasoner*, 13 April 1853; G. J. Holyoake, *The History of the Fleet House* (London, 1856), pp. 5–8; the Agreement, dated 22 May 1851, is in H.C. 421.
41 *Reasoner*, 23 November 1853.
42 *Ibid.*, 5 February 1854.
43 Holyoake, *op. cit.*, pp. 8–10.
44 *Ibid.*, pp. 10–13.
45 Memoranda and list of books, H.C. 776, 777, 778. The agreement was that Watson should close his publishing house and receive £350 compensation, but he was to keep his copyrights and stock and sell through Holyoake's house–Holyoake, *op. cit.*, p. 8.
46 *Reasoner*, 3 March 1861.
47 *Investigator*, June 1855; *Reasoner Gazette*, 1 January 1860.
48 Leaflet in H.C. 985.
49 R. Cooper admitted this was why he started the *Investigator*—*National Reformer*, 12 July 1868.
50 *Reasoner*, 2 January 1850; diary-cum-notebook, 10 November 1849, H.B.
51 Linton to Holyoake [1850], H.C. 365; *Reasoner*, 17 April 1850; diary-cum-notebook, 13 April 1850, H.B. For *Reasoner* prices see appendix III.
52 *Reasoner*, 24 July 1850. But F. W. Newman did not approve—letter to Holyoake [1850], H.C. 395.
53 *Reasoner*, 25 June 1851.
54 *Ibid.*, 10, 24, 31 January 1849; *Cooper's Journal*, 26 October 1850.
55 H. U. Faulkner, *Chartism and the Churches* (New York, 1916), p. 113; R. D. Altick, *English Common Reader* (Chicago and London, 1957), p. 393.
56 *Reasoner*, 8 January 1851.
57 J. Cowen to Holyoake, 12, 16 February 1855, H.C. 736, 739; *Reasoner*, 25 February 1855.
58 *Ibid.*, 13 January 1856; see also *ibid.*, 2 March 1856.
59 E.g. *ibid.*, 25 June 1851.
60 *Saturday Review*, 5 April 1856.
61 *Reasoner*, 23, 30 December 1860, 17 February 1861. Holyoake seems to have had a physical and nervous breakdown, the symptoms of which were acute eczema and swollen glands—diary, 8 March, 29 April, 18 June 1859, H.B.; *Reasoner*, 21 August 1859.
62 *Investigator*, February, March 1856, April, October 1857, 1 November 1858, 15 January, 15 February, 1 April, 1 July 1859, and preface to vols v & vi; *Reasoner*, 11 September 1859.
63 *Ibid.*, 4 March 1860; *Reasoner Gazette*, 18 March, 1, 8, April 1860; *Reasoner*, 6 January 1861.
64 Holyoake, *Fleet Street House*, p. 9; *Reasoner*, 24 March 1861; *National Reformer*, 13 April, 22 June 1861.
65 Cash Book of the Fleet Street House, *passim*, H.B.; *Reasoner*, 19 April 1857, 14 August 1859; *Investigator*, 15 February 1859.
66 Julian Hibbert (1801–1834) gave Carlile at least £2,000. Holyoake thought the amount much higher—*Reasoner*, 1 July 1855.
67 F. M. Leventhall, *Respectable Radical* (London, 1971), pp. 84–6, 93–116.
68 Diary-cum-notebook, entries during autumn 1849, H.B.; J. S. Mill to

Holyoake, 5 April 1856, H.C. 847; Cash Book, 1858–61, H.B.; 'Special Institute Fund Subscription', *Reasoner*, 29 August, 5 September 1858; 'Final Subscription of the Fleet Street House' (1860), H.C. 1262.

69 *Reasoner*, 4 February 1855.

70 *Ibid.*, 20 July 1853 (Blackburn); *National Reformer* 19 January 1861 (Leicester); *Census of Great Britain, 1851. Religious Worship and Education in Scotland* (1854), pp. 94, 91 (Paisley, Glasgow).

71 E.g. by C. Southwell, *Another 'Fourpenny Wilderness'*, p. 22. This was a common charge and was later repeated against Bradlaugh.

72 See printed Appeal, April 1860, in B.L. 78; also D. Tribe, *op. cit.*, pp. 87, 90–1, 99–101, 115–17; and H. B. Bonner and J. M. Robertson, *Charles Bradlaugh . . .*, 2 vols. (second edition, London, 1895), I, p. 98.

73 R. Cooper to R. Owen, 10 July 1847, 20 October 1851, O.C. 1480, 1951; *National Reformer*, 19 July 1868.

74 *Ibid.*, 26 July 1862.

75 *Report of the Select Committee on Public Libraries* (1849), Q. 2434; Holyoake, *Lectures and Debates . . .* [1851]. Bradlaugh also received 2 gns.— H. Turner to W. Hilton, [?1858], B.L. 67.

76 Holyoake to wife, 9 October 1851, 29 April 1852, H.C. 444, 489.

77 Diary, 13 March 1856, H.B.

78 See S. Timmins (ed.), *Birmingham and the Midland Hardware District* (London, 1866), p. 71. Holyoake's family at this time was Eveline (b. 1841), Manfred (b. [?1844]), Malthus (b. 1846), Max (b. 1848) and Francis (b. 1855). Max was killed in a road accident in August 1855.

79 *Reasoner*, 4 June 1854; A. Campbell to R. Owen, 26 October 1855, O.C. 2492.

80 *Reasoner*, 2 December 1857.

81 *Ibid.*, 8 September, 29 December 1852, 21 June 1857, 22 October 1854, 19 May 1852.

82 *National Reformer*, 15 February 1862; *Secular World*, 10 May 1862.

83 *National Reformer*, 4 January 1862; *Reasoner*, 1 April 1865.

84 *National Reformer*, 19 December 1863, 13 February 1864. Holyoake took out a £1 share on 15 December 1863, which he later sold at a profit—H.C. 1517, 1625.

85 *Reasoner*, 13 August 1851, 7 December 1853, 7 September 1856; *National Reformer*, 13 February 1864, 21 October 1866.

86 *Ibid.*, 8 October 1864.

87 B. Simon, *Studies in the History of Education*, p. 230; *Report of S. C. on Public Libraries*, Qs. 2768, 2771, 2773.

88 *Utilitarian Record*, 1 March 1848; *Reasoner*, 2 April 1851.

89 *Ibid.*, 8 July 1855.

90 *Ibid.*, 5 March 1851; see also G. J. Harney to Holyoake, 8 February 1891, H.C. 3283.

91 *Reasoner*, 19 May 1852.

92 'Closing of Thornton's', *Parkin's Almanac* 1925, Huddersfield P. L. Press Cuttings, p. 86, and see also miscellaneous press cuttings. Thornton was treasurer of the W.R.S.U. in 1855—*Reasoner*, 4 November 1855.

93 J. W. Dodds, *The Age of Paradox . . .* (London, 1953), p. 405; *Reasoner* 29 June 1856, 1 July 1860.

94 *Ibid.*, 5 May, 30 October 1858; *Reasoner Gazette*, 28 October 1860;

National Reformer, 14 April, 17 November 1860; *Reasoner*, 20 January, 3 February 1861; *Reasoner Gazette*, 21 October 1860.

95 *Reasoner*, 3 April 1859; *National Reformer*, 14 April, 10 November 1860; A. Briggs, 'David Urquhart', *Bradford Antiquary*, x (1962), p. 203.

96 *Reasoner*, 29 July 1860; [D. Urquhart], *The Turkish Bath, with a view to its Introduction into the British Dominions* (London, 1856), pp. 59, 61.

97 *Reasoner*, 15 January 1854, 1 April 1855; *National Reformer*, 7 July, 18 August 1860, 7 September 1861.

98 *Notes to the People*, ii, p. 585.

99 *National Reformer*, 30 August 1862.

100 Page 204.

101 *Reasoner*, 22 July 1855; W. E. Adams, *Memoirs of a Social Atom*, pp. 313–318; see also A. Plummer, *Bronterre* . . . (London, 1971), pp. 204–5, 242–3.

102 For the social side of Owenism, see E. Yeo, 'Robert Owen and radical culture', in S. Pollard and J. Salt (eds.), *Robert Owen*, pp. 84—114.

103 *Reasoner*, 17 November 1852, 1 January 1854, 2 March 1856, 8 March 1857.

104 *Scripture Reader's Journal*, January 1856, quoted by F. Meyrick, *Outcast and Poor of London* (London, 1858), pp. 89–90.

105 *National Reformer*, 2 May 1863.

106 Handbill (1859), H.C. 1078.

107 *Reasoner*, 14 October 1857, 9 October 1859; *National Reformer*, 19 September 1863.

108 *Investigator*, May 1855.

109 *National Reformer*, 22 June 1861; *Reasoner*, 1 July 1865; *National Reformer*, 18 June 1864.

110 *Lancashire Beacon*, no. 12 [19 October 1849]; *National Reformer*, 8 August 1863.

111 *Reasoner*, 4 February 1855, 15 July 1857; *National Reformer*, 12 September 1863.

112 *Ibid.*, 24 May 1862.

113 *Reasoner*, 10 July 1859.

114 W. N. Molesworth, *The History of England*, 3 vols. (London, 1876), ii, p. 236—see H.C. 2265.

115 Quoted in *Reasoner*, 9 April 1854.

116 *Ibid.*, 29 October 1854; *Annual Report of the Leeds Unitarian Domestic Missionary Society* (1858), p. 22, quoted by J. F. C. Harrison, *Learning and Living, 1790–1960* (London, 1961), p. 157.

117 *Reasoner*, 23 September 1846; *National Reformer*, 15 September 1860; *Investigator*, no. 5 [29 April 1843].

118 F. Bishop, *Twenty First Report of the Ministry to the Poor* (Manchester, 1858), pp. 11–12; *Manchester City Mission Magazine*, November 1854.

119 John Layhe, *20th Report of the Ministry to the Poor* (Manchester, 1854), p. 14.

120 *Reasoner*, 19 December 1849, 10 November 1847; *Utilitarian Record* 15 September 1847; *Reasoner*, 20 September 1848.

121 *Ibid.*, 21 April 1847; *Movement*, 29 January 1845 and G. J. to Austin Holyoake [March 1858], H.C. 1014.

122 P. Ahier, *The Story of Castle Hill* . . . (Huddersfield, 1946), pp. 51–5.

123 See above, p. 210; also A. Fein, 'Victoria Park: its origin and history', *East London Papers*, v (1962), pp. 73–90.

124 *British Banner*, 24 July 1850.
125 *National Reformer*, 22 June 1861; *Reasoner*, 27 October 1852; F. Meyrick, *op. cit.*, p. 92.
126 See *Reasoner*, 22 July 1846, 27 October 1852.
127 *Northern Star*, 23 February 1850; *Reasoner*, 25 February 1852.
128 *Ibid.*, 24 January 1849; Lord Shaftesbury to Lord John Russell, 15 November 1851 (quoted by S. Maccoby, *English Radicalism 1832–52* (London, 1935), p. 313); W. R. Greg, *Rocks Ahead*, p. 130 (quoted by S. Maccoby, *English Radicalism, 1853–86* (London, 1938), p. 133); 'Aliquis' to Holyoake, 25 July 1854, H.C. 682; *Reasoner*, 16 February 1848.
129 *Ibid.*, 19 February 1860.
130 *Reasoner*, 1 October 1851; Carlile to Holyoake, 16 October 1842, H.C. 79; E. Yeo, *op. cit.*, pp. 94–5; E. Royle, *Radical Politics*, pp. 11–14, 97–8.
131 J. D. Chambers, *Workshop of the World* (London, 1961), p, 166.
132 *National Reformer*, 22 June 1861.
133 See appendix III.
134 *Reasoner*, 6 August 1851; W. O. Chadwick, *The Victorian Church, Part 1,* (London, 1966), p. 334; and see appendix IV.
135 L. Faucher, *Manchester in 1844*, p. 122; *Northern Star*, 25 December 1847 (some editions only); Ludlow and Jones, *Progress of the Working Class* pp. 18–19.
136 *Reasoner*, 23 September 1857, 17 June 1860.
137 D. Bythell, *The Handloom Weavers* (Cambridge, 1969), pp. 92–3, 221–2; H. Ashworth, *The Preston Strike*, pp. 35–6.
138 A modified version of this map was issued with J. H. Clapham, *An Economic History of Modern Britain: Free Trade and Steel, 1850–1886* (Cambridge, 1932).
139 L. Faucher, *op. cit.*, pp. 26–7; also anon., *Manchester as it is* (Manchester, 1839), p. 29; D. Bythell, *op. cit.*, p. 92.
140 Ludlow and Jones, *op. cit.*, pp. 102–3; H. Perkin, *The Origins of Modern English Society* (London, 1969), pp. 393–4.
141 W. B. Crump and G. Ghorbal, *History of the Huddersfield Woollen Industry* (Huddersfield, 1935); K. G. Ponting (ed.), *Baines's Account of the Woollen Manufacture of England* (Newton Abbot, 1970), p. 75.
142 *Northern Star*, 17 December 1842; *Jones's Directory of Halifax, Huddersfield, Dewsbury etc.* (1863–4).
143 Ludlow and Jones, *op. cit.*, pp. 6–7.
144 A. Briggs, *Victorian People* (London, 1965), p. 213; R. J. Morris, 'The history of self help', *New Society*, 3 December 1970.
145 See appendix IV.
146 *Reasoner*, 21 November 1858 (Turner); handbill in O.C. 2078 (Campbell); *Huddersfield Examiner*, 6 October 1967 (Balmforth); Census Return (1851) for 110 Honley Moor Bottom, Honley near Huddersfield, and *Reasoner*, 3 February 1861 (Jagger).
147 *National Reformer*, 17 December 1864 (Barker); 18 July 1863 (Mallalieu); 8 March 1862 (Hampson); 16 July 1865 (Brook); 26 March 1865 (Wilding).
148 *Secular World*, 1 January 1864.
149 R. K. Webb, *Modern England* (London, 1969), pp. 278–327.

6

Secularism in action

a
Political reform

> The Secularist has two fields to occupy. *He* sees but a very little way before
> him who does not discern that politics is the Secular field of the state. The
> public evil of theology consists in holding the veil of speculation before the
> arcana of political misrule. The purpose of tearing the veil away is to see
> what is going on behind, and to take part in putting an end to the
> mischief.[1]

So Holyoake thought that the Secularist ought to be involved in political
and social affairs, but he never made it clear whether Secularists as
Secularists should be identified with the various reform efforts. If
Secularism were concerned only with theology, then politics ought to be
left out. This was J. B. Bebbington's point of view when he criticised
Holyoake for wanting to use the Temple Secular Society in 1858 to
examine the effect of a rating franchise in St Bride's parish, Fleet Street.
Similarly, politics ought to leave out theological questions, and this is
what Holyoake had done on his 1859 lecture tour of the north. In fact
this rigid distinction between Secularism and reform politics was rarely
maintained. As one contemporary complained, 'It often happens, that
when any liberal-minded man or party recommends measures calculated
to advance the interests, improve the health, or in any way to benefit
society, the Secularists are ready to claim to themselves the credit.'[2]

Not all Secularists held the same political views. Percy Greg, F. W.
Newman, R. W. Mackay, Evans Bell and Edward De Pentheny O'Kelly,
all middle-class sympathisers, were unable to share 'the liberal political
views' frequently expressed in the *Reasoner*, and Joseph Barker returned
from America disillusioned with a democracy which had imposed the
Maine Law, and in favour of a broad Established Church under Palmerston and Russell, rather than a disestablished one under a Methodist-
style Conference. He was also said to be in sympathy with Louis
Napoleon's regime in France, and later sided with the south in the
American Civil War.[3] Most Secularists, however, adopted those radical
attitudes expressed in the philosophy of Rationalism, though they still
differed on how radical they should be.

There were two approaches to radical reform in the 1840s. One saw the Whigs and the Anti-Corn Law League as the chief enemy; this was anti-millocrat and became anti-Liberal. The other saw the Tory party and the landed aristocracy as the principal opponents of reform. To some extent this division reflects a difference between local and national politics. In the Lancashire and West Riding towns in particular, the middle classes, entrenched in power since the 1830s as Poor Law Guardians, electors, and—in those towns which were incorporated— town councillors, were anathema to working-class radical leaders. So Joshua Hobson ended his days as a Tory-radical, as befitted a supporter of Richard Oastler.[4] In London, on the other hand, the opponents of reform in Parliament were plainly the aristocracy, and, although this included the Whigs, after Peel's death it especially meant the Tories. The real campaigners for reform, still excluded from power at the centre despite the reforms of the 1830s, were those Manchester School radicals who were so detested as millocrats in their native north. Chartist leaders had to choose between Bright the opponent of factory reform and Bright the proponent of parliamentary reform. Here was fruitful material for bitter controversy.

Holyoake did not hesitate. He was a Manchester School man. In 1847 he championed the cause of W. J. Fox in the Oldham election, although Fox was not the Chartist candidate—which is not surprising, considering Fox's association with the Anti-Corn Law League. Fox was, however, also a champion of freethought, and Holyoake had no doubt where his loyalties lay. The *Northern Star* was not pleased. After 1848, therefore, when Holyoake emerged as a leader of moderate Chartism, he was usually to be found as an advocate of co-operation with the middle classes and this further alienated a number of other prominent Chartists.[5]

He continued to associate himself with moderate reform throughout the 1850s, joining the National Parliamentary and Financial Reform Association in 1849, the Residential Suffrage Association in 1856 and the Political Reform Union in 1860. Despite his adherence to nominal Chartism and his membership of the Chartist executive he advocated Cobden's 'Little Charter', thereby incurring the wrath of G. J. Harney and hastening the break-up of the National Charter Association.[6] This policy was not typical of the Secularists, though, and when Thomas Wilcock spoke up for Holyoake at Bradford in 1852 he did so to defend the latter's honesty and not his views. By 1858, when he began to advocate an 'intelligence franchise', he had clearly travelled far in the direction of the middle-class moderates and had left many of his own supporters behind.[7] W. E. Adams was probably voicing the opinion of a majority of the rank and file when he wrote in Bradlaugh's *Investigator*, condemning any system which treated England as 'a National School, within whose rules the pedagogue is purveyor of the prize of civil freedom'.[8] Yet Holyoake remained a Chartist in principle, and worked loyally for Joseph Cowen's Northern Reform Union. He differed over means not ends, and it would be as wrong to assume that he was untypical as it would be to assume that the Adams–Bradlaugh view was typical. Robert Cooper, for example, who had an impeccably radical career, was also prepared to defend compromise with the middle classes and was a founder of the middle-class Reform Union, while both Bradlaugh and Holyoake were on the council of the more extreme Reform League.[9]

Collaboration with the middle classes, at first hesitant and then enthusiastic, was also the pattern of events in foreign radical affairs. The major difference was this: in domestic affairs the extremists gradually moderated their demands, whereas in foreign affairs everyone was more extreme. Even the ultra-radicals had baulked at revolution at home, and certainly the Secularists would not have counted themselves among the revolutionaries; but middle-class radicals—even Mr Gladstone himself—were quite happy to favour revolution abroad, and in the 1850s the British freethinkers became closely associated with activities of foreign revolutionaries and refugees.

Republicanism was the political doctrine of freethought and the struggles of the Continental liberals could be seen in theological terms. 'Clericalism is the enemy,' as Léon Gambetta later said. 'We welcomed any social disorder in any part of Italy, as likely to be annoying to the Papacy,' Edmund Gosse recalled.[10] The Italian leaders held unorthodox religious views—Mazzini was a theist; Garibaldi, a sentimental atheist. The ultra-radicals were at last able to share in the attack which the European republicans were making on the Vienna settlement of 1815, by which the military power of the conservative, clerical, aristocratic governments of Europe had imposed reactionary regimes on the liberal peoples of the struggling nations. Holyoake made his Fleet Street House in the 1850s a refuge for foreigners. There, in 1859, he published Italian, Spanish, French and German radical newspapers.[11]

The year of revolutions, 1848, naturally made a great impact, both on the London radicals and on the radical scene in London, and as disillusioned refugees fled to England after 1849 the sense of brotherhood was deepened. Italy and Hungary were cast in the roles of victims; Russia, Austria, France (after the rise to power of Louis Napoleon) and Britain (symbolised by Lord Palmerston) were cast in the roles of tyrants for the rest of the decade. Committees to aid the republican cause proliferated: by 1852 there existed a Kossuth Fund, a Polish Refugee Fund, an Italian Loan Fund, and several others. Southwell urged Britain to intervene on behalf of Hungary; Italy begins to appear as a topic of concern in Holyoake's diaries.[12]

The radicals were at first divided into socialists and non-socialists: the former, led by Harney and Louis Blanc, approximated to the extreme Chartist wing of the domestic reform movement; the latter, led by W. J. Linton, Kossuth and Mazzini, had more middle-class support. The two came together in the early 1850s, especially after Harney had joined forces with Joseph Cowen, junior, in Newcastle in December 1853.[13] Holyoake was also drawn into active participation in the republican cause by Cowen, and his strained relationships with Harney were somewhat healed.

In February 1852 the various efforts on behalf of the refugees were co-ordinated to some extent when Mazzini, Kossuth, Cowen and Linton created a European Democratic Committee to raise a Shilling Subscription Fund on the same lines as the Sixpenny Fund started by the Association for the Repeal of the Taxes on Knowledge. Holyoake joined in this effort after a personal appeal from Mazzini, and he organised a propaganda committee for the purpose. By October he was able to send to the treasurer the first thousand shillings which he had raised through the *Reasoner*.[14] This kind of involvement continued for the rest of the 1850s. In 1855, he was offered membership of the Republican Brotherhood, recently founded in Newcastle by Cowen and Harney, and his correspondence shows him to have been in regular contact with Louis Blanc, Kossuth and Mazzini, the leading refugees, as well as with Joseph Cowen, James Stansfeld and P. A. Taylor, their principal English sympathisers.[15] Holyoake was also involved in a rather more sinister fashion when he agreed to take some bombs, manufactured in Birmingham for the revolutionary Owenite, Thomas Allsop, and to test them on his lecture tours. This he did, but probably not till later did he learn that the bombs were the prototype of those used by Orsini in his attempt on the life of Louis Napoleon in 1858.[16]

The British radicals helped with arms in a small way, and with money on a rather larger scale. Their third activity—and most important so far as British politics was concerned—was to watch over the rights of the refugees in their land of exile, and to guard zealously their own freedom to speak and act as they wished. Attempts by the government to restrict the refugees could easily spill over into a question of English civil liberties.

Following the Orsini affair, Dr Simon Bernard, a socialist follower of Fourier, was put on trial at the Old Bailey. Allsop fled to New Mexico for a few months; and Palmerston's government introduced an Anti-Conspiracy Bill. The latter reunited the Urquhartites, who hated Lord

Palmerston, and the other radicals, who hated Louis Napoleon. James
Stansfeld, W. H. Ashurst (son of Owen's lawyer), William Shaen and
Holyoake formed an Anti-Conspiracy Bill committee at 147 Fleet Street,
and Milner Gibson raised the matter in the House, supported by a
mammoth demonstration in Hyde Park on 21 February 1858. Palmerston's ministry was defeated on the Second Reading of the Bill. English
liberties had been defended, and the radicals had learned the power
of a well-organised mass meeting in Hyde Park.[17]

Louis Napoleon, as the radicals insisted on calling Napoleon III, was
at the heart of the next crisis also. In 1855 Felix Pyat had written a *Letter
to the Queen*, which was an attack, issued by the Commune Revolu-
tionnaire of France, on Napoleon and on Queen Victoria for visiting him.
The letter was quoted in *L'homme*, the newspaper of the French exiles
in Jersey, and so the Governor expelled the refugees. Then in 1858
Pyat, Besson and Talandier wrote a *Letter to Parliament and the Press*
on a similar theme, which was published by another of the refugees,
Stanislaus Tchorzewski—Holyoake had, with typical caution, refused to
handle it 'because it *might* be misconstrued' and later, 'because it was
disrespectful to Lord Derby's Government' which had just dropped the
Anti-Conspiracy Bill. The anti-Napoleonic theme was taken up at the
same time by W. E. Adams in a pamphlet on *Tyrannicide: is it Justifiable?* which Holyoake also refused to publish—this time on the grounds
that he was handling a similar work for Mazzini.[18] Edward Truelove,
the John Street socialist who had set up as a bookseller and publisher
at 240 Strand, agreed to publish for Adams instead. For this he was
bound over to appear at the Old Bailey and Tchorzewski also was
prosecuted. A Press Prosecution Defence Committee was set up to defend
the two publishers, with James Watson as treasurer and Charles
Bradlaugh as secretary. Holyoake then announced his intention of
re-publishing the Pyat Letter as the issue had now broadened from a
foreign one into a question of English liberties. The outcome was a
triumph for the refugees. Truelove, Tchorzewski and Bernard were all
acquitted, Allsop was granted a free pardon, and no action was taken
against Holyoake.[19] It was a victory as impressive as that over the Anti-
Conspiracy Bill, and set a precedent for the benevolent neutrality of
the British government in the next crisis to arise, which was the Italian
war of independence.

Italy was a major concern of the radicals, not only because of the
influence of Mazzini, Garibaldi, Orsini and other refugees, but also
because, as Henry Clinton pointed out, a liberal British-German-Italian
alliance with a Mediterranean fleet would be the best foundation for an
anti-Russian foreign policy, and Italy was the weakest link in the chain

of states under the Austro-Russian tyrannies. As early as 1856 Holyoake had re-printed from *Italia e Popolo* an appeal for money to buy a thousand rifles for the first Italian province to rise, and he had collected a number of subscriptions, the first being £1 from Cowen, but not until 1859 did the Italian liberation movement gain pace. In that year Piedmont, helped by France, attacked the Austrian occupying forces in northern Italy. The radicals were not quite sure what to make of this unholy alliance. Bradlaugh chaired a meeting for Dr Bernard to lecture on 'Napoleon the Third, Italy and the Pope' at St Martin's Hall on 9 March, and in the *Reasoner*, Percy Greg speculated that when Napoleon had made peace with Austria by deserting Italy, he would turn his 100,000 troops, in alliance with Russia, against England. Such fears were turned to joy when the news came through in June 1860 of Garibaldi's military successes in Southern Italy.[20]

There were already two Italian Funds in existence in May 1860 when the first Garibaldi demonstration was held in St Martin's Hall to launch a Garibaldi Fund with Ashurst as treasurer, but on 27 August the several different funds were consolidated by the creation of a Garibaldi Committee under the chairmanship of E. H. J. Craufurd. Holyoake was assistant secretary, and in fact was the effective secretary throughout the existence of the Committee, while Austin Holyoake acted as secretary to 'Captain Styles', the recruiting officer for the Garibaldi Legion.[21] The idea of a volunteer Legion went back to the Spanish Legion of which Southwell had been a member in the early Carlist wars: it was illegal, but a satisfactory verdict when J. Baxter Langley was brought before the Newcastle Police Court charged with violating the Foreign Enlistment Act, ensured that the attitude of the government would be one of benevolent neutrality.[22] Holyoake's contribution to the work was outstanding. By October 1860 the *Reasoner* had raised £50 for the Legion Fund; and he missed only a few committee meetings—and those through illness—between 27 August 1860 and 1 March 1861, although meetings were held at least twice a week. In February 1861 he became general secretary in theory as well as practice, at a time when the committee had to raise £1,000 to meet current debts, and in June he sent a letter from Garibaldi to the *Daily News,* which promoted a new Italian Committee to work for the liberation of Venice and Rome.[23]

The Roman issue in particular underlined the religious nature of the Italian liberation movement. The ultra-radicals were by no means all atheists, but the attack on the ancien regime and the attack on the Pope were inseparable, as became obvious in September 1862 when, at a Hyde Park meeting called to protest against the French occupation of Rome, the English radicals clashed with the Irish—'Cardinal Wiseman's lambs', as *Punch* called them.[24] And Ireland itself, soon to replace Italy as a major concern of the Liberal party, was to provide serious ideological problems for radicals who were in favour of Home Rule but opposed to Rome Rule.

Despite the religious and political sympathies which bound many Secularists to the European republican cause, however, and despite the important part played by Holyoake and his followers in the Italian liberation movement, it would be misleading to conclude that Secularism was an important force in radical politics in the 1850s and early 1860s. The links were personal rather than organisational. This became increasingly true also of the co-operative movement which, starting from an Owenite position, rapidly moved to one of independence.

b
Socialism and the co-operative movement

The old socialists, many of them active Secularists in the 1850s, remained true to the principles of socialism and faithful followers of the Social Father, despite his conversion to spiritualism in 1853, until his death in 1858. A prominent item in Holyoake's election address at Tower Hamlets in 1857 was that 'home colonies' should be established by the government on waste land, both for the relief of the poor and for the training of emigrants, and this had actually been done in the early 1850s by the Sheffield Poor Law Board under the guidance of Isaac Ironside.[25]

Robert Owen never gave up trying. He arranged to commence the millennium on 14 May 1855 at St Martin's Hall in London. Preliminary meetings were held, Robert Cooper and Holyoake promised their help, and the latter became Owen's publisher.[26] But the millennium was inevitably postponed, and it was not brought much nearer in March 1857, when Owen again offered himself for election at St Marylebone, or in May of the same year, when a 'Congress of the advanced minds of the world' was called at St Martin's Hall, in which leading Secularists played a prominent part. John Maughan was secretary of a committee appointed by the congress, Robert Cooper read all Owen's speeches as the old man's sight and hearing were failing, and Holyoake gave extensive coverage to the congress in the *Reasoner*.[27] Later the same year, Owen attended the inaugural meeting of the Association for the Promotion of Social Science in Birmingham, and in November he saw the formation of the Social Science League, with James Rigby, the Owenite, and J. M. Ludlow, the Christian Socialist, as joint secretaries.[28] Owen wrote to Holyoake shortly before his death in 1858, urging him to take up the cause of the Social Science League, as 'The rights of Secularism are now fully established.'[29]

Holyoake doubtless questioned this, but he also had in hand far more practicable schemes than enigmatic associations dreamed up by Robert Owen. He had kept in close touch with the Owenites of Rochdale who in 1844 had opened their co-operative store in Toad Lane, and in 1857 he narrated their history in a series of articles written for the *Daily News*, and published as a volume the following year.[30]

The new co-operative movement, which rapidly spread throughout the North on the Rochdale model in the 1850s, was linked to Secularism by history and by personalities. Owenism, co-operation and Secularism were, in many ways, parts of the same movement. Robert Cooper, for example, who with James Rigby had been Owen's closest companion until his death, was a prominent member of the Robert Owen Memorial Committee, and among the names of local secretaries sending contributions to him were those of a number of men who had become leading local Secularists: John Beswick of Oldham, Charles Hindle of Stockport, Willis Knowles of Hyde, Josiah Meadowcroft of Ashton and Jeremiah Olive of Halifax.[31] Such men were often the founders of local co-operative stores: James Campbell, president of the Manchester Secular Society in 1859, had been a member of a co-operative committee inspired in the north by the Christian Socialists in 1851, and in 1859 he was a leading member of the Hulme co-operative store, which transferred its original premises to the Secular Society when it moved to a larger shop in that year. Willis Knowles was similarly involved both in Hyde Secularism and the Hyde Branch of the Dukinfield Co-operative Society. At Holmbridge, Bradlaugh reported, the store was run by 'an intelligent Freethinker', and John Howarth was secretary of both the Secularist and Co-operative Societies in Bradford. Charles Cattell was prominent in both movements in Birmingham, and Abraham Greenwood and William Cooper were leading Secularists and co-operators in Rochdale.[32] Yet co-operation was distinct. When Holyoake inquired into the religious backgrounds of the Rochdale Pioneers in 1861, Abraham Howard quoted from the 1860 Almanac:

> The present Co-operative Movement does not intend to meddle with the various religious or political differences which now exist in society, but by a common bond, namely, that of self-interest, to join together the means, the energies and the talents of all for the benefit of each.[33]

As the personalities who had belonged to both movements retired or died, co-operation left its infidel past behind. The new co-operative movement owed as much to Christian Socialism as it did to Secularism, and the later development of consumers' co-operation was based as much on economic pragmatism as on ideology. Indeed Holyoake was to find that the men who most shared his co-operative ideology were the Christian Socialists. The co-operative movement, despite its origins, cannot be identified with the organisation of Secularism.

In a number of other reform movements no such distinction can be made. The Secularists were not a large body and could exercise little significant influence on large movements, but as a small pressure group they could and did play a vital role in smaller agitations. This was to be their particular contribution to nineteenth-century radicalism, as they worked for freedom of expression and the secularisation of the Victorian state.

c

Sunday observance

One of the most controversial reform issues of the 1850s was the question of the use and abuse of Sundays. 'Socialism, Secularism and Sunday Leagueism are but three forms of one and the same thing,' announced a hostile Coventry newspaper in 1857, and this was broadly true.[34] Opposition to the Christian Sabbath was a fundamental part of the Painite tradition. 'They might as well talk of the Lord's month, of the Lord's week, of the Lord's hour, as of the Lord's day,' Paine had written.[35] The Secularists could find a better use for the Sabbath than attendance at chapel, church or public house. Holyoake told Grant in 1853:

> Secularism would take, when necessary, the poor factory-jaded Sunday scholars into fields—that school-room of nature; It would throw open the Clyde on the Sunday to the Sunday steamer, that the poor Glasgow weaver might gaze on Ben Lomond on the Lord's-day. It would give the mechanic access to museums, and botanical gardens, and crystal palaces, and even to the theatre on that day.[36]

An agitation was begun in the early fifties by Robert Le Blond for the opening of the Crystal Palace on Sundays, and Holyoake made the opening of public buildings on Sunday afternoons part of his election programme when he stood at Tower Hamlets in 1857.[37]

The agitation took a more violent turn in the middle 1850s when the issue of Sunday trading was raised. Sunday trading had long troubled Christian consciences and the police. The problem was that employers often paid wages at public houses on Saturday nights, and that the working men were then induced to loiter around, in various states of inebriation, until Sunday morning when they spent what was left of their earnings on food at the street traders' stalls, much to the discomfiture of the well-to-do on their way to church. The crisis broke in June and July 1855 over Sir Robert Grosvenor's Sunday Trading Bill, which was described by Holyoake as 'a mere Church monopoly act, for the protection of religion from competition'.[38] Riots occurred in Hyde Park on Sunday afternoons throughout the summer. They began on 24 June with the mobbing of fashionable people in the park, but the most serious clash came the following Sunday. More people came to the park, attracted by the events of the previous week. The police also attended in force, and the information which alerted the police illustrates the way in which the agitation had grown to embrace a whole spectrum of radical causes: a French police report to Napoleon III had warned of a 'Chartist' demonstration to be held in Hyde Park on Sunday 1 July, organised by G. W. Reynolds, Ledru-Rollin and other French refugees, 'à l'occasion du projet de Bill présenté par Lord Grosvenor sur l'observation du dimanche'. This information was passed on to the Foreign Office, which informed the Home Office, which gave instructions to the metropolitan police. The outcome was a number of violent clashes between demonstrators and police so severe that an inquiry was subsequently held in which the conduct of some of the police was criticised. Unrest continued throughout the summer. A Republican Society encouraged its members to attend, and contingents were expected from Birmingham and Sheffield. As late as October 1855 Lord Dartmouth was still protesting that his sister's windows overlooking Hyde Park had been broken by rioters. Thomas Frost saw in these riots, and the subsequent withdrawal of Grosvenor's Bill, a precedent for the Anti-conspiracy Bill demonstration of 1858.[39]

The Secularists took a keen interest in these occurrences but they could claim very little credit for them. The riots merely show the general strength of popular feeling against a controlled Sabbath, and illustrate the favourable nature of the environment within which the Secularist agitators worked. The riots were the occasion of Bradlaugh's first public demonstration since his release from the army and return to civilian life and he later gave evidence to the Commission of Inquiry, but Holyoake kept out of the way. On the other hand, the Secularists did involve themselves in the agitations which arose out of the riots. The first of these was the campaign of the National Sunday League which originated in the summer of 1855 among the gold- and silver-smiths for the opening of the British Museum on Sundays. Their agitation was expanded under the presidency of Sir Joshua Walmsley into a general movement for freeing the Sabbath. Walmsley made little progress on the matter in Parliament, but the Secularists and others took up the campaign in the provinces, while the *Reasoner* devoted some of its pages, entitled the *Free Sunday Chronicle,* to reporting the progress of the 'Free Sunday League'. Branches of the National Sunday League were organised by Secularists in many places, such as Halifax, Manchester and in the East End at Philpot Street, where Bradlaugh was the local secretary.[40]

The Secularists also contributed to three further agitations. First, they took part in the campaign for Sunday music. On 13 April 1856, Sir Benjamin Hall, Commissioner of Woods and Forests, had given permission for military bands to play in the metropolitan parks on Sundays but, following a request from the Archbishop of Canterbury, this decision had been reversed by the Prime Minister, Lord Palmerston. The agitators for a freer Sunday therefore hired private bands to play on Sundays both in London and in the provinces. Bands were hired at Manchester, Stalybridge and many other places in the north. At Newcastle 15,000 people were said to have gathered on the Town Moor to hear a band on a Sunday evening, and 86,000 were reported in Victoria Park, London.[41]

Secondly the Secularists drew attention to the severity of the Sunday trading laws by bringing to the public notice petty examples of their enforcement. In 1858, for example, there was the case of Peter Kay of Preston, a cripple who sold nettle beer on Sundays and was prosecuted under a law of 29 Charles II which restricted the Sunday opening of inns. While Holyoake was convalescing at Silloth in Cumberland in 1859 he came across the case of Widow Elizabeth Hodgson of Wigton who was prosecuted for selling hot mutton pies a few minutes after midnight on a Saturday night. The case was taken up by the local press and Holyoake lectured at Wigton. In Leeds three men were reported by two Sunday School teachers for selling 'Spices and Cigars in the Borough of Leeds' on a Sunday morning. Two were fined five shillings but a third, William Ridge, who was a Secularist, argued with the magistrates and was fined fourteen shillings.[42]

Thirdly the Secularists demonstrated their attitude towards Sunday in a very positive way by organising Sunday excursions and entertainments for their members and others. In London there were the open-air meetings in Victoria Park; for Glasgow, Holyoake demanded Sunday excursions on the Clyde; and in Lancashire, Southwell had identified himself with organised trips to Fleetwood. The climax of this activity came at the end of the decade, especially in the north with the Tandle Hill, Woodhead, Bills o'Jacks, Shipley Glen and Castle Hill camp meetings. Holyoake saw these gatherings as a demonstration of an important point of principle, and the authorities did what they could

to prevent them. At Castle Hill in 1860, for example, a policeman
stopped Jeremiah Olive's son from selling freethought papers, so Bradlaugh sold them instead and asked that all complaints be referred to
him. Olive's contingent from Halifax had already suffered once that
day from Sabbatarian zeal when the Halifax Station authorities had
refused to allow the special excursion train to stop there.[43] These
camp meetings show, if not the popularity of Secularism, then at least
that a large number of working men agreed with the Secularists that
it was better to spend the Sabbath in the open-air, listening to the
Holmfirth or Royton brass band, than in a closed chapel—whether
they believed the doctrines preached there or not.

The campaign to free the Sabbath, though, had not progressed very
far by 1866, and energetic Secularists continued for many years in
their attempts at changing public opinion on this matter. How far
they eventually contributed to the diminution of Sabbatarian feeling
in Britain is difficult to tell. One suspects that secularity has been of
more significance than Secularism.

d
The taxes on knowledge

By contrast, the aims of the Association for the Repeal of the Taxes
on Knowledge had largely been achieved by 1866, and were completely
realised within the next three years. Though the Association was not
exclusively atheistic, the Secularists did play a very real part in its
work and success. The rationalistic outlook of freethought presupposed
that the press should be unfettered and cheap, and the freethinking
booksellers, not least Hetherington, had been largely responsible for
the liberalisation of the law in 1836. This work was continued until
the Advertisement Duty was repealed in 1853, the Stamp Act in 1855,
the Paper Duty in 1861, and the Securities System in 1869. First Holyoake, and then Bradlaugh, carried on the work of Hetherington, trying
the law until it failed and making themselves a nuisance to the
authorities.

At the suggestion of Francis Place, a Newspaper Stamp Abolition
Committee had been formed in 1849, drawing its inspiration from
the Chartist movement and in particular from the People's Charter
Union. The original members included Francis Place, C. D. Collet,
Henry Hetherington, Richard Moore and James Watson, to whom
G. J. Holyoake and James Stansfeld, among others, were added shortly
afterwards. At the same time other committees were formed to agitate

for the repeal of the Advertisement and Paper Duties. Holyoake was entrusted with the job of co-ordinating these movements, and he did so successfully when, on 21 January 1851 at a London Tavern meeting, he moved that Cowan's Paper Duty agitation should include the more general objects of Stamp and Advertisement Duty repeal. This was followed by the formation of the Association for the Repeal of the Taxes on Knowledge, a committee which contained a large number of prominent middle- and working-class radicals, including Holyoake, with Thomas Milner Gibson, M.P., as president. Holyoake was also busy collecting sixpences in the *Reasoner* for an agitation fund, and of the committee's first year's income of £51 in 1850, £11 came from the *Reasoner*; all together £25 was collected through the Secularists' organisation.[44]

The agitation in the 1850s, according to J. S. Mill, converted the government department, which converted the government, which converted the House of Commons. This was broadly true, and certainly in 1852 the agitators appeared to have a long way to go when the House firmly rejected the repeal of all three duties.[45] The campaign began by seeking a definition of a newspaper. The 1836 Act had not made clear whether any paper containing news was a newspaper, or only one which was published at intervals of not more than twenty-six days. In a case brought against Charles Dickens's *Household Narrative* in 1851, the Barons of the Exchequer ruled that the twenty-six day interval of the 1712 Act did apply to the 1836 Act and that, therefore, monthly publications, although containing news, were not liable for the tax. Next, on behalf of the Association, Frank Grant—who, though he was a regular contributor to the *Reasoner,* was not an atheist— began the *Stoke-upon-Trent Narrative of Current Events and Potteries Advertiser* to try the law on monthly publications which had a publication date in the middle of the month, contrary to the Act of 60 George III cap. 9, sec. 4. The government refused to prosecute him, thereby depriving the Association of a clear judicial decision, but a similar case involving the *Dunfermline News* showed that the government was prepared to concede that monthly publications could be issued at any time of the month.[46]

Attention was then turned to the question of whether a weekly trade journal was a newspaper or not. In 1850 Thornton Hunt and Charles Bray had petitioned against papers such as *Punch* and the *Builder* which used to stamp only those copies which were to be sent through the post, although all copies contained news. Grant and Collet wished to contest this practice, so they began a *Potteries Free Press* to question the legality of the *Athenæum*, the *Builder* and the

Racing Times in their avoidance of the stamp. The London publisher of the *Free Press*, Edward Truelove, was summonsed for selling the paper and so the practice of the Stamp Office in excepting trade journals was shown to be illegal. By this means the Association was able to bring either the Stamp Office, or the Law, or both, into ridicule.[47]

Immediate success then came with respect to the Advertisement Duty, and in an unexpected way. The repeal of this duty, which hit rich and poor press alike, had never excited the same opposition as had met efforts to repeal the Stamp Duty. A motion by Milner Gibson in 1853 for repeal was carried with the support of the Tories, so Gladstone inserted in the 1853 Budget a provision for the duty to be reduced from 1s 6d to 6d. An amendment to the Budget by Milner Gibson, proposing total abolition, was defeated, but late at night when government supporters had left the House, E. H. J. Craufurd succeeded in moving that 0d be substituted for 6d. Gladstone therefore acquiesced and by 16 and 17 Victoria cap. 63, sec. 5, the Advertisement Duty was repealed.[48]

On the advice of Cobden, the Association then decided to go for an all-out attack on the Newspaper Stamp, leaving the Paper Duties, which were purely a financial question, to Mr Gladstone's love of free trade. The repeal of the Advertisement Duty had meant that papers which were primarily advertisers might now be classed as newspapers for the purposes of the Stamp. So Novello, the treasurer of the Association, brought out his monthly *Musical Times* at fortnightly intervals, with over 50 per cent of the space filled with advertisements, and Holyoake issued a *Fleet Street Advertiser* of two pages, one blank and one full of advertisements, solely for the benefit of the government. These publications forced the government to make it clear that advertisers were, in fact, newspapers.[49]

The next point of law which Holyoake set out to clarify was whether an unstamped paper which was declared by its proprietor to be a newspaper, thereby obtaining a Stamp, could travel freely through the G.P.O. Many periodicals had resorted to this device to obtain cheap circulation, but such a practice encouraged the existence of the Stamp, which the Association were trying to make as obnoxious as possible. The *Reasoner* was a periodical and therefore not liable, so Holyoake applied for a Stamp. The Treasury replied that he could have a Stamp if he made the declaration that his paper was a newspaper, which it plainly was not. By adhering to the letter of the law he demonstrated its absurdity and he was able to show that the *Quarterly List of the Additional Curates Society* and other worthy publications were openly defrauding the Treasury by making false statements at which the

Treasury was conniving. Holyoake succeeded in persuading the government to remedy this situation, but the projected Bill was lost with Mr Gladstone's resignation in 1855, so Holyoake recommenced his work by beginning proceedings against John Crockford for making false statements about his *Critic, London Literary Journal* and *Clerical Journal*, until the government, which was already considering a general Stamp Bill in the Lords, gave way.[50]

The final impetus for repeal came from outside the scope of the Association's efforts, when the great appetite for news generated by the Crimean War resulted in a general measure for reforming the Press Laws. Several unstamped daily and weekly war papers were begun in 1854 and were soon threatened by the government with prosecution. Following cautions to William Strange about his *Strange's Army and Navy Dispatch* and *War Chronicle,* Holyoake took over the latter in December 1854 and published it in a dubiously legal fashion as follows:

9 December, *Collet's War Chronicle*
16 December, *Moore's War Chronicle*
23 December, *Hoppy's War Chronicle*
30 December, *War Chronicle*

The government was unmoved and finances were low, so Holyoake abandoned the *War Chronicles* for a two-page, unstamped halfpenny *War Fly Sheet*, which was issued as a supplement to John Hamilton's *Empire*. He did this weekly between 13 December 1854 and 22 June 1855, ignoring summonses to attend the Exchequer Court and incurring potential fines of over £600,000. The law was clearly unenforceable, and on 15 June the Stamp was at last made optional for all papers, its use being retained solely for purposes of transmission by the G.P.O.[51] Holyoake was able to claim proudly that he was one of 'the last persons prosecuted for Atheism, and for publishing unstamped newspapers'.[52]

The repeal of the compulsory Stamp made the Paper Duty all the more conspicuous. It was against the interest of all papers and against Mr Gladstone's principles, but so long as the war lasted there was little possibility of repeal, and the defeat of the radical M.P.s in the 1857 election further set back the campaign. Holyoake urged Secularists to join in the fight against a duty which made a penny *Reasoner* a practical impossibility, and he drafted for them a model petition to Parliament.[53]

Milner Gibson was returned to Parliament at the Ashton by-election in December 1857, and, following his defeat of the Palmerston ministry in 1858, he renewed the agitation inside and outside Parliament. He attacked Disraeli's Budget in June and a motion condemning the Paper Duty was actually carried. Then in September a campaign for repeal was launched at a meeting of the representatives of the metropolitan newspaper and periodical press. Holyoake was put on a committee chosen at the meeting, and the *Reasoner* announced a new appeal for four hundred sixpences. By 1860 Mr Gladstone had become convinced that the duty was untenable: the agitation had converted the Exchequer, Mr Gladstone was able to carry the government, but Parliament remained to be convinced. To compensate for the loss of duty which repeal would entail, Gladstone had to put a penny on the income tax. The House of Lords readily accepted this measure, but rejected repeal. Their action turned the campaign against the duty into a general one for parliamentary and constitutional reform, but the repeal of the Paper Duty was assured because it had been presumed in the terms of the commercial treaty negotiated by Cobden with France in 1860. Gladstone therefore included repeal in his 1861 Budget, which also reduced the income tax again. He became the idol of the radicals.[54]

All that now remained of 60 George III cap. 9 was the securities system, which meant that a deposit had to be paid against the commission of blasphemous and other libels by the press; also, by 39 George III cap. 79, printers, presses, proprietors and papers had to be registered. This law had originally been aimed at the popular, anonymous press which flourished in the crisis immediately after the onset of the revolutionary wars, and it had not been rigorously enforced in more recent times. As registration had normally taken place when the stamped paper was acquired, the repeal of the compulsory stamp threw the whole question of registration into confusion. In 1856, for example, the Urquhartite paper, the *Sheffield Free Press,* was not registered and yet the government refused to prosecute, but in 1857 a circular was issued reminding the unstamped press that registration was still required, and the *Bury Times* was prosecuted.[55] Now that there were no financial reasons for such a system, it was obvious that the only purpose of the law was solely to keep a check on the press and to impose a kind of censorship. The object of the Association was to remove all 'previous' restrictions (i.e. restrictions imposed before a paper could even be published, as opposed to 'subsequent' restrictions, i.e. the laws of libel enforced in the courts of law), so the campaign continued. Holyoake began by querying whether pamphlets, as defined by 60 George III cap. 9, sec. 8, should be treated as newspapers, under 6 & 7 William IV cap. 76. After hesitation, the Board of Inland Revenue

S

ruled that this was so, which meant that the securities system applied
to publishers of pamphlets as well as newspapers. If enforced, this
ruling would have made the law even more obnoxious—which is what
Holyoake wanted—but the government wisely declined to make any
martyrs and an uneasy truce was maintained between Whitehall and
Fleet Street. Meanwhile, in Parliament, A. S. Ayrton unsuccessfully
introduced measures to secure the amendment of the law.[56] The agitation revived in 1866, when Joseph Timm of the Inland Revenue Board
retired and was replaced by William Mebrill, a solicitor who was not
prepared to let the law lie dormant. In this he may well have been
influenced by the worsening of the political situation in London, with
the Hyde Park riots of 1866 and the defiance of the government by the
Reform League in Hyde Park the following year. Certainly this is what
Bradlaugh thought when his *National Reformer* became one of the
Stamp Office's chosen victims. Bradlaugh contested his case in the
courts, but before a decision was reached Gladstone was returned to
power and A. S. Ayrton was appointed Secretary to the Treasury, a
position which enabled him to introduce in 1869 a Bill for the final
abolition of the securities system.[57] In the words of C. D. Collet,
secretary of the Association for the Repeal of the Taxes on Knowledge
throughout its long career, 'the Georgian Code fell'. The obnoxious
provisions of 60 Geo III cap. 9 had at last been removed, and all the
'previous' restrictions on the press, except the law requiring that the
name and address of the printer appear on every publication, had
finally been abolished.[58] The radical campaign against the restrictions
on the press had united parliamentary and working-class radicals in a
long struggle, and freethinkers had played a full part in the final
victory.

The same techniques were also applied by them in a number of
other agitations of a similar nature aimed at the 'subsequent' restrictions on the freedom of expression and publication, and other laws
which discriminated against freethinkers on account of their non-
Christian beliefs.

e
Law reform

The Fleet Street House had as its second aim 'Securing equal civil
rights for all now excluded from them by conscientious opinion not
recognised by the state'.[59] The Victorian State was a Christian institution and the laws of the state worked to the advantage of Christi-

anity. The Secularists attacked three aspects of the law, relating to
Church rates, blasphemy, and the Christian oath in courts of law and
Parliament.

Ecclesiastical taxation was obnoxious, not only to Secularists but
also to Nonconformists, and in the light of the failure of the latter
to end it the Secularists were powerless to do more than protest.
Easter dues, Church rates and tithes had long been a source of great
bitterness between the radicals and the Church, and reports of clerical
inhumanity to the poor occur in most popular radical papers. Holyoake recalled the Easter dues his mother had had to pay in 1829
when his baby sister lay dying; John Loft, a poor weaver from Almond-
bury who was an infirmary outpatient with a wife and two children to
support, had a clock and two chairs seized in 1842 when he was unable
to pay his Easter dues. In London, Holyoake and Truelove regularly
defied the authorities. In 1855, for example, for refusing to pay tithes
of 12/4d., Holyoake lost an eight-day clock valued at three guineas;
he made an offering in kind—volume XVII of the *Reasoner*—but this
was refused. The broker removed three reams of paper from Truelove's
premises in 1858, but the following year Bradlaugh, acting on behalf
of Truelove, challenged the Church rate in the parish of St Clement
Dane, and the churchwardens, after taking legal advice, dropped
their claim. This was an isolated achievement, though, and ecclesiastical taxation remained a source of grievance and anti-clericalism. All
the Secularists could do was to keep up their pressure on public
opinion. In 1860, for example, Bradlaugh attended an anti-Church
rate rally at Park Gate, near Rotherham, which had been organised by
the Sheffield Secular Society, and he delivered an address 'remarkable
for its effect'. Whether this effect was merely oratorical or not, the
report does not say.[60]

The blasphemy laws were challenged over the case of Thomas Pooley,
a Cornish well-digger, who was imprisoned for twenty-one months for
writing on the gate of the Reverend Paul Bushe, Rector of Duloe:
'Duloe stinks of the monster Christ's Bible—Blasphemy—T. Pooley',
and for saying that the ashes of burnt Bibles would cure the potato
disease and that Christ was 'the forerunner of all theft and whore-
dom'. This case raised two points. First, there may well have been a
miscarriage of justice, for Pooley was plainly insane. Secondly, this
was the first successful application of the Blasphemy Acts in England
since Hetherington had prosecuted Moxon in 1841 as a counter-
measure to the action taken against himself over Haslam's *Letters to
the Clergy*. Pooley's case looked like a dangerous revival of obsolete
practice, and, moreover, the infidels also thought that the Blasphemy

Acts could be enforced only by the Law Officers of the Crown. The Pooley case, therefore, seemed to threaten all the achievements of the early 1840s.[61]

Pooley was tried at Bodmin assizes on 31 July 1857 before Mr Justice Coleridge, and the prosecution was conducted by his son, John Coleridge.[62] Holyoake first heard of the case in August and immediately wrote to Pooley, taking up his case 'on behalf of the Society of the Promoters of Freethought'. He went down to Cornwall and made a full journalistic exposure. William Coningham, the Member for Brighton and a friend of Holyoake, took up the case with the Home Secretary and procured a free pardon for Pooley in December 1857. Although Pooley was not a Secularist but an anti-clerical pantheist, his release was a major triumph for the Secularists and for Holyoake in particular. The radicals, including T. H. Buckle and J. S. Mill, regarded the outcome as a triumph for liberty, and even though the blasphemy laws still stood and were by no means dead, they were, at least on this occasion, thoroughly discredited.[63]

The most consistent form of legal discrimination against freethinkers occurred over the taking of a Christian oath. The nineteenth century saw the gradual relaxation of this law with regard to Unitarians, Quakers and Jews, but atheists were, throughout this period and until the Evidence Amendment Acts of 1869 and 1870, without legal rights because they were unable to take an acceptable oath. The case law on this subject was in utter confusion, as various magistrates had interpreted statute law in a number of different ways. In 1839 George Connard, a socialist lecturer in Oldham, was imprisoned for debt because he would not take the oath; in 1842 a law officer named William Simpson, who had been assaulted, could not give evidence on his own account because he was an atheist; in 1850 Holyoake was allowed to explain that he took the oath as a legal formality and not as a statement of belief (*Russell v. Jackson*), but this privilege was denied to him in a different court in 1852. Edward Truelove tried to make an affirmation under the law as applied to Jews and Quakers when he wished to prosecute a man for stealing a book in 1854, but he was told that the affirmation was allowed only when the oath was objected to on religious grounds, and this did not apply to atheists. Joseph Turner of Park Gate in Yorkshire found that his doctor's bill included items which he had not received. He refused to pay, was prosecuted, and was winning his case when the prosecution asked him his theological views. He did not believe in Hell, so his oath was declared to be invalid and he lost his case. In 1857 and 1860 Holyoake was summoned for Jury service and then rejected because he would not take the oath. Atheists were not the only people to suffer. In 1851 John Denman, a Roman Catholic, refused to swear on the Protestant Bible and his case against his wife was dismissed.[64]

Holyoake's attitude towards the oath was that which he had expressed in *Russell v. Jackson* in 1850. He was prepared to take it only if he were allowed at the same time to explain what he meant by it, and in 1854 he sent a petition to this effect to Lord John Russell, who ignored it.[65] The Affirmation Act of 17 and 18 Victoria further complicated matters: cap. 125, ss. 20 and 21, set out that

> If any person called as a witness, or required or desiring to make an Affidavit or Deposition shall refuse or be unwilling from alleged conscientious motives to be sworn, it shall be lawful for the court or judge or other presiding Officer or person qualified to take affidavits or depositions, *upon being satisfied of the sincerity of such Objection,* to permit such person, instead of being sworn, to make his or her solemn affirmation or declaration in the words following; *videlicet,* 'I *A.B.* do solemnly, sincerely, & truly affirm & declare, That the taking of any oath is, *according to my Religious belief, Unlawful;* . . .[66]

This law had several drawbacks, as was pointed out to Holyoake by T. B. Baines in the letter from which this extract is quoted. If interpreted liberally it gave the Secularists all they wanted. D. Wallwork, the Dudley Secularist leader, was permitted to make an affirmation at the Worcester Sessions in 1857 under this Act, but a ruling at the Old Bailey stated that the Act applied only to Quakers, Mormons and Separatists. Holyoake thought that the Secularists were covered by the Act in civil cases; George Henness, a *Reasoner* correspondent, thought it applied in all cases.[67] The drawbacks of the Act, underlined by Baines in the quoted extract, were that the sincerity of non-theists might be questioned, the religious nature of unbelief might be doubted, and the non-theist might be thought to be amoral and therefore not capable of conceiving of the oath as unlawful. Bradlaugh gave it as his opinion in 1858 that Secularists could not be sure of protection until incompetency on the grounds of a want of religious faith had been totally abolished. Without such a radical reform, cases such as *Hole v. Barlow,* in which Mr Justice Byles had held that any conscientious objections came within the meaning of the Act, were exceptions, irrelevant to the main course of the law.[68]

The Secularists differed over what should be done to change this position. Some thought with Charles Newman that what the Secularists had to do was 'to take the oath as it stood, and throw the responsibility of the incongruity on the imposers of it'. Bradlaugh followed this line and preferred to argue the case law in court. He thought that the agitation for the Secular Affirmation Bill was 'a waste of time, strength and resources'. Holyoake took the opposite view. He regarded the oath question in the light of the 1841 crisis in Owenism, and his conclusion was still the same: 'The cause of "Freethought" cannot be advanced by the weapons of the Jesuit'.[69]

The agitation gained strength as Sir J. S. Trelawney prepared to introduce an Affirmation Bill into Parliament in 1861. Holyoake set up an 'Evidence Committee' at 147 Fleet Street to gather arguments against the existing law: 'It is intended to act on the policy of Bentham, and to carry the bad law into operation, until all the mischief it can produce makes an impression upon the Legislature.'[70] This was the same technique as had been used against the Taxes on Knowledge. A collusive action was arranged with John Bigg, a Unitarian Secularist and former follower of Carlile, who was a baker in Lenham near Maidstone. Jane Bottle had stolen a shawl from his shop, and there were only two witnesses of this incident, Bigg and his wife. Bigg could not take the oath, and he had arranged for his wife to have a medical certificate excusing her from giving evidence. He and Holyoake then arranged for Jane Bottle to be defended and for an objection to be raised against Bigg by this defence.[71] Other cases arose without this elaborate planning. Four poachers who beat up a gamekeeper could not be punished because the keeper was an infidel and could not give evidence; in 1853 a man had actually been imprisoned for not taking the oath, while the man whom he was prosecuting for theft escaped; Henry Clark of Derby was unable to appear as a witness for a plaintiff in a debt case but, in June 1861 at Marylebone County Court, a plaintiff in a debt case was allowed to give evidence although he did not believe in Hell.[72]

The most renowned case of all, and one which became a rallying cry for the whole Secularist movement, was *Maden v. Cattenach* at Rochdale in 1860–1861. Mrs Maden, a former Wesleyan school teacher, and her husband, Samuel Maden, an artist and a Secularist, lived with her mother and step-father, Mr Cattenach. When the young couple moved their home Cattenach would not let Mrs Maden take her piano with her, so she sued him for £6 3s damages. Mrs Maden had become noted as a freethinker because of her correspondence in the *Rochdale Spectator* following Bradlaugh's lectures in the district. The judge at Rochdale County Court therefore refused Mrs Maden's request to take the oath and non-suited her because she did not believe in a future state of rewards and punishments.[73] The Rochdale Secular Society took up the case and arranged for an appeal to the higher courts, and the Manchester Secular Society raised forty guineas for a new piano which was presented to Mrs Maden at a great Secularist gathering at Rochdale in the spring of 1861.[74]

A re-trial of the case was held in Rochdale in January 1861, with E. H. J. Craufurd, M.P., who had carried a Scottish Affirmations Bill, for Mrs Maden. The judge again refused to accept evidence from Mrs Maden. The legal issue was whether the defence had the right to question Mrs Maden about her beliefs. Trelawney and Coningham raised the matter in the House but the Home Secretary upheld the judge. A new summons was therefore taken out on which to ground an appeal to London. The case was heard at Rochdale on 27 April. The judge refused Mrs Maden's evidence, non-suited her and suggested an appeal. The sum sued for was raised to £25 to justify this, and the case was heard in the Court of the Exchequer on 11 November 1861 before the Lord Chief Baron (Baron Bramwell) and Barons Channell and Wilde. Craufurd acted as Counsel for Maden, with Zach Mellor (the Rochdale Town Clerk) and Ashurst and Morris as attorneys. The judgement was, in the words of Holyoake's *Counsellor*, that the law afforded 'no relief to those who declined to take the oath. For this relief, we must go to Parliament.'[75]

But Trelawney's attempts to carry a Secular Affirmations Bill in Parliament all met with failure. In June 1861, his first Bill was lost on the Second Reading by 66 votes to 136; in June 1862 leave was given to introduce a Bill by 88 votes to 56, but the reformers decided not to press forward until a new campaign had been mounted. Meanwhile further examples of abuse occurred, and Truelove was refused his request to affirm in a case involving stolen books in 1862. The next Bill was defeated in March 1863, by 112 votes to 158, but Holyoake was now more hopeful. He calculated that there were over two hundred Members who, at one time or another, had voted for the Bill, including Lord Palmerston and four other members of his Cabinet. The tide was clearly turning but, like so much other liberal legislation, secular affirmations were not secured in the courts until 1869 when Gladstone's First Ministry saw the passing of the Evidence Further Amendment Act. Bradlaugh then took over the campaign to have this Act applied without exceptions, and especially to the highest court of all, Parliament.[76]

The Secularist's efforts to secure equal civil rights for Christians and non-Christians had met with considerable success. The secular foundations of the modern state were laid in the mid century decades, and, as J. S. Mill wrote to Holyoake in 1869, 'It is a great triumph of freedom of opinion that the Evidence Bill should have passed both houses without being seriously impaired. You may justly take to yourself a good share of the credit of having brought things up to that point.'[77]

The same might have been said, to some extent, of the many agitations in which the Secularists shared under Holyoake's leadership in the 1850s and 1860s, and it is as a civil rights movement that Secularism is best remembered.

Notes

1 *Reasoner*, 25 March 1855.
2 T. Lond, *Secularism: What Is It?* . . . (London, 1859), p. 32.
3 *Reasoner*, 4 September 1859, 29 January, 12 February 1860; *National Reformer*, 13 July 1861; *Barker's Review*, 5 October 1861.
4 *Huddersfield Weekly News*, 13, 20 May 1876.
5 *Northern Star*, 22 May 1847, 5 August 1848; *Spirit of the Age*, 3 March 1849.
6 *Northern Star*, 18 October, 17 January 1852; *Star*, 27 March 1852.
7 G. J. Holyoake, *The Workman and the Suffrage* (London, 1859).
8 *Investigator*, 15 April, 1, 15 May 1859; also *National Reformer*, 14 April 1860.
9 *Ibid.*, 26 July 1868; R. Cooper to J. Cowen, 28 July 1862, C.N. C.1738.
10 J. M. Robertson, *History of Freethought*, II, p. 463; G. F. A. Best, 'Popular Protestantism in Victorian Britain', in R. Robson (ed.), *Ideas and Institutions of Victorian Britain* (London, 1967), p. 119.
11 Holyoake, *Bygones*, I, pp. 220–1; *Reasoner*, 20 February 1859.
12 *Ibid.*, 25 February 1852; *Lancashire Beacon*, no. 3 [17 August 1849].
13 A. R. Schoyen, *The Chartist Challenge* (London, 1958), p. 231.
14 *Reasoner*, 25 February, 10 November 1852; Mazzini to Holyoake [1852], C.N. A.171; also papers in H.C. 534, 535.
15 Harney and Cowen to Holyoake, 21 January 'Year 1' [1855], H.C. 728; *Reasoner*, 21 January, 15 April 1855; also papers in H.C. 743, 799, 803, 804, 806.
16 Holyoake, *Sixty Years*, II, pp. 19–25; McCabe, *Life of Holyoake*, I, pp. 249–250; M. St J. Packe, *The Bombs of Orsini* (London, 1957), pp. 240–3.
17 Holyoake, *op. cit.*, II, pp. 31–5, 48–57; McCabe, *op. cit.*, I, pp. 250–4, II, pp. 3–5; *Reasoner*, 24 February 1858; handbill in H.C. 1003.
18 *Reasoner*, 4 November, 23 December 1855; A. R. Schoyen, *op. cit.*, pp. 242–262; *Letter to the Parliament and the Press by Felix Pyat* . . . (second edition, London, 1858), publisher [Holyoake]'s preface, p. v; also Holyoake, *Sixty Years*, II, pp. 63–8.
19 W. E. Adams, *Memoirs*, II, pp. 356–72; *Reasoner*, 24 February, 31 March, 7, 21 April, 7 July 1858; *Investigator* 15 March 1858; letters between G. J. and Austin Holyoake, March 1858, H.C. 1012, 1013, 1014.
20 *Reasoner*, 15 May 1859, 14, 21 September 1856; *Investigator*, 15 March 1859; *Reasoner*, 31 July, 7 August 1859.
21 *Reasoner Gazette*, 17 June, 8 July 1860; *Reasoner*, 3 June, 29 July 1860; minute book of the Garibaldi committee, 1860–61, 27 August, 6 September, 28 December 1860, H.B.; A. Holyoake to J. Cowen, 15 August 1860, C.N. C.1488.
22 *Newcastle Journal*, 25 August 1860.

23 *Reasoner Gazette,* 21 October 1860; Garibaldi Minute Book, 11, 16, 23 October 1860, 1, 21 February 1861; *Reasoner,* 30 June 1861.

24 *Punch,* 25 October 1862.

25 *Reasoner,* 29 March 1857; W. H. G. Armytage and J. Salt, 'The Sheffield Land Colony', *Agricultural History,* xxxv (1961), pp. 202-6.

26 *Reasoner,* 3 December 1854; J. Rigby to R. Owen, 4 May 1855, O.C. 2397.

27 *Reasoner,* 29 March, 3 May 1857; *Investigator,* June 1857.

28 *Reasoner,* 28 October, 11 November 1857, 6 January 1858; *Investigator* November 1857, January 1858.

29 *Reasoner,* 7 July 1858.

30 *Self Help by the People: history of co-operation in Rochdale. Part 1. 1844–1857* (London, 1858).

31 *Reasoner,* 12 June 1859.

32 T. Christensen, *Christian Socialism,* p. 197; *Reasoner,* 11 September, 9 October, 4 December 1859; *Reasoner Gazette,* 15 April, 4, 18 November 1860; *National Reformer,* 20 December 1868.

33 G. D. H. Cole, *Century of Co-operation,* p. 95.

34 *Investigator,* June 1857.

35 Paine, *Reply to the Bishop of Llandaff,* Foner, II, p. 778.

36 *Holyoake—Grant Discussion, 1853,* p. 26.

37 *Reasoner,* 13 April 1853, 29 March 1857.

38 Report (1832) on Sunday Trading, sent to the Home Office, 15 May 1845, as part of a general investigation by Sir James Graham—H.O. 45 O.S.1091; see also H.O. 45 O.S. 4631; *Reasoner,* 8 July 1855.

39 *Ibid.,* 1, 8 July, 5 August 1855; H.O. 45 O.S. 6092 (nos. 1, 21, 38, 40); T. Frost, *Forty Years' Recollections,* p. 262; B. Harrison, 'The Sunday Trading Riots of 1855', *Historical Journal,* VIII (1965), pp. 219–245.

40 D. Tribe, *Charles Bradlaugh,* pp. 44–6; *Reasoner,* 23 September 1855, 15 June 1856; F. E. Gillespie, *Labor and Politics in England, 1850–1867* (Durham, N. Carolina 1927). p. 121; S. Maccoby, *English Radicalism 1853–86,* p. 56; *Reasoner,* 2, 9, 16 March, 6 April 1856.

41 *Ibid.,* 18, 25 May, 15, 22 June, 14 September 1856; Maccoby, *op. cit.,* pp. 56–7.

42 *Reasoner,* 21 July 1858, 28 August, 25 September, 2 October 1859.

43 *Ibid.,* 12 August 1860.

44 C. D. Collet, *History of the Taxes on Knowledge,* I, pp. 85–6, 90, 126–30; *Reasoner,* 1 August 1849, 12 March 1851; diary-cum-notebook, 21 January 1851, H.B.; Collet, *op. cit.,* I, pp. 136–7, 99.

45 *Ibid.,* pp. 130–1 168–9.

46 *Ibid.,* pp. 65, 151–3, 155–64; *Reasoner,* 10 March 1852.

47 Collet, *op. cit.,* I, pp. 109–14, 179–87; *Reasoner,* 16 March 1853.

48 Collet, *op. cit.,* I, pp. 190–7.

49 *Ibid.,* pp. 204–5, 211–13.

50 Holyoake, *The Government and the Working Man's Press* (London, 1853), pp. 6–7; *Reasoner,* 2 July, 20 August 1854, 25 February, 29 April 1855; Collet, *op. cit.,* II, pp. 12–14, 20–1.

51 *Reasoner,* 3, 10, 17 December 1854, 21 January 1855; Holyoake, *Bygones,* I, pp. 118–23; Collet, *op. cit.,* II, pp. 14–16.

52 *Reasoner,* 15 July 1855.

53 *Ibid.,* 15 February 1857.

54 Collet, *op. cit.*, II, pp. 66–135; *Reasoner*, 5 September 1858.

55 *Ibid.*, 15 February 1857; Collet, *op. cit.*, II, pp. 49–53, 57–60.

56 *Reasoner*, 9, 23 December 1857; Collet, *op. cit.*, II, pp. 49–60, 73–4, 155–65.

57 *Ibid.*, pp. 180, 196; *National Reformer*, 20 December 1868.

58 Collet, *op. cit.*, II, pp. 175–6, 207.

59 *Reasoner*, 8 January 1860.

60 Holyoake, *Bygones*, II, p. 219; *Northern Star*, 3 September 1842; *Reasoner*, 3 June, 15 July 1855; *Investigator*, 15 May 1858, 1 May 1859; *Reasoner Gazette*, 9 September 1860. Compulsory Church Rates were abolished in 1868.

61 *Reasoner*, 19, 26 August, 30 September 1857; and see Pooley's correspondence with Holyoake, H.C. 987, 991, 993, 994, 1006, 1009, 1023.

62 Mr Justice Coleridge had become famous for his lenient treatment of J. H. Newman in the Achilli trial (1851–53)—W. O. Chadwick, *Victorian Church, Part 1*, pp. 306–8. John Coleridge was later judge in the G. W. Foote blasphemy trial (1883)—D. Tribe, *100 Years of Freethought* (London, 1967), p. 158.

63 Mary Pooley to Holyoake, 19 August 1857, H.C. 944; *Reasoner*, 19 August, 23, 30 September, 25 November, 9, 16, 23 December 1857, 15, 22 May 1859.

64 *N.M.W.*, 24 August, 7 September 1839; *Oracle*, 7 May 1842; H. Ludlow to Holyoake, 29 May 1850, H.C. 374; *Reasoner*, 21 April, 15 December 1852, 19 February 1854; *Investigator*, December 1854; *Reasoner*, 26 August 1857, 15 July 1860, 15 January 1851.

65 *Ibid.*, 26 February 1854.

66 T. B. Baines to Holyoake, 5 March 1855, H.C. 744.

67 *Reasoner*, 20, 27 January 1858, 18 November, 9 December 1857.

68 *Investigator*, 15 November 1858; *Reasoner*, 14 July 1858.

69 C. R. Newman to Holyoake, 11 June 1861, H.C. 1339; *Reasoner*, 2 June, 28 April 1861.

70 *Ibid.*, 17 March, 28 April 1861.

71 Correspondence between Bigg and Holyoake, February–March 1861, H.C. 1277, 1280, 1282, 1283, 1285, 1286, 1287, 1289, 1291.

72 Bigg to Holyoake, 8 March 1861, H.C. 1291; R. Cameron to Holyoake, 20 March 1861, H.C. 1301; *Reasoner*, 16, 23 June 1861.

73 *Ibid.*, 30 December 1860; *National Reformer* 22 December 1860; Holyoake, *A Plea for Affirmation in Parliament* (London, 1882), p. 8.

74 *Reasoner Gazette*, 23 December 1860; *National Reformer*, 12 January 1861; *Reasoner*, 10 March, 14, 21 April 1861.

75 *Ibid.*, 13 January, 3, 10, 24 February, 5, 26 May 1861; *Counsellor*, December 1861; see also H.C. 1252, 1253, 1265, 1279, 1284, 1307, 1315, 1367, 1379, 1381, 1392, 1393.

76 *Secular World*, June 1863; also *National Reformer*, 12 July 1862. There remained some doubt as to whether atheists could affirm in courts of arbitration, but this was remedied in 1870. Further loopholes, concerning jury service and Scottish law, were closed by Bradlaugh's Act in 1888.

77 J. S. Mill to Holyoake, 8 August 1869, H.C. 1883.

7
Bradlaugh and national unity

In 1859 Secularism, particularly in London, had reached its lowest point. Trade at Holyoake's Fleet Street House had fallen by half in the preceding two years and the circulation of the *Reasoner* was stagnant. Austin Holyoake was very gloomy about the future: the only national advocate of Freethought in the country, he wrote, was Charles Bradlaugh, 'and he does not do much'. Many people blamed G. J. Holyoake himself for this failure, because he no longer seemed to be giving the movement any clear lead. His moderate Secularism was lacking in appeal to the rougher followers of Carlile, Southwell and Robert Cooper, and they were disappointed and disillusioned with his respectable approach towards Christians and the middle classes.[1]

These criticisms began to make an impact, and in 1859 Holyoake stirred himself for a new campaign. A Secular meeting hall was to be acquired in London, promises were made of more platform speaking and an annual conference, and the publishing department at Fleet Street was made over to Austin so that G. J. Holyoake could 'be more free to promote those objects to which he has devoted his life'. His eventual aim was to create a Secular Tract Society, modelled on the Anti-Corn Law League and the Religious Tract Society.[2]

This was Holyoake's last chance, and he failed. The scheme for the hall was abandoned because of his repeated ill-health and severe attacks of eczema during 1859, but he promised greater platform advocacy for 1860. This too he failed to accomplish. In the first half of 1860 he stayed in London while the Reform Bill was before Parliament. Then the Garibaldi Committee occupied most of his time for a further season. When he did venture again into the provinces it was not to speak on Secularism but on Italy. He even went so far as to refuse to debate 'the personal existence of God and man's responsibility to him' at Birmingham, because it was a 'mere abstract question'.[3] Holyoake had virtually abdicated from platform advocacy, and in June 1861 he also abandoned the *Reasoner*. Privately, he may have been conscious that he was fighting a losing battle, though it was also true that he needed a rest. He had been involved in agitation since 1842 and had brought out the *Reasoner* weekly since 1846 with only one disastrous break, in 1859, when he had

allowed Percy Greg, the middle-class Tory son of W. R. Greg, to be
editor during his illness. In 1861 he was involved in five other major
issues: Parliamentary Reform, Paper Duties, Harmony Hall, the Oath,
and Italy. He was also hoping to go to the United States for a while,
though this last idea was abandoned because of the Civil War.[4] The Fleet
Street House continued to be a financial burden. Even after the fund
of 1858 there remained debts of over £1,000, Holyoake was still dependent upon his middle-class sympathisers for money, and the Cash Book
for the House was not even balanced after 1858—in marked contrast to
the carefully kept Minute Book of the Garibaldi Committee. Holyoake
recognised in 1860 that 'The original error was incurring the liabilities
above mentioned [when the House was opened] without the means in
hand of meeting them.' Weakened by further illness and tired of the
worry of the debt, he agreed to let J. G. Crawford and W. Turley raise
another fund to pay off the money once and for all. This was done at a
meeting held at Anderton's Hotel on 14 May 1861. The lease of the
House ran until 1868 but the Holyoake brothers kept the place on for
only a few months longer. They could not make it pay so Holyoake
agreed to throw in his lot with Bradlaugh. Austin was appalled and
wanted his brother to raise a new loan from his wealthy friends, but
he refused. The business had—in a word which Austin could not bring
himself to use—failed.[5]

By the end of 1861, therefore, Holyoake's leadership appeared to be
at an end. He had withdrawn from platform advocacy, he had given up
the *Reasoner*, and he was about to close the Fleet Street House. Meanwhile Charles Bradlaugh had been far from inactive. He had already
gone a long way towards reviving Secularism in the North and the new
movement was rallying behind him: since 1858 he had been establishing
himself as one of the best orators in the movement, and in April 1860
he had been invited with Joseph Barker to edit the Sheffield Secularist
newspaper, the *National Reformer*. He was now equipped to take over
from Holyoake and to give a new lead and a new direction to the British
freethought movement.

But in 1861 Holyoake could not be entirely forgotten by the movement
which he had done so much to create. The pattern which had emerged
in 1861 after two years of steady Secularist growth was shortly to be
broken in pieces; Holyoake's popularity was to revive again; and
national unity under Bradlaugh's leadership was to be delayed for a
further five years.

The joint editorship exercised by Bradlaugh and Barker over the
National Reformer did not long survive the *Reasoner*. Barker was
rapidly abandoning his 'advanced' political and religious views, and the

Secularist movement under Bradlaugh's influence was growing increasingly distasteful to him. The two men finally parted over Bradlaugh's attitude towards George Drysdale's book, *The Elements of Social Science; or, Physical, Sexual, and Natural Religion*, first published in 1854, and republished in 1857 and again in 1861. Barker found this work disgusting, and—to judge from the extracts quoted by Barker in a review article in the *National Reformer*—this opinion was not entirely without foundation, since one of Drysdale's contentions was 'that seduction is a physiological virtue' and that intercourse outside marriage and easy divorce are morally and physically desirable.[6] Barker, one suspects, welcomed this pamphlet as a *casus belli*. He was already hostile to Bradlaugh on personal grounds, and disagreed with him on practically every issue discussed in the *National Reformer*. He left that paper at the end of August 1861 and a week later started his own *Barker's Review*, a weekly periodical for 'Conservative Reformers'. He now regarded 'the Churches and professional teachers' as 'natural human necessities', he deplored 'wholesale' political change as 'neither desirable nor possible', and he plainly dissociated himself from what he termed the 'Unbounded Licence Party' of neo-Malthusians. In theory much of what Barker said made good sense, and Holyoake in particular might have been expected to be sympathetic towards his views, but in practice the Secularists suspected—quite rightly—that Barker was not so much moderating his views as going through another change of heart. By 1862 he was finding even household suffrage too radical, and in 1863 he again became a Christian.[7]

Bradlaugh made a tactical error, though, when he espoused neo-Malthusian ideas in the *National Reformer*. Many column inches were devoted to articles by 'G.R.' and 'R.D.N.' which advocated the obnoxious doctrine. 'G.R.', indeed, was thought to be the author of *The Elements of Social Science* and he was said to be the inspiration behind the Malthusian League which was launched in 1861 with Bradlaugh as secretary. Bradlaugh also published his own pamphlet, *Jesus, Shelley and Malthus*, at this time.[8] Barker was not the only person to be shocked. Holyoake, who was not opposed to neo-Malthusianism as such (though he was rather inconsistent in his attitude), had commented unfavourably on the *Elements* in a *Reasoner* review in 1857; W. H. Johnson, who, as editor of the *Investigator* in 1857, had then welcomed the book, wrote to *Barker's Review* in 1861 saying he had changed his mind. Robert Cooper stated that the *Investigator* had certainly not advocated such views while he was editor. The most implacable and important of all Bradlaugh's opponents, though, was John Maughan, the London leader. He announced in 1861 that he would not accept Bradlaugh's leadership of Secularism so long as he persisted in identifying it with his neo-Malthusian propaganda. Critics of Secularism, like John Brindley, were, of course, delighted with Bradlaugh's attitude and used the 'immorality' argument against Secularism with renewed vigour.[9]

It was in these circumstances that Holyoake announced to his surprised brother that he intended to support Bradlaugh and the *National Reformer*, and to appeal for funds for the latter rather than for their own Fleet Street House. G. J. Holyoake did many petty things as leader of Secularism, and he was to do many even pettier things in the future, but this was not one of them. His aim was to unite Secularism under its two most popular leaders, and for a few months the two men almost achieved their purpose. When Barker and Bradlaugh had quarrelled, a shareholders' meeting of the *National Reformer* Company had been called in Sheffield on 26 August to decide the fate of the paper. The Company was very nearly wound up there and then, but this drastic step was avoided by 113 votes to 64, and by 41 votes to 18 Bradlaugh was chosen as sole editor in preference to Barker. Bradlaugh was henceforward determined never to share the editorship with anyone again, but he reached an agreement with Holyoake whereby the latter was to become 'chief contributor', having sole command over the first three pages. His payment was to be two guineas a week, the initial contract was to be for either six or twelve months, and during that time Bradlaugh was not to advocate neo-Malthusianism (as expressed in the *Elements*) in his part of the paper. Holyoake, who had started a monthly *Counsellor* on closing the *Reasoner* in June 1861, ended this independent expression of his views in December and commenced the new year with the new agreement.[10]

There followed one of the most discreditable episodes in the history of the freethought movement. The rights and wrongs of the issue are too complex for a final and impartial judgement to be passed upon them, but what happened appears to have been as follows. The directors of the *National Reformer* Company wanted to reduce the format of the *National Reformer* from that of a newspaper to that of a foolscap periodical. Bradlaugh was opposed to this but Holyoake was in favour and the directors appear to have tried to go over the head of the editor in this matter. Bradlaugh resigned in protest, and then decided to put himself up for re-election. Meanwhile Holyoake had agreed to stand for the post, and Bradlaugh seems to have suspected him of conspiring with the directors to take over the paper. A meeting of shareholders was held on 23 March in Sheffield when the merits of the two men were debated. Some said that Holyoake 'was too refined for the office; that his articles were more fitted for the gentleman and the scholar than for the working man, etc., while others said that it was he who had made Freethought respectable'. Eighteen votes were cast for Bradlaugh and nine for Holyoake. John Child of Leeds, who supported Holyoake, demanded that proxy votes be counted as well. There were now eighty-five votes for Holyoake, but a hundred and six for Bradlaugh. James Dodworth and the two other directors immediately resigned, and Bradlaugh assumed full control over the paper with its circulation of 3600.[11]

The day before this meeting, Bradlaugh had tried to alter the terms of the agreement with Holyoake. He offered to continue to pay him two guineas a week, but for two columns only. Holyoake was outraged. For him to give up control over the first three pages would be tantamount to his resigning the virtual editorship of that part of the paper and he would thereby be sacrificing his only outlet for his weekly opinions; it would also mean Bradlaugh would be free to advocate his neo-Malthusian ideas again. Bradlaugh's meaning was underlined by a further letter a week later which informed Holyoake 'Your connection is now that of a contributor only', meaning Bradlaugh could now edit or even refuse Holyoake's material. Holyoake immediately withdrew his latest copy, which was already with the printer, his brother Austin. The question now was, who had broken the contract first? Bradlaugh claimed that Holyoake had withdrawn; Holyoake that Bradlaugh had dismissed him, and he claimed £100 compensation from Bradlaugh plus his fees for the rest of the year. The matter went before two arbitrators, as provided for in the initial agreement—W. J. Linton and J. G. Crawford—with the possibility of reference to an umpire if the arbitrators disagreed. Linton (one of Holyoake's most long-standing and bitter critics), assisted by M. R. Leverson (Bradlaugh's employer) as solicitor, naturally found for Bradlaugh; Crawford (a staunch supporter of the Fleet Street House), assisted by W. H. Ashurst as solicitor, just as naturally found for Holyoake. The umpire, William Shaen, was therefore called in and in July 1863 he ruled in favour of Holyoake's claim for fees. The *National Reformer* hailed a Bradlaugh triumph—presumably because Holyoake had been forced to drop his excessive claim for compensation—but privately Bradlaugh was angry and refused to make any payment. Holyoake felt vindicated, though one may doubt whether he was morally justified in the avaricious way he had pressed the badly-off Bradlaugh for money.[12]

This was the parting of the ways for the two men. Throughout the 1850s Holyoake had maintained himself supreme in the movement and, although he had managed to quarrel with every other recognised leader at some time or other, his position had never been shaken for long.

Indeed some of his most violent opponents who were most ready to criticise his conciliatory attitude themselves became Christians while Holyoake himself continued to soldier on as a dogged—if apparently lukewarm—atheist.[13] But in Bradlaugh Holyoake at last met his match: in both intellectual and organisational abilities Bradlaugh was by far his superior, and after the two men had parted in 1862 there was to be no permanent reconciliation between them. Henceforward Secularism was to be divided into two parties and, though the cracks were papered over from time to time, the bitterness was to survive among followers of both men well into the present century and has dogged a balanced historical understanding of the movement ever since. Bradlaugh always led the larger and more popular party, advocating militant atheism, while Holyoake persisted on a more moderate course, occasionally winning support from the Bradlaugh camp whenever Bradlaugh's popularity suffered a temporary set-back. But Holyoake was never again to shake Bradlaugh's dominance over the movement as a whole.

With the leaders at one another's throats, the plans for Secularist unity which had been made with such high hopes at the end of 1861 came to nothing. The first Castle Hill camp meeting in 1860 had been followed on 7–8 October by a Convention held in the Odd Fellows' Hall, Halifax. National organisation had been debated and with bureaucratic deliberation a committee of five had been set up (Bradlaugh, Holyoake, John Watts, Barker and Maughan) to consider various plans and to report back to the next Convention, which was to be held in 1861. Unfortunately, the five committee-members were never in the same place at the same time and their appointment was fruitless. Barker was later made a scapegoat for this failure, and certainly his reluctance to join in any organisation was at least partly responsible for this lack of progress.[14] Finally, late in 1861, Bradlaugh and Holyoake, who had just come together on the *National Reformer*, cut the Gordian knot by announcing a National Secular Association to be formed at 147 Fleet Street. Enraged, John Maughan objected to their 'Napoleonic policy' of creating a National Secular Association, and he issued an address on behalf of his own society, the General Secular Reformers. To ratify their position, Holyoake and Bradlaugh called a meeting at the City Road Hall of Science on 18 December to arrange for the formation of a National Secular Society based at 147 Fleet Street. At this meeting Holyoake spoke in favour of 'a party where diversity of view is not only permitted, but justified'; Maughan followed this up with a counter-proposition for a much more rigorous form of organisation, such as he had proposed at the Halifax Convention in 1860, and a speaker named Corfield went as far the other way, proposing that all action should be postponed; but

Bradlaugh threw his weight behind Holyoake's plan and urged the formation of a society based on Holyoake's *Principles of Secularism*, and a provisional committee was at last approved, with Holyoake as chairman, John Watts as vice-chairman, and Joseph Jagger as secretary and missionary. The subscription was to be a shilling a quarter.[15]

The new society was doomed from the start. Barker would have no part in it; Maughan and his influential London followers were opposed to it. Most support came from Lancashire and Yorkshire, newly united under the Lancashire Secular Union and the Yorkshire Secular Association respectively, but the headquarters were fixed with Holyoake at 147 Fleet Street. The survival of the National Secular Association depended upon the one organ of national communication, the *National Reformer*, which was the basis of the policy of 'One Paper and One Party' inaugurated by the Bradlaugh–Holyoake reconciliation. All hopes were dashed when the two men quarrelled so bitterly in March 1862, and the National Secular Association faded for lack of funds during the course of the year. Secularist history now began to repeat itself, and 1863 was another year like 1859. The movement was struggling through another crisis, all semblance of national unity had been abandoned, and the builders had to begin again from the foundations.[16] Branches were divided amongst themselves; districts were divided from each other; local rivalries added to the conflict of personalities. John Maughan's group issued their own paper, the *Stepping Stone*, and the metropolis was deprived of that leadership which the General Secular Benevolent Society had offered since the decline of the London Secular Society. Geographical rivalry was expressed by John Child of Leeds who had originally supported the National Secular Association but who in 1863 wrote, 'The attempt was not successful, and, had it been so, it would have entailed disgrace on every provincialist joining it, and ultimately endangered his self-respect.' The fragmentation was complete. Sheffield, which had led the Bradlaugh revival of 1860, was split in three ways. Henry Turner, the hard-working secretary of the *National Reformer* Company and of the Sheffield Secular Society, supported Barker's views on birth-control and became a leading Barkerite, even going so far as to set up a separate society. Jeremiah Olive of Halifax and Thomas Ranford of Birmingham went the same way, and influential Barkerite groups seem to have flourished also in Huddersfield, Burnley and Ashton.[17] In County Durham, where the official Secularist leadership had scarcely penetrated, Barker made a considerable impact as he rallied supporters and even held revival meetings in a tent at West Auckland.[18]

Here Barker was clearly building not on his Secularist past but on the Methodist–Barkerite–Chartist legacy of his long and varied career.

T

Undoubtedly his popularity and success in setting up rival societies damaged the Secularist movement as a whole. Sheffield split again over the Bradlaugh–Holyoake quarrel, with the bulk of the society remaining faithful to Bradlaugh, while Leeds and Huddersfield, led by John Child and W. R. Croft, probably glad to seize the initiative back from Sheffield, were more decisively pro-Holyoake. Lancashire, on the contrary, seems to have favoured Bradlaugh.[19] At the local level, though, the division between Bradlaugh and Holyoake was never so serious as the division between Barker and the rest, and most societies were happy to receive visits from either of the two great leaders and to praise them indiscriminately. On top of these divisions one might further add those personal quarrels such as marked the regular course of freethought history. The antagonism of J. P. Adams to Holyoake which went back to the mid-1850s, continued and in 1865 it assumed the form of the long-felt rivalry between City Road Hall of Science Secularists and the John Street Institution Secularists for the leadership of London, the former being the Adams-Bradlaugh headquarters while the latter provided Holyoake with a regular London platform.[20]

The initiative in the early 1860s lay firmly with the provinces. 'As a rule,' wrote John Child, 'the oldest and best organised societies exist in Lancashire and Yorkshire. The largest number of Secularists live in these two counties.' But in 1862 Yorkshire was weakened in Bradlaugh's eyes by the adherence of the leaders of the Yorkshire Secular Association to Holyoake's views, while the Lancashire Secular Union was thoroughly tested by and pre-occupied with the Cotton Famine. Its greatest achievement, and source of subsequent strength, was that it survived the harrowing experience of mass unemployment, poverty and near starvation in 1862–3. During these years of Secularist weakness the men who appear to have nurtured the movement were Frank Field of Dewsbury, W. R. Croft of Huddersfield, Thomas Ellis of Manchester, Thomas Slater of Bury, and, above all, Thomas Saville Oates of Rochdale, the secretary and backbone of the Lancashire Secular Union.[21] The national leaders supplemented the work of these local men where they could, but the comparative independence of the north and the self-sufficiency of its organisations augured well for the future. The men of London could offer little. Holyoake was, for a time, in semi-retirement, still suffering from the effects of exhaustion and disappointment (or sulking like Achilles in his tent, depending on the point of view); Bradlaugh had to keep himself and his small family by working as a solicitor's clerk, company promoter, and financial odd-job man, but although he managed to spend much time in the lecture field, he could not be everywhere at once and his health was not good; Austin Holyoake emerged as a lecturer during these years, mainly in London, but after 1864 he was kept busy by 'Austin & Co.', his new printing and publishing business. John Watts took on the editorship of the *National Reformer* in 1863, which often kept him in London; his brother Charles only started public lecturing in 1864; and, though Harriet Law continued her provincial lecture tours, she was very much a free-lance at the service of the local societies rather than giving leadership. This lack of national direction was in one way fortunate: it relieved the local societies of the burden of any further personality clashes between the leaders. Bradlaugh was winning the movement over in a gradual and almost imperceptible way. Holyoakism was gone, and Bradlaughism had not yet been born. The provinces flourished. Bradlaugh was only slowly establishing himself through the columns of the *National Reformer* and by means of his matchless platform oratory. He conquered his rivals and won the provincial movement by sheer ability. Holyoake with his *Secular World*, which was started in May 1862 to continue the *Reasoner* series, although generously supported—especially in Yorkshire—could only appear as second best.[22]

The signs of Secularist revival again became apparent in 1864. As in 1860 and 1861 close co-operation was established across the Pennines and regional activity was again inspired elsewhere, especially in the north-east and in west Scotland.[23] The number of local societies grew steadily and the roots struck deep. Hopes for national organisation again revived. Holyoake re-emerged on the scene to defend his own particular brand of Secularism—becoming increasingly more moderate and disinclined to war with the churches—and he was widely and enthusiastically received. The Paisley society which, if the *National Reformer* alone were to be believed, had ceased to exist, re-appeared as healthy as ever and as pro-Holyoake as ever, and Glasgow appointed the latter as their permanent lecturer, a sign of the prestige he still had where Owenite memories were long.[24] But the *National Reformer* was now the chief organ of communication, and as John Watts's brief life ebbed away —he died of consumption, aged thirty-two, in October 1866—Bradlaugh's voice became dominant as he spoke with a lawyer's certainty in its columns. In June 1866 he appealed for statistical information concerning local Secularist societies and, though not much seems to have been forthcoming, he learned enough to proceed with plans for a new organisation. Suggestions and good advice were not wanting and the old formula was again repeated—a provisional committee, a national conference in Lancashire or Yorkshire, Holyoake and Bradlaugh as joint leaders. But Bradlaugh was not content this time to leave matters to be settled according to these vague proposals, and in the *National*

Reformer of 9 September he published a proposed programme for a national Secular society and the conditions of membership. He decided initially on a form of individual membership rather than affiliation through local societies: he did not want another umbrella organisation which no-one would look after, but, rather, a new society to which all Secularists could be personally pledged. Two weeks later the National Secular Society was formally announced with Charles Bradlaugh as president and Charles Watts as secretary. A general conference was promised for the following year, though it did not meet until December. By this time the names of members had slowly begun to trickle in, and after fifteen years of failure a durable national organisation for the Secularist movement had at last been established.[25]

The history of this society, which still exists, has never fully been told, and in the absence of further research, particularly into local history, only a few generalisations can be made. In one respect the Secularist movement was now Bradlaugh's movement—he was so authoritarian that some of the men who had criticised Holyoake in the 1850s now transferred their vituperations to Bradlaugh.[26] Through the National Secular Society and the *National Reformer* he was able to give to ultra-radicalism a well-organised and tightly-controlled organisation which in the early 1870s he used to the full to stir up the only real republican movement in Victorian Britain and the last serious manifestation of republican feeling which Britain has known. In the 1880s he again used his movement, this time for a new civil rights campaign to support his efforts to sit in Parliament. But the N.S.S. is not the whole of the story and, though societies as well as individuals were allowed to affiliate themselves to the N.S.S., not all local societies did so. Bradlaugh's strength lay mainly in London, and an independent Secularist movement survived in the provinces. Harriet Law never came under central control, Holyoake continued to enjoy pockets of support, and occasionally two secular societies—one local and one a branch of the N.S.S.—are to be found side by side in the same town.[27] When the birth control issue came to the fore again with the prosecution of the Knowlton Pamphlet in 1877, a rival British Secular Union was started by Holyoake, Watts and G. W. Foote. The Union did not last long, but in 1881 Foote started his own paper, the *Freethinker*, which has long survived the *National Reformer*, while Watts's son and Holyoake eventually helped create a fruitful middle-class freethought organisation in the Rationalist Press Association. In the late 1880s another revolt against Bradlaughism found its outlet in W. Stewart Ross and the *Secular Review*, and when Bradlaugh died in 1891 relations were very strained between Foote, who inherited the N.S.S., and Mrs Hypatia Bradlaugh Bonner, who inherited the *National Reformer* and the task of defending her father's reputation against all-comers—not least Holyoake, who survived until 1906.[28]

These late Victorian infidels must be the subject of a further study. They were more diverse than the Bradlaugh story alone would suggest, and they owed considerably more than they were often prepared to admit to those earlier Victorian infidels who had perpetuated and yet modified the tradition of Paine and Carlile and who had turned the remnants of Owenism, Chartism and Zeteticism into the beginnings of a permanent freethought movement.

Notes

1 Austin to G. J. Holyoake, 15 July 1859, H.C. 1113; T. Lond, *Secularism*, p. 6.

2 *Reasoner*, 24 July, 21 August, 3 July, 20 February, 27 March 1859; Holyoake, *The Public Purposes of the Fleet Street House* (1861), pp. 1–2; *Secular Institute Report, 1858–9* [1859], p. 4.

3 *Reasoner Gazette*, 24 June, 23 September 1860; *Reasoner*, 9 September 1860; *Counsellor*, December 1861.

4 Diary, 1861, note added in the front by Holyoake in 1896, H.B.

5 *Reasoner Gazette*, 1 April 1860; *Reasoner*, 19 May 1861; Austin to G. J. Holyoake, 3 November 1861, H.C. 1366; *Secular World*, August, September 1862.

6 *National Reformer*, 31 August 1861.

7 *Barker's Review*, 7 September 1861, 5 July 1862; *National Reformer*, 6 June 1863.

8 *Barker's Review*, 28 September 1861; *National Reformer*, 31 August 1861; F. H. Amphlett Micklewright, 'The Rise and Decline of English Neo-Malthusianism', *Population Studies*, xv (1961), pp. 35–6.

9 *Reasoner*, 7 May 1857; *Investigator*, August 1857; *Barker's Review*, 7, 14 September 1861; *National Reformer*, 24 August 1861; *Barker's Review*, 15 December 1861.

10 G. J. to Austin Holyoake, 3 November 1861, H.C. 1366; *National Reformer*, 31 August, 7 September 1861, 4 January 1862; *Secular World*, 10 May 1862; *Counsellor*, 6 December 1861. Holyoake's articles, signed 'Quasimodo', begin on 2 November 1861 with an attack on Barker.

11 G. J. Holyoake, *Mr Holyoake's Disconnection with the 'National Reformer'* . . . (London, 1863); J. Dodsworth, *An Account of the Proceedings at the Shareholders' Meeting* . . . [1862]; *National Reformer*, 5 April 1862.

12 Minutes of Evidence taken by the Arbitrators between Holyoake and Bradlaugh, 26 December 1862–25 April 1863, and miscellaneous correspondence 13 May 1862–9 December 1863, B.L. 92–140 *passim*, especially 100.

13 E.g. W. H. Johnson and J. H. Gordon—J. Robertson, *Secularists and their Slanderers* (London, 1858), p. 14; Leeds Secular Society, *The Converted Lecturer* . . . (Leeds, 1862).

14 *Reasoner Gazette*, 7, 21 October 1860; *National Reformer*, 13 October, 24 November 1860; *Secular World*, 1 April 1864.
15 *National Reformer*, 16 November, 7, 14, 21 December 1861, 4 January 1862.
16 Ibid., 15, 29 March 1862, 15 August 1863; *Secular World*, 1 October 1863.
17 *National Reformer*, 8 August 1863, 31 August 1861; *Barker's Review*, 9 November 1861, 1 February, 31 May 1862.
18 *Ibid.*, 7 December 1861, 1 February, 16, 30 August 1862.
19 *Secular World*, 17 May 1862; *National Reformer*, 24 May 1862.
20 *Propagandist*, 3, 31 May 1862; *Secular World*, 1 October 1863; *National Reformer*, 16 January 1864, 18 June 1865.
21 *Ibid.*, 8 August 1863, 6 December 1862. Oates had earlier been a leading member of the W.R.S.U.—*Reasoner*, 18 May 1856.
22 *National Reformer*, 31 January 1863, 16 January 1864; *Secular World*, 17 May 1862.
23 Non-Lancashire societies were invited to join the L.S.U. in 1865—*National Reformer*, 30 April 1865; see also *ibid.*, 2 July, 5 November 1864 (North East); *Reasoner*, 1 October 1865 (Scotland).
24 *National Reformer*, 3 December 1865.
25 *Ibid.*, 10 June, 19 August, 23 September 1866, 1 December 1867.
26 E.g. W. H. Johnson was behind the libellous *Life of Bradlaugh*, nominally written by C. R. Mackay in 1888—B.L. 1630, and D. Tribe, *Charles Bradlaugh*, pp. 265–7.
27 E.g. Newcastle in 1877, Manchester in 1878, Leeds in 1880, Bradford in 1884.
28 For a brief account of Secularism, see J. E. McGee, *A History of the British Secularist Movement* (Girard, Kansas, 1948).

Conclusion

Compared with the power and influence of the earlier Chartist and Owenite movements, Secularism under Holyoake seemed a small, narrowly based and uninfluential organisation—hardly a movement at all. 'SOCIALISM or OWENISM is dead; Secularism or Holyoakism is dying. This, the last phase of modern Infidelity, is likely to have but a brief existence,' thought a contributor to the *Manchester Review* in 1858. 'So far as my experience goes, infidelity, in the common acceptation of the term, is of very rare occurrence indeed,' reported Mr Harrop from the Hulme branch of the Manchester Ministry to the Poor in 1860.[1] This was true, and to some extent Secularism had failed: it had failed to become the broadly based philosophy which was to unite working class unbelief and respectable doubt; it had failed to attract the support of the thousands for whom the institutions of organised religion were meaningless; it had remained, instead, a small sect a few thousand strong. Holyoake's liberal and open approach had been rejected by Bradlaugh in favour of an exclusive atheism. Secularism, divorced from the political wing of the radical movement, had proved wanting in appeal to the leaders of the working class.

Yet the record is not one of total failure. As a hostile critic, T. Lond, wrote in 1859:

> There is no party—social, political, or moral—that, with a like paucity of numbers and machinery, has obtained the same amount of notoriety. It is a question whether the whole party could number one thousand registered members; and one recognised organ, a penny weekly, which had dragged out a lingering existence by persevering mendicity or regular weekly begging, is all that they can command. Yet, notwithstanding, there is scarcely a pulpit, metropolitan or provincial, in which discourses have not been delivered against its doctrines, and the attention of the public directed to its errors.[2]

Secularism had made this impact because, however insignificant as a movement, it had become very important as a pressure group. Holyoake saw that this was the real nature of all agitations. Some sought to bring pressure to bear by weight of numbers or by threats of violence, but the failure of Chartism had discredited these measures in his eyes. Like the

287

early Robert Owen, rather, he sought the realisation of his aims by the conversion of those in authority. Holyoake's achievement, and that of Secularism under his leadership, was that, by persuasion, by a controlled agitation, and by a demonstration of the sweet reasonableness of his position, he helped convince the influential and powerful in the land of the justice of secularisation. ' "The king reigns but does not govern"— public opinion governs in Great Britain . . .' was the axiom on which he built his life's work.[3]

There had been great changes in public opinion between 1841 and 1861. When Holyoake began the *Reasoner* 'There existed no relations with the outside press. Few books sent for review were ever noticed, and if they were noticed, they were howled at.' By 1861 Holyoake was on the way to becoming an established member of Fleet Street. The *Reasoner* was respected, even by its opponents. Reputable *Reviews* had written at length on Secularism. In 1864, when Holyoake listed 'The Changes in Religious Opinion in England since 1841', he included the improved tone of controversy; the discrediting of the blasphemy laws; the decline of rigid belief in original sin, eternal punishment, the Atonement and the infallibility of the Bible; and the greater courage with which public men spoke out on controversial matters of belief.[4]

This was certainly true, though Holyoake was always ready to give himself too much of the credit. Liberal clergymen and thinkers, such as Thomas Binney, James Martineau, F. W. Newman and W. R. Greg, had modified religious thought, and the Christian Socialists had most notice-ably compensated for the harshness of some Christian practice. Palmer-ston was not influenced by the Secularists when he told the Moderator of the Presbytery of Edinburgh that the best way to prevent the cholera was sanitation, not fasting, though his ideas happened, on this occasion, to be the same as theirs.[5] The clergy had long been aware of the problems of life in the slum areas of towns. The importance of Secularism in contemporary eyes is that it focused a topic of growing importance to many respectably and serious-minded Victorians. It rose on the crest of a mounting tide of public concern.

Yet orthodox opinion still held sway, and a great deal still needed to be changed in the 1860s. Britain was, and continued to be, a heavily religious country. Before 1848 unbelief had meant 'the demoralisation of the people', and this long remained so for many people. In 1853 F. D. Maurice was compelled to resign his Chair at King's College, London, and a less august person, J. Stephenson, who was employed in the locomotive workshop at Swindon, was dismissed in the same year for the same reason—namely, 'That he did not believe in any other hell than the gnawing of a man's conscience.' A riot outside the Philpot Street Hall in 1860 forced the East London Secular Society to close down.[6] Even when Holyoake was accepted, Bradlaugh was still mobbed and locked out of halls, and Holyoake himself at times still met with prejudice. One of his greatest tactical errors was to overestimate the extent to which public opinion had changed by the early 1860s. Ironically, he received a sharp reminder of this in 1864 when he proposed to deliver his lecture on 'Changes in Religious Opinion in England since his Imprisonment from Cheltenham in 1841' at the Corn Exchange, Cheltenham. Religious opinion had scarcely moderated in Cheltenham since those days, and the lord of the manor cut off the gas to the Corn Exchange and gave the lessee notice to quit. A large room in a local hotel had to be hired instead.[7]

Yet there were chinks of light to be seen. Legislative improvement had begun: the press had been freed from burdensome taxation, Jews had been admitted to Parliament, the Affirmations Bill had come near to success, and the seeds of reform had been sown in the mind of Government. Political, educational, administrative and 'Secular' reforms were to follow within the next decade, Mr Gladstone being given most of the credit and earning for himself Holyoake's lifelong adulation. Official opinion was undoubtedly changing. When the Rye magistrates wrote to the Home Office in 1850, sending a book by H. C. Clark entitled *Consistency versus Inconsistency*, which was an average sort of freethought work, an official at the Home Office noted, 'I should think it impolitic to call attention to this by a Prosecution'.[8] The campaigns of Carlile and Hetherington and the Anti-Persecution Union had made their impact. Public opinion in the country was also changing, though more slowly and erratically. The 'odium theologicum' was losing its power. James Stansfeld was returned for Parliament for Halifax in 1859, despite being called 'an infidel, an atheist, and one who did not believe in the Bible'.[9] In 1867 Jacob Bright wrote to Holyoake,

> They tried to damage me in Manchester by associating your name with mine—They forget that though your name is feared by some it is respected by more. Their absurd attack I think did me more good than harm.[10]

It is hard to imagine this being said in 1840.

Holyoake naturally had many weaknesses and, as architect of the Secularist movement, he imparted a great many of them to his organisation and its ideology. He was not a deep or logical thinker, and his theories at times seemed confused and were open to criticism from both inside and outside the movement. Sophia Dobson Collet accurately observed that Holyoake was a practical rather than a speculative thinker. He therefore pursued the end and forgot the philosophy on which his

ideas were supposed to be based. Secularism was essentially a practical
philosophy. It was, therefore, right in Holyoake's eyes for him to
co-operate with Christians, simply because it was possible. He never
inquired whether belief could legitimately be separated from practice,
and, as his daughter remarked many years later, 'he did not quite realise
that it was their religion which turned Kingsley and other Christian
Socialists to the work of raising the condition of the workers, and they
adopted the co-operative method to do it'.[11] Robert Cooper thought the
same way as the Christian Socialists had on this issue: both agreed that
neutrality was logically impossible where belief was the mainspring of
action. Holyoake does not seem to have worked out whether Secularism
as a party, one object of which was to attack all harmful superstition,
was compatible with Secularism as a bond of unity in which men of
all or no beliefs could work together. He also does not seem to have
realised the consequences for his rationalist philosophy of his adopting
the subjective and emotional morality of conscience. As J. A. Langford,
a Christian radical and old school-friend of Holyoake's, pointed out in
a pamphlet in 1854:

> [Man] is as much endowed by Nature with a religious sense as he is
> with a geometric one; and the one requires as much cultivation as the
> other . . . Religion is as much a want as is hunger: the religious faculty
> as natural as the desire for love, friendship and esteem. It provides for
> and answers these faculties and these desires. Secularism denies, or, at
> least, silently ignores them.[12]

Despite the influence of F. W. Newman, W. R. Greg and other theists,
Holyoake continued to make the rationalist's mistake of underestimating
the power of feeling. Even fellow Secularists recognised this deficiency:
J. B. Bebbington, in a hostile though shrewdly perceptive article on
Holyoake's character, wrote in 1862:

> Mr Holyoake wants the deep, earnest, sympathetic nature. The head is
> there, but the heart is wanting. There is the directing controling [sic]
> power; but there is nothing to direct or control. A boast has been made
> that he is "impassive". Here is the key to his whole character. Impassive
> as marble he certainly is; it would be difficult to find a man with less of
> feeling in his nature. A plaster bust would be as easily excited to passion
> as Mr Holyoake. While listening to him you are painfully conscious of
> the utter absence of that earnestness which can only arise from deep
> feeling. The idea of God seems to him illogical; he, therefore, in the
> coldest and most methodical manner flings a syllogism at it.[13]

Holyoake had been a teacher of mathematics, and he made the mistake
of relying on rational, logical thought in all spheres of life. He really
believed that, given freedom of thought, the rational and the good would

inevitably triumph, and he was by no means alone in this self-delusion. More than this, Holyoake was also deficient as a pure reasoner—though, considering his lack of elementary education, his accomplishments were considerable. His faults were those of the autodidact, and Francis Place once complained that Holyoake suffered from Lord Brougham's trouble of mistaking knowledge for wisdom.[14] For one so determined to be a freethinker, he was sadly uncritical of 'respectable' liberal opinions, and woefully uncritical of his own opinions. When criticised by his equals in the freethought movement, his instinctive reaction was a self-protective counter-attack, not a searching re-examination of himself.

Nevertheless, Holyoake achieved much. Freethought when led by Paine, Carlile, and even by Owen, was feared by the respectable classes who made no attempt to understand it. Under Holyoake's leadership it was presented in such a way as to win serious consideration. 'The chief merit of the editor [of the *Reasoner*] is, perhaps, the improved moral tone which he has introduced into the literature of unbelief', wrote the Manchester Domestic Missionary in 1851. Holyoake contributed considerably to that development, noted by Mary Maison in her study of the Victorian novel, whereby the wicked sceptic of the 1840s became the honest doubter of the 1880s. The tone of his correspondence and of the public reaction to him in the 1850s is epitomised in a letter from a clergyman writing in 1854: 'You have—even amidst your cool, daring, dreadful blasphemies—at times evinced thought and feeling—and always apparently a curtesy [sic]—which have affected my heart.'[15]

Holyoake was a pioneer, and Secularism was a pioneering movement. Before the publication of those books which shook the intellectual world from the end of the 1850s—Mill's essay *On Liberty,* Buckle's *History of Civilisation,* Darwin's *Origin of Species,* the *Essays and Reviews,* and Colenso's *Pentateuch*—Holyoake was arguing and acting out the opinions and attitudes expressed in those works. 'You can now claim as allies a host of mighty names,' wrote Alexander Bain of Aberdeen in 1876.[16] The time was when Holyoake had been almost alone in making his controversial and unfashionable views public. He spoke the worst fears of many men, and yet won their respect for it.

Furthermore, he not only brought the religious views of some of the lower orders to the sympathetic notice of the educated and respectable classes, he also exercised some influence in the opposite direction. Holyoake's eclecticism might sometimes be denigrated as the mere repetition of other men's ideas or as the deliberate adoption of respectable opinions for selfish ends, but this is to miss the importance of the man. He served the function of a clearing house: he tried to heal the divisions—religious and political—between men of enlightenment and goodwill from all classes. One is staggered more by the impertinence of the effort than by its comparative failure; and there were some successes. To the freethought canon of Paine and Carlile, of Volney and Voltaire, he added Comte and F. W. Newman; works by Mill, Buckle, Spencer and Darwin were introduced to the bibliographies of the old tradition. The horizons of popular freethought were widened.[17]

The exact role of Holyoake and Secularism in the changing society of the 1850s is not easy to determine, but in one particular respect some positive comments can be offered. Secularism as a movement was basically an agitation for a scheme of rights: the right to think for oneself; the right to differ; the right to assert difference of opinion; the right to debate all vital opinion.[18] The progress of the campaign to achieve these rights in mid-Victorian England owed something to the early Secularists. Holyoake was not, as he claimed, the last man to be tried by jury for Atheism in England, but he probably was the last man to be prosecuted for honestly and moderately expressing blasphemous views in England. Looking back on the events of 1842 and Holyoake's subsequent agitations, men could see this as a turning point. By his conduct he had changed hostility to sympathy.[19] The release of Thomas Pooley in 1857, which was largely the result of Holyoake's work, further discredited the courts, though it did not abolish the law. The Holyoake brothers were also the last men to be summonsed under the Stamp Acts in 1855, and G. J. Holyoake's resolute opposition to the oath greatly aided the cause of secular affirmation. Much still remained to be done in 1866, and a great deal of the work was to be continued and shared by Bradlaugh, culminating in his famous struggle to enter Parliament, but this would not have been possible had Bradlaugh not been able to build on the movement he inherited from Holyoake.

In 1861, in the last number of the *Reasoner,* Holyoake wrote:

> Mr John Stuart Mill has shown that society owes everything to the unresting spirits who ceaselessly struggle for the dominion of right. Mr Buckle has shown that all new truth owes it prevalence to the thankless labours of obscure minorities—who count it better to perish in some forlorn hope of intrepid progress, than rot in cynical apathy or selfish ease. To have been the co-worker of such persons, renders life a privilege.[20]

With unusual modesty, he had summed up his own position and that of the Secularist movement. The best commentary on the aims of Secularism is still J. S. Mill's essay *On Liberty,* and the development in Britain of the liberal society advocated in that work is partly attributable to the efforts begun by George Jacob Holyoake in the 1850s, when he first organised the Victorian infidels and gave them a positive programme of reform in the Secularist movement.

Notes

1 *Manchester Review*, 17 April 1858; 'Station at Tomlinson Street, Hulme, Mr Harrop's Report', given at the twenty-sixth Annual Meeting of the Ministry to the Poor—*Report* . . . (Manchester, 1860), p. 25.
2 T. Lond, *Secularism*, pp. 6–7.
3 Holyoake, *Organisation* . . . (London, 1853), p. 24.
4 *Reasoner*, 1 January 1860; 'Opinions of authors and of the Press during the publication of the *Reasoner*', H.C. 4347; *Westminster Review* n.s. XXI (1862), pp. 60–97; Holyoake, *The Suppressed Lecture at Cheltenham* (London, 1864), pp. 5–7.
5 *Reasoner*, 30 November 1853.
6 T. Christensen, *Christian Socialism*, pp. 338–9; *Reasoner*, 7 December 1853, 12, 26 June 1859.
7 H. B. Bonner, *Charles Bradlaugh*, I, pp. 194–202; *National Reformer*, 17 December 1864.
8 H.O. 45 O.S.3017 (1850).
9 B. Wilson, *Struggles of an Old Chartist* (Halifax, 1887), p. 30.
10 Jacob Bright to Holyoake, 5 December 1867, H.C. 1751.
11 *Reasoner*, 22 September 1852; Mrs Holyoake-Marsh to W. H. Brown, 22 July 1923, quoted in W. H. Brown, *Charles Kingsley* (Manchester, 1924), p. 69.
12 J. A. Langford, *Christianity not Secularism* . . . (London and Birmingham, 1854), pp. 8–9.
13 *Propagandist*, 3 May 1862.
14 F. Place to Holyoake, 3 March 1849, H.C. 303.
15 John Layhe, *Seventeenth Report of the Ministry to the Poor* (Manchester, 1851), p. 46; M. Maison, *Search Your Soul, Eustace* (London, 1961), pp. 212, 223; Rev T. Phillips to Holyoake, 18 July 1854, H.C. 680.
16 A. Bain to Holyoake, 5 January 1876, H.C. 2344.
17 See F. W. Newman to Evans Bell, 22 March 1875, H.C. 2298.
18 *Reasoner*, 2 April 1854.
19 E.g. Rev. J. S. Jones to Holyoake, 16 July 1894, H.C. 3474.
20 *Reasoner*, 30 June 1861.

Appendix I

Distribution of provincial Secularism, 1837–66

The following lists of areas of freethought activity and the accompanying graph are based principally on notices of meetings in the various periodicals of the freethought movement, together with reports of meetings and lecture tours and other incidental references. The pattern of development is therefore distorted by the quality of the periodicals and of the reporting in any one year. Between 1837 and 1845 the figures for Owenite societies are reasonably reliable, as reports of the proceedings of the Annual Congresses, given in the *New Moral World* and elsewhere, have details of all active branches. In the late 1850s and early 1860s the picture is also a full one, as the *Reasoner* in these years and the *National Reformer* made their weekly 'Guide to the Lecture Room' as complete as possible. The lack of reported societies in the intervening years is in part a weakness of the source material, but this in itself suggests an overall organisational weakness between the failure of the Rational Society and the development of Secularism. Societies which had less than three years of continuous existence have been omitted from the list of organisations, but are included in the numbers indicated on the graph.

Some localities had activity but no apparent organisation—places without societies but which sent representatives to district and national conferences or shared in district organisations (especially in 1852, 1856 and 1861), and localities which sent contributions to the various appeals (especially to the Theological Utilitarians in 1847 and to Holyoake's Special Institute Fund in 1858). The upper line on the graph includes these places, while the lower one shows organisations only. In the Owenite period, 1837–45, and in Secularism after 1859, the closeness of the two lines plotted on the graph suggests a high degree of formal organisation, while the wide discrepancy between the number of positive societies and the total number of localities with activity in the years 1846–58 indicates the rudimentary nature of the organisation of freethought in these years. Three further conclusions can be drawn from the figures: first, the post-Owenite freethinkers in the provinces extended neither their organisation, nor even their influence, as far as the Owenites did around 1840; secondly, the steady growth of the 1850s represented not a breaking of new ground but an establishment of societies in previous areas of influence; and thirdly, the foundations of the National Secular Society in the provinces rested on the narrow basis of a few strong societies, particularly in Lancashire and Yorkshire, and not on a strong national movement.

Major provincial freethought organisations, 1837–66

Locality	Owenite Branch or class (if any)	Floruit (more than two successive years)
East Anglia		
Norwich	Branch 51	1837–44, 1860–66
Yarmouth	Branch 38	1838–43, 1860–62
Ipswich	Class 5	1841–44, 1846–50
South-east		
Chatham	Branch 46	1837–42
Maidstone	Class 2	1841–44
Canterbury		1839–41
Dover	Class 1	1840–44
Brighton	Branch 45	1838–45, 1855–59
South and south-west		
Reading	Branch 54	1839–42
Trowbridge	Class 4	1841–43
Bath	Branch 21	1838–41
Bristol	Branch 5	1837–50, 1855–59
Plymouth and Devonport		1855–61
West and west Midlands		
Cheltenham	Branch 44 and Class 8	1838–44
Worcester	Branch 13	1837–44
Leamington	Class 7	1841–43
Coventry	Branch 18	1838–62
Stourbridge	Branch 55	1839–45
Birmingham	Branch 4	1837–44, 1854–66
Dudley		1852–61
Bilston	Branch 35	1838–43
Longton and Shelton		1856–58
Burslem		1838–40
Tunstall	Branch 56	1839–41, 1847–49
East Midlands		
Northampton	Branch 58	1838–49, 1854–62, 1864–66
Leicester	Branch 26	1838–48
Derby	Class 10	1856–59
Nottingham	Branch 65	1840–43, 1851–54, 1858–65
Mansfield	Branch 57	1839–41

Yorkshire

Sheffield	Branch 31	1838–66
Doncaster	Branch 36	1839–43, 1850–53
Huddersfield	Branch 6	1837–43, 1847–66
Honley	Class 19	1842–61
Holmfirth		1856–62
Slaithwaite		1854–56
Halifax	Branch 8	1837–42, 1854–64
Dewsbury		1855–66
Bradford	Branch 11	1837–46, 1851–66
Keighley		1852–55
Leeds	Branch 20	1837–47, 1850–66
Hull	Branch 39	1838–44, 1846–48

Lancashire and the north-west

Manchester and Salford	Branches 1 and 34	1837–66
Middleton	Branch 42	1837–42
Ashton under Lyne	Branch 29	1837–50, 1852–66
Stalybridge	Branch 29	1837–42, 1852–60
Hyde	Branch 23	1837–51, 1854–61
Stockport	Branch 3	1837–43, 1851–55
Mottram	Branch 22	1838–42
Tintwistle		1855–59
Macclesfield	Branch 17	1838 44
Congleton	Branch 60 and Class 12	1839–43
Warrington	Branch 30 and Class 14	1838–43
Liverpool	Branch 12	1838–50, 1854–66
Wigan	Branch 40	1838–44
Leigh	Branch 14	1837–42
Bolton	Branch 2	1837–47, 1852–62
Radcliffe Bridge	Branch 49	1838–41
Chowbent	Branch 33	1838–42
Failsworth	Branch 28	1839–45
Oldham	Branch 19	1837–45, 1851–66
Rochdale	Branch 24	1837–47, 1849–66
Todmorden		1850–58, 1860–62
Burnley	Class 9	1840–55
Padiham	Branch 27 and Class 18	1840–42
Pendleton		1857–59
Accrington		1857–59
Blackburn	Branch 10	1837–44, 1852–54, 1856–58
Preston	Branch 41	1837–42, 1851–54, 1857–61
Lancaster		1859–61

North-east

Darlington	Branch 50	1838–42
Cockfield		1856–59

Sunderland and Bishop's
  Wearmouth   Branch 47   1838–42, 1853–58
Newcastle upon Tyne   Branch 43   1838–44, 1852–66

Scotland

Aberdeen   1840–43, 1846–48
Stonehaven   1846–48
Arbroath   1840–43
Dundee   Branch 52   1838–47; 1860–63
Kirkcaldy   Class 16   1843–45
Edinburgh   Branch 61   1840–48, 1855–66
Glasgow   Branch 7   1837–66
Paisley   Branch 9   1837–66

Wales

Abergavenny   1864–66

Ireland

Dublin   Class 15   1842–44

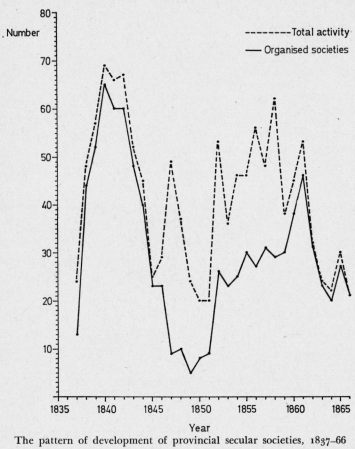

The pattern of development of provincial secular societies, 1837–66

Appendix II

Distribution of London freethought, 1837–66

The sources for the list and the graph derived from it are the same as for provincial freethought, though interpretation of the material is more difficult because of the complicated nature of the London organisations. Societies were easily formed and disbanded, lecture halls could be hired for occasional meetings without any presumption of formal organisation, and such societies as there were changed their locations and even their names several times in as many years. The list of organisations and activity cannot therefore be regarded as a complete record. The first column shows the general distribution of freethought activity, indicating those areas of London which usually had one or more freethought meetings near at hand: the City and the East End predominate. The second column shows the major organisations only, and the names given to them are those usually used in the late 1850s or early 1860s. Two non-Secularist societies have been included: the South Place Chapel, Finsbury (W. J. Fox), and the Free Church, Newman Street, Oxford Street (P. W. Perfitt). The information from both columns has been plotted on the graph, which indicates a steady growth in London freethought throughout the period.

The high number of localities involved in the late 1840s suggests the unsettled nature of radicalism in London at this time, with freethinkers attending and reporting ephemeral groups which were later not thought of as being especially Secularist in nature. As in the provinces, the later consolidation of organisation is indicated by the closeness of the two lines on the graph. The general pattern of development is similar to that in the provinces, but there are two clear differences: first, freethought was always stronger in London than Owenism had ever been; and secondly, freethought did not collapse in London as it did in the provinces in the late 1840s.

A comparison between appendix I and appendix II suggests two further points: the comparative importance of London in the freethought movement was at its least in the Owenite period and in the late 1850s and early 1860s; but London was overwhelmingly important in the late 1840s when Holyoake was propagating Theological Utilitarianism, and there are signs of a move back to London in the mid-1860s, when Bradlaugh started the National Secular Society.

London freethought organisations and areas of activity, 1837–66

Freethought localities	Freethought organisations	Owenite branch (if any)	Floruit (more than two successive years)
South			
Gravesend			
Woolwich	Woolwich and Plumstead Secular Society		1854–56, 1860–66
Greenwich	Greenwich and Deptford Secular Society	48	1838–44, 1862–66
Walworth The Borough Blackfriars Road Lambeth	South London Secular Society	53	1839–66
West-north-east			
Harlington, Mddx.		59	1839–42
Kensington		37	1838–41
Paddington Marylebone	Society of Materialists West London Secular Society Society of Free Inquirers		1847–51, 1854–57, 1859–63
Chelsea			1848–51
Leicester Square			
Westminster			
Oxford Street	Free Church		1861–66
Soho			1849–53, 1864–66
John Street Cleveland Street	Metropolitan Institute Society of Materialists	32 and A1	1837–66
Euston	Society of Free Inquirers		1846–50, 1855–57
Tavistock Place			1854–56
Somers Town King's Cross	North London Secular Society		1856–58
Islington			
Kentish Town			
Edgware Road			
High Holborn			1844–53
Leather Lane, Holborn	General Secular Benevolent Society; General Secular Reformers' Society		1860–66
Fleet Street	Temple Secular Society, 147 Fleet Street		1857–60
Shoe Lane			
Snow Hill	Farringdon Hall		
Aldersgate Street			
Clerkenwell	Clerkenwell		1852–59
Sadler's Wells			

City Road	Hall of Science ⎱ London Secular Society ⎰		1838–40, 1844–66
Finsbury	South Place Chapel		1837–66
	Finsbury Institution, Goswell Road	16	1838–47
	Bunhill Row		1846–50
Barbican	City Forum, Red Cross Street		1850–54, 1858–61
	East City Discussion Hall, Beech Street		
Liverpool Street			
Doctor's Commons			1855–58
Gould Square			
Leadenhall Street			
Shoreditch	Freethought Propagandists		1861–66
Philpot Street	East London Secular Society		1851–60
Hoxton	North East London Secular Society		1855–57
Hackney	Hackney		1850–54
Bethnal Green	Bethnal Green	62	1850–53
Whitechapel	Whitechapel Institution ⎱	63	1847–52
Tower Hamlets	Tower Hamlets ⎰		1840–45
Limehouse			
Poplar			

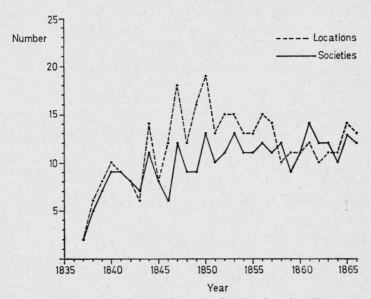

Temporal distribution of London freethought, 1837–66

Appendix III

Circulation of the Reasoner, *1846–61*

The income from sales of the *Reasoner*, volumes I–XX, is given by Holyoake
in his *History of the Fleet Street House*. Details of income from volumes
XXI, XXII and XXVI do not seem to be available. Those for volume XXIII are
given in the cash book of the Fleet Street house under 1858, and for volumes
XXIV and XXV in the *Reasoner* itself.[1] In 1852, when the *Reasoner* was 1*d*,
Holyoake stated that the trade price was 7½*d* per dozen of thirteen.[2] Circulation figures have been calculated from income on the assumption that this
rate was maintained throughout the period. The figures so derived corres-
pond with those occasionally mentioned elsewhere in the *Reasoner*. For
example, the sales of the *Reasoner* from July to September 1852 are said
to have been 3,029 copies per week: the graph shows the figure to have been
around the 3,000 mark.[3]

The main points indicated by the graph are as follows:

A The turn in the fortunes of the *Reasoner* began in 1850, at the same time
as the upturn in London freethought, but just before the provincial
recovery.

B The exceptional peak of circulation was reached between the two debates
with Brewin Grant, January 1853–November 1854.

C The generally high level of circulation began to fall off in 1856 at a time
when criticism of Holyoake's leadership was becoming vocal.

D Even after that date, though, the *Reasoner* still maintained a body of
support higher than that enjoyed in the late 1840s.

Notes

1 Holyoake, *Fleet Street House*, p. 9; *Reasoner*, 24 March 1861; Cash Book of
the Fleet Street House, H.B.

2 *Reasoner*, 23 June 1852.

3 *Ibid.*, 29 September 1852.

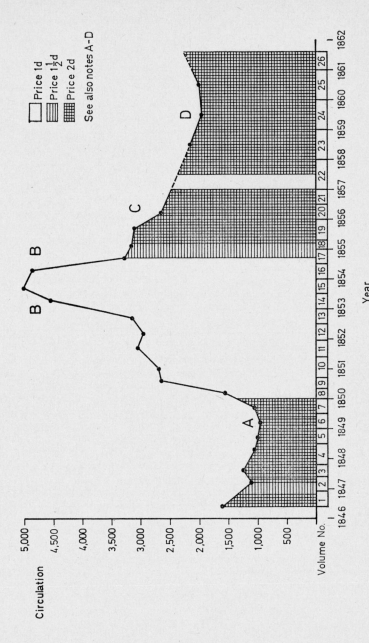

Reasoner circulation, 1846–61

Appendix IV

Occupational structure of Secularist membership

Notes

1 661 names have been drawn at random from all the periodicals of freethought between 1837 and 1866, particularly from the 'Special Institute Fund Subscription' list, printed in the *Reasoner*, 29 August 1858. The information regarding occupations is taken principally from trade directories, usually *White's* or *Slater's* (see bibliography).

2 For 241 of these people occupations can clearly be identified. Where a man appears to have two occupations, both are included in the figures.

3 A further fifty-eight people have names in common with other entries in the directories, but the inclusion of such ambiguous cases makes little difference to the final percentages.

4 Another sixty-six names occur so often in the directories as to yield no reliable information at all, and these have been omitted.

5 The remaining 296 names are not to be found in the directories. Some of these might be traced in the census returns, but this would be difficult, as addresses are rarely given in the periodicals for the sort of person whose name does not occur in the directories. One of the directories used for Manchester, however (*Slater's*, 1851), is much fuller than usual and helps to break down the unknown figure. It suggests that, whereas a number of people may have been omitted from the directories for a variety of reasons such as the timing of their periods of residence, a considerable proportion has been left out because the occupations were too lowly to warrant an entry. This is to some extent borne out by the shortage of directory entries obtainable for some of the textile towns, such as Accrington and Macclesfield, where most of the names are taken from the 1858 subscription list, which represents the rank-and-file membership in those towns. In the following table I have therefore assumed that at least half the unknown names are those of semi-skilled or unskilled workers, and the figures have been adjusted accordingly. The Secularist movement appears in the table to have appealed to a wide range of social groups, but was basically a working-class movement with a strong leaven of lower middle-class leadership.

6 London membership has been excluded from this appendix because of the special difficulties involved. The lack of geographical precision in the metropolitan area means that the likelihood of finding names in the directories is very much reduced. The thorough search required would simply produce a large number of ambiguous identities. Some occupations are given in the periodicals, and these suggest that the London leadership, at least, came from very much the same social group as in the rest of the country.

Higher classes   %

Manufacturers (those who appear likely to have been employers of labour) 4
Others (professional men etc).   3

Lower middle classes

Booksellers (including stationers and newsagents)   10
Innkeepers (including keepers of beer houses and retailers of beer)   4
Temperance hotel, coffee rooms, etc, keepers   2
Shopkeepers, general retailers and employees of co-operative stores   13

Upper working classes

Craftsmen (including those who may have kept their own shops;
    tailors, plumbers, joiners, hairdressers, blacksmiths, etc.)   13
Cobblers and shoemakers   5
Others (miscellaneous trades of a lower middle or upper working-class
    status)   8

Other working classes

Semi-skilled (including weavers and factory workers)   2
Unskilled   2
Presumed working-class (half the unknown occupations)   34

Appendix V

1 *Biographical summaries*

The following list includes most of the important people involved in the freethought movement in the period covered by this book. Fuller details can be found in the secondary sources consulted. The most important of these are J. M. Wheeler, *A Biographical Dictionary of Freethinkers of all Ages and Nations* (London, 1889); J. McCabe, *A Biographical Dictionary of Modern Rationalists* (London, 1920); F. Boase, *Modern English Biography containing many thousand concise memoirs of persons who have died during the years 1851–1900* (three volumes and three volumes of supplements, Truro, 1890–1921); J. M. Bellamy and J. Saville (eds.), *Dictionary of Labour Biography*, vol. 1 (London, 1972); and the *Dictionary of National Biography*. There are also a number of useful Co-operative biographies in A. Bonner *British Co-operation* (Manchester, 1961), pp. 481–504. Other major sources are indicated briefly in parentheses after each entry; full details of titles are given in the bibliography.

Adams, George: cabinet-maker and radical bookseller in Cheltenham; imprisoned at the same time as Holyoake, 1842; emigrated to America, 1851; his wife Harriet, was also a freethinker.

Adams, J. P.: introduced to politics by the Anti-Corn Law League agitation; became a Unitarian under the influence of W. J. Fox; became an atheist after hearing Emma Martin and Charles Southwell; leading London freethinker at the City Road Hall of Science; founded the Society of Materialists in opposition to Holyoake, 1857; assisted W. H. Johnson with the *Investigator*, 1857–58; supporter of Charles Bradlaugh.

Adams, William Edwin: b. Cheltenham, 1832; apprenticed to a printer; supported Chartism in the 1840s, then the foreign republican cause; assisted Linton with the *English Republic* at Brantwood, 1854–55; came to London and wrote *Tyrannicide: is it Justifiable*, 1858; worked as a reader and compositor in Manchester; contributed political articles to the *National Reformer* over the name 'Caractacus'; went to Newcastle upon Tyne to work on Joseph Cowen's *Newcastle Chronicle*, c. 1863; became editor, 1864–1900; d. May 1906. (W. E. Adams, *Memoirs of a Social Atom*.)

Annet, Peter: b. Liverpool, 1693; dissenting minister, then schoolmaster; lectured on deism in London and wrote against the resurrection; edited the *Free Inquirer*, the first freethought periodical, 1761; sentenced to a year's hard labour and a pillorying, 1762; d. 1769. (E. Twynam, *Peter Annet*).

Ashurst, William H.: b. London, 1792; solicitor; patron of Robert Owen and his followers; supported Italy and other radical causes; helped Holyoake formulate his version of Secularism; used the pseudonym 'Edward Search' in his writings for Secularism: d. 1855. (*Reasoner,* 11 November 1855.)

Ashurst, William H.: son of the above; b. 1819; solicitor, friend of Garibaldi and Mazzini; d. 1879.

Barker, Joseph: b. Bramley, near Leeds, 1806; Methodist New Connexion preacher; opponent of socialism; expelled and formed his own 'Barkerite' sect, 1841; became a Unitarian, 1845; a leading West Riding Chartist; his *People* sold 20,000 weekly copies in 1848; elected to Leeds town council, 1848; emigrated to America, 1851; became a freethinker, 1853; returned to England, 1854, for a brief visit, and again in 1860; edited the *National Reformer* with Charles Bradlaugh, 1860–61; broke with Bradlaugh over birth-control propaganda; edited *Barker's Review,* 1861–63; became a Primitive Methodist, 1863; returned to America, 1868; d. 1875. (J. T. Barker (ed.). *The Life of Joseph Barker; Reasoner,* 23 January 1859.)

Barmby, John Goodwyn: b. 1820; founded the Communist Propaganda Society, 1841; edited the *Promethean,* 1842; a religious socialist, but became a Unitarian minister; d. 1881.

Bebbington, J. B.: a journeyman potter; became a freethinker; worked for Holyoake at 147 Fleet Street in charge of the Provincial Newsagency, 1857; attacked Holyoake in the *Propagandist,* 1862, which he edited; became a Christian, 1863.

Bell, Thomas Evans: b. London, 1825; spent most of his life in the Indian army; deputy commissioner of police, Madras, 1861–3; supported Holyoake and chaired early Secularist meetings, 1852; wrote for *Reasoner* as 'Undecimus'; d. 1887. (Evans Bell, *The God of the Bible* [a reissue of *The Task for To-day* (1851)] (1943), publisher's preface.)

Birch, William John: b. 1811; educ. Balliol and New Inn Hall, Oxford; one of the leading contributors to freethought funds; supporter of Italy, where he spent much of his later life.

Bradlaugh, Charles: b. Hoxton, 1833; became a freethinker after hearing speakers in Victoria Park; left home and lived with the Sharples-Carlile family at the Warner Street Temperance Hall, 1850; joined army, 1850–53; employed as a solicitor's clerk, 1854–63, and involved in company promotions; lectured and wrote under the name 'Iconoclast', 1854–68; president of the London Secular Society, 1858; founder-president of the National Secular Society, 1866; edited the *Investigator,* 1858–59, and the *National Reformer,* 1860–63, 1866–91; owned the *National Reformer,* 1862–91; stood for Parliament (Northampton), 1868, 1874; elected, 1880, but could not take his seat until 1886 because of the oath controversy; d. 1891. (H. Bradlaugh Bonner, *Charles Bradlaugh;* D. Tribe, *President Charles Bradlaugh.*)

Campbell, Alexander: b. Kintyre, 1796; manager of the Orbiston Community under Abram Combe, 1826–28, and imprisoned for the community's debts; founder of the first Glasgow Co-operative store, 1830; lectured on Co-operation and advocated the 'divi' principle; secretary of the Glasgow Carpenters' Union, 1834; imprisoned for publishing an unstamped newspaper, 1834; secretary of the Committee of Trades Delegates which assisted the leaders of the cotton spinners' strike, 1837; became social missionary, 1838; lived at the Ham Common Concordium, 1842; edited the *Spirit of the Age* 1848, and was member of the League of Social Progress, 1849; returned to Glasgow, 1856, and wrote for the *Glasgow Sentinel* on trade union matters; edited the paper, *c.* 1863; member of Glasgow Co-operative Association, and of the Glasgow Trades Council, 1858; collaborated with Alexander Macdonald of the Miners' union in an agitation against the Master and Servant law, 1864–67; d. 1870. (W. H. Marwick, *The Life of Alexander Campbell.*)

Carlile, Eliza Sharples: second wife of Richard Carlile; came from Lancashire to help Carlile and Taylor during their imprisonment, 1831; lectured at the Rotunda and elsewhere; edited the *Isis* and used this as a pseudonym; entered the Ham Common Concordium after Carlile's death, 1843, and later kept the Warner Street Temperance Hall, 1850, where she gave hospitality to Charles Bradlaugh; d. 1861.

Carlile, Richard: b. Ashburton, 1790; settled in London, 1813; started selling radical pamphlets, 1817; published the *Republican*, 1819–26, and the works of Paine; imprisoned 1817, 1819–25, 1832–33, 1834; advocated materialistic atheism after *c.* 1821, but was converted to an allegorical interpretation of Christianity *c.* 1834; took out a licence to preach, and attacked both Owenites and Chartists; d. 1843. (G. D. H. Cole, *Richard Carlile.*)

Cattell, Charles C.: b. 1830; leader of Secularism, Republicanism and the Co-operative movement in Birmingham; founded the Birmingham Eclectic Institute, 1852; founder of the Birmingham Republican Club and organiser of the Republican conference held in Birmingham, 1873; d. 1910.

Chilton, William: b. Bristol, 1815; started as a bricklayer, but became a compositor and then a reader on the *Bristol Mercury*; a founder and sub-editor of the *Oracle of Reason*; a regular contributor to freethought journals on biology, geology, etc; author of the 'theory of regular gradation'; d. 1855. (*Reasoner* 10 June 1855.)

Collet, Collet Dobson: b. 1812; son of John Dobson, a merchant in Old Jewry; educ. University College, London; training for the bar interrupted by lack of money; became a teacher of music; director of music at South Place Chapel; member of the National Political Union, 1831, the National Association, 1842, and the People's Charter Union, 1848; became secretary of the latter, and of the Newspaper Stamp Abolition Committee, 1849; secretary of the Association for the Repeal of the Taxes on Knowledge, 1851–70; his early official correspondence is signed John Dobson Collet or J. C. Dobson Collet; d. 1898. (M. D. Conway, *Autobiography*, p. 39; *Reasoner*, 5 August 1855.)

Collet, Sophia Dobson: sister of the above; b. 1822; member of the South Place Chapel, for which she composed several hymns; supporter and friendly critic of Holyoake; wrote for the *Reasoner* as 'Panthea'; her later writings were concerned with India; d. 1894. (M. D. Conway, loc. cit.)

Cooper, James R.: Manchester radical publisher and bookseller; member of the Manchester Secular Society, and occasional lecturer on Owenism and Secularism; elder brother of Robert Cooper.

Cooper, Robert: b. 1819; son of a Manchester radical; brought up an Owenite; prominent lecturer on Owenism and Secularism from the age of sixteen; lived in London, 1847–58; closely associated with Robert Owen until the latter's death in 1858; founded and edited the *London Investigator,* 1854–57; suffered from bronchitis and retired to Manchester, 1858; active member of the Union and Emancipation Society during the American Civil War; formed the Manchester Working Man's Parliamentary Reform Association to advocate moderate reform; assisted in the formation of the National Reform Union; d. 1868. (*Investigator* May 1855 and November 1857; autobiography in *National Reformer* 14 June–26 July 1868.)

Cooper, Thomas: b. Leicester 1805; Chartist and poet; imprisoned for sedition, 1843; started as a Methodist; became a freethinker in the early 1850s; on the council of the People's International League, 1847; president of the People's Charter Union, 1848; baptised 1859, and became a Baptist preacher; d. 1892. (T. Cooper, *Life of Thomas Cooper.*)

Cooper, Walter: b. Aberdeenshire, 1814; came to London and worked as a tailor; active Chartist and freethinker; joined the League of Social Progress, 1848; lectured with Southwell in Manchester, 1849; attracted to the Christian Socialists, and was responsible for bringing Holyoake into touch with them; manager of the Working Tailors' Association. (T. Christensen, *Christian Socialism,* pp. 98–9.)

Cooper, William: b. 1822; hand loom weaver, and one of the founders of the Rochdale Pioneers, 1844; leading Rochdale Co-operator and Secularist; d. 1868. (*National Reformer* 20 December 1868.)

Cowen, Joseph, junior: b. 1829; Newcastle upon Tyne radical republican; educated at Edinburgh University; entered his father's fire brick and clay retort works at Winlaton; encouraged G. J. Harney, G. J. Holyoake and most other British ultra radicals and foreign refugees; started the *Northern Tribune,* 1854–55; owned the *Newcastle Daily Chronicle* and the *Newcastle Weekly Chronicle,* from 1859/60; treasurer of the Northern Reform Union, 1858–62, and of the Northern Reform League, 1866–67; involved in industrial, educational and Co-operative affairs; M.P. for Newcastle on his father's death, 1873–86; became an imperialist in foreign affairs; d. 1900. (E. R. Jones, *Joseph Cowen*; W. Duncan, *Joseph Cowen.*)

Detrosier, Rowland: b. 1800 (Wheeler says 1796); an illegitimate child; patronised by Joseph Brotherton of Manchester, and became a Bible Christian preacher at Mount Brinksway Chapel, Stockport, 1823; attracted to Carlile and the Zetetics; leading Manchester radical, in association with John Doherty, 1829; went to London and became secretary of the moderate National Political Union, 1831; d. 1834. (G. A. Williams, *Rowland Detrosier*.)

Dodworth, James: a Sheffield palette knife manufacturer; leading Secularist and chairman of the *National Reformer* Co., 1860–62; d. 1876. (*Sheffield Telegraph* 17 April 1876.)

Farrah, Frederick: London radical publisher and bookseller; in charge of book sales at 147 Fleet Street, 1856; set up in his own business, Farrah and Dunbar, 1857; opened the Strand House at 282 Strand, to continue the work of the Fleet Street House, 1864.

Finch, John: b. Dudley 1784; settled in Liverpool, 1818; became a prosperous iron manufacturer; leading Co-operator and temperance advocate in Liverpool; founded the Liverpool Temperance Society, 1830; a national temperance lecturer, 1830–1836; espoused Owenism and expelled from the Temperance Society, 1837; a trustee of Queenwood, 1839; acting governor, 1839–40; chairman of the Rational Society Congress, 1844; took over the community from John Buxton, 1846; experimented with co-partnership at his Windsor foundry, 1851; d. 1857. (R. B. Rose, 'John Finch', *Tr.H.S.L.C.* vol. 109 (1957).)

Fox, William Johnson: b. Suffolk, 1786; unitarian minister at Chichester, 1813–17, and at the Parliament Court Chapel, Bishopsgate, 1817–24; went as minister with the latter when it was moved to South Place, 1824, and remained there until 1852; leader writer on the *Morning Chronicle*, 1839–43, and 'Publicola' of the *Weekly Dispatch*; Anti-Corn Law League orator; M.P. for Oldham, 1847–63; d. 1864 (G. Wallas, *W. J. Fox*.)

Galpin, William: a leading member of the Home Colonisation Society; secretary to the Rational Society Central Board, 1842–44; became a White Quaker.

Gimson, Josiah: b. 1818; head of a Leicester engineering firm; president of the Leicester branch of the Rational Society, 1845; leading Secularist in Leicester, and member of the town council; d. 1883. His son, Sidney Ansell Gimson, was a prominent figure in the Ethical movement. (F. J. Gould, *Leicester Secular Society;* Holyoake, *Secular Prospects in Death*.)

Gordon, John Henry: b. Carlisle; had a religious upbringing, but became a secret unbeliever; started contributing to the *Reasoner*; used the pseudonym, B.B.B., but in November 1860 he lost his position on a Carlisle daily paper on account of his beliefs; appointed Secularist lecturer in Leeds, where he became an extreme freethinker; converted back to Christianity, 1862. (J. H. Gordon, *A Public Statement*.)

Gottheil, Elias: London Freethinker; a photographic artist by trade; secretary of the East London Secular Society, and editor of the *Secularist*, 1856.

Grant, Brewin: b. 1821; son of a Leicestershire wool-worker; studied in London, then won a scholarship to Glasgow University, 1843–45; a Congregationalist minister in Birmingham, 1848–53; he went on a mission against Secularism, 1853–55; minister at Sheffield, 1856–68; then struck off and was ordained priest, 1871; debated with most of the leading Secularists: Holyoake (1853, 1854), Barker (1855), Bradlaugh (1858); d. 1892.

Greg, Percy: b. 1836; son of W. R. Greg; attended London University and became a Secularist; wrote as 'Lionel H. Holdreth'; edited the *Reasoner* during Holyoake's illness, 1859; lived in Manchester most of his life, and for a time worked on the *Manchester Guardian*. (*Manchester Guardian* 30 December 1889.)

Gurney, Joseph: leading Northampton Owenite and Secularist; elected to the town council, 1858; president of the Secular Society and supporter of Bradlaugh in his parliamentary campaign; secretary of the Northampton Town and County Benefit Building Society, 1853–90, and president, 1891–4; d. 1894. (D. Tribe, *President Charles Bradlaugh.*)

Gwynne, George: patron of Secularism; contributed to the *Reasoner* and *National Reformer* as 'Aliquis'; d. 1873. (*National Reformer*, 12 October 1873.

Hagen, Benjamin: b. 1791; a Quaker brewer, attracted to Owenism, *c.* 1841; retired in 1843 to spend more time on Owenism; president of the Derby Secular Society, 1853; the backbone of Derby freethought until he moved to Brierly Hill; d. 1877. (*Reasoner* 6 August 1851.)

Harney, George Julian: b. Deptford, 1817; joined the National Union of the Working Classes, 1833, and became one of Hetherington's shop boys; imprisoned for selling unstamped newspapers at Derby, 1834; started the East London Democratic Association 1837; outspoken, ultra-radical Chartist; stationed in Sheffield, 1841; came to know Holyoake there; sub-editor, then editor, of the *Northern Star*; advocated international republicanism; set up the Fraternal Democrats, 1845; broke with O'Connor, 1849, and started the *Democratic Review*, followed by the *Red Republican*, 1849, and the *Friend of the People*, 1850; became more moderate; split with Ernest Jones, 1851, and left for Cowen's Newcastle, 1853; edited Cowen's *Northern Tribune*, 1854, and founded the Republican Brotherhood, 1855; settled in Jersey, 1855–62, then emigrated to the United States; returned, 1888, and settled in Surrey; contributed to the *Newcastle Weekly Chronicle*; d. 1897. (A. R. Schoyen, *Chartist Challenge.*)

Haslam, Charles, Junius: b. Northumberland, 1811; went to Manchester, 1829, and was an active Owenite and Chartist; wrote *Letters to the Clergy of All Denominations*, 1838; removed to Newcastle, 1860, and started business as a chemist; retired, 1879; d. 1902. (*Newcastle Weekly Chronicle* 22 February 1902.)

Hetherington, Henry: b. Soho, 1792; radical printer and publisher, best known for the *Poor Man's Guardian*; Owenite and moderate Chartist; member of the Anti-Persecution Union; d. of cholera, 1849. (A. G. Barker, *Henry Hetherington*; *Reasoner* 5 September 1849.)

Hobson, Joshua: b. Huddersfield, 1810; worked as a handloom weaver, then as a joiner; involved in the Short Time agitation in the 1830s; imprisoned for publishing an unstamped paper, the *Voice of the West Riding*, 1833; moved to Leeds where he published the *New Moral World* and the *Northern Star*; edited the latter in Leeds and London, 1843–45; returned to Huddersfield, 1846; appointed an Improvement Commissioner, 1848–54; resigned and joined the *Huddersfield Chronicle*, 1855, and the *Huddersfield Weekly News*, 1871 —both Tory papers; opponent of Whig landlord, Sir John Ramsden, over tenant right; d. 1876. (*Huddersfield Weekly News* 13, 20 May, 1876.)

Hollick, Frederick: b. Birmingham, 1813; educated at the mechanics' institute; became a Socialist lecturer; emigrated to America and wrote several popular medical works; d. 1900.

Holyoak, W. H.: b. 1818; Leicester bookseller, and leader of Leicester Secularism. (F. J. Gould, *Leicester Secular Society*.)

Holyoake, Austin: b. Birmingham, 1826; younger brother of G. J. Holyoake; became an Owenite and freethinker; started as a printer, 1847, and managed the printing side of the Fleet Street House, 1853–62; assisted with the *Reasoner*; publisher at Fleet Street, 1859–62, and as Austin & Co. at 17 Johnson's Court, 1864–74; sub-editor of the *National Reformer*, 1864–74; member of the Garibaldi Committee, 1861, the Association for the Repeal of the Taxes on Knowledge, the Reform League, and the London Republican Club; d. 1874. (*National Reformer* 19 April, 10 May 1874.)

Holyoake, George Jacob: b. Birmingham, 1817; educated at the mechanics' institute; Owenite lecturer at Worcester, 1840, and Sheffield, 1841–42; imprisoned for blasphemy, 1842–43; freethought lecturer and writer; creator of the Secularist movement in the 1850s; member of the last Central Board of the Rational Society, 1846, and of the last Executive of the National Charter Association, 1851; acting secretary of the Garibaldi Committee, 1861; prominent Co-operative propagandist and radical agitator; d. 1906. (McCabe, *Life and Letters of G. J. Holyoake*.)

Hornblower, John Griffin: Birmingham friend of G. J. Holyoake; married his sister, Caroline Holyoake; printed the *Reasoner* until 1847; emigrated to Australia.

Hunt, Thornton Leigh: b 1810; son of Leigh Hunt; founder and editor of the *Leader*, 1850; contributor to the *Spectator*, 1840–60; acting editor of the *Daily Telegraph*, 1855–72; d. 1873.

Ironside, Isaac: b. Masborough, 1808; apprenticed to a stove-grate fitter; founder member of the Sheffield Mechanics' Institute; leading member of the Sheffield Socialists at the Rockingham Street Hall of Science; converted to freethought by the lectures of Frances Wright; member of the Central Board, 1843;

a Sheffield town councillor; became a follower of David Urquhart, 1855; d. 1870. (J. Salt, 'Isaac Ironside', *Co-operative Review* vol. 34 (1960), pp. 218-19.)

Johnson, William Harral: b. 1834; Yorkshire Secularist leader; lived in Huddersfield, 1850–55, and in Blackburn, 1855–c.1860; promoted many attempts at regional organisation; assistant editor of the *Yorkshire Tribune*; editor of the *Investigator*, 1857–58; sometimes used the pseudonym of 'Anthony Collins'; was at first an extremist opponent of Holyoake, then he retired from freethought at the request of his family, but in 1865 he reappeared as a Secularist lecturer in London; collaborated with W. S. Ross and C. R. Mackay in libelling Bradlaugh, 1888. (D. Tribe, *President Charles Bradlaugh*.)

Jones, John Gale: b. 1771; leading member of the London Corresponding Society; supported Carlile's efforts after 1819; kept the Rotunda open with Eliza Sharples, 1831; d. 1838.

Jones, Patrick Lloyd: b. Cork, 1811; a fustian cutter; came to Liverpool, then Manchester; converted to Owenism and helped found the Salford Co-operative Store, 1831, and run the schools there; appointed a social missionary, 1837; settled in London after 1846; a moderate Chartist; started the *Spirit of the Age*, 1848; member of the League of Social Progress, 1849; attracted to Christian Socialism; leading advocate of the Co-operative movement; d. 1886. (Christensen, *Christian Socialism*; see also the memoir added to L. Jones, *Life of Robert Owen*.)

Law, Harriet, Mrs: b. London, 1832; a Baptist, converted after hearing John Watts; became a freethought lecturer; edited the *Secular Chronicle*, 1876; d. 1897.

Linton, William James: b. Stepney, 1812; apprenticed to Bonner, the wood engraver; came under influence of W. J. Fox; introduced to Chartism by James Watson; met Mazzini, 1841; worked as an engraver on the *Illustrated London News;* became a leading republican; started the People's International League, 1847; edited the *Cause of the People* with Holyoake, 1848; projected the *Leader* with Thornton Hunt, 1850, but soon quarrelled with Hunt's lukewarm editorial policy; lived in the Lake District, at Miteside, 1849, and at Brantwood, 1852; published the *English Republic*, helped by W. E. Adams and Joseph Cowen, junior; member of the Garibaldi Committee, 1860–61; emigrated to America, 1866; d. 1897. (W. J. Linton, *Memories*.)

Maccall, William: b. 1812; educated at Glasgow University; became a Unitarian minister, 1837–46; then came to London as a Pantheist; leading contributor to *Propagandist*, 1862; d. 1878.

Martin, Emma, Mrs: b. Bristol, 1812; brought up a strict Baptist; began to doubt after hearing Alexander Campbell, 1839; left her husband and became a freethought lecturer; also practised midwifery; d. 1851. (*Reasoner* 22 October 1851.)

x

Maughan, John: London freethought leader; opponent of Holyoake and the Fleet Street House; promoter of many attempts at organisation in the 1850s; secretary of the General Secular Benevolent Society; against Bradlaugh's neo-Malthusian policies; edited the *Stepping Stone*, 1862; d. 1875.

Moore, Richard: b. London, 1810; a wood carver; married a niece of James Watson; moderate Chartist and follower of Lovett; treasurer of the People's Charter Union, 1848; chairman of the Newspaper Stamp Abolition Committee, 1849, and of the Association for the Repeal of the Taxes on Knowledge, 1851–70; d. 1878. (W. J. Linton, *James Watson*.)

Newman, Francis William: b. 1805; fellow of Balliol College, Oxford, 1826–30; Professor of Classical Literature at New College, Manchester, 1840–60; Professor of Latin at University College, London, 1846–63; started life as an extreme Evangelical; became a deist after going on a mission to Bagdad, 1830–33; joined the Unitarian Association, 1876; his works, *The Soul, its Sorrows and Aspirations* (1849), and *Phases of Faith* (1850) had a profound effect on Holyoake; d. 1897. (B. Willey, *More Nineteenth Century Studies*.)

Owen, Robert: b. Newtown, 1771; rapid social advancement through the cotton trade; assumed control of the New Lanark Mills, 1800; became internationally famous for his work there; increasingly absorbed in social problems; denounced religious influences in *A New View of Society* (1812–14) and in his London Tavern speeches, 1817; outlined a plan for communities in his *Report to the County of Lanark*, 1821; inspired communitarian and co-operative efforts by working men; his major communities were New Harmony, Indiana, 1824; and Queenwood, Hampshire, 1839; both failed; became a spiritualist, 1853; d. 1858. (F. Podmore, *Robert Owen*; R. Owen, *Autobiography*.)

Owen, Robert Dale: b. 1800; eldest son of Robert Owen; went to New Harmony, 1825; became a United States citizen, 1827; edited the *Free Enquirer* with Frances Wright, 1828–32; elected to the House of Representatives, 1842; U.S. Minister in Naples, 1853–58; d. 1877. (R. D. Owen, *Threading My Way*.)

Paine, Thomas: b. Thetford, 1737; political and religious pamphleteer in the American and French revolutions; published *Common Sense* (1776), the *Rights of Man* (1791–92) and the *Age of Reason* (1793–95); d. 1809. (M. D. Conway, *Thomas Paine*.)

Paterson, Thomas: outspoken freethinker; assisted Holyoake at Sheffield, 1841–42; took a prominent part in the agitations of the Anti-Persecution Union, 1842–43; imprisoned at Perth, 1843–44; edited the *Oracle of Reason*, 1842–43; emigrated after several scandals, 1845. (Southwell, *Confessions*.)

Pare, William: b. 1805; apprenticed to a cabinet maker; became a reporter and kept a tobacconist shop in Birmingham; founder member of the Birmingham Co-operative Society, 1828; Co-operative and Owenite missionary; member of the Birmingham Political Union, 1830, and elected to the first Town Council, 1830; first Civil Registrar in Birmingham, 1837–42; acting governor of the Queenwood Community, 1842–44; later became the successful manager of ironworks near Dublin, and in Liverpool and Chepstow; d. 1873.

Pitkethly, Lawrence: Huddersfield general draper; leading member of Oastler's Short Time Committee, and the anti-Poor Law, Chartist and Socialist agitations in the West Riding; d. 1858 (J. T. Ward, 'Lawrence Pitkeithly' [*sic*], *Huddersfield Examiner* 2 June 1958).

Perfitt, Philip William: b. 1820; liberal preacher at South Place and elsewhere; founder of the Free Church, Newman Street; edited the *Path-finder*, 1859–61.

Powell, Thomas: b. Newtown; became one of Hetherington's shop boys in London; returned to mid Wales as a Chartist leader; then secretary of the London Atheistical Society and the Anti-Persecution Union; emigrated to Trinidad; d. 1862. (W. J. Linton, *James Watson.*)

Roalfe, Matilda: b. 1813; converted to freethought by questions asked by her Sunday School class; volunteered to help in the Edinburgh campaign, 1843–44; opened a bookshop; imprisoned for two months, 1844; published the *Plebeian*; married Walter Sanderson and settled in Galashiels; d. 1880. (*The Scotch Trials.*)

Ryall, Maltus Questell: b. c. 1809; member of the Lambeth branch of the Rational Society; the son of an engraver, or perhaps an engraver himself; worked as an advertising agent; spent what money he had in the cause of freethought; helped with the *Oracle* and was secretary of the Anti-Persecution Union, 1842; lived with a woman who was not his wife, and adopted her children as his own; died in poverty, 1846. (*Herald of Progress* 14 March 1846; M. Q. Ryall to William Berwick, 21 October 1844, H. C. 129.)

Saull, William Devonshire: b. 1784; London wine merchant; had a fine geological collection and was F.G.S., F.R.A.S.; founder and patron of the John Street Institution; d. 1855.

Shaen, William: b. 1821; fellow of University College, London, 1846; solicitor, 1848; a Unitarian; supporter of Holyoake and the Fleet Street House; arbitrated in the *National Reformer* dispute between Holyoake and Bradlaugh, 1863; d. 1887.

Southwell, Charles: b. London, 1814; freethought lecturer and social missionary; published the *Oracle of Reason*, 1841, and sentenced to 12 months in prison and a fine of £100 for blasphemy, 1842; took a prominent part in the Scottish agitation, 1843; edited the *Investigator*, 1843; lectured in South London, Manchester, and Glasgow; edited the *Lancashire Beacon*, 1849; emigrated to New Zealand, 1856; edited a Wesleyan magazine without declaring his views; d. in Auckland, 1860. (C. Southwell, *Confessions*; *Reasoner* 2 December 1860.)

Taylor, Robert: b. Edmonton 1784; trained as a surgeon, and then took holy orders under the influence of Charles Simeon at Cambridge; converted to deism after reading Gibbon, 1818; lectured as a deist in Dublin and then London, 1824; worked with Richard Carlile; imprisoned for blasphemy, 1828; wrote the *Diegesis*; went on an infidel mission with Carlile, 1829; lectured from his 'Devil's Pulpit' in the Rotunda, 1830–31; imprisoned for blasphemy, 1831–33; then married a wealthy supporter and retired to Tours; d. 1844. (G. A. Aldred, *Devil's Chaplain*; H. Cutner, *Robert Taylor*.)

Trevelyan, Arthur: b. 1802; second son of Sir John Trevelyan, 5th baronet; total abstinence advocate and supporter of radical causes; d. 1878.

Truelove, Edward: b. 1809; secretary and bookseller at the John Street Institute; went to Harmony Hall, 1844; antiquarian bookseller and freethought publisher at 240 Strand, 1852; prosecuted for publishing W. E. Adams, *Tyrannicide*, 1858; moved to 256 High Holborn, 1867; imprisoned for publishing R. D. Owen, *Moral Physiology*, 1878; d. 1899.

Turner, Henry: secretary of the Sheffield Secular Society and of the *National Reformer* Co., 1860; leading West Riding Secularist; became a follower of Joseph Barker.

Watson, James: b. Malton, 1799; became a radical in Leeds, 1818; volunteered to help Carlile, 1822; imprisoned for selling Palmer's *Principles of Nature*, 1823; first store-keeper at the Red Lion Square Co-operative store, 1828; Co-operative missionary, 1830; assisted Hetherington in the unstamped press struggle, 1831–4; bookseller at the City Road Hall of Science, 1837, at St Paul's Alley, 1843, and at 3 Queen's Head Passage, 1846; transferred stock to Holyoake at 147 Fleet Street, 1854; first president of the London Secular Society, 1853; prominent in many radical agitations, including Chartism and Owenism; d. 1874. (W. J. Linton, *James Watson*.)

Watts, Charles: b. Bristol, 1836; father a Wesleyan minister; came to London, *c.* 1852; helped his brother (see below) with the *National Reformer*, 1864 and was a sub-editor until 1877; prominent Secularist lecturer; took over the publishing business at 17 Johnson's Court on Austin Holyoake's death, 1874; broke with Bradlaugh over birth control, 1877; emigrated to Toronto, 1886; returned, 1891, and resumed freethought lecturing; a founder of the Rationalist Press Association; d. 1906. ('Saladin' [W. S. Ross], *Charles Watts*.)

Watts, Charles, Albert: b. 1858; son of Charles Watts; apprenticed to Austin Holyoake at 17 Johnson's Court; took over the business from his father, 1882; published G. W. Foote's *Freethinker*; founder of the Rationalist Press Association; d. 1946. (F. J. Gould, *Pioneers of Johnson's Court*.)

Watts, John: b. Bristol, 1834; elder brother of Charles Watts; worked at 147 Fleet Street as a printer, 1858; set up on his own, 1860; sub-editor of the *Reasoner*, then of the *National Reformer*; editor, 1863–66; d. 1866. (*National Reformer* 11 November 1866.)

Watts, John: b. Coventry, 1818; son of a weaver; assistant secretary and librarian at the mechanics' institute, 1831–38; became an Owenite; moved to Manchester, 1841; Ph.D. from Goessen University, 1844; member of Lancashire Public Schools Association, 1847–53; responsible for sale of Campfield Hall of

Science to Manchester Town Council for use as a public library, 1851; secretary of the Owen's College Extension Committee; leader of educational reform and Co-operative efforts in Manchester; d. 1887.

Wright, Frances (married, d'Arusmont): b. Dundee, 1795; visited U.S.A., 1820; returned and became a citizen, 1824; became a radical freethought lecturer, 1828; started a community at Nashoba for freed slaves; visited New Harmony and became friendly with William Maclure; assisted R. D. Owen with the *Free Enquirer*, 1828–32; d. 1858. (W. R. Waterman, *Frances Wright;* A. J. F. Perkins and T. Wolfson, *Frances Wright; Northern Star* 1 June 1844.)

Young, Frederick Rowland: from Diss, Norfolk; attracted by Holyoake, 1853; worked at 147 Fleet Street; became a Unitarian minister, 1855.

2 Pseudonyms

The following are the principal pseudonyms used in the various periodicals of the freethought movement in the period covered in this book:

Aliquis   George Gwynne
Anthony Collins   W. H. Johnson
B.B.B.   J. H. Gordon
Caractacus   W. E. Adams
Christopher Charles   Charles C. Cattell
Edward Search   W. H. Ashurst (father and son)
Eugene   George Hooper (a clerk from Oxford who helped Holyoake with his university studies)
Henry Tyrrell   Henry Tyrrell Church (a leader of London freethought)
Iconoclast   Charles Bradlaugh (used until 1868)
Ion   G. J. Holyoake (used mainly in the *Leader*)
Isis   Eliza Sharples-Carlile
Lionel H. Holdreth   Percy Greg
Panthea   Sophia D. Collet
Quasimodo   G. J. Holyoake (used in the *National Reformer*)
Spartacus   W. J. Linton
Undecimus   T. Evans Bell
Zulu, a London   G. J. Holyoake (used in his *Cummings Wrong* pamphlet, 1863)

Bibliography

1 *Manuscript sources*

International Institute of Social History, Amsterdam

Association of All Classes of All Nations: minute book of the Central Board, 26 May 1838-13 April 1840
National Community Friendly Society: minute book of directors, 4 June 1838-29 April 1839 (continued in the A.A.C.A.N. minute book, 16 April 1840-21 July 1842, 2 April 1843-28 September 1843)
Rational Society: minute book of directors, 1 October 1843-5 March 1845.

Co-operative Union library, Manchester

Robert Owen papers: approximately 2,000 letters, etc., covering the later years of Owen's life, 1821-58
G. J. Holyoake collection: over 4,000 manuscript items, chiefly letters to Holyoake, 1840-1906

Bishopsgate Institute library, London

G. J. Holyoake collection: includes extracts from Holyoake's early diaries in two log books, 1831-45, and in a diary-cum-notebook, 1845-52; pocket diaries for almost every year, 1849-1905; a notebook of early lecture notes, 1838-39; the rules of the London Atheistical Society, 1842-43; a copy of the deed of the *Leader* Newspaper Company, 1850; the Garibaldi Special Fund Committee minute book, 1860-61; the cash book of the Fleet Street house, 1858-61; and miscellaneous correspondence.

British Museum

Harriet Martineau–G. J. Holyoake correspondence, Add. Mss. 42,726
Charles Babbage–G. J. Holyoake correspondence, Add. Mss. 37,193
Leigh Hunt–G. J. Holyoake correspondence, Add. Mss 38,111

Newcastle upon Tyne public library

Joseph Cowen, junior, papers: items on domestic and foreign republicanism and radical politics

National Secular Society, London

Charles Bradlaugh collection: over 3,000 letters and papers covering the whole of Bradlaugh's public career.

The following unpublished works have also been consulted:

Budd, S., 'Militancy and expediency–an account of the Secular movement in the nineteenth century', a paper presented to the *Past and Present* Conference on Popular Religion, London, 7 July 1966.

Campbell, C. B., 'The conceptualization of irreligion', a paper presented to the Society for the Scientific Study of Religion, New York, 23 October 1970.

— 'The pattern of irreligious denominationalism in England', a paper read to the Society for the Scientific Study of Religion section of the International Congress of Learned Societies in the Field of Religion, Los Angeles, September 1972.

Francis, M., 'British Secularism, 1840–85', an essay submitted in partial fulfilment of the requirements for a Master of Arts degree in the Department of History, University of Toronto, May 1969.

Wilmer, H., 'Dechristianisation in England in the nineteenth and twentieth centuries', a paper read at the Ecclesiastical History Colloquium, Cambridge, 24–27 September 1968.

2 Official papers and other reports

Public Record Office

Petitions: H.O. 54, 33 (1839); H.O. 54, 34 (1840); H.O. 54, 35 (1841–54); H.O. 56, 25 (1838–53)

Entry books: H.O. 57, 3 (1837–40); H.O. 57, 4 (1841–45); H.O. 57, 5 (1846–1850); H.O. 57, 6 (1850–53); H.O. 57, 7 (1853–61)

Blasphemy papers: H.O. 45. O.S. 3017 (1850); H.O. 45. O.S. 3537(1851)

Disturbances: H.O. 45. O.S. 6092 (Hyde Park Sunday Trading Riots, 1855)

Press, laws and liberty: H.O. 45. O.S. 929 (1845); H.O. 45. O.S. 1993 (1847)

Socialists: H.O. 45. O.S. 92 (1841); H.O. 45 O.S. 338 (1842); H.O. 45. O.S. 981 (1845)

Sunday trading: H.O. 45. O.S. 1091 (1845); H.O. 45. O.S. 4631 (1853)

Parliamentary reports

Hansard, *passim*.
Journal of the House of Lords, passim.
Journal of the House of Commons, passim.
Report from the Select Committee on Public Libraries, 1849.
Report from the Select Committee on Newspaper Stamps, 1851
Report of the Religious Census: England and Wales, 1852–53.
Report of the Educational Census: England and Wales, 1852–53.
Report of the Religious and Educational Census: Scotland, 1854.

Law reports:

Law Journal, new series, vol. xxx, Chancery Division (1861); pp. 742–9; Pare v. Clegg

Mission reports:

Reports of the Ministry to the Poor, Manchester: 1837, 1840–54, 1858–61
(Unitarian)
Manchester and Salford Town Mission Reports: 1838–1841, 1853–1856, 1858–
1862 (Evangelical, interdenominational)
Manchester City Mission Magazine, 1853–1861 (contains further reports of
the above)
Reports of the Leicester Domestic Missionary Society: 1846–62 (Unitarian)

3 Newspapers and periodicals

1819–26. *Republican* (2*d* to 7 January 1820, then 6*d*), vols. I–XIV: London
weekly, 27 August 1819–29 December 1820; 4 January 1822–29 December
1826, ed. Richard Carlile and others.

1828–29. *Lion* (6*d*), vols. I–IV: London, weekly, 4 January 1828–25 December
1829, ed. Richard Carlile.

1830–31. *Prompter* (3*d*), one volume only: London, weekly, 13 November
1830–12 November 1831, ed. Richard Carlile.
1831–32. *Devil's Pulpit* (2*d*), vols. I–II: London, weekly, 4 March 1831–
20 January 1832, ed. Robert Taylor.
1831–35. *Poor Man's Guardian* (1*d*), vols. I–IV: London, weekly, 9 July 1831–
20 December 1835, ed. J. Bronterre O'Brien.

1833–34. *Gauntlet* (3*d*), one volume only: London weekly, 9 February 1833–
30 March 1834, ed. Richard Carlile.

1833–34. *Voice of the West Riding* (1*d*), vols. I–II: Huddersfield, weekly,
1 June 1833–(?) 7 June 1834, ed. Joshua Hobson.

1834–45. *New Moral World* (1*d* to 14 March 1835, then 1½*d* to 20 October
1838, then 2*d* to 27 June 1840, then 3*d* (4½*d* stamped) to 26 June 1841, then
2*d* (3*d* stamped)), vols. I–III, No. 135: London, weekly, 1 November 1834–
3 June 1837; vol. III, No. 136–IV, No. 188: Manchester, weekly, 10 June 1837–
2 June 1838; vols. IV, No. 189–V (new series, I): Birmingham, weekly, 9 June
1838–6 July 1839; vols. VI (n.s. II) –X (third series, III), No. 16: Leeds, weekly,
11 July 1839–16 October 1841; vols. X (third series, III), No. 17–XIII (third
series, VI), No. 32: London, weekly, 23 October 1841–1 February 1845; vol.
XIII (third series, VI), Nos. 33–61: Harmony Hall, weekly, 8 February–23
August 1845, ed. Robert Alger to 3 June 1837, and Robert Owen during the
summer of 1842, otherwise by G. A. Fleming. (*Note.* Vol. XIII (third series,
VI), Nos. 62–4, were issued as an anti-Owenite paper, London, weekly,
30 August–13 September 1845, ed. James Hill.)

1837–52. *Northern Star* (4½*d*), vols. I–VIII, No. 367: Leeds, weekly, 17 November
1837–23 November 1844; vols. VIII, No. 368–XV, No. 749: London, weekly,
30 November 1844–13 March 1852; ed. William Hill to [? August 1843], then
Joshua Hobson to [? October 1845] then G. J. Harney to May 1849, then
[? William Rider], then G. A. Fleming. (*Note.* Vol. XV, Nos. 750–4, 20 March–

17 April 1852, were published as the *Star*, which was then taken over by Harney as the *Star of Freedom*, see below).

1839. *The Natural Mirror, or Free Thoughts on Theology*: (1*d*), 4 issues only: Manchester, n.d., ed. 'An Owenian'.

[? 1841]. *Rational Religionist and Independent Inquirer*: (2*d*), Nos. 1–3: Manchester, n.d., ed. Robert Buchanan.

1841–3. *Oracle of Reason*: (1*d*), vols. I–II: London, weekly, 6 November 1841–8 January 1842, 12 February 1842–2 December 1843, ed. Charles Southwell to 8 January 1842, then G. J. Holyoake to 27 August 1842, then T. Paterson to 3 June 1843, then W. Chilton.

[1842–3]. *Freethinker's Information for the People*: (1*d*), vols. I–II: London, weekly, n.d., ed. Henry Hetherington.

1843. *Investigator*: (2*d*), one volume only: London, weekly [1 April]–October 1843, ed. C. Southwell.

1843–5. *Movement*: (1½*d* to 10 August 1844, then 2*d*), vols. I–II: London, weekly 16 December 1843–2 April 1845, ed. G. J. Holyoake and M. Q. Ryall.

1845. *Circular of the Anti-Persecution Union*: 1*d*), one volume only: London, monthly, May–August 1845, ed. G. J. Holyoake.

1845. *Moral World*: (2*d*), Nos. 1–11: London, weekly, 30 August–8 November 1845, ed. G. A. Fleming.

1845–6. *Herald of Progress*; (1*d*), one volume only: London, fortnightly, 25 October 1845–23 May 1846, ed. John Cramp.

1846–61. *Reasoner*: (for prices, see appendix III), vols. I–XXVI: London weekly, 3 June 1846–30 June 1861, ed. G. J. Holyoake.

1846–8. *Utilitarian Record*: (issued with *Reasoner*), weekly with *Reasoner*, 2 December 1846–24 November 1847, ed. G. J. Holyoake.

1848. *Cause of the People*: (1*d*), one volume only: London, weekly, 20 May–22 July 1848, ed. W. J. Linton and G. J. Holyoake.

1849–[?1850] *Lancashire Beacon*: (1*d*), one volume only: Manchester, weekly, [3 August 1849–? early 1850], ed. C. Southwell.

1850. *Cooper's Journal*: (1*d*), one volume only: London, weekly, 5 January–29 June, 5 October–30 October 1850, ed. Thomas Cooper.

1850. *People's Review of Literature and Politics*: (1/-), Nos. 1–3: monthly, February–April 1850, ed. G. J. Holyoake and others.

1850–60. *Leader*: (6*d*), vols. I–XI: London, weekly, 30 March 1850–24 November 1860, ed. Thornton Hunt.

1850. *Red Republican*: (1*d*), Nos. 1–24: London, weekly, 22 June–30 November 1850, ed. G. J. Harney.

1850–1. *Friend of the People*: (1*d*), Nos. 1–35: London, weekly, 7 December 1850–26 July 1851, ed. G. J. Harney.

1852. *Star of Freedom*: (1d), Nos. 1–27: London, weekly, 24 April–27 November 1852, ed. G. J. Harney.

1854–6. *Secular Miscellany*: (1d), Nos. 1–6: London, periodically, 1854–1856.

1854–7. *London Investigator*: (2d), vols. I–III: London, monthly, April 1854–March 1857, ed. Robert Cooper.

1857–9. *Investigator* (continuation of the above): (2d. to September 1857, then 1d), vol. IV: London, monthly, April 1857–March 1858; vol. V: London, fortnightly, 15 April 1858–1 March 1859; vol. VI: London, fortnightly with gaps, 15 March–1 August 1859, ed. W. H. Johnson to 28 October 1858, then C. Bradlaugh.

1855–6. *Yorkshire Tribune*: (1d), one volume only: London, monthly, July 1855–September 1856, ed. W. Mitchell (assisted by W. H. Johnson, July–December 1855).

1856. *Secularist*: (2d), one issue only: London, January 1858, ed. Elias Gottheil.

1856–7. *Half-Hours with the Freethinkers*: (1/- to 15 March 1857, then 1/1d), Nos. 1–24: London, fortnightly, 1 October 1856–15 September 1857, ed. C. Bradlaugh, W. H. Johnson and J. Watts.

1860. *Reasoner Gazette*: (issued with *Reasoner*), weekly with *Reasoner*, 1 January–23 December 1860, ed. G. J. Holyoake.

1860–7. *National Reformer*: (2d), vols. I–X: London, 14 April, 12 May, 2 June 1860, then weekly–29 December 1867 (publication continued until 1893), ed. C. Bradlaugh (with Joseph Barker to 31 August 1861) to 21 February 1863, then John Watts to 22 April 1866, then Charles Bradlaugh (until 1891).

1861. *Counsellor*: (1½d), one volume only: monthly, August–December 1861, ed. G. J. Holyoake.

1861–2. *Barker's Review*: (2d), vols. I–II: London, weekly, 7 September 1861–30 August 1862, ed. Joseph Barker.

1862. *Propagandist*: (2d), Nos. 1–2: London, 3 May, 31 May 1862, ed. J. B. Bebbington and William Maccall.

1862. *Secular World* (*Reasoner* series vol. XXVII): (2d to 19 May 1863, then 1½d to September 1863, then 2d), vol. I, Nos. 1–9: London, weekly, 10 May–5 July 1862; vol. I, No. 10–11, no. 13: London, monthly, August 1862–June 1864, ed. G. J. Holyoake.

1864. *English Leader*: (2d), Nos. 1–20: London, weekly, 4 June–15 October 1864, ed. G. J. Holyoake.

1864–5. *Half-Hours with the Freethinkers*: (1d), Nos. 1–24: London, weekly, 1 September 1864–9 February 1865, ed. John Watts and Charles Bradlaugh.

1864. *Secular World* (continued from June 1864): (1d), vol. II no. 14: London, 1 December 1864, ed. G. J. Holyoake.

1865. *Reasoner and Secular World* (*Reasoner* series vol. xxviii): (1*d* to May 1865, then 2*d*), one volume only: monthly, January–December 1865, ed. G. J. Holyoake.

1866. *English Leader*: (2*d* to 3 February 1866, then 6*d*), nos. 21–48: London, 6 January, 3 February, then weekly to 14 July 1866, ed. G. J. Holyoake.

Note. A complete list of the periodicals edited by G. J. Holyoake is given in C. W. F. Goss, *A Descriptive Bibliography of the Writings of George Jacob Holyoake* (London, 1908), pp. 65–72.

4 Directories

Birmingham: White (1855); anon. (1861).
Brighton: anon. (1854).
Bristol: Hunt & Co. (1848).
Cheshire: Kelly (1857).
Derby, etc.: Slater (1850); White (1848, 1854, 1858).
Derby: White (1857).
Durham: anon. (1856, 1861).
Glasgow: Slater (1857).
Hull: Wright (1863).
Kent: Bagshaw (1847).
Lancashire: Slater (1858).
Leeds: White (1847, 1866).
Leicester: Hagar & Co. (1849).
Manchester: Slater (1851, 1858, 1863); Whellan (1853).
Newcastle: White (1847).
Northumberland: Ward (1850).
Norwich: Blyth (1842); Mathieson (1867).
Nottingham: White (1853).
Oxford: Hunt & Co. (1846).
Scotland: Kelly (1852, 1860); Slater (1852).
Yorkshire: Kelly (1857, 1861); Jones (1863–4).

5 Contemporary printed sources

Date of first edition, where known, if different from that used in this work, is given in parentheses before the place of publication. Authors' real names are used where known. For a key to pseudonyms see appendix v(*b*).

(a) Freethought books and pamphlets

Barker, Joseph, *What Atheism can say for Itself by Mr. Joseph Barker, extracted from a Discussion between himself and Mr. Thomas Cooper, at St. George's Hall, Bradford, September 1860.* Leicester, 1870.
Bell, T. Evans, *The God of the Bible. A Searching Study of the Christian Creed.* (1851), new ed., London, 1943.

[Bentham, Jeremy], *Analysis of the Influence of Natural Religion on the Temporal Happiness of Mankind, by Philip Beauchamp*, London, 1822.

Bradlaugh, Charles, *Has Man a Soul? A Lecture delivered by Iconoclast in the Temperance Hall, Townhead Street, Sheffield, March 29, 1859.* London, 1859.

— *A Review of the Work of the Rev. E. Mellor, M.A. entitled 'The Atonement, its Relation to Pardon'. A Lecture delivered by Iconoclast, in the Odd Fellows' Hall, Halifax, November 22nd 1859.* London, [1859].

— *New Life of Abraham* (1860). London, 1861.

— *New Life of David* (1860). London, 1861.

— *The Bible: What it Is.* London, 1861.

— *Is there a God?* London, [1861].

— *Jesus, Shelley, and Malthus; or Pious Poverty and Heterodox Happiness.* London, 1861.

— *New Life of Jacob.* London, 1861.

— *New Life of Moses.* London, 1861.

— *What Did Jesus Teach?* London, [1861].

Bray, Charles, *The Philosophy of Necessity.* London, 1841.

Carlile, Richard, *An Address to Men of Science; calling upon them to stand forward and Vindicate the Truth from the Foul Grasp and Persecution of Superstition; and obtain for the Island of Great Britain the noble appellation of the Focus of Truth; whence mankind shall be illuminated, and the black and pestiferous clouds of Persecution and Superstition be banished from the face of the earth; as the only sure prelude to universal Peace and Harmony among the Human Race. In which a Sketch of a Proper System for the Education of Youth is submitted to their judgment.* London, 1821,

— *Church Reform: the only means to that end, stated in A Letter to Sir Robert Peel, Bart, First Lord of the Treasury, &c. by Richard Carlile, to which is prefaced a Correspondence with the Bishop of London on the same subject.* London, 1835.

Chubb, T., *Discourse on Miracles.* London, 1741.

Cooper, Robert, *A Contrast between the New Moral World and the Old Immoral World; a lecture delivered in the Social Institution, Salford.* Second edition, Hulme, 1838.

— *A Lecture on Original Sin, delivered in the Social Institution, Great George Street, Salford.* Second edition, Hulme, 1838.

— *The Holy Scriptures Analyzed, or Extracts from the Bible, showing its contradictions, absurdities, and immoralities.* Third edition with additions, London, 1843.

— *The Infidel's Text Book, being the substance of Thirteen Lectures on the Bible.* Hull, 1846.

— *The Immortality of the Soul, Religiously and Philosophically Considered.* London, 1852.

'Cosmopolite', *The Bible an improper book for Youth, and dangerous to the easily excited brain; with immoral and contradictory passages from Holy Writ.* Edinburgh, 1843.

Deism, Fairly Stated, and Fully Vindicated from the Gross Imputations and Groundless Calumnies of Modern Believers, wherein some of the Principal Reasons contained in Dr. Benson's Answer to Christianity not founded on

*Argument are fully considered, and proven to be far from conclusive. In
a letter to a Friend. By a Moral Philosopher*. Second Edition, London,
1746.

Diderot, D., *Thoughts on Religion*. London, 1819.

Dodworth, James, *An Account of the Proceedings at the Shareholders' Meeting of the National Reformer Co., Held at Sheffield, March 23, 1862. Giving
a true version of The Way in which the Editor was Re-elected*. [1862].

Ellis, John, *Marriage; as practised by the priesthood, in all ages, contrasted
with the principles of reason, and the views of the Rational Society. An
Address delivered in the Institution, John Street, Tottenham Court Road
by John Ellis, S.M. together with a report of the celebration of matrimony,
in accordance with the New Marriage Act, on Sunday, March 15th, 1845*.
London, [1845].

Foote, George William, *Secularism Restated; with a Review of the Several
Expositions of Charles Bradlaugh and George Jacob Holyoake*. London
1874.

Gordon, J. H., *The Exodus of the Priests; a Secularist's Dream of Better Times*.
London, 1860.

Hetherington, Henry, *Cheap Salvation; or, An Antidote to Priestcraft: being
A Succinct, Practical, Essential, and Rational Religion, deduced from the
New Testament, the general adoption of which would supersede the necessity of a hireling priesthood, and save this over-taxed nation fifteen millions
per annum!!! Written at the Express Desire of the Rev. D. Ruell, (Chaplain
of Clerkenwell Prison)*. Second edition, London, [1832].

Holyoake, George Jacob, *The Advantages and Disadvantages of Trades'
Unions (based on a lecture delivered at the Rockingham Street Hall of
Science, on Sunday Evening, 28 November 1841)*. Sheffield 1841.

— *A Sketch of the Life and a Few of the Beauties of Pemberton, compiled and
selected chiefly with a view of Developing the Causes which Generated
the Talent and Moral Greatness of this Extraordinary Man*. Leeds,
1842.

— *The Spirit of Bonner in the Disciples of Jesus; or the Cruelty and Intolerance
of Christianity Displayed, in the Prosecution for Blasphemy of Charles
Southwell, Editor of the Oracle of Reason*. London, [1842].

— *A Short and Easy Method with The Saints*. London, [1843].

— *Paley refuted in his own words*. London, [1843].

— *Practical Grammar; with Graduated Exercises*. (1844), eighth ed., London
1870.

— *A Visit to Harmony Hall! (Reprinted from the 'Movement'). With a New
and Curious Vindicatory Chapter, Dedicated to the Socialists of England
and Scotland*. London, 1844.

— *The Value of Biography, in the Formation of Individual Character, illustrated by the Life & Writings of Charles Reece Pemberton, (A Lecture
delivered, May 12, 1844, to Branch A 1 of the London Communists)*. (1845),
London 1855.

— *Rationalism. A Treatise for the Times*. London, 1845.

— *Literary Institutions: Their Relation to Public Opinion. An Essay written
for the London Literary and Scientific Institution*. London, 1849.

— *The Last Trial for Alleged Atheism in England. A Fragment of Autobiography* (1850). Third edition, revised, London, 1861.

Holyoake, George Jacob, *The Logic of Death; or, Why should the Atheist Fear to Die?* (1850), thirteenth thousand, London, 1852.

— *Lectures and Debates: their terms, conditions and character.* 1851.

— *The Philosophic Type of Religion, as developed by Professor Newman, stated, examined and answered.* (1851) (in *Reasoner* XI nos. 264-266).

Mr. Geo. J. Holyoake's Three Lectures, in Heywood, in Answer to Mr. E. Grubb's Lectures, entitled Infidelity Unmasked'. Manchester and London, [1852].

— *Why do the Clergy avoid Discussion, and the Philosophers Discountenance It?* London, 1852.

— *The Government and the Working Man's Press, Reprinted from the 'Leader' Newspaper. Two Letters to the Right Hon. Thomas Milner Gibson, M.P.* [London, 1853].

— *Organisation, Not of Arms—but Ideas.* London, 1853.

— *(Proposed) Address from the Democrats of England to the Democrats of the United States Issued by George Jacob Holyoake, Richard Moore, J. Coleman Burroughs, sec. from the 'Leader' office.* [1853].

— *Freethought Directory: a Catalogue of Works published or supplied by Holyoake & Co., 147 Fleet Street.* London, [1854].

— *Secularism, the Practical Philosophy of the People.* London, 1854.

— *Secularism, distinguished from Unitarianism.* London, 1855.

— *The History of the Fleet Street House. A Report of Sixteen Years.* London, 1856.

— *The Case of Thomas Pooley, the Cornish Well-Sinker, sentenced to a year and nine months' imprisonment for writing on a clergyman's field gate.* (Report made at the instance of the Secularists.) London, 1857.

— *To the Electors of the Tower Hamlets.* 1857.

— *British Secular Institute Report of Communication and Propagandism. Report of the Fleet Street House, Part II, for 1857.* [1858].

— *The Trial of Theism* (1858), London, [1877].

— *Secular Institute Report, 1858-9.* [1859]

— *The Workman and the Suffrage, Letters to the Right Honourable Lord Russell, M.P. and the 'Daily News'.* London, People's edition, 1859.

— *The Logic of Life, Deduced from the Principle of Freethought.* London, [1861].

— *Public Purposes of the Fleet Street House. Reply of Mr. Holyoake on the Presentation of the Final Subscription, at Anderton's Hotel, May 14, 1861.* [1861].

— *Joseph Barker, and his expulsion from the secular body. Dr Perfitt, and the Unbounded Virtue Party.* London, [1862].

— *Cummings Wrong: Colenso Right. A reply to the Rev. Dr. Cummings's "Moses Right, Colenso Wrong", by a London Zulu.* London, [1863].

— *Mr. Holyoake's Disconnection with the "National Reformer" and the Correspondence which accounts for it.* London [1863].

— *The Suppressed Lecture, at Cheltenham.* London, 1864.

— *A Plea for Affirmation in Parliament.* London, 1882.

— *Secular Prospects in Death. The Late Councillor Josiah Gimson, addresses by George Jacob Holyoake.* London [1883].

— *To the Members of the Leicester Liberal Association.* Leicester, 1884.

Holyoake, George Jacob, *The Origin and Nature of Secularism. Showing that where Freethought Commonly Ends Secularism Begins.* London, 1896.
— *The Warpath of Opinion. Strange things seen thereon.* London, 1896.
— *History of the Travelling Tax.* (Reprinted from the "Co-operative Wholesale Societies' Annual of England and Scotland for 1901.*) London, 1901.
Jeffery, Henry, *The Day of Judgment. A Discourse delivered in the Clyde Street Hall, Edinburgh.* Edinburgh, 1842.
Knowlton, Charles, *The Fruits of Philosophy, or the private companion of Adult People.* (1832), third edition, London 1841.
Leeds Secular Society, *The Converted Lecturer, or, Mr. Gordon's Repudiation of Secular Principles Examined.* London & Leeds, 1862.
Manchester Public Library Tracts on Secularism: *First Annual Report of the Lancashire Secular Union.* (Local History Library T.440/21); Leaflet advertising meetings of the Manchester Secular Society, n.d., (Local History Library, Newspaper Cuttings, Societies—Secular, 149.7).
Martin, Emma, *First Conversation on the Being of God.* London n.d.
— *Second Conversation on the Being of God.* London n.d.
— *A Few Reasons for Renouncing Christianity and Professing and Disseminating Infidel Opinions.* London, n.d.
— *A Funeral Sermon, occasioned by the death of Richard Carlile, preached at the Hall of Science, City Road, London (Sunday Evening, 26 Feb. 1843).* London, [1843].
— *Prayer.* London, n.d.
— *Religion Superceded, or the Moral Code of Nature sufficient for The Guidance of Man.* London, n.d.
Owen, Robert, *The Catechism of the New Moral World.* Manchester & London, n.d.
— *A New View of Society: or Essays on the Formation of the Human Character Preparatory to the Development of a Plan for gradually ameliorating the Condition of Mankind.* Third edition, London, 1817.
— *A New View of Society: extracted from the Daily Papers of 30th July and 9th and 10th of August, 1817.* [1817].
— *Outline of the Rational System of Society, Founded on demonstrable Facts, developing the Constitution and Laws of Human Nature; Being the Only Effectual Remedy for the Evils Experienced by the Population of the World.* London, n.d.
— *A New View of Society* (1813-14) and *Report to the County of Lanark* (1821), edited with an introduction by V. A. C. Gatrell. London, 1969.
— *The Book of the New Moral World, containing the Rational System of Society founded on demonstrable facts, developing the Constitution and Laws of Human Nature and of Society.* part I (1836), parts II, III (1842), parts IV–VII (1844), London, 1849.
Owen, Robert Dale, *An Outline of the System of Education at New Lanark.* Glasgow, 1824.
— *Moral Physiology; or, A Brief and Plain Treatise on The Population Question* (New York, 1830), eighth edition, London, 1832, re-issued by E. Truelove, n.d.
Paine, Thomas, *Complete Writings,* ed. P. Foner, 2 vols., New York, 1945.
— *The Rights of Man* (1791-92), edited with an introduction by Henry Collins, London, 1969.

Priestley, Joseph, *Disquisitions relating to Matter and Spirit, to which is added The History of the Philosophical Doctrine concerning the Origin of the Soul, and the Nature of Matter; with its Influence on Christianity, especially with Respect to the Doctrine of the Pre-existence of Christ,* London, 1777.

— *The Doctrine of Philosophical Necessity Illustrated; being an Appendix to the Disquisitions relating to Matter and Spirit. To which is added An Answer to the Matters on Materialism, and on Hartley's Theory of the Mind.* London, 1777.

— *Letters to a Philosophical Unbeliever,* Part I (1780, second edition, 1787) and Part II (1787), (as published in *The Theological and Miscellaneous Works, etc. of Joseph Priestley, LL.D. F.R.S. etc.* vol. IV. London [1818].

Pyat, Felix, *Letter to the Parliament and the Press, by Felix Pyat, Beeson, and A. Talandier. With a Preface by the Publisher* [Holyoake]. (1858), second edition, London, 1858.

Robertson, James. *Secularists and their Slanderers: or, the 'Investigator' Investigated. Mr. Holyoake and his Assailants, their defeat, and the Votes of Confidence in Fleet Street House, from Manchester & Elsewhere.* London, n.d.

Southwell, Charles, *Socialism made Easy: or, A Plain Exposition of Mr. Owen's Views.* London, 1840.

— *Reply to a 'Discourse on the Subject of Deity, by a Philosophical Inquirer, delivered in the Church of Mount Brinksway, near Stockport on Sunday, September 9, 1827'.* London, 1842.

— *The Difficulties of Christianity, stated in a series of letters to the Archbishop of Canterbury.* London [?1843].

— *An Apology for Atheism: addressed to Religious Investigators of every denomination, by one of its apostles.* London, 1846.

— *An Antidote to Deism.* London, [1848].

— *The Impossibility of Atheism Demonstrated: with Hints to Nominal Atheists: in a Letter to the Freethinkers of Great Britain.* London [1852].

— *Another 'Fourpenny Wilderness'. In which may be found More Nails for the Coffin of Nonsense called Atheism. More Hints to Freethinkers, and A Reply to George Jacob Holyoake's 'Examination' of Charles Southwell's 'Impossibility of Atheism Demonstrated'.* London, 1852.

— *Review of a Controversy between The Rev. Brewin Grant and G. J. Holyoake, in the Cowper Street School Room, City Road, On the question 'What Advantages would Accrue to Mankind Generally, and to the Working Classes in Particular, by the Removal of Christianity and the Substitution of Secularism in its Place?'* London 1853.

Taylor, Robert, *The Diegesis: being a discovery of the Origin, Evidences, and Early History of Christianity, never yet before or elsewhere so fully and faithfully set forth.* (1829), second edition, London, 1841.

Turley, William, *Mr. Holyoake and his Detractors. An Address to the Friends of Progress.* London, [1858].

Turner, Henry, *Phrenology: its evidences and influences. With criticisms upon Mr. Grant's Recent Lectures.* Sheffield, 1858.

G. T., *Occasional Essays in Philosophy. No. 1—Existence of Evil. No. 2—The Religious Sentiment, being an Examination into the belief in the Supernatural.* London, 1860.

(b) *Reports of trials*

The Trial of Charles Southwell, (Editor of 'The Oracle of Reason') For Blasphemy, before Sir Charles Wetherall, Recorder of the City of Bristol, January the 14th, 1842. specially reported by William Carpenter. London, 1842.

The Trial of George Jacob Holyoake, on an indictment for Blasphemy, before Mr. Justice Erskine and a common jury, at Gloucester, August the 15th, 1842, from notes specially taken by Mr. Hunt. London, 1842.

The Man Paterson. God versus Paterson. The Extraordinary Bow-Street Police Report. London, [1843]. [edited by W. J. Birch & M. Q. Ryall].

The Scotch Trials. The Trial of Thomas Paterson for Blasphemy, Before the High Court of Justiciary, Edinburgh, with The Whole of his Bold and Effective Defence, also The Trials of Thomas Finlay and Miss Matilda Roalfe (for Blasphemy), In the Sheriff's Court. With notes and a special dissertation on Blasphemy Prosecutions in General by the Secretary of the 'Anti-Persecution Union' [Holyoake]. London & Edinburgh, 1844.

(c) *Discussions*

Barker, Joseph, *Origin and Authority of the Bible. Report of A Public Discussion between Joseph Barker, esq., and The Rev. Brewin Grant, B. A. Held at Halifax on Ten Nights, namely, January 22nd, 23rd, 26th, 30th, and 31st; and February 1st, 2nd, 6th, and 8th, of the Year 1855.* Glasgow, [1855].

Bradlaugh, Charles, *A Full Report of the Discussion, between The Rev. Brewin Grant, B.A., and 'Iconoclast', in the Mechanics' Hall, Sheffield, on the 7th, 8th, 14th & 15th June 1858.* London and Sheffield, 1858.

— *Christianity and Secularism Contrasted. Report of the Debate at Wigan, between 'Iconoclast' and Mr. W. M. Hutchings.* London, 1861.

— *A Full Report of the Discussion between Mr. Mackie (Editor of the 'Warrington Guardian') and 'Iconoclast' (Mr. C. Bradlaugh) in the Music Hall, Warrington on Wednesday and Thursday, April 10 & 11, 1861.* London, [1861].

— *Are the Doctrines and Precepts of Christianity, as Taught in the New Testament, Calculated to Benefit Humanity? Report of the Three Nights' Debate at Liverpool, between 'Iconoclast' and the Rev. J. H. Rutherford.* London, [1861].

— *The Existence of God: A Discussion between Rev. Woodville Woodman, Minister of the New Jerusalem Church, Kersley, Lancashire, and 'Iconoclast', Editor of the 'National Reformer' held at Wigan, on February 18th to 21st, 1861.* London, [1861].

— *Is the Bible a Divine Revelation? A Discussion between Rev. Woodville Woodman, (Minister of the New Jerusalem Church, Kersley, Lancashire) and 'Iconoclast' (Editor of the 'National Reformer'): held at Ashton-under-Lyne, on October 21st, 22nd, 28th and 29th.* London, [1861].

Hollick, Frederick, *The Substance of the Two Nights' Discussion, In the Social Institution, 69, Great Queen Street, London, On Friday and Saturday, 14th & 15th December, between the Rev. Joseph Baylee and Frederick Hollick, Social Missionary, on The Genuineness, Authenticity, and Inspiration of The Bible.* London, 1839.

Hollick, Frederick, *Public Discussion on Socialism, held at the New Theatre, Leicester, on the evenings of Tuesday and Wednesday, April 14th and 15th, 1840, between Mr. Brindley, and Mr. Hollick, Socialist Missionary. From the Leicester Journal, 17 April 1840.* Leicester, [1840].

Holyoake, George Jacob, *The Report on the Four Nights' Public Discussion at Bradford, between George J. Holyoake of London, Editor of 'The Reasoner' etc. and John Bowes, of Manchester, Editor of 'The Truth' etc. on The Truth of Christianity and The Folly of Infidelity, 22nd, 23rd, and 24th April. The Free Agency of Man and the Formation of Character, on the 25th.* London, 1850.

— *A Report of the Public Discussion, between George J. Holyoake and David King, Held in the Hall, John Street, Tottenham Court Road, London, on 3 Evenings in September, 1850. Questions: What is the Christian System? What are its legitimate effects?* London, [1850].

— *Townley and Holyoake. Atheistic Controversy. A Public Discussion on the Being of a God.* London, [1852].

— *Christianity and Secularism. Report of a Public Discussion between the Rev. Brewin Grant, B.A., editor of 'The Bible and the People', and George Jacob Holyoake, Esq., editor of 'The Reasoner', held in the Royal British Institution, Cowper Street, London, on six successive Thursday evenings, commencing January 20th and ending February 24th, 1853, on the question, 'What Advantages would Accrue to Mankind Generally, and the Working Classes in Particular, by the Removal of Christianity, and the Substitution of Secularism in its Place.'* London, 1853.

— *Christianity versus Secularism. A Public Discussion in Newcastle-upon-Tyne, between The Rev. J. H. Rutherford and Mr. G. J. Holyoake, on the Evenings of 1st, 3rd and 5th August 1853.* London, 1854.

— *Discussion on Secularism. Report of Public Discussion between the Rev. Brewin Grant, B.A., and George Jacob Holyoake, Esq., held in the City Hall, Glasgow, on Monday and Thursday Evenings, commencing October 2, and ending October 19, 1854, on the Question, 'Is Secularism inconsistent with Reason and the Moral Sense, and condemned by Experience? —By Secularism is meant that Phase of Modern Free Thought, represented by Mr. Holyoake's Writings, and in the Publications edited, recommended, or approved of by him.'* Glasgow, 1854.

— *Public Discussion on Teetotalism and the Maine-Law: between George Jacob Holyoake, Esq., and Dr. Frederic R. Lees.* London, 1856. (Printed in the *Works of F. R. Lees*, vol. III Appendix.)

— *Report of a Discussion on the Maine Law, between Mr. G. J. Holyoake, Editor of the 'Reasoner', London, and Mr. G. E. Lomax, of Manchester. In the Theatre Royal, Blackburn, on the Evenings of November 16 & 17, 1857.* Second edition, Blackburn, 1858.

— *Secularism, Scepticism and Atheism. Verbatim report of the proceedings of a Two Nights' Public Debate between Messrs. G. J. Holyoake & C. Bradlaugh, Held at the New Hall of Science, 142 Old Street, City Road, London, on the evenings of March 10 and 11, 1870.* London, 1870.

Jones, Lloyd, *The Influence of Christianity. Report of a Public Discussion which took place at Oldham, on the evenings of Tuesday and Wednesday, February 19th and 20th, 1839 between The Rev. J. Barker, of the Metho-

dist New Connexion, Mossley, and Mr. Lloyd Jones, of Manchester, Social Missionary, on The Influence of Christianity. Manchester 1839.

—*Socialism. Report of A Public Discussion, between John Bowes, minister of the Gospel, Liverpool, and Lloyd Jones, social missionary, Glasgow; in the Queen's Theatre, Christian Street, Liverpool, May 5th, 6th, 7th, and 27th, 1840; 'On the Five Facts, and Constitution and Laws of Human Nature, as propounded by Robert Owen', Mr. Bowes being at Liberty to express his views of their inconsistency with Christianity. Also on the Marriage System of Socialism, as taught in the writings of Robert Owen, Esq.* London, 1840.

Owen Robert, *Public Discussion between John Brindley and Robert Owen, on the questions 'What is Socialism; and What would be its practical effects upon Society?' held in the Amphitheatre, Bristol, on the evenings of January 5th 6th and 7th, 1841. Moderator, John Scandrett Harford, esq.* Birmingham, [1841].

Southwell, Charles, *A Report of the Public Discussion, between Mr. John Bowes, of Manchester, and Mr. Charles Southwell, of London, at the Lecture Room, Nelson Street, Newcastle-upon-Tyne, on the Evenings of the 13th, 14th, 15th and 16th of August, 1850.* Newcastle, 1850.

(d) *Pamphlets, etc, by Christians and other opponents*

Barker, Joseph, *The Abominations of Socialism Exposed, in Reply to the 'Gateshead Observer'.* Newcastle on Tyne, 1840.

Batchelor, Henry, *The Logic of Atheism. Three Lectures, by the Rev. Henry Batchelor, delivered in the Large Temperance Hall, Sheffield.* London and Sheffield, 1858.

Beard, J. R., *The Religion of Jesus Christ defended from the Assaults of Owenism.* London, 1839.

Buckland, William, *Viniciae Geologicae, or, The Connection of Geology with Religion Explained.* Oxford, 1820. (Bodleian Library copy, with marginal notes and alterations in manuscript.)

Chew, Sanders J., *Mr. G. J. Holyoake Refuted in his own Words.* London and Leicester, 1853.

[Collet, Sophia Dobson], 'Recent Aspects of Atheism in England' *Christian Examiner*, LXVII (November 1859), pp. 339–79, reprinted as *Phases of Atheism described, examined and answered.* London, 1860.

Davies, Charles M., *Heterodox London: or, Phases of Free Thought in the Metropolis.* London, 1874.

Earnshaw, Samuel, *The Church and the Artizan. A Sermon preached on Sunday Morning, Feb. 10th, 1861, in the Parish Church, Sheffield.* London, 1861.

Ellison, W. S., *Statement delivered by W. S. Ellison (Formerly a Secularist) in Ebenezer Chapel, Leeds, on Wednesday Evening, Oct. 8, 1862, containing his reasons for having abandoned Secularism, and an account of his conversion.* Leeds, 1862.

Farrar, Adam S., *A Critical History of Freethought, in reference to the Christian Religion. The Bampton Lectures for 1862.* London, 1862.

French Philosophy, or a Short Account of the Principles and Conduct of the French Infidels. Sheffield, 1798.

Gordon, John Henry, *The Public Statement of Mr. J. H. Gordon (Late Lecturer to the Leeds Secular Society) with reference to his Repudiation of Secular Principles, and his adoption of the Christian Faith. (Delivered in the Music Hall, Leeds, on Tuesday, August 5th, 1862. The Rev. G. W. Conder in the Chair.)* Leeds and London, 1862.

Grant, Brewin, *An Apology for Christianity or Modern Infidelity Examined, in a series of letters to Robert Owen.* London and Leicester, 1840.

— *Shall we open the Free Library on Sundays? No!* [London, 1858].

Gregory, J. etc., *Modern Atheism: or the Pretensions of Secularism Examined. A Course of Four Lectures, delivered in the Atheneum, Thornton, Bradford, by the Rev. J. Gregory of Thornton, Rev. G. W. Conder of Leeds, Rev. J. A. Savage of Wilsden, Rev. E. Mellor, A.M., of Halifax.* London, 1853.

Hall, Robert, *Modern Infidelity Considered, with respect to Its Influence on Society.* new. ed., London, 1831.

Hindmarsh, Robert, *Christianity against Deism, Materialism, and Atheism. occasioned by A Letter addressed to the Author by Richard Carlile.* Manchester, 1824.

Hinton, John Howard, *Secular Tracts, No. 1. A Lecture delivered at the Royal British Institution, Cowper Street, London, March 3rd 1853, on the Conclusion of the Discussion Between Mr G. J. Holyoake and the Rev. Brewin Grant.* London, 1853.

Langford, John Alfred, *Christianity, not Secularism, the practical Philosophy of the People: a reply to G. J. Holyoake's Tract, 'Secularism, the Practical Philosophy of the People'.* London and Birmingham, 1854.

Linton, W. J., *'Holyoake versus Garrison. A Defence of Earnestness', from English Republican,* 26 March 1853, pp. 257–60.

— *G. J. Holyoake Exposed: a Supplement to the 'Reasoner' of Nov. 9, 1853.* [London, 1853].

Lond, Thomas, *Secularism: What Is It? Answered by a working man.* London, 1859.

McCann, James, *Anti Secularist Lectures. A Course of Six Lectures by the Rev. Jas. McCann, MA, FRSL, FGS, with an appendix containing Secularist Objections to the Bible, notes, etc.* Huddersfield and London, 1867.

McInnes, D., *Modern Infidelity Tried on Its Own Merits; or A Reply to some of the Statements of Mr G. J. Holyoake, in his Discussion with the Rev. B. Grant, in Glasgow, in the month of October, 1854.* Glasgow, 1854.

Martin, William, *The Logic of Holyoake's 'Logic of Death;' or, why The Atheist Should Fear to Die.* Glasgow, 1854.

Meyrick, Frederick, *The Outcast and the Poor of London; or our present duties towards the poor: a course of sermons preached at The Chapel Royal, Whitehall.* London, 1858.

Miall, Edward. *The British Churches in relation to the British People.* London, 1849.

Molesworth, William Nassau, *The History of England,* 3 vols., London, 1874.

Murray, Charles, *A Letter to Mr George Jacob Holyoake; containing a brief review of that Gentleman's conduct and policy as a Reformer, with especial reference to his Reply to Mr Linton and the 'Boston Liberator'; His Criticism upon the Stranger of the 'Leader' Newspaper, and Defence of the Cobden Policy; with the writer's opinion upon free-trade measures:*

and on the position and interests of the Middle and Working Classes; etc. etc. etc. London, 1854.

Paley, William, *Natural Theology, or Evidences of the Existence and Attributes of the Deity. Collected from the Appearances of Nature.* (1802), sixth edition, London, 1803.

Parker, Joseph, *Six Chapters on Secularism: or the Secular Theory Examined in the Light of Scripture and Philosophy.* London, 1854.

— *Helps to Truth Seekers: or Christianity and Scepticism, An Exposition and a Defence.* London, 1857.

Phillpotts, Henry, Bishop of Exeter, *First Speech of the Bishop of Exeter, in the House of Lords, January 24, 1840.* [1840].

— *Second Speech of the Bishop of Exeter, in the House of Lords, February 4, 1840.* [1840]

Reid, William Hamilton, *The Rise and Dissolution of the Infidel Societies in this Metropolis: including, The Origin of Modern Deism and Atheism; the genius and conduct of those associations; their lecture-rooms, field-meetings, and deputations; from the Publication of Paine's Age of Reason till the present period. With General Considerations on the Influence of Infidelity upon Society; answering the various objections of Deists and Atheists; and a Postscript upon the present state of Democratic Politics; Remarks upon Professor Robison's late Work, etc. etc.* second ed., London, 1800.

Satchwell, Thomas, *Satchwell and Christianity versus Holyoake and Atheistical Infidelity. Mr T. Satchwell's Two Speeches delivered during his Discussion with Mr. G. J. Holyoake, formed from notes taken during the time, by several of his friends, and from his own recollection; and to the best of his ability Without Any Omission or Addition.* Northampton, 1847.

Vanderkiste, R. W. *Notes and narratives of a six-years mission, principally among the dens of London.* London, 1852.

Woodman, Woodville, *The Doctrine of a Supreme Being Vindicated, and the Fallacy of Infidel Arguments Exposed and Refuted; being strictures on a Lecture delivered at Heywood, June 16, 1852, by Mr G. J. Holyoake, of London, 'On the Development of the Principles of Free Inquiry etc.'* [1852].

'The Secular Press', *Saturday Review*, 1 (5 April 1856), pp. 453–4.

'The Religious Heresies of the Working Classes', *Westminster Review*, new series, XXI. (1862), pp. 60–97.

(e) *Autobiographies*

Adams, W. E., *Memoirs of a Social Atom.* London, 1903; [repr. 1968, ed. J. Saville].

Bamford, Samuel, *Early Days.* ed. H. Dunckley, London, 1893.

— *Passages in the Life of a Radical* ed. H. Dunckley, London, 1893.

Barker, Joseph, *Confessions of Joseph Barker, a Convert from Christianity.* London, 1858.

— *An Answer to the Question How Did You Become An Infidel? with some account of My Religious Experience.* London, [1859].

Barker, John Thomas (ed.), *The Life of Joseph Barker written by himself, edited by his nephew.* London, 1880.

Conway, M. D., *Autobiography. Memories and Experiences of Moncure Daniel Conway.* 2 vols., London, 1904.

Cooper, Thomas, *Life of Thomas Cooper.* London, 1873.

Frost, Thomas, *Forty Years' Recollections: Literary and Political.* London, 1880.

Holyoake, Austin, *Sick Room Thoughts Dictated Shortly before his death.* [London, 1874].

Holyoake, George Jacob, *Sixty Years of an Agitator's Life.* 2 vols., London, 1892.

— *Bygones Worth Remembering.* 2 vols., London, 1905.

Linton, W. J., *Memories.* London, 1895.

Lovett, William, *The Life and Struggles of William Lovett, in his pursuit of Bread, Knowledge, and Freedom: with some short account of the different associations he belonged to, and of the opinions he entertained.* London, 1876.

Owen Robert, *The Life of Robert Owen, written by himself, with selections from his writings and correspondence.* vol. 1, London, 1857; and vol IA, *containing a series of reports, addresses, memorials and other documents.* London, 1858.

Owen, Robert Dale, *Threading My Way. Twenty-seven years of autobiography.* London, 1874.

Quin, Malcolm, *Memoirs of a Positivist.* London, 1924.

Southwell, Charles, *The Confessions of a Freethinker.* London, [?1850].

(f) *Other contemporary sources*

Ashworth, Henry, *The Preston Strike, an enquiry into its Causes and Consequences, the substance of which was read before the Statistical Section of the British Association, at its meeting, held in Liverpool, September 1854.* Manchester, 1854.

Biggs, William, *National Education.* Leicester, 1849.

Buckle, T. H., 'Mill on Liberty', *Frazer's Magazine* vol. 59 (1859), pp. 509–42.

Chambers, Robert, *Vestiges of the Natural History of Creation.* [1844], reprinted Leicester, 1969.

Combe, George, *The Constitution of Man in relation to The Natural Laws.* [1828], Edinburgh and London, 1893.

Engels, Frederick, *The Condition of the Working-Class in England.* [1845], London, 1892, reprinted Moscow, 1962.

English Aid to Garibaldi on his invasion of the Sicilies. Is it Lawful and Just? Correspondence between The Manchester Foreign Affairs Association and Mark Philips, esq.: also between the former and R. P. Greg, esq. Manchester, [?1860].

Essays and Reviews. London, 1860.

Faucher, Léon, *Manchester in 1844; its Present Condition and Future Prospects. Translated from the French, with copious notes appended, by a Member of the Manchester Atheneum.* London and Manchester, 1844.

Greg, W. R., *The Creed of Christendom, its foundations and superstructure.* London, 1851.

Hook, W. F., *On the Means of Rendering More Efficient the Education of*

the People. A Letter to The Lord Bishop of St. David's. (1846), eighth
edition, London, 1846.

Linton, W. J., *Ireland for the Irish. Rhymes and Reasons against landlordism
with a preface on Fenianism and Republicanism.* New York, 1867.

*Manchester and the Manchester People, with a Sketch of Bolton, Stockport,
Ashton, Rochdale and Oldham and their Inhabitants, by a Citizen of the
World.* Manchester, 1843.

*Manchester as it is: or, notices of the Institutions, manufactures, commerce,
railways, etc. of the Metropolis of Manufacturers: interspersed with much
valuable information for the Resident & the Stranger.* Manchester, 1839.

*Manchester Free Public Library: Report of the Proceedings at a Public Meet-
ing held in The Hall, Camp Field, Manchester, on Wednesday, January
8th, 1851, to effect the establishment of a Free Public Library and Museum
in Manchester: To which are prefixed Leading Articles on the Subject from
the Manchester Newspapers.* [1851].

*Manchester Free Library. Report of the Proceedings at The Public Meetings,
held in the Library, Camp Field, Manchester, on Thursday, September 2nd
1852, to celebrate the Opening of the Free Library.* Manchester, [1852].

Newman, Francis W., *Phases of Faith.* (1850), London, 1860, reprinted Leicester
1970.

[Somerville, Alexander], *A Journey to Harmony Hall, in Hampshire, with
some particulars of the Socialist Community, to which the attention of
the Nobility, Gentry, and Clergy, is earnestly requested—Notes from the
Farming Districts. No. XVII—reprinted from Morning Chronicle, Tues.
December 13, 1842.* London, [1843].

[Urquhart, David], *The Turkish Bath, with a view to its Introduction into
the British Dominions.* London, 1856.

6 *Secondary sources—a selective bibliography*

For fuller bibliographies, see the following works listed below: Gilmour, J. P.,
Charles Bradlaugh; Goss, C. W. F., *G. J. Holyoake*; Harrison, J. F. C., *Robert
Owen and the Owenites*; and E. Royle, *Radical Politics, 1790–1900*.

(a) *Books*

Ahier, P., *The Story of Castle Hill throughout the Centuries, B.C. 200–
A.D. 1945.* Huddersfield, 1946.

Aldred, G. A., *The Devil's Chaplain: the story of the Rev. Robert Taylor,
M.A., M.R.C.S. (1784–1844).* Glasgow, 1942.

— *Richard Carlile, agitator: his life and times.* third, revised ed., Glasgow,
1941.

Aldridge, A. O., *Man of Reason: the life of Thomas Paine.* London, 1960.

Altick, R. D., *The English Common Reader: a social history of the mass
reading public, 1800–1900.* Chicago and London, 1957.

Armytage, W. H. G., *Heavens Below: utopian experiments in England, 1560–
1960.* London, 1961.

Arnstein, W. L., *The Bradlaugh Case: a study in late Victorian opinion and
politics.* Oxford, 1965.

Balleine, G. R., *A History of the Evangelical Party in the Church of England.*
London, 1909.

Balmforth, O., *The Huddersfield Industrial Society Ltd: history of fifty years' progress, 1860–1910*. Manchester, 1910.

Barker, A. G., *Henry Hetherington, 1792–1849: pioneer in the freethought and working class struggles of a hundred years ago for the freedom of the press*. London, 1938.

Beer, M., *A History of British Socialism*. single vol. ed., London, 1940.

Bellamy J. M., and Saville, J. (eds.), *Dictionary of Labour Biography*. vol. 1, London, 1972.

Best, G. F. A., *Mid Victorian Britain, 1851–75*. London, 1871.

Boase, F., *Modern English Biography, containing many thousand concise memoirs of persons who have died during the years 1851–1900*. 3 vols. and 3 vols. of supplements, Truro, 1890–1921.

Bonner, A., *British Co-operation: the history, principles, and organisation of the British Co-operative Movement*. Manchester, 1961.

Bonner, H. B., and Robertson, J. M., *Charles Bradlaugh, a record of his life and work by his daughter with an account of his Parliamentary Struggle, Politics and Teaching by J. M. Robertson*. Second edition, 2 vols., London, 1895.

Bray, R. A., *Labour and the Churches*. London, 1912.

Brierley, B., *Failsworth, my native village; with incidents of the struggles of its early reformers*. Oldham, 1895.

Briggs, A., *Press and Public in Early Nineteenth Century Birmingham*. (Dugdale Society occasional paper, no. 8), Oxford, 1949.

— *Victorian People*. (1954), London, 1965.

Briggs, A. (ed.), *Chartist Studies*. (1959), London, 1965.

Brown, W. H., *Charles Kingsley: the work and influence of Parson Lot*. Manchester, 1924.

Burn, W. L., *The Age of Equipoise: a consideration of the era, 1850–68*. London, 1964.

Burrow, J. W., *Evolution and Society: a study in Victorian social theory*. Cambridge, 1966.

Bury, J. B., *A History of Freedom of Thought*. London, 1913.

Butt, J. (ed.), *Robert Owen: Prince of Cotton Spinners*. Newton Abbott, 1971.

Bythell, D., *The Handloom Weavers: a study in the English cotton industry during the Industrial Revolution*. Cambridge, 1969.

Campbell, C. B., *Towards a Sociology of Irreligion*. London, 1971.

Campbell, T. C., *The Battle of the Press as told in the story of the life of Richard Carlile, by his daughter*. London, 1899.

Chadwick, W. O., *The Victorian Church*. 2 vols., London, 1966–70.

Chambers, J. D., *Workshop of the World: British economic history from 1820 to 1880*. London, 1961.

Charlton, D. G., *Secular Religions in France, 1815–70*. Oxford, 1963.

Christensen, T., *Origin and History of Christian Socialism, 1848–54*. (Acta Theologica Danica, vol. III), Aarhus, 1962.

Clapham, J. H., *An Economic History of Modern Britain*. 3 vols., Cambridge, 1926–38.

Cockshut, A. O. J., *The Unbelievers: English agnostic thought, 1840–1890*. London, 1964.

Cole, G. D. H., *A Century of Co-operation*. Manchester, [1945].

— *Chartist Portraits* (with an introd. by A. Briggs). New York, 1965.

Cole, G. D. H., *Richard Carlile*. (Fabian Society biographical series, no 13), London, 1943.
— *Socialist Thought: the forerunners, 1789–1850*. (1953), New York, 1965.
— *The Life of Robert Owen*. (1925), third ed., London, 1965.
Cole, G. D. H. and Filson, A. W., *British Working Class Movements: select documents, 1789–1875*. London, 1965.
Collet, C. D., *History of the Taxes on Knowledge, their origin and repeal*. 2 vols., London, 1899.
Conway, M. D., *Centenary History of the South Place Society, based on Four Discourses given in the Chapel in May and June, 1893*. London, 1894.
— *The Life of Thomas Paine, with a history of his Literary, Political and Religious Career in America, France, and England, to which is added a sketch of Paine by William Cobbett*. 2 vols., New York and London, 1892.
Croft, W. R., *The History of the Factory Movement, or, Oastler and his times*. Huddersfield, 1888.
Crump, W. B., and Ghorbal, G., *History of the Huddersfield Woollen Industry*. Huddersfield, 1935.
Cutner, H., *Robert Taylor, (1784–1844), the Devil's Chaplain*. London, n.d.
Daniel, G., *The Idea of Pre-history*. (1962), London, 1964.
Derry, J. W., *The Radical Tradition: Tom Paine to Lloyd George*. London, 1967.
Dodds, J. W., *The Age of Paradox: a biography of England, 1841–51*. (1952), London, 1953.
Draper, J. W., *A History of the Conflict between Religion and Science*. London, 1875.
Driver, C., *Tory Radical: the life of Richard Oastler*. New York, 1946.
Duncan, W., *Life of Joseph Cowen (M.P. for Newcastle, 1874–86): with letters, extracts from his speeches, and verbatim report of his last speech*. London and Newcastle, 1904.
Eiseley, L., *Darwin's Century: evolution and the men who discovered it*. London, 1959.
Faulkner, H. U., *Chartism and the Churches: a study in democracy*. (Columbia University Studies in History, Economics and Public Law, vol. 73), New York, 1916.
Fisher, H. A. L., *The Republican Tradition in Europe*. London, 1911.
Gammage, R. G., *History of the Chartist Movement, 1837–1854*. (1854), London, 1894, reprinted 1969.
Garnett, R. G., *Co-operation and the Owenite Socialist Communities in Britain, 1825–45*. Manchester, 1972
— *The Ideology of the Early Co-operative Movement* (The first Kent Co-operative Endowment Lecture, delivered at the University of Kent at Canterbury on 25 May, 1966). Canterbury, 1966.
Gibbon, C., *The Life of George Combe, author of 'The Constitution of Man'*. 2 vols., London, 1878.
Gillespie, F. E., *Labor and Politics in England, 1850–67*. Durham, N. Carolina, 1927, reprinted London, 1966.
Gillispie, C. C., *Genesis and Geology: a study in the relations of scientific thought, natural theology, and social opinion in Great Britain, 1790–1850*. Cambridge, Mass., 1951.

Gilmour, J. P. (ed.), *Charles Bradlaugh; Champion of Liberty: collected writings and speeches, with comments.* London, 1933.

Gleason, J. H., *The Genesis of Russophobia in Great Britain: a study of the interaction of policy and opinion.* Cambridge, Mass., 1950.

Goss, C. W. F., *A Descriptive Bibliography of the Writings of George Jacob Holyoake: with a brief sketch of his life.* London, 1908.

Gould, F. J., *The History of the Leicester Secular Society.* Leicester, 1900.

— *The Pioneers of Johnson's Court: a history of the Rationalist Press Association from 1899 onwards.* London, 1929.

Gray, E. M., *Old Testament Criticism: its rise and progress from the second century to the end of the eighteenth: a historical sketch.* New York, 1923.

Greene, J. C., *The Death of Adam: evolution and its impact on Western Thought.* Iowa, 1959.

Grisewood, H. J. G. (ed.), *Ideas and Beliefs of the Victorians: a historical revaluation of the Victorian Age.* London, 1949.

Halévy, E., *The Growth of Philosophical Radicalism*, trans. M. Morris. (1928), London, 1952.

— *History of the English People in the Nineteenth Century:* vol. IV. *The Victorian Years*, trans. E. I. Watkin with a supplementary section by R. B. McCallum. (1948, 1951), London, 1961.

Hammond, B., *William Lovett, 1800–77* (Fabian Tract no. 199: Fabian Biographical Series, no. 8). London, 1922.

Harrison, B., *Drink and the Victorians: The Temperance Question in England 1815–1872.* London, 1971.

Harrison, J. F. C., *The Early Victorians, 1832–51.* London, 1971.

— *Learning and Living: a study in the history of the English adult education movement.* London, 1961.

— *Robert Owen and the Owenites in Britain and America: the quest for the new moral world.* London, 1969.

Harrison, R., *Before the Socialists: studies in labour and politics, 1861–1881.* London, 1965.

Hazlitt, W., *Political Essays with Sketches of Public Characters. Robert Owen.* Second edition, London, 1823.

Headingly, A. S., *The Biography of Charles Bradlaugh.* London, 1880.

Henriques, U., *Religious Toleration in England, 1787–1833.* London, 1961.

Hinton, R. J., *Brief Biographies: English radical leaders.* New York, 1875.

Hobsbawm, E. J., *Primitive Rebels: studies in archaic forms of social movement in the 19th and 20th centuries.* Manchester, 1959.

Hoggart, R., *The Uses of Literacy: aspects of working class life with special reference to publications and entertainments.* (1957), London, 1963.

Hollis, P., *The Pauper Press: a study in working-class radicalism of the 1830s.* Oxford, 1970.

Holyoake, G. J., *Essay on the Character and Services of Thomas Paine.* London, [1861].

— *In Memoriam. Austin Holyoake. Died April the 10th, 1874.* [1874].

— *The History of Co-operation.* 2 vols., London, 1906.

— *The History of the Rochdale Pioneers. Part 1, 1844–57. Part 2, 1857–77.* (1858, 1878), tenth edition, revised and enlarged, London, 1893.

— *The Life and Character of Richard Carlile.* London, 1849.

Houghton, W. E., *The Victorian Frame of Mind, 1830–1870.* (1957), Yale, 1963.

Humphrey, A. W., *Robert Applegarth: trade unionist, educationalist, reformer*. Manchester and London, 1913.

Hunt, J., *Religious Thought in England in the Nineteenth Century*. London, 1896.

Inglis, K. S., *Churches and the Working Classes in Victorian England*. London, 1963.

Jefferys, J. B. (ed.), *Labour's Formative Years, 1849–1879*. London, 1948.

Jephson, H., *The Platform: its rise and progress*. 2 vols., London, 1892.

Joll, J. B., *The Anarchists*. London, 1964.

Jones, E. R., *The Life and Speeches of Joseph Cowen, M.P.* London, 1885.

Jones, L., *The Life, Times and Labours of Robert Owen*. (With a note on Lloyd Jones by William Cairns Jones). (1890), fifth edition, London, [1912].

Kent, W., *London for Heretics*. London, 1932.

Kingsley Martin, B., *The Triumph of Lord Palmerston: a study of public opinion in England before the Crimean War*. (1924), revised edition, London, 1963.

Koch, G. A., *Republican Religion: the American Revolution and the cult of Reason*. New York, 1933.

Kuczynski, J., *The Rise of the Working Class*, trans. C. T. A. Ray. London, 1967.

Lees, F., *Dr. Frederic Richard Lees, F.S.A. Edin.: a biography, with an introductory appreciation and bibliography by Frederic Arnold Lees, L.R.C.P. (Lond.) , M.R.C.S.(Eng)*. London, 1904.

Leventhall, F. M., *Respectable Radical: George Howell and Victorian Working Class Politics*. London, 1971.

Linton, W. J., *James Watson. A Memoir of the Days of the fight for a free press in England and of the agitation for the People's Charter*. Manchester, 1880.

Ludlow, J. M., and Jones, L., *Progress of the Working Class, 1832–67*. London, 1867.

McCabe, J., *Life and Letters of George Jacob Holyoake*. 2 vols., London, 1908.

— *A Biographical Dictionary of Modern Rationalists*. London, 1920.

Maccoby, S., *English Radicalism, 1832–52*. London, 1935.

— *English Radicalism, 1853–86*. London, 1938.

McGee, J. E., *A History of the British Secular Movement*. Girard, Kansas, 1948.

Magnus, P., *Gladstone: a biography*. (1954), London, 1963.

Maison, M. M., *Search Your Soul, Eustace: a survey of the religious novel in the Victorian Age*. London, 1961.

Martin, D., *A Sociology of English Religion*. London, 1967.

Marwick, W. H., *The Life of Alexander Campbell*. Glasgow, [1964].

Mather, F. C., *Public Order in the Age of the Chartists*. Manchester, 1959.

Morley, J., *The Life of Richard Cobden*. (1881), 2 vols., London, 1896.

Neill, S., *The Interpretation of the New Testament, 1861–1961*. London, 1964.

Nethercot, A. H., *The First Five Lives of Annie Besant*. London, 1961.

Packe, M. St. J., *The Bombs of Orsini*. London, 1967.

Patterson, A. T., *Radical Leicester: a history of Leicester, 1780–1850*. Leicester, 1954.

Perkin, H. J., *The Origins of Modern English Society, 1780–1870*. London, 1969.

Perkins, A. J. G., and Wolfson, T., *Frances Wright, Free Inquirer: the study of a temperament*. New York, 1939.

Plummer, A., *Bronterre: a political biography of Bronterre O'Brien, 1804–1864*. London, 1971.

Podmore, F., *Robert Owen: a biography*. (1906), single vol. ed., 1923.

Pollard, S., and Salt, J. (eds.), *Robert Owen: prophet of the Poor*. London, 1971.

Ponting, K. G. (ed.), *Baines's Account of the Woollen Manufacture of England*. Newton Abbott, 1971.

Post, A., *Popular Freethought in America, 1825–50*. (Columbia University Studies in History, Economics and Public Law, vol. 497), New York, 1943.

Putnam, S. P., *400 Years of Freethought*. New York, 1894.

Raven, C. E., *Christian Socialism, 1848–54*. London, 1920.

Read, D., *The English Provinces, c. 1760–1960: a study in influence*. London, 1964.

Reardon, B. M. G. (ed.), *Religious Thought in the Nineteenth Century, illustrated from writers of the period*. Cambridge, 1966.

Robbins, C., *The Eighteenth-century Commonwealthman: studies in the transmission, development and circumstance of English liberal thought from the restoration of Charles II until the war with the thirteen colonies*. Cambridge, Mass., 1959.

Robbins, W., *The Newman Brothers: an essay in comparative intellectual biography*. London, 1966.

Robertson, J. M., *A History of Freethought in the Nineteenth Century*. 2 vols., London, 1929.

— *A Short History of Freethought*. London, 1899.

Robinson, G., *David Urquhart: some chapters in the life of a Victorian Knight-Errant of Justice and Liberty*. Oxford, 1920.

Robson, R. (ed.), *Ideas and Institutions of Victorian Britain: essays in honour of George Kitson Clark*. London, 1967.

Rosenblatt, F. F., *The Chartist Movement in its Social and Economic Aspects*. (Columbia University Studies in History, Economics and Public Law, vol. 73), New York, 1916.

[Ross, W. S.], *Sketch of the Life and Character of Charles Watts, by 'Saladin'*. London, n.d.

Royle, E., *Radical Politics 1790–1900: religion and unbelief*. London, 1971.

Sargant, W. L., *Robert Owen and his Social Philosophy*. London, 1860.

Saville, J., *Ernest Jones: Chartist: selections from the writings and speeches of Ernest Jones with introduction and notes*. London, 1952.

Schoyen, A. R., *The Chartist Challenge: a portrait of George Julian Harney*. London, 1958.

Shipley, S., *Club Life and Socialism in Mid-Victorian London*. (History Workshop Pamphlets, no. 5), Ruskin College, Oxford, 1971.

Silver, H., *The Concept of Popular Education: a study of ideas and social movements in the early nineteenth century*. London, 1965.

Simon, B., *Studies in the History of Education, 1780–1870*. London, 1960.

Smith, F. B., *The Making of the Second Reform Bill*. Cambridge, 1966.

— *Radical Artisan: William James Linton, 1812–97*. Manchester, 1973.

Smith, W. S., *The London Heretics, 1870–1914*. London, 1967.

Stephen, J. T., *Social Redemption: or the fifty years' story of the Leicester Co-operative Society Ltd., 1860–1910*. Leicester, 1911.

Stephen, L., *History of English Thought in the Eighteenth Century*. 2 vols., London, 1876.

Symondson, A. (ed.), *The Victorian Crisis of Faith.* London, 1970.
Taylor, E. R., *Methodism and Politics, 1791–1851.* Cambridge, 1935.
Taylor, G. H., *A Chronology of British Secularism.* London, 1957.
Thomis, M. I., *Politics and Society in Nottingham, 1785–1835.* Oxford, 1969.
Thompson, E. P., *The Making of the English Working Class.* London, 1965.
Thrupp, S. L. (ed), *Millennial Dreams in Action: essays in comparative study.* The Hague, 1962.
Timmins, S. (ed.), *Birmingham and the Midland Hardware District.* London, 1866.
Tribe, D. *100 Years of Freethought.* London, 1967.
— *President Charles Bradlaugh, M.P.* London, 1971.
Twynam, E., *John Toland, Freethinker, 1670–1722.* Privately printed, 1968.
— *Peter Annet, 1693–1769. London,* [1938].
Veitch, G. S., *The Genesis of Parliamentary Reform.* (1913), London, 1965.
Venturi, F., *Utopia and Reform in the Enlightenment.* Cambridge, 1971.
Vidler, A .R., *The Church in the Age of Revolution, 1789 to the present day.* London, 1961.
Vincent, J., *The Formation of the Liberal Party, 1857–1868.* London, 1966.
Wallas, G., *The Life of Francis Place (1771–1854).* London, 1898.
— *Conway Memorial Lecture: William Johnson Fox (1786–1865), delivered at the South Place Institute on March 20, 1924.* London, 1924.
Waterman, W. R., *Frances Wright.* (Columbia University Studies in History, Economics and Public Law, vol. 115), New York, 1924.
Wearmouth, R. F., *Methodism and the Working Class Movements of England, 1800–50.* London, 1937.
—*Methodism and the Struggle of the Working Classes, 1850–1900.* Leicester, 1954.
Webb, C. C. J., *A Study of Religious Thought in England from 1850.* Oxford, 1933.
Webb, R. K., *The British Working Class Reader, 1790–1848: literacy and social tension.* London, 1955.
— *Harriet Martineau: a radical Victorian.* London, 1960.
— *Modern England.* London, 1969.
Webb, S. and B., *The History of Trade Unionism,* London, 1920.
Wheeler, J. M., *A Biographical Dictionary of Freethinkers of all Ages and Nations.* London, 1889.
White, A. D., *A History of the Warfare of Science with Theology in Christendom.* 2 vols., New York, 1896.
White, R. J., *Waterloo to Peterloo.* (1957), London, 1963.
Wickham, E. R., *Church and People in an Industrial City.* London, 1957.
Wickwar, W. H., *The Struggle for the Freedom of the Press.* London, 1928.
Wiener, J. H., *A Descriptive Finding List of Unstamped British Periodicals, 1830–1836.* Oxford, 1970.
— *The War of the Unstamped: the movement to repeal the British newspaper tax, 1830–36.* New York, 1969.
Willey, B., *The Eighteenth Century Background: studies in the idea of Nature in the thought of the period.* (1940), London, 1962.
-- *Nineteenth Century Studies: Coleridge to Matthew Arnold.* (1949), London, 1964.

Willey, B., *More Nineteenth Century Studies: a group of honest doubters*. London, 1956.

Williams, G. A., *Artisans and Sans-culottes: popular movements in France and Britain during the French Revolution*. London, 1968.

— *Rowland Detrosier: a working-class infidel, 1800–1834*. (Borthwick Institute of Historical Research, Borthwick Papers no. 28), York, 1965.

Williams, R., *Culture and Society, 1780–1950*. (1958), London, 1963.

Wilson, B., *The Struggles of an Old Chartist, what he knows, and the part he has taken in various movements*. Halifax, 1887.

Wilson, B. R. (ed.), *Patterns of Sectarianism: organisation and ideology in social and religious movements*. London, 1967.

Young, G. M. (ed.), *Early Victorian England, 1830–1865*. 2 vols., London, 1934.

Young, R. M., *Mind, Brain and Adaptation in the Nineteenth Century: cerebral localization and its biological context from Gall to Ferrier*. Oxford, 1970.

(b) *Articles*

Armytage, W. H. G., 'Manea Fen: an experiment in agrarian communitarianism', *Bulletin of the John Rylands Library*, xxxviii (1956), pp. 288–310.

Armytage, W. H. G., and Salt, J., 'The Sheffield land colony: failure of a "Back to the Land" scheme', *Agricultural History*, xxxv (1961), pp. 202–6.

Black, A., 'The Owenites and the Halls of Science', *Co-operative Review*, xxix (1955), pp. 42–4.

Briggs, A., 'David Urquhart and the Foreign Affairs Committees', *Bradford Antiquary*, x (1962), pp. 197–207.

Brock, P., 'Polish democrats and English radicals, 1832–62: a chapter in the history of Anglo-Polish relations', *Journal of Modern History*, xxv (1953), pp. 139–56.

Budd, S., 'The loss of faith: reasons for unbelief among members of the secular movement in England, 1850–1950', *Past and Present*, No. 36 (April 1967), pp. 106–25.

Eros, J., 'The rise of organised freethought in mid-Victorian England', *Sociological Review*, ii (1954), pp. 98–120.

Fein, A., 'Victoria Park: its origins and history', *East London Papers*, v (1962), pp. 73–90.

Gossman, N. J., 'Republicanism in nineteenth century England', *International Review of Social History*, vii (1962), pp. 47–60.

Harrison, B., 'The Sunday trading riots of 1855', *Historical Journal*, viii (1965), pp. 219–245.

Harrison, B., and Hollis, P., 'Chartism, liberalism and the life of Robert Lowery', *English Historical Review*, lxxxii (1967), pp. 503–535.

Harrison, J. F. C., 'The Owenite socialist movement in Britain and the United States: a comparative study', *Labor History*, ix (1968), pp. 323–337.

— 'The visions of the Leeds redemptionists: one of the last experiments in Owenite socialism', *Manchester Guardian* 22 June 1955.

Herrick, F. H., 'The second reform movement in Britain, 1850–65', *Journal of the History of Ideas*, ix (1948), pp. 174–192.

Holland Rose, J., 'The unstamped press, 1815–36', *English Historical Review*, xii (1897), pp. 711–726.

Inglis, K. S., 'Patterns of worship in 1851', *Journal of Ecclesiastical History*, XI (1960), pp. 74–86.

Learoyd, N., 'The late Mr Joshua Hobson: with a tribute to his memory', *Huddersfield Weekly News* 13, 20 May 1876.

Micklewright, F. H. Amphlett, 'The rise and decline of English Neo-Malthusianism', *Population Studies*, XV (1961), pp. 32–51.

Morris, R. J., 'The history of self-help', *New Society*, 3 December 1970.

Murphy, H. R., 'The ethical revolt against Christian orthodoxy in early Victorian England', *American Historical Review*, LX (1955), pp. 800–817.

Murphy, J., 'Robert Owen in Liverpool', *Transactions of the Historical Society of Lancashire and Cheshire*, CXII (1960), pp. 79–103.

Neale, R. S., 'Class and class-consciousness in early nineteenth century England: three classes or five?', *Victorian Studies*, XII (1968–1969), pp. 4–32.

Rose, R. B., 'John Finch, 1784–1857: a Liverpool disciple of Robert Owen', *Transactions of the Historical Society of Lancashire and Cheshire*, CIX (1957), pp. 159–184.

Royle, E., 'Mechanics' Institutes and the working classes, 1840–60', *Historical Journal*, XIV (1971), pp. 305–321.

Salt, J., 'The creation of the Sheffield Mechanics' Institute', *Vocational Aspect*, XVIII (1966), pp. 143–150.

— 'Isaac Ironside, the Sheffield Owenite', *Co-operative Review*, XXXIV (1960), pp. 218–219.

— 'The Sheffield Hall of Science', *Vocational Aspect*, XII (1960), pp. 133–138.

Thompson, D. M., 'The religious census: problems and possibilities', *Victorian Studies*, XI (1967–1968), pp. 87–97.

Walker, R. B., 'Religious changes in Cheshire, 1750–1850', *Journal of Ecclesiastical History*, XVII (1966), pp. 77–94.

— 'Religious changes in Liverpool in the nineteenth century', *Journal of Ecclesiastical History*, XIX (1968), pp. 195–211.

Ward, J. T., 'Centenary of Lawrence Pitkeithley's death: he fought with Oastler for shorter hours in mills', *Huddersfield Examiner*, 2 June 1958.

Weisser, H., 'Chartist internationalism, 1845–48', *Historical Journal*, XIV (1971), pp. 49–66.

Index